β

D0983311

THE SHIP THAT
WOULD NOT DIE

THE SHIP THAT WOULD NOT DIE

Rear Admiral F. Julian Becton, USN, Ret.
With Joseph Morschauser III

Prentice-Hall Inc., Englewood Cliffs, New Jersey

Designer, Donna Kurdock
Art Director, Hal Siegel

The Ship That Would Not Die
by Rear Admiral F. Julian Becton, USN, Ret.
With Joseph Morschauser III
Copyright © 1980 by F. Julian Becton and
Joseph Morschauser III

Photos courtesy U.S. Navy, except where noted.

Englewood Cliffs, New Jersey 07632
Printed in the United States of America
Prentice-Hall International, Inc., London
Prentice-Hall of Australia, Pty. Ltd., Sydney
Prentice-Hall of Canada, Ltd., Toronto
Prentice-Hall of India Private Ltd., New Delhi
Prentice-Hall of Japan, Inc., Tokyo
Prentice-Hall of Southeast Asia Pte. Ltd., Singapore
Whitehall Books Limited, Wellington, New Zealand

10 9 8 7 6 5 4 3 2 1

Library of Congress Cataloging in Publication Data

Becton, F   Julian, date-
    The ship that would not die.

    1.   Laffey (Ship)   2.   World War, 1939-1945—Personal
narratives, American.   3.   Becton, F. Julian, date-
4.   World War, 1939-1945—Naval operations, American.
5.   United States. Navy—Biography.   6.   Admirals—
United States—Biography.   I.   Morschauser, Joseph,
joint author.   II.   Title.
D774.L3B42   940.54′5973   80-16263
ISBN 0-13-808998-1

Dedicated to my shipmates, living and dead,
who fought so gallantly and who saved our ship.

ACKNOWLEDGMENTS

In reconstructing this action years after it occurred, I am indebted to many of my shipmates who answered questionnaires and my numerous queries in conversations at reunions and elsewhere to complete this account. Their own experiences enlivened the official report submitted at the time.

I want to express my thanks to those in the Department of the Navy who have gathered and passed on to me copies of historical records and documents which have helped me prepare this book. Among these are Captain Paul B. Smith, USN, Retired; Lieutenant Commander William Steadley, USN, Retired; and Mr. Franklin P. Greenman. Officials in the Naval Historical Center, Washington, D.C., who were most helpful are Dr. Dean C. Allard, Head of Operational Archives; Mr. John C. Reilly, Jr., Staff of the Ship History Branch; and Mr. Donald R. Martin, Staff of the Curator Branch.

As in past wars we had to call on the Reserves to help us win World War II. Our pre-Pearl Harbor regulars were the nucleus for the vast manpower expansion for our fleet. Eighty-five percent of our crew were Reserves. They came from high schools and colleges across the land. I often wondered about some of ours that looked too young to be of draft age. They were willing youngsters and doing a good job so I didn't question their ages. I learned later that some were as young as sixteen when they enlisted. A few of our men had a year or two of college, but most of them came straight from high school. They had had only five weeks of recruit training. Young and inexperienced as were most of them, they were patriotic and eager to do what they could to win the war. The task of training them into an efficient fighting team was a tremendous challenge, but it had to be done.

Among our officers only two thirds were Reserves. Of our eighteen or so officers three of them—our assistant engineer officers Jim Fravel and Harvey Shaw, and our torpedo officer, "Gag" Parolini—had former enlisted service. Three of us were graduates of the Naval Academy—our executive officer, Charlie Holovak, our assistant gunnery officer Paul Smith, and I. My officers and I had quite a job facing us.

In double-checking operations of other ships mentioned in this book, I referred to several well-known authoritative histories and historical listings, among which were: Theodore Roscoe's *United States Destroyer Operations in World War II* (U.S. Naval Institute, Annapolis, Maryland, 1953); Samuel Eliot Morison's comprehensive fifteen-volume *History of United States Naval Operations in World War II* (Little, Brown Co., Boston, 1950s); Paul S. Dull's *A Battle History of the Imperial Japanese Navy 1941-45* (Naval Institute Press, Annapolis, Md, 1978); General Omar N. Bradley's *A Soldier's Story* (Holt, Rinehart & Winston, Inc., New York, 1951); and *The Divine Wind* by Captain Roger Pineau, USN, Captain R. Inoguchi, and Commander T. Nakajima (U.S. Naval Institute, Annapolis, Md., 1958). Certain technical facts and designations were double-checked in such source books as *Janes Fighting Ships*, various editions (Arco, New York); the Ian Allan *Navies of World War II* book series, *U.S. Warships of World War II* by P. H. Silverstone (Ian Allen Ltd., Shepperton, UK, 1965 and 1977) and *Japanese Warships of World War II* by A. J. Watts (Ian Allen Ltd., 1966, Doubleday, New York, 1973); Peter Cooksley's *Flying Bomb, Story of Hitler's V-Weapons* (Scribner's, New York, 1979); Anthony Preston's *Destroyers* (Prentice-Hall, Inc., Englewood Cliffs, N.J., 1977); and *Destroyer Weapons of World War 2* by Hodges & Friedman (Naval Institute Press, 1979) as well as with Navy historical sources.

I would also like to thank Ms. Patty Maddocks of the U.S. Naval Institute, who loaned me pictures of Japanese suicide planes, and Captain Frank S. Bayley, Jr., USNR, Retired, who provided the first pictures taken of the *Laffey* following the action. I want to thank Rachel Carr, who initiated the chain of events that brought together Mr. Joseph Morschauser III and me. Without Mr. Morschauser's help this history would not have been published. And finally I want to thank my dear wife, Betty, who endured the long months while this story was written.

F. Julian Becton

CONTENTS

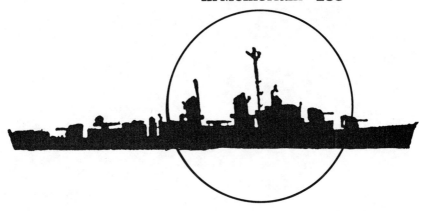

THE SHIP THAT WOULD NOT DIE

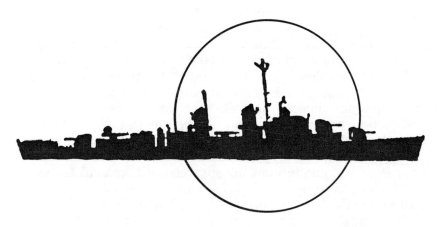

ONE

The original U.S. warship named *Laffey* died gallantly on Friday the thirteenth, November 1942. My own ship at that time, the *Aaron Ward,* was about a mile astern of her in the opening round of the three-day naval conflict between the Japanese and the Americans, the Battle of Guadalcanal. Though outgunned and overwhelmed, the *Laffey* fought to the last and helped set the stage for an American victory. Later on in World War II, when it came time for me to take *Laffey*'s successor into battle, I could never forget the example she set for us all in those brief final minutes of her life. Thus the story of the first *Laffey*'s last fight is an inseparable part of the tale I have to tell.

The first *Laffey* was a destroyer, a DD in naval terminology, a can in naval slang. Some think the latter means tin can, because destroyers have no armor and very thin plates. Actually, to those who know the history of destroyers and value their accomplishments, the word is a compliment. It stands for "Can do," the traditional reply of a destroyer skipper to any and all requests or orders.

Destroyers were thoroughbred workhorses of our fleet and other navies in both world wars, but the first destroyers built in the early 1900s were specialized ships. They were designed solely to protect a battle line against high-speed torpedo boats. In World War I they began to take on the jobs of protectors and torpedo boats, and soon had others as well. By the end of that war destroyers had not only engaged enemy warships with their guns and delivered lightning torpedo attacks, but they were

1

equipped with depth charges and listening devices for antisubmarine work. And by 1942 they also carried numerous small, automatic antiaircraft guns to protect not only themselves but other ships from air attack. Despite their small size and relatively frail structures, destroyers had become all-purpose warships.

The first *Laffey* was long and narrow—347¾ feet overall with 36¼ foot beam. Almost a third of her hull was packed with boilers and high-pressure steam turbines. She was fast. When necessary, she could charge an enemy at what, for a ship, was a very high speed—something approaching thirty-seven land miles per hour. With her ammunition, her supercharged power plant, her depth charges, torpedoes, and a full load of fuel oil, she was a floating bomb. Those who rode her and other destroyers into battle knew it wouldn't take much to set her off.

The *Laffey*, DD 459, was a 1,620-ton ship built at the Union Iron Works in San Francisco. She was commissioned on March 31, 1942. Her skipper was Lieutenant Commander William E. Hank, USN, a fine sailor and dedicated officer. At the end of her fitting-out period the Battle of Midway was imminent. The need for destroyers in the Pacific was so urgent she was sent to Pearl Harbor without any shakedown training at all, and went from there directly to the South Pacific.

I was then an executive officer, the second in command of a similar destroyer, the *Aaron Ward*, and my ship was soon working with the *Laffey* in the seas bounding the Solomon Islands. In the months between August 1942 and February 1943, these waters were to be the scene of more naval battles than the U. S. Navy had fought since the American Civil War. So frequent and intense was the fighting that the waters north of Guadalcanal Island and bounded by Savo and Florida islands gained the nickname "Iron-bottom Sound" because so many warships were lost there.

The Solomons were two roughly parallel chains of tropical, disease-infested jungle islands located about eight hundred miles northeast of Australia. Running from below the equator several hundred miles down to the southeast, these two island chains were like swords pointed at the vital sea-supply routes between Australia and the United States. With little equipment, few arms, and many of her men fighting half a world away in North Africa, these supply routes were Australia's lifelines. Whoever held the Solomon Islands held the key to that vast but sparsely populated country's future.

In mid-1942 the Japanese began building a base and airfield

on the island of Guadalcanal, one of the southernmost in the string of islands nearest Australia. They had by then already developed a seaplane base at Tulagi, about twenty miles north, near Florida Island. But the base and airfield near Lunga Point on Guadalcanal was a far more serious threat. Aware of the danger to our supply lines and to Australia, we struck back. We seized Tulagi and, on August 7, 1942, the U. S. Navy landed ten thousand Marines on Guadalcanal, capturing the half-finished base and airfield. The airstrip was put in order, named Henderson Field in honor of Major L. R. Henderson—a Marine aviator lost at the Battle of Midway—and shortly became a major base for Marine aircraft.

The Japanese lashed out furiously on land, sea, and in the air. They sent ships loaded with troops and supplies down the Slot, as the sixty-mile-wide, deep-water area between the two chains of Solomon Islands came to be called. Their soldiers ashore pressed Marine defenders who protected the airfield. And they sent wave after wave of planes to knock out Henderson and destroy its aircraft.

The Marines hung on. New aircraft were shuttled up from bases far to the south to replace those lost. The distance between those bases and Henderson exceeded the range of our aircraft. But we kept an aircraft carrier, usually the *Enterprise*, midway between to act as a refueling stop for the planes. It was a desperate gamble because during that time the *Enterprise* was frequently the only operational carrier we had. Yet it paid off. Henderson's aircraft were right on the spot, close to the battle area, while the Japanese had to fly some three hundred miles before reaching Marine positions. As a result, the Slot became too hot for daylight intrusions by Japanese warships.

With Japanese losses from daylight attacks on their ships mounting, Admiral Isoruku Yamamoto, their naval Commander in Chief, ordered his ships to shift to night supply and bombardment operations in the Solomons. At night, U. S. aircraft were grounded; and each night, down the Slot came what the Marines called the Tokyo Express. These enemy warships would land reinforcements and supplies for the Army ashore and bombard Henderson with shells. On four nights in early November 1942, the Japanese—using twenty destroyers—landed their entire 38th Army Division on Guadalcanal.

Neither side would budge. We had to hold Henderson and supply the Marines on Guadalcanal because there was no other choice. And the Japanese, in stubborn rage, kept sending more and more warships and replenishments down the Slot. The series of costly night naval actions that resulted drained resources on both sides. We were just hanging on, but we knew our losses could be replaced if we hung on long enough. But for the Japanese the Solomons became an open wound, a naval Stalingrad. They won some of the night surface actions but in so doing lost ships at a rate at which they could never replace them. This attrition soon began to sap the naval superiority they had had since Pearl Harbor.

In almost every one of those naval actions in the Solomons, the U. S. Navy fought against odds. The Japanese usually had more ships or equal numbers of ships of greater power. And the battles were night actions, a type of warfare in which the Japanese Navy had specialized in prewar training. Though the radar on some of our ships gave us an improved ability to locate the enemy, this training often gave them the edge. In addition, their torpedoes were more powerful, faster, and had a longer range than ours; and torpedo attacks played a major role in many of the battles.

The *Laffey* was lost in an action that was typical of these deadly night engagements in most aspects save one. Though it began in the usual way, for the usual reasons, it was intended by the Japanese to be a prelude to a major naval thrust. Admiral Hiroaki Abe's two battleships, his light cruiser, and eleven destroyers were only the spearhead of what Admiral Yamamoto hoped would be a knockout blow. At bases to the north of the Solomons he had assembled a massed fleet that included battleships, carriers, cruisers, and destroyers to back up Abe. In numbers of ships and total power, this fleet was far superior to U. S. Navy forces in the South Pacific. Once Abe had destroyed Henderson Field, Yamamoto intended to use that great superiority to finish us once and for all.

On the afternoon of November 12 some U. S. Navy attack cargo ships were unloading at Guadalcanal as Admiral Abe pushed south. My ship was part of the destroyer screen near the cargo ships. Rear Admiral Richmond Kelly Turner was anxious to get the job done and his cargo ships away. At 8:30 that morning a B-17 had sighted strong Japanese naval units heading toward the Slot.

Unloading was interrupted in midafternoon by twenty-five Japanese torpedo planes escorted by eight Zero fighters. We had been alerted by coast watchers and were ready for them. They came in low, met our wall of antiaircraft fire, and Marine fighters from Henderson helped finish them. Only four Jap planes survived, and the torpedoes they launched ran too deep, leaving our ships unharmed. Unloading resumed at an even faster pace to make up for lost time. Then at 6:30 P.M. the supply and transport ships cleared out, heading for Espíritu Santo far to the south. All destroyers and cruisers in the area saw them well on their way before returning.

We were glad to see the supply ships get away because by that time we knew something was up. *Aaron Ward* and the *Laffey* and six other destroyers joined five cruisers under the overall command of Admiral Daniel J. Callaghan, who had orders to steam out to meet the enemy heading for Guadalcanal. Tall, gray-haired Admiral Callaghan knew the enemy force included battleships. He also knew that the two U. S. battleships in the South Pacific, the *Washington* and *South Dakota*, were still too far away to the south to give him support. Yet despite the overwhelming odds, he took his thirteen ships back to Guadalcanal determined to do the impossible.

Callaghan formed us into a long line to pass through the narrow Lengo Channel north of Guadalcanal. In the lead was the destroyer *Cushing*, commanded by Lieutenant Commander E. N. Parker. She had the commander of Destroyer Division 10, Commander T. M. Stokes, aboard.

Cushing was followed by *Laffey*, then the destroyers *Sterett* and *O'Bannon*. Next in line was the antiaircraft cruiser *Atlanta*, so designated because she mounted only dual-purpose five-inch guns instead of the six-inch guns of a regular light cruiser. She carried six twin mounts, twelve main battery guns in all, but these were similar to those on destroyers and lacked the punch of six-inchers.

Following *Atlanta* were 2 eight-inch-gun heavy cruisers, the *San Francisco* and the *Portland*. The former was Admiral Callaghan's flagship. Then came the six-inch-gun light cruiser *Helena*. Directly astern of her was the *Juneau*, a sister ship of—and identical to—the cruiser *Atlanta*. She was followed by the destroyers *Aaron Ward* (my ship), the *Barton, Monssen*, and *Fletcher*.

In terms of gun power and armor we were a mighty thin gray battle line that sailed toward the Japanese that night. And our numbers weren't exactly impressive either.

Even under the best of circumstances—and those that night were not—steaming toward a naval action in darkness is an unnerving experience. Each ship is blacked out, isolated from the rest. The shroudlike gloom surrounding a ship presses in on every man aboard, even those at stations below. Forward and aft, port and starboard, unseen danger lurks. At any moment a searchlight or flare may bathe the ship in a blinding glare, and torpedoes or shells tear her apart.

You try to concentrate on your work, yet even that effort can be dangerous. Too much concentration may numb your senses, hobble your reflexes at a moment you need them most. And such a moment may come even before battle is joined. In the blackness, ships can get out of formation, and a ship—even an agile destroyer—cannot be maneuvered easily. Collision is an ever-present danger, one that can sink you just as surely as enemy action.

Just about the time the Japanese torpedo planes attacked the supply ships off Guadalcanal, Admiral Abe's flagship, *Hiei*, catapulted its scout plane. Not long after, the enemy force ran into a violent tropical rainstorm. Visibility was cut to zero, but Abe's ships continued at a steady eighteen knots. Finally the scout plane reported that there were more than a dozen American warships off Lunga Point on Guadalcanal. Lunga was used as a navigational landmark by both sides.

Admiral Abe steamed on, his ships in three parallel columns. The central column was led by the light cruiser *Nagara*, which was followed by the battleships *Hiei* and *Kirishima*. Though both of these battleships were old, they were thoroughly modernized, and carried eight 14-inch guns each, in addition to a number of 6-inch guns as secondary armament. And a considerable proportion of their huge displacements of more than 31,000 tons was thick steel armor. In any gun action they would be formidable opponents.

Six Japanese destroyers were in the port (easterly) column. Five others, led by the *Yudachi* and *Harusame*, made up Abe's starboard (westerly) column. We were outnumbered in destroyers, and the two enemy battleships far outclassed our cruisers in firepower and armor.

After suffering hours of darkness and receiving a report from the Japanese Army observation post on Guadalcanal that the weather there was very bad, Admiral Abe ordered his formation to reverse course. He apparently felt his ships were moving with the storm at about the same speed. He knew the course reversal would delay his arrival off Henderson Field, but he hoped the maneuver would allow the storm to move away from his line of approach. Then something more than a half hour later, Admiral Abe ordered another reversal back to the original course.

These two course changes threw his formation into disarray. Bad weather and darkness make station keeping very difficult for even the most experienced seaman. The effect was to put the destroyers *Yudachi* and *Harusame* far ahead of the others in the Japanese starboard column. Had they continued, they would have run aground on Guadalcanal. Instead they turned easterly on an angle which took them across the front of the Japanese formation.

The sea was calm that night in our area, with only a light breeze blowing from the east. We could see low-lying clouds, occasionally broken to reveal stars, but the thin curve of the new moon had long since disappeared. The only illumination in the sky came from occasional stabs and flashes of lightning stretching in an arc across the horizon ahead of us. It was the edge of a tropical storm. At midnight it began to appear as if we would be in it before we made contact with the Japanese.

With the weather still bad and the seas through which he was steaming kicking up, Admiral Abe's scout plane could not return to land near *Hiei* and be hoisted aboard. As his fuel ran low, the pilot headed for Bougainville Island to land. This deprived Abe of an important tool for a night engagement, because scout floatplanes often were used by the Japanese to drop flares to illuminate enemy ships. But Admiral Abe apparently was not concerned. His mind was on the bombardment of Henderson Field, not on thoughts of a surface action against enemy warships; and Bougainville would send floatplanes to drop flares for the bombardment.

Flare illumination of Henderson for naval bombardments was a standard Japanese tactic. In fact it had become so routine a measure that Marines at Henderson would dive for foxholes the minute one flare was dropped. It always was a signal for shells to start roaring in.

Henderson had been plastered quite often, but none of the bombardments had interrupted operations for very long. The giant fourteen-inch projectiles ready in the magazines aboard *Hiei* and *Kirishima* might have produced a different result; yet as it turned out, this shore-bombardment ammunition was to prove more of a liability than an asset to the Japanese.

Our own battle line was still intact as Admiral Abe's ships neared us. We were steaming in a northwesterly direction at

1:20 A.M. when the *Helena*'s radar picked up a skunk—a contact that could neither be land nor friendly. *Helena* and *O'Bannon* were the only two ships in the forward part of our formation with up-to-date SG surface-search radars. They were Admiral Callaghan's "eyes."

He immediately ordered a course change to the north, which each ship in our line was to execute as she reached the turning point of the ship ahead. We knew we were closing the enemy, but exact details of the situation were unclear. Both *Helena* and *O'Bannon* were separated from the flagship by other ships, and Admiral Callaghan had to rely solely on short-range voice radio signals for information from them and then to send his orders. The TBS (talk between ships) channel was not ideal for such communication. It was soon overloaded with tactical information messages.

My ship, the *Aaron Ward,* had not yet reached the turning position in line when Commander Stokes in *Cushing* reported visual contact with enemy ships. So close were the *Yudachi* and *Harusame,* that the fast-running *Cushing* had to turn hard to port (her left) to avoid a sure collision and to get herself into position for launching torpedoes. Stokes requested immediate permission to fire torpedoes, and it was granted. The *Laffey,* just astern of the *Cushing,* also had to swing hard to port, but the *Sterett* and the rest of the ships in Admiral Callaghan's line of battle were able to maintain a northerly course. Very soon then, *Cushing* and *Laffey* found themselves separated from the others, alone and about to be engulfed by a large enemy formation.

Aboard the *Yudachi* the Japanese sighted *Cushing,* and *Laffey* following her. Then the masthead lookout aboard Admiral Abe's flagship, *Hiei,* spotted four more of us. Abe's thoughts of the bombardment were swept away as he realized he now faced a battle against warships. He was in trouble. The relatively thin-skinned one-ton bombardment ammunition ready in the magazines of the two battleships was not really suitable for such an action if he faced heavily armored American ships. The difficulty was that he didn't know exactly what kinds of ships confronted his own. He must have been swept by panic, for he gave an order he must have known would be almost impossible to execute. He told his men to shift the ammunition in the magazines so they could use armor-piercing shells stored deep within them. The result was pandemonium in both battleships.

It was now about 1:43 A.M. Shortly thereafter the entire

American line became disorganized, all its ships charging almost headlong into the teeth of the Japanese formation. For some time the TBS was strangely silent. Then Admiral Callaghan finally gave the order to open fire. Why he delayed no one knows, nor ever will, because he was killed soon after when Japanese shells struck the *San Francisco*.

As a naval officer, now retired, I am reluctant to compare what happened next to a land battle, yet in this case the confused drive of our ships right into the middle of the Japanese formation did somewhat resemble that charge immortalized by Tennyson. Every American ship took the bit and raced at Admiral Abe's forces. We were in among them before they knew what was happening, firing every gun that would bear, launching torpedoes port and starboard. It was disorganized. It was individual, with every ship for herself. Perhaps if Tennyson had seen it he would have called it magnificent.

Cushing got there first, but *Laffey* wasn't far behind. Both ships opened fire at 1:50 A.M. Moments later their lookouts reported they were head to head with a giant. It was the *Hiei*.

While her gunners fired at enemy destroyers, *Cushing* went after the battleship with torpedoes. They were the only weapons she carried that could handle *Hiei*—and the run to the *Hiei* was less than one thousand yards, a short range. Yet *Cushing*'s torpedoes either missed or, more likely, failed to explode. *Hiei* took evasive action, illuminating *Cushing* with her searchlights, then pounding the destroyer into a flaming junk pile with her guns.

In trying to avoid *Cushing*'s torpedoes, *Hiei*'s bow swung dead on the *Laffey*. With a shock, Lieutenant Commander Hank and his men saw what must have looked like a giant's ax head cleaving the waves toward them less than three hundred yards away. It was *Laffey*'s turn to take evasive action. She swung just in time as the *Hiei* crossed her wake.

Hiei came so close Hank could have hit her with a slingshot. He didn't have one, but he let go with torpedoes. These bounced off the battleship's thick hide like pebbles off a sea turtle's shell. Our torpedoes had to run a certain distance before their arming mechanism was activated; the narrow span of water between the two ships wasn't enough for that.

Laffey was doomed, and everyone aboard must have known it. Though *Hiei* had been hit by our fire, she was still mostly unharmed. She was like a slightly wounded bull, enraged by pain and determined to smash the little matador challenging her. Her guns trained toward the *Laffey*, their gaping muzzles ready to deliver tons of shell and explosive. But the destroyer was still too close for *Hiei*'s main battery to depress enough to hit her. *Laffey* had a few minutes left and she made good use of them.

Even a thickly armored battleship has its weak spots, and the gunners aboard the destroyer found *Hiei*'s. *Laffey*'s little 5-inch guns and her smaller, automatic antiaircraft cannon elevated and poured a torrent of steel at the giant's superstructure. They concentrated on the tall, pagodalike mast forward where the bridge was located. On that bridge was Admiral Abe and the *Hiei*'s captain. *Laffey*'s gunners tried to do what Ulysses—that hero of ancient Greek mythology—did to the giant, one-eyed Cyclops. They tried to blind her.

By naval standards, *Laffey*'s small automatic antiaircraft cannons could not be considered heavy weapons. The explosive shells they fired were hardly worthy of the name, averaging only a few inches long and with the diameter of large cigars. Such shells could have little effect on real armor plate because they were mainly for use against thin-skinned aircraft or small enemy boats and ships. But fired against the thin, light steel that forms the protective screen in the bridge area of many ships, these shells could inflict terrible damage. Each shell was small, but the cumulative effect of a steady stream of rounds poured machine-gunlike at a target would rip, tear, and batter. It would also set fires.

Such automatic antiaircraft cannons are in fact machine guns, and intermixed with their other shells were tracer rounds. Tracers have phosphorus imbedded in an adhesive at the shell's base. Ignited when the shell is fired, it burns with a high heat, thus marking the trajectory of the shell with a trail of bright light. If a still-burning tracer strikes anything that will burn, it starts a fire just like a larger explosive shell such as a five-incher. And at short range, *Laffey*'s tracers arrived at their target still burning.

Laffey's gunners sent her streams of shells at the *Hiei*'s bridge; shattering, chopping, and chewing away at its thin steel; further confusing and threatening Admiral Abe. He was stunned, others near were wounded. Captain Suzuki, Abe's Chief of Staff, was killed. Meanwhile, other hits continued to set more fires. Flames and smoke blurred Abe's vision. All the rounds that struck *Hiei* did not come from the *Laffey*, but many of the streams of tracers that sliced through the choking smoke certainly did. *Laffey* blinded the Cyclops and threw the most important brain aboard *Hiei* into a state of near panic. Abe was a rear admiral, an experienced naval officer, but he was still just a man. *Laffey* had gotten to him, personally and directly.

The irony of it all was that it was not the guns of *Hiei* that began the destruction of the *Laffey*. Ensign David Stafford Sterrett, one of her survivors, who told historians of the Navy Department his recollections of the action and sinking of his ship, made this point.

Sterrett estimated that the *Laffey* was only about twenty feet from the bow of the *Hiei* when the destroyer swung clear. The battleship's guns were silent, but soon *Laffey*'s gunners were about their deadly work. Exactly how long they had to do their job, Sterrett wasn't sure, but he remembered that suddenly the destroyer was hit in the stern by a torpedo. A torpedo—not a shell from *Hiei*.

The explosion of the warhead smashed the destroyer's fire mains and started a bad fire. With the fire mains out of action, there was no way to flood the ship's magazines, and attempts by the crew to extinguish the blaze met with no success.

While this was happening, Japanese warships would race by and throw heavy salvos of shells at the ship. Sterrett especially remembered a cruiser not more than 1,500 yards away lighting up the ship with her searchlights, then opening up with her guns. Her shells struck home with loud blasts that shook the vulnerable destroyer, and quickly began to turn her into a complete wreck.

There were hits in the engineering spaces—her fire rooms and engine rooms—and more in the director, the bridge, and the forward part of the ship. Gun crews still firing their weapons were wiped out to a man, and others who escaped were badly wounded. Finally the order had to be given to abandon ship.

Sterrett told his interviewers that he was in no hurry to jump in the water. He said he remembered that the *Duncan*, another destroyer hard hit in a night battle about a month before, had stayed afloat for hours, and he felt he could keep away from the sharks a little longer that way. The waters around Guadalcanal were heavily infested with sharks, and many sailors had been killed by them after their ships went down. But Sterrett had another reason to stay aboard for a while: His life jacket was missing.

He just had time to find a mattress and heave it over the side when he saw his skipper, Lieutenant Commander Hank, come round from the port side. Hank took a few steps toward the break in the forecastle and *wham*, the whole ship lifted out of the water with a blast. Sterrett never saw Hank again. He ended up in the water shortly after and finally got on the mattress. Luckily, he was far enough away from the *Laffey* by the time she dived so that her suction did not pull him with her.

Another survivor, Lieutenant Eugene A. Barham, USN, was also in the water at that time, though he did not see Sterrett. Barham was *Laffey*'s chief engineer. He had made his way to the bridge a short time before to report the total destruction of the destroyer's power plant and to recommend abandoning the ship. After hearing his summation of the damage, Hank reluctantly agreed. Minutes later, as Barham was in the water, he called up to Hank asking if he was coming. Hank called back that he was, then disappeared around a corner of the superstructure. Not long after that the massive explosion ripped out the ship's bottom, throwing chunks of steel into the air. Barham thinks falling debris killed his skipper.

The *Laffey*'s giant adversary, *Hiei*, roared on after her guns and those of her consorts finished the destroyer. But by this time *Hiei* was suffering too. Fires aboard her, many set by *Laffey*'s guns, had made her a perfect target for American ships. She had been and continued to be hit and hit again. Her control tower was wrecked. Her steering mechanism was smashed. She was soon a virtual derelict, one that Admiral Abe would be forced to abandon some hours later.

All during this time things had hardly been dull aboard my own ship, *Aaron Ward*. The skipper, Lieutenant Commander Orville Gregor, had had to maneuver her like a quarterback on a broken field run to avoid collisions, to keep her guns trained on the enemy, and to dodge enemy fire. I recall one instance when I was in the pilothouse with the skipper, the destroyer squadron commander, Captain Robert Tobin, and others. A target crossed our bow about seven thousand yards away. We pumped a number of five-inch salvos into her, but then Gregor had to shout, "Check fire! All engines stop! All engines back full!" Our chance to rake what possibly was the *Hiei* with more shells disappeared as we narrowly averted collision with the *Helena*. It was an incident typical of that wild melee in which *Laffey* was lost.

We had other chances to pound the enemy, but like a number of other American ships in that battle, *Aaron Ward* too was heavily hit. We lost steam power, and for a while we were in complete darkness. I can understand how Admiral Abe must have felt aboard his burning, careening flagship. A naval ship heavily damaged in a night action seems completely isolated, vulnerable, and alone. And if the damage produces fires and smoke which further blind and confuse, the situation appears critical to a point of despair. Your only weapon against it is your training and your determination not to give in.

Admiral Abe did no damage to Henderson Field. By about 2:00 A.M. on Friday the thirteenth of November, 1942, both sides had suffered terrible damage and losses. We had lost more ships, however, and had Abe continued to press us our losses that morning might have been more severe. We could not have stopped his ships. But Admiral Abe apparently never realized this at the time.

What the guns of the *Laffey* and other U. S. Navy ships had done to the *Hiei* during the action made Abe believe he faced impossible odds. With smoke and flames blinding him, he issued no orders to his other ships until the very end. He remained as mute as the dead Admiral Callaghan throughout the fighting until, in apparent desperation and confusion, he ordered a withdrawal.

This was *Laffey*'s accomplishment, even though fire from many other American warships contributed to it. Her very gall in remaining almost unmoving in the glare of *Hiei*'s searchlights as she poured streams of tracers up toward Abe's station seemingly unnerved him. Destroyers were designed for hit-and-run torpedo attacks against battleships. They were not supposed to challenge them head on with their small-caliber guns.

Admiral Abe's warships paid dearly for his confusion and panic. That brief and violent battle in the early morning darkness of Friday the thirteenth was followed by wave upon wave of attacks we launched during the next seventy-two hours. *Hiei*, of course, had to be scuttled. But Abe's other battleship, the *Kirishima*, was so battered in subsequent fighting that she too was scuttled. The three-day naval Battle of Guadalcanal ended in a U. S. victory the likes of which we had not experienced in many long, terrible months.

This battle was a turning point. Admiral Yamamoto was furious with Admiral Abe, whom he quickly relieved of his command. Not only was the loss of two battleships a staggering blow to Yamamoto's plans, but it ended forever any real possibility of a truly massive Japanese Navy victory over the U. S. Navy in the South Pacific. Japan could not afford the kind of losses such a battle was sure to entail.

The USS *Laffey*, DD 459, was not a supership. She did not

win the naval Battle of Guadalcanal all by herself, though she did much to make it possible. She was just a destroyer, one faced with impossible odds, who sold her life dearly. She made the enemy pay a high price before he could overcome her.

Aaron Ward went on. Although hit by nine shells during the battle, three of them fourteen-inchers, she was finally towed to safety. Repaired at Pearl Harbor, she soon returned to the South Pacific.

Soon afterward, I became *Aaron Ward's* skipper. I did not hold my command long: Within three weeks bombs from enemy planes caused serious underwater damage to her hull. We fought to control the flooding, but we lost. She went down less than a mile from safety without an enemy plane or ship in sight.

Long after it happened I continued to feel I could have done more to prevent it. Though my superiors commended us for our efforts to save her, and my fellow officers did their best to cheer me up, the feeling of depression and loss stayed with me for a very long time. I was not the only one—many of my shipmates shared my sorrow.

Months later, when I learned I would be given command of a new destroyer, I prayed she would not be forced to suffer the same end as the *Aaron Ward.* I hoped that, if her turn came, she would have the opportunity to make the enemy pay dearly just like the *Laffey.* Yet I did not intend for her to suffer that fate either. I wanted her to match *Laffey's* record of accomplishment in battle. But I also wanted her to do that with as few or fewer casualties as we had had when *Aaron Ward* was lost. I swore a silent oath that I would do everything in my power to make this possible. Odds or no odds, we were going to both win *and* survive.

I suppose it was a foolish oath. I had seen enough of war and of battle by then to know that even the best-trained, bravest men in the most efficient ship in the world may not be able to prevail against circumstance. Yet I have a stubborn streak—I had faith we could do it. I was at the time so intent on my determination, and remained so, that I ignored such a possibility. Perhaps it was just as well. There were a lot of those circumstances ahead.

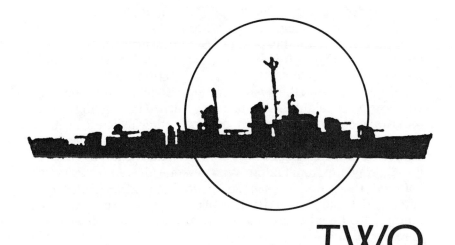

TWO

A captain of a warship, even one who has had command of her for only a short time, quickly starts to think of her as more than just a responsibility. To him she becomes something special, a fondly regarded companion and partner in the constant battle with the sea and elements, a right arm in the deadly struggle to defeat the enemy. If he loses her, he can never forget her.

Aaron Ward went down on April 7, 1943, in forty fathoms of water off Tinete Point in the Solomons. I knew we had done everything possible to save her, and that her sinking was just one more tragic incident in the costly war we were fighting. Yet her loss depressed me and my memories of it were painful. I hoped that when I was given command of another destroyer, she too would be named *Aaron Ward.*

I also hoped my new assignment would come soon. But with heavy fighting still raging in the South Pacific, and with the need for experienced officers great, this was not to be. Instead, I was made operations officer on the staff of the commander of Destroyer Squadron Twenty-one.

It was an important job and the experience it gave me was vital to my continued development as a naval officer. We tangled often with the enemy, usually coming out on top. I had the opportunity to work with and learn from many fine officers. Still, I continued to long for a command of my own. In November, when I finally received orders to proceed to the States, I was very pleased. I knew my wish would soon be fulfilled.

I boarded a plane at Henderson Field, Guadalcanal, and flew to Noumea on the island of New Caledonia. From there I went on to Hawaii and got another plane for San Francisco. On that plane I found three officers from the destroyer *Chevalier* with whom I had worked in the South Pacific. The *Chevalier* had been sunk, and they too were on their way home for reassignment to another ship. We got to talking and, when they learned I was going home to assume command of a new destroyer, they asked if I could arrange to have them assigned to it. Their own skipper had suffered a broken leg before his ship went down, and the injury would delay him from taking over a new one for some time. I was flattered that they seemed so anxious to serve under my command. I said I would try, because I knew all three to be fine officers, good men whom I would be proud to have aboard my ship.

I didn't know anyone in San Francisco so, as the plane neared the West Coast, I suggested we all get together that night at the Top of the Mark, a popular restaurant atop the Mark Hopkins Hotel. I told them that by then I might know more about my ship, where she was being built, and whether it was possible for them to become part of her complement. They agreed at once, promising to meet me at eight that evening.

We landed in midafternoon, and I reported to the commandant of the Twelfth Naval District for further orders and to find out where I would be quartered while in the city. In late November 1943, San Francisco was a major distribution center for officers and enlisted personnel going to and coming from the Pacific. I discovered that all regular quartering facilities were filled up, but this turned out to be a lucky break. I was assigned instead to the Sir Francis Drake Hotel, where the Navy had leased space. After months of Spartan living aboard ship in the South Pacific, I welcomed a chance to enjoy the comfort of civilian surroundings. I hurried to the hotel as fast as I could, but by the time I got to my room, it was almost 4:00 P.M. That meant it was about 7:00 P.M. in Washington, D.C.: too late to call there. I knew I'd have to wait until the next morning to find out about my new ship. I was disappointed, but I quickly put it out of my mind. I had too many other things to do.

First, I needed some clothes—a blue uniform and a raincoat. Like everyone else aboard, I'd lost a lot of personal gear when *Aaron Ward* went down, and it was cold in Frisco. There's an old saying that those who have spent a lot of time in a hot climate have thin blood. I never believed it, but I sure felt then as if it were

16

true. I found a shop with an accommodating tailor close to the hotel. He promised to have my new uniform ready by 5:00 P.M. the next day. Gratefully, my new raincoat pulled close around me, I walked back to my room and picked up the phone.

I called my family in Hot Springs, Arkansas, and talked to my mother. She was happy. She had not been well and, like any mother with a son off at war, she had worried about me. And, like any grown son in a similar situation, I did my best to reassure her I was fine. I also told her I would be home soon.

After we finished talking, I put in another long-distance call, this time to New York. When Imogen's voice came on it was warm, friendly, and I was elated she was happy to hear from me. I'd been corresponding with Imogen Carpenter for over a year; her letters had meant a great deal to me during those months in the South Pacific. I told her I was to get some leave and that I would come to New York to see her as soon as I could.

When I hung up the phone I sat there thinking about Imogen, of how we'd first met, and of how lucky I was to have a beautiful young woman like her as a good friend.

That first meeting was back in January of 1942. It had all come about by sheer chance. My sister, Virginia, and her husband, Philip Winston, had come up to New York from their home in Memphis. I was then waiting for the *Aaron Ward* to be completed over in the Federal Shipyard at Kearny, New Jersey, and I got together with them in New York on a Sunday.

That afternoon, my brother-in-law said he wanted to get in touch with a Memphis friend due in New York the next day. The friend was planning to stay at the Hotel Pierre over on Fifth Avenue at Sixty-first Street, and Philip intended to leave a message for him at the desk.

The Pierre was one of the finest, most luxurious hotels in the city, and it housed a plush and glamorous dining room-lounge, the Cotillion Room. As my sister and I stood in the lobby waiting for her husband, I suddenly noticed a large picture of one of the most beautiful girls I had ever seen. Under it was her name, Imogen Carpenter, and the announcement said that she was then appearing as a performer at that famous Cotillion Room. Not only was her face somewhat familiar, but so was her name.

I turned to my sister and asked, "Do you think she could be the Imogene Carpenter who lived a few blocks from us in Hot Springs years ago?"

When I went off to prep school, there was a ten-year-old girl in my hometown who was already being talked of as a superb pianist. She was also said to have a beautiful voice. Of course I was a few years older, and back then I never paid any attention to her. But if this was the same Miss Carpenter, even though her first name lacked the last *e*, then she had surely grown into a beautiful woman. And her talent must have carried her to a considerable success in the entertainment world. The Cotillion Room was noted for engaging only the best entertainers in the business.

"Let's leave a note for her and see," my sister replied, probably with a twinkle in her eye that I missed because I was too busy looking at the picture.

We did. I called the hotel the next week—sure enough, she was that former ten-year-old from Hot Springs. Not very long after that we met. Like me, she wasn't married, and she seemed pleased when I asked her for a date. To say that I was happy when she accepted would be an understatement. She was not only beautiful—with a fine figure, wonderful blue eyes, and raven black hair—but she was a refined gentlewoman. She had a warm, friendly personality, a superbly musical voice, and a keen sense of humor. And on top of all that, we got on well together; in part, I think, because we shared many memories of the past in Hot Springs.

Other dates followed, and we became fond of each other. She fascinated me: She was fun to be with, and the entertainment world in which she worked was a whole new experience for me.

Not long after our first date she was soon taking part in nightly rehearsals for a new Broadway show, *High Kickers*, starring Sophie Tucker and George Jessel. Whenever we dated, we usually had dinner in the theater district, very often at a place called Dinty Moore's. Imogen had a Navy man's preference in food: She loved steak, as did I, and the brine-soaked baked potatoes they served there along with it set the meal off with a salty tang. I felt right at home. But the pleasure of her company alone would have been enough to make these dinners memorable.

A couple of times I went with her to rehearsals, sitting down front in the semidarkness watching the development of various parts of *High Kickers*. Though little that went on there even remotely resembled the world I was used to, it did strike me that there was at least one similarity between the theater and the Navy. In both cases, the drills had to be endlessly practiced until every participant could respond perfectly when the curtain went up. Theater rehearsals and Navy exercises both required discipline, dedication, and concentration.

When the *Aaron Ward* left for the South Pacific, Imogen promised to write to me. Her letters were not only welcome, but were one of the things that helped lift my sagging spirits when my ship was lost in April 1943. She always wrote that she thought of me often, especially when there was news of some major naval battle.

Our considerable interest in each other led to one amusing incident. Out in the Solomons, someone gave me a clipping from the New York *Daily Mirror*, a newspaper that featured many photographs. The clipping was a picture of Imogen. She was wearing some diamond earrings, and the caption stated that these had been a gift from me.

She wrote me about it, embarrassed, and explained what had happened. She apparently had mentioned me to her friends and those she worked with. When she was picked to model the jewelry for a newspaper publicity photo, her manager decided it would be published more readily if he wrote a caption saying the earrings were a present to her from her Navy man overseas.

Her manager's instincts about what would catch the eye of the paper's editor were good, but his knowledge of the Navy was a little faulty. Though I was certainly fond enough of Imogen to have given her such a present, the possibility of any officer of my rank doing so was very remote. None of us were paid enough to be able to buy that sort of gift.

Imogen knew all this, and that's why the incident embarrassed her. But to me it was just plain funny, and I reassured her, telling her I really didn't mind. It wasn't her doing, and besides, I was secretly pleased because it meant she was thinking of me as much as I was of her.

I stayed in my hotel room after these calls, thinking about Imogen, my family, what I would do on leave, and my new ship. Suddenly, about 7:00 P.M., I realized I was getting hungry. I got my coat and walked up the hill to the Mark Hopkins. The food at the Top of the Mark was delicious, a real treat after all those meals at sea on a destroyer. There is nothing wrong with Navy food, but Navy cooks and stewards can do only so much with what they have. And most of them are not trained as master chefs.

I had just finished when the three officers from the *Chevalier* walked in. They were anxious to know about my ship and whether there appeared to be any possibility they could join her. We talked for a while, had a couple rounds of drinks. When we broke up I again reassured them I would request they get orders assigning them to my destroyer.

Promptly at 8:00 the next morning I put in a person-to-person call to the destroyer detail officer in the Bureau of Naval Personnel in Washington. The voice that came over the wire was that of an old friend. Commander Bernie Fuetsch had graduated from Annapolis with the class of 1930 a year earlier than I. This was an example of one thing I have always liked about being in the Navy: No matter where you were, you usually ran into an old friend, and dealing with old friends always makes any task easier.

"Julie," he said, "it's nice to hear your voice again. You are getting a destroyer. Which coast would you prefer? We have them building on both the West and East coasts."

I didn't need to ponder that one very long. "East Coast, Bernie," I said. I knew it didn't matter to the Navy. And all the people I wanted to see were in the East. If my ship was building and put in commission on the East Coast, I knew I'd probably have more chances to see them because travel time would be held to a minimum.

"Then you'll get the *Laffey*," Bernie's voice came back.

I've already mentioned that I had had a very slim hope that I might get the new *Aaron Ward.* Very slim because I knew such things rarely worked out that way. Actually, though I did not know it at that time, a new *Aaron Ward* was not to be commissioned until May 1944. But when Bernie Fuetsch mentioned *Laffey*, it shook me a little.

"The *Laffey*," I said. I suppose I sounded as if I didn't believe him.

"Yes, Julie," Bernie went on. "She's an Allen M. Sumner-class 2,200-tonner being built at Bath, Maine. I'll get dispatch orders out to you this afternoon. You'll get leave, of course."

"That's fine, Bernie." I replied, now recovered somewhat from my initial shock on hearing the name *Laffey*. But memories of that morning off Guadalcanal over a year ago flashed through my mind. It was going to take some doing to live up to her record.

"Do you have anyone with you?" Bernie went on.

"Yes, yes, I do," I said. "Three officers I know. They are survivors from the *Chevalier*. They have all asked to be assigned to my ship and I'd like to have them, if it's possible."

20

"OK," said Bernie. "Give me their names."

I spelled them out, and he went on.

"I can't promise you'll get all three, Julie. But I'll see what I can do."

I thanked him again, then hung up. By that time I had managed to come to terms with what he'd told me about my new ship. I was excited, but after a bit I suddenly realized that the flutters in my midsection were being caused by something else: A good, leisurely breakfast would take care of them. After that, a walk in the crisp, bright morning air would be just the thing, give me a chance to review what I'd learned with a clear head.

During the day I had lunch with a friend who lived in a small community outside San Francisco, and did a little research on the origin of the name *Laffey*. Then I met my *Chevalier* friends again in the evening and told them about my conversation with Bernie. I said I'd put in a request for them and that I hoped to get orders the next day. If they came in, I intended to get a plane for the East as soon as I could. One of the officers, Brad Collins, gave me the phone number of their quarters, asking me to call them again before I left.

The next day I stayed around my hotel waiting for a call from district headquarters. Right after lunch it came. The communications watch officer said I could pick up my orders in about an hour. I packed my bag, then called the officer in charge of the bachelor officers' quarters at the Alameda Naval Air Station. I wanted to stay there that night so I could get the first available space on a plane heading east.

I called Brad Collins, but none of the three *Chevalier* officers had orders yet. I tried to cheer them up, saying I would see them at Bath. I guess I shouldn't have been so reassuring—things never did work out the way they wanted. All three ended up on the destroyer *John D. Henley;* the next time I saw them was in Bermuda on *Laffey*'s shakedown cruise. What Robert Burns, the eighteenth-century Scot poet, said about "The best laid schemes o' mice and men" went double for World War II Navy men. All their plans were twice as likely to "Gang aft a-gley"—meaning not work out.

I picked up my orders, then hitched a ride in a car going out to Alameda to meet an admiral inbound from Hawaii. By 7:00 A.M. the next day I was aboard a C-47 rolling down the runway and lifting off for Memphis Naval Air Station. It was clear, though still almost dark, and as the plane climbed for more altitude, you

21

could see dots of light spread out below in the semigloom. But even over San Francisco the sky lacked its usual bright glow, because the brilliant illumination of the city was dimmed by wartime brown-out regulations.

The C-47 was a service version of the dependable prewar Douglas DC-3 commercial transport plane. By today's modern jet standards, it flew low and slow. I settled back in my seat as the plane bucked and jumped through the occasional air pocket, knowing it would be many hours before we touched down at Memphis. I was anxious to get home, but my years of contact with the Navy and in service had taught me patience, how to wait out long periods of time without frustration. This, in fact, had been one of the first lessons I had had to learn.

I thought back to those days. It was 1925 and I was nearing graduation from high school when my Aunt Mary had sent some pictures of Annapolis to my brother John. In her letter she had included a lot of descriptive information about the Naval Academy.

My brother wasn't really interested, but I was fascinated. I decided then I wanted to go to Annapolis and become a naval officer. A career as a Navy regular appealed to me, even though my only knowledge of the service and the sea came from reading. My choice of a career was not unusual. The inland states of this country have produced many deep-water sailors and outstanding naval officers throughout the nation's history.

Wanting to go to the Naval Academy and getting there were two different things. One had to be appointed, then pass a series of difficult tests. I wrote a letter to our senator, Joe Robinson, a man who was to be the Democratic vice-presidential nominee three years later; but he quickly wrote back, replying that the soonest he could fill my request was two years hence. To a boy of my age, that sounded like a very long time. I made other inquiries, but the response was the same. There were no current openings.

I was impatient, annoyed, but I was also concerned. In two years I would be nineteen. The Academy's entry age limit was twenty. If something went wrong, I would miss out completely. Yet I soon resigned myself to waiting those two years, and meanwhile became determined to make sure nothing would go wrong when the time came. With the help of my Aunt Mary, my family found a good school in the South that specialized in preparing young men for the service academies.

I went back to high school after graduation, and spent a year taking mathematics courses. Then I went to Marion Institute in Alabama. In June of the following year I was accepted at Annapolis. In four more, I graduated with the class of 1931, and was a new ensign in the U. S. Navy.

It had all taken much more time than I had supposed back when I made my decision on a naval career, but it had been worth it. Further, the patience it taught me served me well in the years thereafter.

Flying east from San Francisco to Memphis, you have to cross some of the highest mountains of the Rockies. Even with the good weather we were having, this was not an easy job in a C-47, with its relatively limited maximum operating altitude. Where possible, to minimize such higher altitude flying, the pilot kept our plane over valleys between peaks.

There were times when I could look out of the small windows and see snow-covered, rocky mountain walls to port and starboard. With the noise and vibration of our motors and the occasional rocking and jolts from air pockets, it reminded me of the sensation one gets in a small motorboat sailing in beam seas through the troughs of great waves. It made me feel at home, but as a seaman I had to admit that I would have preferred a mile or two of ocean brine below to that chill, thin mountain air. Not only that, but as a deep-water sailor I had an instinctive dislike of being in a channel between two rocky outcrops—but in a plane there was a difference. No destroyer could climb above and over shoaling rocks to port and starboard.

After a while I began to study my fellow passengers, finally glancing at the man sitting next to me. He had on the uniform of a lieutenant junior grade of the Coast Guard. Though in peacetime the Coast Guard was an independent service, in war it had become part of the Navy. In other words, he was a brother officer; when he looked at me, I nodded and smiled, introducing myself.

I can't recall his name after all these years, but I think it was something like Jackson, Johnson, or maybe Johnston. It doesn't really matter—what did was that he seemed to want company and to chat. I suppose he was restless, bored, yet had hesitated to speak before because of my rank. He was en route to Dallas, Texas, on emergency leave. His uncle had died, leaving him heir to a business. The company lawyers had requested he be allowed home on brief leave to sign needed legal documents. And since his ship was in San Francisco for a couple of weeks, his sympathetic skipper had agreed.

"You have been out in the Pacific?" he said after a few minutes.

I nodded and replied that I had, down in the Solomons.

He told me he didn't know very much about that area, only what he'd heard and read, but he said he had had a cousin from Texas who had been killed on the cruiser *San Francisco*. It turned out this had happened during that battle of November 13, 1942, when the *Laffey* was sunk. When I mentioned that my own destroyer, *Aaron Ward*, was in that action, he asked me to tell him more about it.

He was especially interested in more details about his cousin's ship, explaining that his family would be very grateful for anything I could add that did not violate security regulations. Since I knew how limited and carefully worded were official communications to families of those lost in battle, I was more than happy to tell him what I could.

When I was finished he thanked me, saying, "I know it's going to make the family feel better when they find out just how important that battle was and how much it accomplished. It helps a lot when people back home can hear that their son or some close relative gave up his life to win a real victory."

I agreed, thinking of the families of all those good men, from Admiral Callaghan to those on the *Laffey* and the *Aaron Ward*, whose sacrifices did so much to help us defeat the Japanese.

The lieutenant was still looking at me, his young face very serious, when he spoke again.

"Your own ship, Commander, what happened to her? You said she made it to safety. Is she still OK?"

I shook my head slowly, and for just a few moments that feeling of hurt returned. I would have passed on to some other subject, because I had made up my mind not to dwell on the loss of *Aaron Ward*, only to think of the future. But as I looked at his face, I realized he truly wanted to hear the story. What I could tell him might help him later on when he got into battle. Also, I recalled that talking about *Aaron Ward* had always made me feel a little better about her.

I told him how my skipper, Lieutenant Commander O. F. Gregor, had taken the ship to Pearl Harbor after some emergency repairs at Espíritu Santo. When I remarked that Gregor had been awarded the Navy Cross for the way he had fought and maneuvered *Aaron Ward* during the battle, my seatmate interrupted briefly to say Gregor deserved it after what he'd done. Then he added, "You went back to the South Pacific after that. Was Gregor still her skipper?"

I explained that he was, but only for a few weeks after we got there, saying that he got orders to return to the U. S. to take command of a new ship. I said I'd taken over as skipper of the *Aaron Ward* on March 17, 1943, and that we were in the middle of a lot of fighting after that.

"How long did you have her?" he asked.

I said it was only about three weeks, and he remarked that it was a bad break, losing her so quickly.

"Not a bad break," I said. "Things just happen that way sometimes."

I went on with the story, telling him about April 7, the day it happened. I could remember it all so clearly.

It was about 12:30 P.M. when we finished escorting some LCTs (landing craft, tanks) and the fast transport *Ward*, a converted flush-deck, former four-stack destroyer near Guadalcanal. We got word that a big group of enemy planes were headed our way. The coast watchers had reported sixty-seven Val dive-bombers and one hundred Zero fighters were airborne toward Guadalcanal.

Henderson Field put up fighters to meet them, but the odds were more than two to one in the Japs' favor. The condition was very, very red; and almost all the ships in the vicinity were ordered to steam away to the southeast. Unfortunately, the *Aaron Ward* couldn't go with them. We were sent out instead to escort the LST (landing ship, tank) 449, which was then near Tagoma Point, to safety.

"You know how fast an LST can steam," I said. "Out there we used to call them large, slow targets. That one really needed help. After some delays, she was steaming at maximum speed—all of about eleven knots—following us. I had my destroyer zigzagging east at fifteen just ahead of her."

I hesitated for a few seconds, recalling the bright sun, the puffy white cumulus clouds, the specks up there in the sky which kept getting larger. Then I went on.

It was about 3:08 P.M. when the dogfighting was at its hottest. We could see a group of planes over near Tulagi, and my gunnery officer, Lieutenant (j.g.) LeBaron was tracking them with our five-inch guns. Four minutes later, as the ship was swinging to starboard, (our right) three enemy planes came in suddenly in a steep sixty-degree dive right out of the sun.

I shouted, "All engines ahead, flank," meaning the maximum speed *Aaron Ward*'s engines could deliver, and added, "Left full rudder," hoping the sudden maneuver would throw off the dive-bombers. The engineers delivered at once. The ship's stern dug in and she surged ahead, swinging sharply to port (left), the white foam peeling back from her bow. At the same time our automatic antiaircraft cannon, and even some smaller caliber machine guns, opened up, quickly followed by our 5-inch main weapons.

You could hear the whining screech as the dive-bombers zoomed down on us. The Japanese didn't use sirens on their dive-bombers the way the Germans were said to, but that noise they made was bad enough. They came in single file as the ship twisted to throw off their aim. Two of the bombs missed, but blew up in the water close to the ship.The third caught us, hitting the ship three feet in from the edge of the deck midships. It smashed into the after engine room, killing a number of men and knocking out all electric power in the ship.

Before we could recover, three more planes were diving at us. The whole ship vibrated and her hull resounded with the noise of our guns. The rapid, high-pitched cracks of the automatic cannons mixed with the deeper, less frequent, but throaty, roaring cracks of our 5-inchers. It was an orchestration of sounds that had become all too familiar to Navy men facing the Japanese. For those at stations deep inside the ship the chattering, the cracks, the booms must have resembled the sounds of drums played by musicians Gene Krupa or Buddy Rich during wild solo finales on stage with the Benny Goodman or Tommy Dorsey swing bands.

Our gunners raised a wall of hot steel and burning tracers against the oncoming enemy, but two of the planes got through. Their bombs fell close alongside the ship, shaking her, wounding her.

Near misses can be as deadly as direct hits. The bombs that exploded near the ship seemed to be less than five yards away. And water, as any high-school physics student knows, cannot be compressed. It does not absorb force applied to it, but transmits it to whatever is nearby. The bombs were like exploding mines. They appeared to lift us out of the water, and the ship's thin plating took a beating. By the time the attack was over, water was pouring into her engineering spaces in ever-growing amounts.

The fleet tug *Ortolan,* commanded by Lieutenant C. A.

Holland, quickly appeared and came alongside, passing towlines. Then as our damage-control parties got to work and medical personnel cared for the wounded, she began to haul us toward shore as ordered by the Guadalcanal task group commander.

I didn't like the idea of beaching her on Guadalcanal. I had seen what happened to too many ships left stranded on those shores. I requested permission to risk a tow all the way to the protected shelter of Tulagi.

Permission was granted. About forty minutes later another tug, *Vireo*, came along our port side and used her suction hose to help us try to control the flooding below. A boat came out from the island and took off our three-hundred-pound Y-gun depth charges to decrease our topside load. The less we carried the better, because a ship with flooding compartments is always in danger of foundering.

Damage-control parties shored up the watertight doors in the after part of the ship with four-by-four-inch lumber. Though watertight bulkhead doors are secured with heavy metal dogs— pivoting levers that work against wedges by the doors—the pressures of water against them can burst them open without extra support to keep them closed. Meanwhile, parties of sailors moved all loose gear forward to the forecastle and the detonators on our six-hundred-pound depth charges in the stern were removed. The depth charges, antisubmarine ash cans, were then released from their racks to sink harmlessly to the bottom. At the same time, all personnel records, government money, confidential publications, and scarce radar and radio parts were transferred to the tugs.

By 7:00 P.M. the tugs were on either side of us, edging us along. But soon the tension on their towlines began to increase. *Aaron Ward* had developed a pronounced list to starboard, and this was growing with each passing minute.

Many larger warships have their hulls divided by walls, called bulkheads, that run both across the ship from side to side and the length of the ship, often from bow to stern. But a destroyer like *Aaron Ward* was a narrow ship, at her widest only about thirty-six feet. With her large boilers and turbines filling the hull midships, a longitudinal (end-to-end) bulkhead was not built into her. We could not flood compartments on her port side to compensate for her starboard heel. All we could do was move anything that could be moved—ammunition boxes, gas cylinders, heavy spare parts—over to her port side.

None of this weight shifting did much good. She heeled

farther and farther to starboard as we continued. By 9:15 P.M. her list was so great it threatened to part the towlines. These were let go, and the tugs tried to shove us toward shoal water near Tinete Point. I knew now that we could not get her to harbor. The clinometer, an instrument indicating the roll or list of the ship, showed twenty-six degrees. She was fast approaching a critical point.

The bombs had accomplished their purpose. I could feel her list increasing rapidly when we were still far short of our goal. I ordered the tugs to stand clear.

Our crew had been warned to stay topside. Suddenly the ship began to sink rapidly, stern first. Both tugs turned on search-lights and launched boats to pick up our men. It was exactly 9:35 P.M. when she went down, just six hundred yards from safe shoal water; with her went a piece of my heart. Although all aboard were saved, I soon found they shared my feelings. The next morning, standing in line to draw emergency clothing, one sailor, his face sad, said to me, "Captain, we never abandoned her. She abandoned us."

Aboard the C-47 there was a sympathetic look on the face of my Coast Guard friend.

"I'm sorry," he said. "A bad break, especially when you were so close to saving her."

We talked a little more, but not long after we lapsed into silence, each of us returning to his own thoughts. But our conversation and recollections of *Aaron Ward* and the *Laffey* now started me thinking about the future which was waiting up there in Bath, Maine. I'd known the story of *Aaron Ward*'s name for a long time, but only recently did I have a reason to look into *Laffey*'s. My new destroyer had quite a heritage. Part of it, naturally, was the gallant record of Lieutenant Commander Bill Hank, skipper of the *Laffey*, and his men. But like most U. S. Navy destroyers, my *Laffey* was also named for a hero of the past.

Bartlett Laffey was a seaman in the U. S. Navy in the American Civil War who was awarded the Congressional Medal of Honor for his gallant and determined bravery. He had been born in Ireland in 1841, later come to the United States, then had enlisted in the Federal Navy on March 17, 1862.

In 1864, Bartlett Laffey was a sailor aboard the ship *Petrel* on the Mississippi River. On March 5, Confederate forces were attacking Union troops in recently captured Yazoo City, Mississippi. Laffey and others were sent ashore with a rifled howitzer mounted on a field carriage to support the Union Army.

The howitzer was positioned in the streets of the city and was soon under direct assault by Confederate troops. The enemy charged and reached the howitzer. Though not equipped with many small arms, Laffey led the crew in defense of the position. They fought back with anything they could lay hands on. It was a bitter, bloody, seesaw battle in which Laffey rallied the men time and again until at last the enemy gave up and the howitzer was saved.

The name *Laffey* seemed from the beginning to be associated with desperate battles against odds. But unlike the first destroyer named *Laffey*, the original bearer of the name survived and lived to a ripe old age. He died in 1901 in the Soldiers' Home in Chelsea, Massachusetts.

I knew my *Laffey*, like her predecessors, would tangle with the enemy in some desperate battles. Destroyers always did. Yet I was determined to do everything in my power to bring her and her men safely through any ordeal we might face. I had lost one ship and I did not intend to lose another.

The Memphis Naval Air Station was actually located at Millington, Tennessee, some distance from the city. It was dark again as the C-47's wheels touched the runway surface, the daylight period of a winter day quickly exhausted by our passing the westward-moving sun as we flew east. My Coast Guard friend and I got off the plane about 7:30 P.M., our joints somewhat stiff after all those hours in our seats. As there were no service flights to Dallas for another twelve hours, he joined me on a bus ride into Memphis, intending to get a commercial flight at the airport there.

I called my Aunt Mary and arranged to stay at her house overnight before getting a train home. She sent a car. On the way to her house I dropped the lieutenant at the commercial airport, saying goodbye and wishing him well. He was a nice young officer and his company had made a long, tiresome trip far more pleasant. Being able to talk about the past year—and more especially about those memories, which still hurt—had kept me from brooding all the way east.

Arriving home after a long absence, especially one spent fighting a war, is a special experience. Even if you have had a regular correspondence with loved ones and know what has taken place while you've been away, I think you always expect to find everyone and everything as they were when you left. Reason tells you this cannot be true, but subconsciously you always want it to be that way. You are always disappointed.

My mother was the same wonderful person she had always been, but she was changed. She was older and had not been well. It disturbed me to suddenly be brought face to face with the realization that this gentle, loving person—who had guided my brother, sister, and me through the trials of growing up—was no longer strong and enduring. She was the same in some ways. She still insisted on helping people and on never speaking of someone if she could not say something good about them. But she was frail, and worrying about me had not helped her.

My father and brother were not there when I arrived. My father's business required him to travel most of the week; it was not until the weekend that I saw him. My younger brother, John, who worked with him, arrived at the same time. John had tried to get into service but had been turned down because of a physical disability.

In a way I was glad of this. Both my parents were getting on, and having John at home with them meant a great deal. He was there and could help if help was needed. I could not, and with the war grinding on and on, I might never be able to do so.

Like my parents, Hot Springs itself was changed. Most of my friends from high-school days were away in uniform. Only a few who had physical disabilities were around to talk to. Hot Springs, in common with many other communities across the country, was then a place of the old, the infirm, or the very young. I took many long walks, frequently not meeting one person I knew very well. I wasn't lonely because I was with my family; yet in a way, at times I felt out of place, a stranger in my own hometown. I had spent my youth there, but I realized then that my real home had become the Navy.

After some time at Hot Springs, I went on to Memphis again and visited with my aunt, Mary, and uncle, Julian Wilson, a prominent attorney. Seeing them again was a tonic, even though I found my uncle in bed with influenza. He was a great talker, a storyteller, and I'd always loved listening to him.

Many of his stories concerned a favorite character of his, a real Confederate private named John Allen who had served in the Civil War. One of those Private Allen stories was a special favorite of mine. All of them carried some homey message of wisdom, but this particular one made a special impression on me.

Private Allen, according to my uncle, decided after the Civil War that he wanted to run for Congress. His chief opponent was a former Confederate officer, an imposing man and a good speaker. At the climax of the campaign both candidates were invited to address a crowd at a large picnic.

To prove that he was a man who took a serious job seriously, and thus the one voters should pick on election day, the former officer recounted his experience before the Battle of Shiloh. He said he pitched and tossed on his cot in his tent that night, concerned about how things would go for him in the fighting the next day, how well he would lead his men.

Former Private Allen got up and said he remembered that night too, because he was one of the men trudging up and down on guard duty outside the officers' tents to make sure they were not disturbed. He suggested that all officers vote for his opponent and all privates vote for him. What he was saying was that he was the kind of man who stayed on the job instead of just worrying about it like the officer. He said the more numerous privates would decide the outcome, and if that officer had been so concerned, he should have been up seeing to his men instead of tossing on his nice dry cot. Private Allen spent the next sixteen years in Congress.

Command is not a popularity contest, but Private Allen was absolutely correct in what he said. An officer is supposed to worry about his men first, then think about himself. If he did that, they'd back him one hundred percent when the time came, and that kind of backing wins battles.

After visiting my uncle and aunt, I headed for the Memphis Naval Air Station and found an open seat on another C-47. The flight up to New York was a little lonely because the other "passengers" weren't very talkative; in fact they didn't talk at all—they were boxes and crates full of freight. I was the only live passenger on the plane, but I didn't mind. It gave me time to think of Imogen, whom I would soon see, and to feel just plain happy about some news I had received while still at Hot Springs.

Being promoted in any organization is something that always makes a person feel good. But for the professional naval officer, the regular, it is even more of a reason for celebration. The Navy is a highly structured outfit with a great many hard-and-fast rules of organization. It has a ladder of grades, and ranks within grades, and only rarely does a regular officer move up that ladder in any but the usual progression. He may hold a temporary wartime appointment to a much higher grade, but will usually revert to his "regular" permanent status once hostilities are over. And, if he remains at a certain permanent grade beyond a certain time, and past a certain age, there is a good chance he may retire in that grade.

I had been a lieutenant commander for some time. I was still young, and with wartime opportunities I fully expected to rise above that level. Yet there was always the possibility this might not happen. As a result, when I got word in Hot Springs that I was to be promoted to commander, it gave my spirits a great lift.

My philosophy had always been to do my best and to work hard toward promotion, but to accept the disappointment with good grace if promotion didn't come when I hoped for it, and to concentrate on my job. As a commander, I knew there was a good prospect I might eventually advance to captain before retirement, and that pleased me. Promotion beyond captain I did not think about then, because I knew that a very small percentage of eligibles were selected. If I should be one of them, the promotion to rear admiral would be welcome—if unexpected—frosting on the cake.

For someone like myself who was seriously interested in a young lady, this new promotion meant even more. When the war was over and the risks of my being killed or crippled were past, I knew I could stay with my chosen career, yet still have a secure future to offer that young woman in addition to my love. To say I was elated would be an understatement. And it should be plain why I was not bothered by the lack of traveling companions aboard that C-47. My thoughts on that trip were company enough.

It was 10:00 P.M. when I got to New York. As soon as I landed I found a phone and called Imogen's apartment. Of necessity, our reunion would have to be brief at this time, but I was very anxious to see her if only for a short visit. I wanted to reassure myself that she still felt the same way about me as I did about her. Later there would be plenty of chances for us to see each other.

Nina Korda, Imogen's roommate, answered the phone. Imogen wasn't in, but Nina expected her shortly. I said I'd call back as soon as I reached my hotel.

It was 11:30 P.M. when I heard her voice on the line. She sounded very happy to hear from me.

"Can you come over?" she asked. "I'd love to see you, Julie. Are you all right? You weren't hurt or anything like that? How much time have you got before you have to go off again?"

The barrage of questions finally ended, but I saved most of

the answers until I reached the apartment. I knocked at the door and she opened it, a big, pleased smile on her face as she welcomed me. I knew right away that she was still fond of me.

I went inside and sat down, trying to answer her questions even as she asked more. For a short time the conversation between Imogen, Nina, and me must have sounded like an overloaded TBS channel, with half-asked and half-answered questions flying back and forth.

Finally, Imogen got up and said, "I have a bottle of champagne I've been saving for your return. Let's open it!"

There were a lot of things to toast. We drank to my promotion and to my future success with the new *Laffey*, and, of course, to our reunion. Then we toasted Imogen's future. She was rehearsing a new Broadway show—*Mexican Hayride*—which starred June Havoc. I guess our toast had some effect. June Havoc's later misfortune, an injury on stage, forced her to withdraw from the show; Imogen, as her understudy, got the lead part. In addition, she was soon to sing regularly on a WOR radio show. Though a local radio station, it had a very powerful signal and a large group of listeners in many parts of the country.

I left Imogen and Nina after spending several hours with them. Imogen insisted she wanted to go with me the next day when I bought my new uniform cap. Naturally, I was pleased that she was interested. Buying part of a uniform could hardly be called an exciting experience, except of course for myself.

Outside, on the way back to my hotel, it was cold as only New York streets can be on some December nights. But the cold, penetrating air tasted like more of the champagne, and the Christmas decorations and lights in some of the stores added a festive touch. The next day, when I saw Imogen again, the air still tasted like champagne. The streets were full of people, the weather not so good, but the company made up for it all. I hardly noticed because my attention was on her.

Inside the store she watched me try on caps, a half-serious, half-amused smile of approval on her face. When I finally made a selection she grinned and said, "Those scrambled eggs are quite becoming."

She had learned the expression soon after we first met. I had taken her to a dinner dance at the navy yard in Brooklyn. As we were leaving, she'd seen the hatcheck girl hand a commander his cap. Nodding toward it, she'd said, "I like that gold braid."

I'd told her they called gold braid like that scrambled eggs.

She'd smiled, then continued, "I hope you'll be wearing a cap like that someday." And now that I could, she hadn't forgotten the term.

While the salesman put my new cap in the box, Imogen said, "It does look nice. It means you're a captain now, doesn't it?"

"No," I said. "I'm a commander, but I am a prospective captain of a ship. You see, a commander can be a captain of a ship, but so can a lieutenant commander or even a lieutenant. It all depends on the kind of ship he is to command."

There was just the slightest wrinkle of a frown on her face for a moment before she laughed in that musical way of hers.

"I suppose I'll never get it all straight, Julie," she said. "But never mind! The braid looks wonderful and I hope you get lots more of it soon. If it was up to me, I'd see you were an admiral right away."

I thanked her, but I knew she really wasn't confused. She was too intelligent a person for that. She was just having a little fun, trying to make the little ceremony of my buying my new cap into something memorable and important. I was grateful. And I was happy because it was one more sign that she did care for me.

I would have liked to have stayed in New York much longer then, but I had to get on. As I left I consoled myself with the thought that with *Laffey* being built at Bath instead of at a West Coast yard, I would have other opportunities to see Imogen again before I went to sea.

The Navy had established an excellent policy of sending all its prospective skippers to special training schools before they joined their new ships. This applied to all prospective skippers, even those with combat experience. The idea was to give each officer the benefit of the latest information on a variety of tactical techniques and the newest technical devices and weapons. The officer with a lot of recent sea duty could still learn much from such courses because they were the sum total of all that had been learned since the war began.

I first went to sonar school in Key West, Florida. Sonar was a listening device used to locate submerged enemy submarines. Unlike radar, which was based on radiolike electronic waves sent through the air, sonar was based on sound waves that traveled through the water, which radar could not penetrate. It was quite effective and in fact had made a great deal of difference in Allied operations against German U-boats in the Atlantic. Had the Allies not had sonar, the Germans might have been successful in

34

their efforts to choke off the flow of supplies to England.

Our sonar training was based not only on U. S. Navy experiences, but on those of the British Royal Navy, which had been using it since 1939. The British called sonar *asdic*, and had begun to share their knowledge with us even before we entered the war.

We used a simulator. It saved a lot of time and did not tie up destroyers and submarines needed at sea. Using it, I had to maneuver a simulated ship into position where she could drop depth charges on a simulated submarine. Antisubmarine operations were a cat-and-mouse game, but the mouse too had claws. There were cases in WW II of destroyers that were hit by torpedoes fired by submarines they were after. It did not happen often, but the wise destroyer skipper was always aware of the possibility and took measures against it.

Though only a simulation, the training had all the feeling of the real thing. The only difference was that the tracks of both the sub and the destroyer were registered on a small screen and you could study them after each exercise. You got a chance to correct your mistakes—something you never got under actual circumstances.

The intensity of the training made me wonder just where the *Laffey* and I might be headed once she was ready for service. Jap submarines were very active in the Pacific, but from what I had heard they were almost amateurs at this kind of warfare compared with their German allies. Throughout the war, Jap submarine skippers never did achieve the same large measure of success enjoyed by our own American submarines in the Pacific, even though they sank many ships.

After Key West, I went to Norfolk, Virginia, to attend a tactical school for destroyer skippers. The training there included ship-handling exercises and the study of the latest changes in tactical publications. Though I was not long returned from many months at sea on active combat duty, I found this training invaluable. It too was the sum total of the experiences of thousands of Navy officers who had seen active service, and the product of the best staff minds in the Navy.

My training as a PCO (prospective commanding officer) took place at the same time as training for others who would serve with me aboard the *Laffey*. At Norfolk I met one of these men, my prospective executive officer, Lieutenant Charles Holovak, USN, a regular like myself.

I liked Holovak at once. Sparsely built and of medium height, he was the brother of the brilliant Boston College football star, Mike Holovak. He was also highly competent, energetic, and a dedicated professional, a man on whom I knew I could rely.

A good executive officer, one with whom a skipper can work smoothly and easily, is of paramount importance to every warship. The exec is the officer who takes over if the skipper is put out of action; he actually manages the ship under the skipper's direction. He makes sure the skipper's orders are carried out as they should be. He is the administrative director and the immediate superior of those who head the various departments into which warship complements are organized.

In a destroyer, these department heads are the gunnery officer, engineering officer, the first lieutenant and damage control officer, the supply officer, communications officer, and the medical officer. The exec is usually the ship's navigator.

When the ship is in action against enemy forces, the exec also has an immediate responsibility for the CIC or combat information center. The CIC is the brain cell of the ship that digests information and communications, then supplies reports on which the skipper and others aboard base many vital decisions.

Charles Holovak gave me details of some of the kinds of training my other officers and some of my men were receiving. Like my own training, this was highly specialized and based on what had been learned from actual battle and sea experiences. There were men studying and practicing damage control, torpedo use, antisub methods, new gunnery techniques, and fire fighting.

"It's not just theory and book work, Captain," Holovak told me. "Take the fire-fighting school, for example. The way it's set up, they have them crawling through smoke-filled compartments in freezing temperatures just like they might be sometime out in the North Pacific or Atlantic. But the men are doing well. By the time they all get through this you are going to have a bunch that really knows its business."

This gave me a good feeling. I thought back to some of those peacetime years before the war. We had training exercises then and they were good, probably the best we could have done in the 1930s. But they lacked the kind of realism Holovak had mentioned. Then, there had been no recent wartime experiences to base them on, and appropriations for the Navy were limited. We just didn't have the funds for the kind of extensive, realistic exercises possible in 1943.

The results of this lack had shown up in the early months of the war. Our men fought hard and well, but we'd learned that courage alone was no substitute for continuing, realistic training based on actual battle experience.

I left Norfolk just before Christmas, heading for Fairfax, Virginia, where my sister and her husband, who was now a lieutenant in the Bureau of Ordnance, were then living. I knew it was going to be a good holiday because I was relaxed, confident that the men of the *Laffey* would join her well trained in the skills they would soon need. Yet I intended to make sure none of those skills would become rusty. We would all need to practice, practice, and practice again so that when our time came, we could face the enemy with more than just courage to help us win.

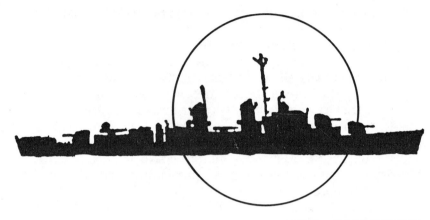

THREE

Soon after Christmas of 1943 I set a course for Bath, Maine, a town about thirty miles up the coast above Portland. As far as I was concerned, it felt like it was thirty miles above the North Pole. Maine winters are not like those in the South Pacific. There was snow everywhere. Even when the sun was out, the sky blue and clear, the cold was penetrating.

In spite of the cold, I was pleased that the *Laffey* was being built by the Bath Iron Works. The yard had a longtime reputation for turning out quality work that dated back to the days when ships were still built of wood. For generations Bath had been a one-industry town, and generations of its people had been shipbuilders. They knew their business.

When people would ask W. S. "Pete" Newell, president of the yard, how many people worked there, he had a stock reply. "About half of them," was an old joke, but given the difficulties of shipbuilding in a Maine winter, there were probably some grains of truth in it. Pete wasn't criticizing his people; he was just stating a fact. In winter those who worked at the yard often had to fight their way along snow-clogged roads in bitter temperatures and freezing winds just to get to their jobs; and when they made it, they had to go to work under the same conditions. At any given time, probably half of them were being defrosted.

As far as I can see, however, none of this seemed to affect productivity or efficiency. During the war the shipbuilders of Bath Iron Works turned out sixty-seven destroyers. That was a record that approached the entire destroyer production of all Japanese shipyards during the same period. As for quality, Bath-built ships were both rugged and durable. Not only did many survive terrible punishment during the war, but some remained serviceable well into the 1970s, and the *Laffey* was one of them.

The first person I saw at Bath was Captain Russell Hitch-cock. He was the Navy's supervisor at the shipyard, the officer on the spot who coordinated naval and civilian efforts. He gave me a brief general summary of *Laffey*'s current state and the work of her nucleus crew, then took me to see Pete Newell.

Pete was an old friend. I'd met him some years before when I was an engineer officer in the destroyer *Gleaves*. When I walked in, he was sitting at his desk studying some papers. But as soon as I came through the doorway, he looked up, stood up, and came forward extending his hand.

"Well, well, look who's back," he said, a grin on his face. "Sent me a good one this time, didn't they! I'm glad to see you again, and a commander too." (I'd been a lieutenant when I first met him.)

I was flattered. Pete was a gracious man, and though I suspected he said something similar to each new skipper who arrived at Bath, I knew he was also an honest man. His words had been truly genuine.

We talked for a while, but Pete didn't keep me long. He knew I wanted to get on to meet some of my officers and men who had arrived before me. The Navy always sent a nucleus crew to study a new ship while she was being built, and Pete was aware of how eager any prospective skipper would be to get to know these key people assigned to his ship.

The nucleus crew was expected to learn every detail of the ship's construction as she progressed, and the workings of the equipment that was being built into her. As a rule, they were always supposed to be experienced people with as much service time as possible under their belts. But with the wartime demands for active-duty personnel, I feared that some of this cadre might not be quite up to standard. If this proved to be the case, I knew I had a difficult job ahead, because the group was supposed to train the others who would join us later.

As it turned out, I need not have worried. The Navy had given me a solid core of thoroughly competent and experienced men. Enlisted technical experts like Chief Gunner's Mate Norman Fitzgerald, Gunner's Mate Warren Walker, Fire Controlman Ralph Peterson, and husky Chief Electrician's Mate Al Csiszar were top grade. After I talked to them and others briefly, there was no question in my mind that they would quickly take any green men in hand and teach them the ropes.

We would have plenty of green men, too; that I knew. They would be men fresh from basic training or with little service experience, and in *Laffey*'s case they would make up eighty percent of our crew. By the end of 1943, dozens of warships were being commissioned each month, and we had no other choice but to man them mostly with men who would need on-the-job training on active duty.

I was both grateful and relieved that two of my officers up there at Bath were men of exceptional talent and quality. For generations, the success of a warship had depended on her ability to "steam and shoot," and my experiences in the South Pacific had confirmed the fact that this hadn't changed. If my *Laffey* was going to survive and live up to her name, she had to have a good engineering and gunnery officer. She had them.

Lieutenant Al Henke, my engineering officer, turned out to be tall and blond, with glasses that gave him the mild-mannered look of a scholar. In one sense he was, for he had an engineering degree from Illinois Tech, and a good academic record. But Al Henke wasn't an inward-turned scholar. He was outgoing, talkative, enthusiastic about his job. He knew just about everything there was to know about the ship's huge boilers, condensers, and massive turbines, and how to fine tune them so they would produce that sixty thousand horsepower which could drive *Laffey* at well over thirty knots when we needed it. Yet he also seemed to know how to lead men. He had already organized those he had at Bath into a solid, smooth-working team, and that was important. The engineering officer on a destroyer like the *Laffey* commanded a third of the ship's crew.

At first glance my gunnery officer, Lieutenant Harry Burns, was not imposing. He wasn't tall, and in build, he tended to a wiry slightness. He had rosy cheeks, black hair, and a Massachusetts accent. But, though quiet in manner, he was aggressively businesslike when it came to gunnery training and practice, and he had a great deal of self-confidence, the product of considerable experience. Harry Burns had served in the Atlantic on a cruiser where he had honed his gunnery skills to near perfection. He would never need any coaching on what to do with *Laffey*'s 5-inch, 38-caliber guns; her 40-mm and 20-mm automatic antiaircraft weapons. Harry knew, and it wouldn't take him long to turn the men he commanded into the same kind of expert gunners.

One of my younger officers who was also at Bath did lack experience, but he made up for this with something else. Ensign Joel Youngquist was the *Laffey*'s supply officer. Handsome, with a ready smile and a friendly manner, "Pay," as he was called, had apparently been born with one ability that was of infinite value aboard any ship in the Navy. He knew how to forage and come up with supplies when we needed them, either in a port like Boston or some out-of-the-way place in the far reaches of the oceans. I am not suggesting Pay ever broke any Navy rules or regulations, but he did seem to have the knack of making friends. And for some reason these friends, whether ashore or on some of the larger ships which carried far more necessities than could *Laffey*, always seemed to be able to spare what we needed.

After meeting these men and others, and reassuring myself that any previous worries I had about them were groundless, I was anxious to get a look at *Laffey* herself. It was hardly the best of days to inspect a ship, nor was she really ready for a formal inspection, but Harry Burns offered to take me on an unofficial tour. I think that Harry, better than some of the others, could understand why I wanted to see the ship at her worst, in a mess, still being built. Looking her over right away would give me an intimate knowledge of her at the very beginning. It was the best way for a skipper to begin a relationship with a new command, and the sooner it began, the better.

Outside in the yard the air was raw and cold, filled with a penetrating dampness, the smells of oil, hot steel, and fresh paint. The sky was a leaden gray-white, the ground covered with dirty ice and snow. I could hear the banging and chattering noises of steel hitting steel, and from time to time I could see the white light of a welder's torch winking and sparkling on one of the dark forms that were all around us.

We started to walk, threading our slippery way through a maze of equipment, gear, and sections of ships that had a patina of orange rust on them. Each time we moved out from behind the shelter of one of these we'd be hit by an icy blast of wind, which seemed to take a devilish delight in finding every opening in my service overcoat. By the time we were partway onto the pier, I was chilled to the bone. Even after a month back from the steamy reaches of the South Pacific, I was still not really acclimatized enough to withstand the assaults of a Maine winter.

Suddenly Harry stopped, pointing a gloved hand, and I saw her for the first time. She was afloat, tied up against the tarred pilings, and from where we stood she was almost bow-on to us. The bow towered over us, high, sharp, and fine, and looked like the edge of a well-honed knife floating—blade upright—in the water. But behind the edge of the blade, it thickened dramatically, and even at that angle I could see the outlines of a bulky superstructure softened with a mantle of dirty white snow.

At first glance, she looked ready to steam away right then. But as we came nearer, our angle of view changing, I could spot tangled webs of lines, electrical cables, and hoses running up into her from the pier. Like umbilical cords, she still depended on these; and I knew it would be a while yet before they could be disconnected. Though she looked a ship, she wasn't one yet.

The closer we came, the more the *Laffey* seemed to grow, longer and wider with each slippery step we took. She was bigger, more massive, than I had somehow expected her to be. With a 376-foot length and a beam of 41 feet, I'd known she was going to be much larger than the *Aaron Ward.* But I just wasn't prepared for the reality that was now before me.

From the bow, her main deck ran aft in one long sweep. Without a step or a break, it sloped gradually down toward her stern. She was a flush-decker, and with her bulk, size, considerable superstructure, and two large stacks, she reminded me more of a light cruiser than a destroyer.

Of course I knew full well she wasn't really that big. But her twin mounts and that sweeping, unbroken deck gave her the look of one of our antiaircraft cruisers. Though such cruisers carried 6 of these twin 5-inch mounts, more than once during World War II Japanese pilots mistook 2,200-ton Allen M. Sumner-class destroyers for cruisers.

The mistake was understandable. *Laffey*, for a destroyer, packed a formidable punch. Her main battery weapons—6 five-inch, thirty-eight-caliber guns—were distributed in three twin-gun mounts instead of single-gun mounts as in earlier destroyers. Two of these mounts were forward—one located about fifty feet aft of the bow, the other about twenty feet farther aft and raised above it. A third mount was positioned about fifty feet from her stern.

All three mounts could rotate, and the 5-inch guns were dual-purpose weapons. They could be used for surface fire against enemy warships or targets ashore, or elevated to a high angle for use against aircraft. A complete round for a gun weighed about

42

seventy-five pounds, approximately two thirds of that being a high-explosive or proximity-fused antiaircraft shell. The mounts themselves were enclosed in turretlike steel boxes which protected the gun crews from muzzle blast, flash, and the weather. But these boxlike shields weren't armored turrets. They were made of very thin steel about a quarter-inch thick which even shrapnel could penetrate. Destroyers, even big ones like the *Laffey*, didn't carry armor plate. It weighs too much.

In addition to her main battery, the *Laffey* also mounted twelve 40-mm antiaircraft guns distributed along her length in open, twin-gun tub mounts and in a quadruple 4-gun open tub mount farther aft. These 40-mm guns were automatics which could spit out high-explosive antiaircraft shells or armor-piercing rounds at a rapid rate. Like the 11 smaller tub-mounted 20-mm antiaircraft guns, the 40's were—for practical purposes —very heavy machine guns.

Both of these automatic weapons had originally been foreign designs. The 20-mm was developed in Switzerland by Oerlikon, and the 40-mm was actually an enemy weapon. A post-World War I development by the German firm of Krupp, which made it in Sweden under the Bofors Company trademark, it had been adopted by the British, then the U. S., in World War II because of its efficiency and reliability.

The open tub mounts for both types of antiaircraft guns were little more than platforms with curved sheet-steel sides which came up to the waists of the crews. The guns themselves revolved on pedestals, and the sides of the tubs gave no protection against enemy fire. Their primary functions were to keep busy gun crews from falling off the platforms, and to provide some shelter from seas that could sweep across decks. Armoring them was out of the question. Had they been armored, these hanging gardens, as one high-ranking U. S. admiral called them, would have made any ship top-heavy.

Laffey mounted 10 torpedo tubes in 2 five-tube mounts. One was located amidships on the deck of the superstructure between the stacks; the other was on the same deck just forward of the after 5-inch mount. Each tube could launch a 21-inch diameter, 20-foot-long torpedo weighing about a ton and a half, 600 pounds of that being explosive warhead.

Laffey also carried Y-gun depth-charge throwers port and starboard on the main deck forward of the aft five-inch mount, and two long depth-charge racks either side of the 20-mm gun tub near the fantail (stern). Each Y-gun could toss two 300-

pound charges well out from the ship. But the 600-pound charges on the fantail racks were just dropped over the stern. This was tricky work done at high speeds. If an ash can went off too quickly, it could damage rudders and screws or even blow off the stern.

All these weapons weighed a great deal, but there were more topsides. There was the large 5-inch-gun fire director towering over her pilot house. Though the guns could—and often did—fire independently, this heavy director allowed the gunnery officer to synchronize and control their fire as a single unit. It was often used in conjunction with the SG and SC radar, and the antennae for these were mounted on the ship's 80-foot mast aft of the pilot house. The SC antenna, used to locate aircraft, was the highest of the two, the largest and heaviest. It looked like a huge bedspring, and weighed a great deal; this height and weight would exert powerful forces against the ship's stability.

All destroyers, because of their narrow beam-to-length ratio, tended to roll heavily in a beam sea. *Laffey* was certainly going to need her 41 feet of beam. She was wider than other destroyers, but with all that weight topsides, she might be difficult to handle under some conditions.

I had no doubts that the ship's basic design was sound. But I also knew that during wartime, equipment tended to be added to a ship as it was needed and because it was needed. Any ship design has its limits, and then and there I made up my mind I'd take the first opportunity to sail aboard a destroyer like the *Laffey* to see how far her limits had been stretched. I had faith in those who designed her and those who were building her, but she was going to be my responsibility. When I went to sea in *Laffey*, I did not want any nasty surprises. With the sea and a ship, there are no second chances.

Harry Burns was waiting for me at the foot of the brow, the gangway that stretched up from the pier to the snow-covered main deck. As I walked toward it, some errant current or swell made *Laffey* move suddenly. She heeled ever so slightly, leaning toward me like a young woman making a curtsy in welcome. And though her decks were cluttered, cold, dirty, and her appearance forbidding, the minute I stepped aboard I felt that she meant it. Like all skippers from the beginning of time, I wanted her all to myself. The sooner I could get the yard workmen off her and make her shipshape, the happier I would be.

Harry Burns took me over most of the ship, except for the

44

engineering spaces, which Al Henke would show me later. I examined her from stem to stern, from pilothouse to bilges, and on the whole I was pleased. I found there was still a lot to be done, but it was being done rapidly and efficiently. And it was being done despite the fact that the cold discomfort topsides was nothing compared to the penetrating, soul-gripping dampness and chill in some of the half-finished spaces.

I don't think there could be a more uncomfortable place to work than in a half-lighted, unheated, and unfinished steel compartment of a ship under construction in the dead of winter. I have been aboard a ship in a subzero gale, steaming through seas that battered and tossed her, and I know the discomfort and danger men must face under such conditions. But a steaming ship is a living thing, and where there is life there is a sense of warmth. There was no such feeling in those unfinished tomblike spaces aboard *Laffey* when I first visited her, and the people who had to endure them commanded my immediate respect.

I came away well satisfied with what I had found during this inspection. She was a stout ship, well built, and a good example of fine workmanship. There were, however, two faults which disturbed me. They had nothing to do with workmanship, materials, or progress. They were faults of design; whose faults of design I didn't know, but they were so evident I could not understand how they had happened.

I am only medium height, yet as I had entered the pilothouse, I almost hit my head. The overhead was too low. Sooner or later, probably in the heat of action, one of my taller men was going to brain himself on that overhead. And as soon as I saw it I had immediate visions of having to file a whole series of casualty reports listing fractured skull as the type of injury. It would have to be corrected!

At first I assumed this low-overhead situation was peculiar to the *Laffey*, but when I checked with some of my fellow officers at Bath, I found out this design error had been propagated aboard a whole group of 2,200-ton destroyers. And no one seemed to know why or how it had happened. The builders had followed the specifications to the letter. The specifications had come directly from the company that had designed the ships, and the company had got these from the Destroyer Design Office. That office was full of people who had practical experience and knew their business. Though they were human and could make mistakes, such mistakes—especially obvious ones like this—

were always caught and corrected very quickly. But there was that low overhead in *Laffey* and a lot of her sister destroyers. The whole thing was incredible.

However, my companions and I had forgotten that this wasn't the old peacetime Navy. It was a greatly expanded service now that the country was at war, and not all the people were experienced professionals. Nor, for that matter, did they always have plenty of time to consider and reconsider everything. We needed ships—lots of ships—in a rush, and that was the root of the problem.

I found out some time later that an executive of the company that had designed the Allen M. Sumner-class destroyers had called the Destroyer Design Office in Washington in a hurry one afternoon. He needed some information right away; without it, work would fall behind schedule. But all the officers who could have given it to him were either out of the building or at conferences.

There was a brand-new, rather young Wave ensign on duty, however, and she did the best she could. This young woman, faced with a critical situation demanding immediate action, took action in the best traditions of the destroyer service. Using what she had, she improvised. She lined up everyone left in the office, measured their heights, then took the average. This measure she telephoned back to the executive as the correct height for the overhead of an Allen M. Sumner pilothouse ceiling.

The young woman's zeal was commendable but, in this instance, there was a small problem. She had never been to sea nor in the pilothouse of a destroyer, because in those days women were banned from such assignments. She did not consider that a ship lifts and plunges, rolls and tosses, and that an extra six inches safety clearance was needed. Before the error was discovered and new measurements fed into the pipeline, a whole group of 2,200-ton destroyers, including my *Laffey*, were built to the potentially skull-fracturing measure supplied by that Wave. Though they were later modified, I have wondered for years how many casualties this misstep caused before it was corrected.

Exactly what circumstances produced *Laffey*'s other design error I have never been able to learn, but in its way it had an even greater potential for creating disasters and damaging the careers of a number of skippers. Destroyer skippers, perhaps more than any others, are often forced to spend days and nights on end on the bridge when their ships are in combat zones or otherwise in jeopardy. During such periods, they can rarely go down to their regular quarters for rest or to care for personal needs. Thus, pilothouses of destroyers (and other warships as well) usually have built into them a small, closetlike captain's sea cabin which contains a small bunk and a head (toilet). Here the skipper of a warship in jeopardy can retire for very brief periods, yet be easily and quickly available should he be needed.

Laffey, however, not only did not have a sea cabin—there wasn't even a head built into or near her pilothouse. It was a critical defect and I soon found that other prospective COs (commanding officers) at Bath shared my consternation. We would be forced to leave the bridge and use the regular captain's cabin one level below. The time involved in transit was more than enough for some crisis to come to a head; the arrangement was unacceptable to us all.

It wasn't the inconvenience that bothered any of us. Warships are not built for the comfort and convenience of those who man them. But no matter what happens aboard a warship or to her, no matter who is at fault, the skipper of that warship is the one who must take the responsibility. That's the way it's always been and that's the way it should be. The skipper is the most experienced man aboard. He's been trained for the job. He is the ship's brain and heart, and everything about her is an extension of his personality. He must always be at or very near his post if the ship is in dire circumstances; and if he is not, he better be dead or incapacitated. There are no other excuses.

Fortunately I, and all other prospective skippers, had to make a weekly report on any unsatisfactory conditions as our future commands neared completion. We knew such reports were given first-priority attention by the Navy Department, and that we would get action. We did. Though there wasn't much then that could be done to rectify the problem of the low pilothouse ceiling, in the case of the missing sea cabin heads, the Navy went all out.

Within hours of the receipt of our first reports, the Navy approached a prominent company with a request to borrow and use its plans for a compact head which could be built into small sea cabins that were to be added to the ships. The situation was critical, but the delay in response was so long, the Navy had to take matters into its own hands.

With no time to waste, the Navy fell back on a time-honored expedient used by fighting men for centuries. It sent out a team of designers and draftsmen with rulers and note pads to get the information it needed where they could get it by "midnight requisition." These valiant individuals climbed aboard countless overnight trains on long, dull trips to nowhere, but during the witching hours each night,they went to work. They sketched all the details of the compact toilet designs aboard, which were so desperately needed on our destroyers, and got them into the works without any further delay.

I suspect that this was the only instance of patriotic, officially sanctioned industrial espionage by the Navy in World War II. Certainly it was necessary, and it worked. But I have often wondered how the men of that Navy midnight-requisition team explained it all to their kids later on when asked, "Daddy, what did you do in the war?" Yet I and a lot of other destroyer skippers could have told them. Those men saved lives and ships.

Despite these important deficiencies and some lesser problems, *Laffey* had some innovative design characteristics which more than made up for the flaws, and were great improvements over arrangements in prewar destroyers. For example, like previous destroyers, the ship was powered by two sets of boilers and two engines. These were arranged in pairs from forward aft. There was a fire room (boiler room) with two boilers forward of the forward engine room. Next came the after fireroom (with two boilers) followed by the after engine room. But unlike prewar destroyers' power plants, these two boiler-steam turbine pairs could either be cross-connected or operated independently as a split plant.

In an operational sense, what this meant was that a destroyer with split-plant capability could retain her ability to move even if she lost one of her boiler-engine room units. That could mean the difference between life or death. A destroyer dead in the water is a sitting duck for enemy bombs, shells, or torpedoes, and at the mercy of the seas. But *Laffey*, like the *Kearny* (DD 432), which had been hit by a German torpedo in the North Atlantic six weeks before Pearl Harbor but had made it back to Iceland despite a wrecked fireroom, could keep moving under such circumstances. A ship that could move was a ship that could survive and fight on.

Impressed as I was over this capability, I was even more so when I saw *Laffey*'s ship-length, interior passageway. None of our previous destroyers had had one.

Previous to this design, destroyers were so packed with boilers and turbines amidships that it was just about impossible to move from one end to the other without going topside. In a heavy sea, the main deck was often awash with seawater, and a bow-to-stern trip could be difficult, dangerous, sometimes impossible. More than one sailor had been swept over the side trying such a trip on our earlier ships. But with *Laffey*'s broader hull—which made this new, below-decks, ship-length passageway possible—this kind of problem was eliminated.

All things considered, I was very pleased with this new ship I was soon to command. And when I got the chance to sail aboard one of her sister destroyers, the *Walke* (DD 723), on a short trip down to Boston, I was thoroughly sold on her. If *Laffey* handled the way the *Walke* did—and since she was identical there was no reason why she shouldn't—we had a bright future ahead together. Though she wasn't perfect, she was mine, and I'd already grown fond of her.

I don't know if all of those men who worked with me at Bath relished those busy days as much as I did, but they certainly put their hearts into it. Considering the difficulties we sometimes faced, I have nothing but praise for both the yard workmen—and women—and the naval personnel who were involved with the *Laffey*. For example, in January the whole area around Bath was buried in one of the worst snowstorms I have ever seen. It wasn't just a storm, it was a blizzard; and until roads were plowed out about two days later, it shut down operations at the Iron Works completely.

That put us behind schedule, but we weren't behind very long. The minute the roads were open, everyone pitched in; the time was made up and in a couple of days more we were right back on schedule again.

Weather problems at Bath were difficult enough, but without the kindness of the citizens of that community, our Navy people would have faced an intolerable situation. Bath wasn't a very big place. With the huge influx of outsiders, housing was in short supply; and though the Bath Iron Works ran a housing office to assist naval personnel, quarters were hard to find.

My assistant gunnery officer, Lieutenant (j.g.) Paul Smith, had an experience that showed just how good-hearted those people at Bath really were. Paul, a ruggedly built young officer, came from Olean, New York. Coming as he did from that part of the country, he was used to bad winters; and having served in the old, four-stack destroyer *Stansbury* in the Atlantic, he knew how to cope with bad weather. But when Paul arrived at Bath, his young wife and newborn baby were with him. Roughing it was out of the question—they had to have a decent place to stay.

The housing office tried and tried, and after a frantic search they finally located an apartment. But when Paul went to see the owner, she told him her elderly parents lived in the house and could not stand noise. She told him she just couldn't take the chance. Yet the following morning she called Paul through the housing office and said he could have the apartment.

Her reason: "I just couldn't sleep last night worrying about your wife and the baby with no place to stay!"

That was neither the first nor the last time something like that happened. The lives of servicemen and their families in communities near many bases in World War II were far from easy, but the people in and around Bath seemed to make a special effort to help. They not only cared about building ships, but they cared about the families of the men who would sail them. For decades they had been sending men and ships down to sea and they knew what this meant for those who would be left behind.

In the middle of January there was a ceremony held at the Bath Iron Works to help raise money for the war effort through the sale of bonds. Officials from the Treasury Department were present, and so were some Navy people from Washington. I don't know how much money this ceremony raised for the war effort, but it sure raised my spirits. I was awarded the Silver Star for my work in the South Pacific.

Although my depressed feelings about the loss of the *Aaron Ward* had vanished, this was a real boost for my morale. I had purposely thrown myself wholeheartedly into my new job as operations officer on the staff of commander, Destroyer Squadron Twenty-one, after the loss in order to blot out the painful memory. But I hadn't expected a medal. I had taken part in some hard-fought battles, but so had many others. More than a few of those brave men had done more than I, and many would never be coming back from the South Pacific. All I had done was my best, in the hope that it would renew my self-confidence. That it had, and that it had made my resolve firmer seemed reward enough. But now, on top of my promotion and in addition to a new ship, here was this Silver Star. To say I was happy would have been putting it mildly.

I think it may have been just as well that Friday was close at hand. I had scheduled a visit to New York for that weekend, and at that point my head was in the clouds anyway, because I expected to see Imogen again. If I hadn't been planning that trip and had stayed at Bath to concentrate on naval matters, I am sure that time would have been completely wasted. I would have tried, but it would have been a lost cause.

I got to New York too late to contact Imogen, but I called her midmorning the next day. I would have done so earlier, but I knew she was still rehearsing for the Broadway show *Mexican Hayride*. Good-natured as she was, she wouldn't have welcomed a ringing phone at 8:00 A.M. after working late the night before. But when I did finally get hold of her on the phone, her voice not only was friendly, but eager. She wanted to see me. Unfortunately, however, there was a problem. She had both an afternoon and an evening rehearsal that day.

I have mentioned before that I can be a determined sort of person when I set my mind to it, and I had no intention of letting a couple of rehearsals spoil this weekend for us. Since it was then past ten and Imogen had some things to attend to, I suggested lunch, and made a mental note to suggest a date for dinner when I saw her. After all, as a naval officer I knew something of the value of advance planning, and this situation called for it.

As a group, naval officers, perhaps because of their training and service at sea, tend to be creatures of habit. Certainly I was somewhat that way, thus it shouldn't surprise anyone that we ended up at Dinty Moore's for lunch. But habit wasn't the whole of it. Both Imogen and I liked the food, and the hamburger steaks served there were the biggest and best I've ever eaten. Or maybe it was just the company that made them seem that way. My head was in the clouds that day. The waiter could have served me a tiny, burned patty of ground chuck and I would have thought it was mushroom-smothered sirloin, because I wasn't concentrating on the food.

Little wonder! Imogen was one of those girls—that's what we called females in those days—who was completely attentive. Once I sat down with her and she'd nodded her head slightly toward any celebrities who happened to be in the restaurant, she'd focus on me exclusively. She would be completely oblivious of anyone else in the room, and made me feel as if she considered me the most important person in the world.

That was pretty heady stuff for any young man, most especially for a young naval officer. From my Academy years on, the one thing I had impressed on me was that I was not the most important person in the world. I was supposed to have self-confidence and have developed leadership abilities. But in the naval scheme of things, self-importance was not considered an acceptable attitude. It was tough on the ego, and though I'd become quite used to it, I was human. I thoroughly enjoyed Imogen's undivided attention. She was a very beautiful girl with a great personality who treated me like I was a four-star admiral.

It was typical of Imogen that the first words she spoke after we were settled at a table were, "Julie, you've got a new ribbon! Tell me about it!"

I guess she had spotted it when I took off my overcoat, and sensed at once that it must mean something important to me. But I was sure she really wasn't interested in a long, detailed account of my experiences with Squadron Twenty-one. Imogen didn't care anything about naval warfare. Very few women do. She had mentioned that ribbon just to give me a chance to talk about it.

I guess women have been doing that sort of thing for centuries. Then, having brought up the subject, they have sat back, put on an interested expression, and endured long, ponderous tales of how the trophies were won. I knew it was a traditional ritual, but when Imogen did it, I liked it. Unless I was wrong, it meant she was really fond of me.

I did my best to keep my story brief. I told her what the ribbon represented, and recounted the sequence of events that led to its being awarded. I downplayed my own part in these events, which wasn't difficult because I felt it had been modest, but she would have none of this. Though she listened patiently and attentively as I tried to explain ship maneuvers and battle actions, she would interrupt every so often and insist on hearing more of what I had been doing. And then, when I'd reluctantly go into more detail, her face would grow serious with concern.

I could understand. The intricate maneuvers of ships and planes were abstracts. To Imogen and thousands like her, battle was only comprehensible in terms of single human beings. Imogen wasn't interested in *the* war. She wanted to know about *my* war.

I hurried on as quickly as possible, all the while secretly cherishing the idea that this beautiful girl apparently cared that much about me. Still, I did not want to turn our lunch date into a somber discussion, and I was glad when our food finally arrived. It diverted our attention and soon we were talking about other things.

Mostly our conversation centered on Imogen, because I kept asking her questions. Her world was similar to mine yet so different, and I was fascinated by it. Her hours, like those of a destroyer skipper, were long; her responsibilities were heavy. Yet she lived and worked in the glare of spotlights, and many of her associates and friends were famous entertainment personalities. Before I had met her, all I had ever known of those personalities was their professional, public image. But by listening to Imogen I had learned to know many as human beings.

Imogen knew I enjoyed this vicarious association with the glamour which was, by then, almost a commonplace element in her life, and throughout the meal she told me a number of anecdotes about various entertainment people she had met. But then as we finished, a mischievous look spread across her heart-shaped face, and suddenly she said, "You're going to meet a few of them too, tonight!"

I looked at her, not quite comprehending. I had mentioned that I planned to get a ticket for the hit *One Touch of Venus*, for that afternoon while she was rehearsing, and hoped to see *Oklahoma!* after we'd had dinner and she had to go back to the theater. I assumed that by "meet" she meant I'd be watching people she knew perform on the stage, and I said so.

She smiled, shook her head, then she laughed lightly, and I suddenly had the feeling I must have sounded very naive.

"No, Julie," she said. "We have been invited to a party after the rehearsal tonight, by the Paul Garretts, some new friends of mine. You will like Lillian and Paul. He's the vice-president for public relations for General Motors. They have a lot of friends, many of them in show business, and some will be there."

That sounded like fun, quite an occasion, and one that called for something special. I had been trying to decide where to take Imogen for dinner, but this settled it.

"Let's eat at 21 tonight," I said.

Imogen beamed. As a rising young singer and actress in the world of show business, she had many opportunities to dine at noted restaurants. But the 21 Club was one of the very best. It wasn't just the food and the atmosphere, both of which were superb, but 21 was frequented by many famous patrons. In those days, just being seen there suggested a performer had joined some magic inner circle of the entertainment world.

"That sounds wonderful," she said, and from her tone, I was suddenly certain it would be.

One Touch of Venus, with its star, Mary Martin, was fine entertainment. I enjoyed it from beginning to end, but the minute I was out of the theater, I forgot it completely; to this day I can't really recall very much about it. As I headed to the theater to meet Imogen and take her to dinner, the reality I knew was ahead was far more interesting and exciting than the fantasy I had just seen on a stage.

The 21 Club, located at 21 West 52nd Street, is in a wide-fronted building of dark, grayish-brown stone which from the outside looks like the residence of some wealthy person. The building has large windows, and an ornate iron fence stands some feet in front of it along the sidewalk, both relics of an era when that section of Manhattan was heavily residential. The only major feature which distinguishes it from a private home is the group of cast-iron figures of jockeys which guard its entrance. These, painted in the colors of famous racing stables, are themselves antiques, and give 21 a well-deserved aura suggesting the conservative opulence and gentility of an exclusive club.

Inside, that same aura was reinforced by the layout of the restaurant and the treatment its staff accorded its patrons. Behind those large, heavily curtained front windows, and stretching deep into the building, there were a number of comfortable medium-sized dining rooms. Imogen explained to me that at times it was difficult to get a table in some of these which were favored by certain well-known, regular customers. But for all I could see, they gave us a good one. We hardly had time to be seated before Imogen was able to tell me about a number of famous theatrical people and one or two movie celebrities who were at tables close by.

Exactly what we had to eat, I can't really remember. But I do recall the food was superb. It must have been steak—steak has always been one of my favorite meals, and Imogen shared my liking for it. Meat for civilian use was rationed during World War II, but good restaurants usually had some steaks available for special patrons and occasions. Since one had only to look at the pair of us to know this was a special occasion, steak was probably offered and we probably ordered it.

Throughout the meal Imogen continued to entertain me with stories about Broadway and its famous and infamous people. Imogen was just about as proper a young lady as you could ever meet, but she did have a great sense of humor which was at once both innocent and sophisticated. Whether the tale was about some slightly risqué episode involving a real individual, or an innocent joke, she could make it very funny.

One of those stories I have never forgotten—mostly, I guess, because subsequently I was to hear variations of it quite a few times and it always brought back memories of that dinner with Imogen at 21. In fact, the first time I was to hear it repeated was about a year later out on Feitabul Island in the Ulithi Atoll, and the person telling it was in show business. He was Eddie Duchin, the pianist and orchestra leader, the father of today's well-known musician, Peter Duchin. Though in my opinion he didn't tell it quite as amusingly as Imogen, hearing it again way out there in the Pacific was wonderful.

Imogen's version went like this:

Once there was this very wealthy and elderly widow who professed to be a good Christian. She prayed often, went to church every Sunday, and prided herself on being a pillar of the community. But, like old Scrooge, she had a fault. Widow Jones considered the less fortunate of the world lazy and shiftless. She did not believe in charity. She and her departed husband, John, had worked like dogs, never received help from anyone, and John had died leaving a fortune.

Then one Sunday the minister gave an especially persuasive sermon on charity which opened her eyes. On leaving the church and coming on a rather seedy-looking man, her heart went out to him. Quickly she reached in her purse and handed him two hundred dollars, wishing him godspeed.

The following Sunday the same seedy man approached her on the street, a grin on his face, and for a moment she began to regret her lapse. But instead of asking her for more money, he held out an envelope. Then he sighed and shook his head, saying, "Lady, you can pick 'em even better than John Jones, and he was the best I've ever known. Here's your ten thousand dollars. Godspeed paid fifty to one."

It was an old joke, but at the time both of us laughed over it so hard that people at other tables nearby looked askance at us. We didn't care! We were having too much fun.

Oklahoma! was fun too, a great show! I walked out of the theater humming that tune about "corn" and something to do with "an elephant's eye"—or I think that's what I was humming. Frankly, I am not sure, because by that time my mind wasn't on *Oklahoma!*. I was thinking about another show in another theater and a star with whom I was going to spend the rest of the evening.

Of all the events and gatherings I attended with Imogen during the war years, that party at the Garretts was, for me, one of the most memorable. I had been to parties in fine homes and clubs before, and I've attended many since, but that one made a tremendous impact. The whole thing reminded me of a scene from a Hollywood musical depicting the glamour and sparkle of New York's world of show business.

I met Imogen at the theater and we took a cab over to the apartment on Park Avenue. When I picked her up, she was so bundled up in her fur coat I could hardly see her, but when we stepped into the elevator, I was stunned. With her coat open, I noticed she had on a beautiful black evening gown, and she looked absolutely gorgeous.

I told her so at once.

She chuckled, saying that flattery would get me nowhere, and when I insisted firmly that I was just telling the truth, she laughed.

"All right, Julian," she said, "have it your way. Besides, whatever it is, I like it."

Paul Garrett met us at the door. He was just then helping a departing guest on with his coat and, after welcoming Imogen and me, he introduced us. The man was a big fellow, his handshake firm, his voice hearty. He apologized for having to leave early.

What a way to start a party! I had never met an opera singer before, much less a Danish opera singer. He was Lauritz Melchior, and I certainly didn't feel he owed me an apology.

Paul's beautiful auburn-haired wife, Lillian, quickly came over to greet us. She had on a striking, silvery evening gown, and it was then that I noticed everyone there was in formal attire. Imogen had described the gathering as a "small, informal party," which was essentially correct—except for the dress. It was one of those times I was especially thankful about being a naval officer. My uniform fitted in perfectly.

The apartment was large, with high ceilings that gave it an air of spacious comfort one rarely finds in apartments today. The walls and the draperies were a soft, light-brownish color which I think is called beige. It increased the feeling of spaciousness considerably.

On the right side of the living room there was a long sofa; across from it were two matching love seats facing each other. All three were covered with a rich velvet fabric. There were some other chairs, one or two tables with lamps, and at the far end of the room stood the centerpiece of the whole layout—a grand piano. It was a Hollywood set designer's vision of a New York Park Avenue apartment. But this was no vision. It was real.

There were a fair number of people present, but given the size of the place it was far from crowded. Some guests, like Lauritz Melchior, had had to leave earlier. Others would be stopping in later to replace them. Though easy and relaxed, the party had a precision that almost suggested naval planning. Paul and Lillian Garrett really knew how to entertain.

We were introduced around, and spent some time talking

with several of the other guests. Among these were Army Colonel Edgar Garbisch and his wife, Bernice. She was the daughter of an auto magnate named Chrysler, and he had been a star football player at West Point some years before I had gone to Annapolis.

I have always been a football fan, and got quite a kick out of talking with Colonel Garbisch about it. But there were a few elements of pain in these recollections. In one game Edgar Garbisch had led Army to a 12-0 victory over Navy by kicking four field goals, something any Navy man would prefer to forget.

Not long after I began talking with Colonel Garbisch, Lillian Garrett called for our attention and made an announcement. One of her guests was going to sing for us, and Imogen would accompany her on the piano. It was a real treat. Ethel Merman was a great star and to hear her like that in person, singing four song hits from her Broadway shows, was a unique experience.

Under other circumstances I would have been disappointed that Miss Merman and her escort, Robert Levitt, had to leave soon after, but Lillian Garrett then asked Imogen to take over. She sang some Gershwin tunes, a couple of numbers from current Broadway shows, plus a few from *Showboat*. And then she sang "Bill," and that really was wonderful.

It was then that a man sitting next to me—whose name I don't recall—leaned over and whispered to me. "I've heard Helen Morgan sing that one," he said, "but this girl is every bit as good."

I passed the remark on to Imogen, and it pleased her considerably. The individual who had spoken to me was apparently someone whose opinion Imogen valued—and Helen Morgan was a show business legend. "Bill" had been her song, her trademark, the tune Helen Morgan did better than anyone. Yet now here was an authoritative opinion that placed Imogen's rendition of the song on a par with Morgan's. No wonder she was pleased.

That incident, I think, put the final touch on what was a very wonderful evening.

The transition from the glitter, glamour, and excitement of Broadway and Park Avenue to the drab, gray reality of Bath wasn't really difficult at all. Even the cold in Maine didn't bother me as much as it had to begin with. I think the glow I brought with me from New York kept me warm. But there was also the work I found waiting for me when I arrived. *Laffey* now had only two more weeks to endure the indignities of welding and hammering, pounding and painting, and the inevitable mess topside and below. Yet though her birth pangs were just about over, those last two weeks as her prospective commanding officer were crammed with activity and work that kept me constantly on the move.

Typically, and perhaps also because Mother Nature didn't want any of us to forget her, that day we left Bath the mercury in the thermometer was concentrated at the bottom of the glass. The wind was blowing a brisk little gale as *Laffey*'s bow at last began to bite into the leaden-gray waves of the Atlantic. Soon a thick confetti of snow was sweeping across her in chill welcome. It cut visibility, isolating us in our own little world as we steamed south toward Boston, but even this meteorological trick could not dampen our spirits. Everyone aboard was keyed up to a pitch of expectancy. *Laffey* was no longer a cold, still form tied to the land. She was alive and vital, challenging those white-capped rollers without hesitation.

When we arrived safely at Pier 1 at the navy yard (in Boston), the rest of the ship's officers and men were waiting for us. As soon as the lines and cables had us snugged against the pier and the brow was rigged, they began to pile aboard. Some moved with the assurance of veteran seamen. But it was easy to see that the majority, despite their attempts to emulate the seasoned hands, were brand-new to the Navy. This was their first ship. They had a lot to learn and not much time to learn it. Yet their obvious willingness, as they got the snow shoveled off the decks and the gear stowed away, was very reassuring. Green they might be, but none of them showed any evidence of slackness.

As I watched them work, something else struck me about them. Though they were mostly strangers to each other, right from the start this alphabet soup of Americans worked well together—as if they had been doing it for years. From an Adams, Asadorian, a Bell, and a Doyle, to a Falotico, Neifah, Revels, and a Yuochunas, they pitched right in as a team.

This was very important and augured well for our future together. In coming months, those men down there would have to live and work together more closely and intimately than many ever had before. We would need a strong spirit of teamwork and tolerance to succeed and survive.

Considering the circumstances, it didn't take long for my officers and men to get the *Laffey* shipshape. Then, as soon as the work was finished, everyone changed into clean blues and tried to look like sailors. Watches were posted just in time to receive the flood of friends, relatives, and guests who began to pour aboard. We'd made it! This was the big moment.

In midafternoon of February 8, 1944, with the temperature hovering at about 15 degrees and the sky heavily overcast, the ship joined the Navy. Officially, she became the USS *Laffey*, DD 724, and I became her commanding officer. She was mine at last.

The commissioning ceremony was relatively brief and, fittingly, my remarks had a "musical" accompaniment. To those working at the Boston Navy Yard who were responsible for keeping production rolling, *Laffey* was just one more ship in the long gray line that stretched from the U. S. to the battlefronts. Her commissioning was no reason to stop work.

As I stood up to speak, I knew that uppermost in the minds of parents, wives, and loved ones was what the future might have in store for the ship and her men. I wish I could have told them, but since I was not an oracle, I did the next best thing. I talked about the ship's heritage, recounting the story of Bartlett Laffey's heroic feats that brought him the Medal of Honor. I told them of the courageous and gallant struggle of the first *Laffey*, and how Bill Hank and his men took on the Jap battleship *Hiei*. I pledged to them that this new *Laffey* would uphold the Laffey tradition. When it came time for us to go into battle, we would be ready to give the best possible account of ourselves, and I ended by saying that if we did, I was sure the Almighty would surely bring us home victorious in safety.

When it was over, the band played the National Anthem and then we showed our guests around the ship. Imogen had come up to Boston with her roommate, Nina Korda, for the ceremony, and naturally, this pleased me a great deal. I took them on a brief tour and we talked for a while, but unfortunately, as host I couldn't stay with them as much as I might have liked. I had to meet everyone there—from the father of Sonarman Charles Bell to the parents of young Ensign Jerome B. Sheets. It was my duty, but it was also my pleasure.

Charlie Bell was later to become a key man on *Laffey*'s bridge. He served as my telephone talker, the man who relayed my orders and messages to the rest of the ship. Jerry Sheets developed into a fine, loyal, and dependable officer, and was to write a moving article about the ship which captured the affection every man aboard eventually came to feel for the *Laffey*. Sadly, this article became Jerry's symbolic legacy to the rest of us. He was later killed in action, fighting to help save the ship during the greatest struggle she was ever to face.

During the postceremonial festivities one of my officers, whom I had sent ahead from Bath to Boston on a very special assignment, came up and drew me aside to report on his mission. In a low voice, Pay Youngquist, the ship's supply officer and paymaster, told me he had been successful.

"That machine you wanted will be aboard tomorrow, Captain!" he said, and I nodded and grinned at him.

"Good work, Pay," I told him. It was the best news I'd heard that day.

Whatever else a ship's crew must have, they must have good morale—and that machine would help. Once we went off to war, we'd be isolated and living a pretty spartan life. Anything that would temper this general discomfort, the tedium, the boredom, would help my men keep their spirits up, and good food was one of those things. We were supposed to have an ice-cream maker aboard, and I wanted to be sure we got it. The Navy was good, but the Navy was big, and it wasn't perfect. I'd sent Youngquist to make sure there weren't any slipups.

Pete Newell was in Boston to get his receipt for the ship from the naval district commandant's office, and he came over to say goodbye and wish us well. I was glad to see him. It gave me a chance to thank him for his kindness, hospitality, and for the fine ship he had turned over to me.

Characteristically, the ever-courteous Pete Newell replied with a compliment, saying he hoped the ship was as good as her skipper.

Being human, I was flattered, but being a realist I felt Pete had turned things around. Maybe I hadn't done too badly in the past, but *Laffey* was a great ship. There was a lot of doing ahead before I and the men I commanded could match her quality—a lot of doing . . . .

FOUR

To the civilians who had gathered at the Boston Navy Yard for *Laffey*'s commissioning ceremony, I am sure that the ship and her men looked ready to go off to sea immediately. But they were far from ready. There was much to be done in the next three weeks and I didn't want to waste any time in getting started. The very next morning I called all my officers together in the wardroom. To make a good start, those who lacked real experience—and the rest, too—all had to know exactly what I expected of them. They had to be told and told right away.

The wardroom of a warship is the officers' mess and lounge area. Aboard *Laffey* it was located below the forward superstructure, which contained the pilothouse, captain's cabin, the combat information center, the radio room, and other important areas. Crammed as the ship was with men, equipment, and weapons, the wardroom was the only suitable place in officers' country where I could address all of my seventeen officers privately. It was a tight fit to squeeze everyone in, and it would get even tighter later in the war when we had twenty-five officers aboard.

My initial concern was safety, both for the ship and her men. Even at that stage, *Laffey* was undergoing some alterations ordered by the various bureaus of the Navy Department. Alterations meant acetylene cutting torches and welding torches—the ever-present possibility of fire. Fire aboard a ship, even if she is moored to a pier and can get outside help, can be deadly.

With most of the crew being new Reserves, the ship would be

unfamiliar to them. I stressed to my officers that the first thing they should do was to show the men their fire stations. They had to know where the fireplugs, hoses, and other fire-fighting equipment was located; the second thing they had to know was what to do in case of fire.

I emphasized that this sort of preparation and concern for the men was something I would always expect of my officers. It would not only assure the welfare of the ship and those aboard her, but it was the best way of gaining the crew's respect and confidence. We had to have that respect and confidence or we could accomplish nothing, I told them, but we had to earn it.

I gave them another example of how this could be done. I noted that in about a month the ship would be in Bermuda for shakedown training. They were to be sure that every man in their charge had a white summer uniform before we sailed. Without one, a man would be denied liberty ashore.

"To some of you," I said, "that might not sound very important. But it is! If a sailor loses his chance for liberty because his officer hasn't made sure he has the proper uniform, that sailor is going to start wondering about that officer. Next time, that officer could forget something that could cost that sailor his life."

I also cautioned my officers against using foul language in the presence of their men. I said it wasn't a matter of manners but of common sense. Swearing doesn't impress sailors. They hear a lot of it from their shipmates. But if an officer blows up and swears at every little frustration, it suggests to his men that he has no self-control. Those men, I said, are soon going to start wondering how that officer will act when the chips are down. Despite his authority, they aren't going to give him their full backing.

I wasn't worried about my experienced officers. I knew they understood fully, yet I wondered if the rest had gotten my message. I paused for a moment to let my words sink in, but when I saw their faces, I knew I didn't have to worry. Reassured, I went on.

As for the ship herself, I told my officers that one of our most important responsibilities right then was to make sure she had a full store of spare parts and equipment. One of the lessons I had learned in the South Pacific was that once a ship was at sea, the more spares she had aboard the better. The Navy's supply system was efficient, but at times there was just no substitute for a little insurance.

"If you need any help," I said, "go to Charlie Holovak." He was the executive officer. "He should be able to help you get what you want, but if he can't pry it loose, come to me. My door will always be open."

Good as Holovak was, I knew that sooner or later I would have to take a hand. Charlie knew his way around the Navy, but not quite as well as I did; and sure enough, not long after he came up against a blank wall. Al Henke, our chief engineer, had tried to get some additional electrical fittings and cable. Even with Holovak's help, he had been unsuccessful. The regular channels of supply couldn't give him what he wanted and Henke didn't know where else to go.

I wasn't surprised. With the Boston Navy Yard filled with new ships, all of which needed equipment, Henke's problem required a traditional rather than an official solution. I asked him to send the senior yard electrician working on board to me at once so I could inquire about a fellow named Daugherty.

As engineer officer in the destroyer *Gleaves*, I had first met Joe Daugherty at the Boston Navy Yard in 1940. I had gotten to know him quite well. We were good friends, and when he showed up at 7:30 at the door of my cabin two mornings later, he was as glad to see me as I was to see him.

Joe wouldn't accept breakfast. He'd already eaten, but over coffee—when I casually mentioned our problem—he looked thoughtful, grinned, and nodded understandingly. That was enough. I didn't press the subject; I knew I didn't need to. When Joe left later on, he told me with a wink to have one of my "boys" give him a call.

Three days later, Al Henke came to me with welcome news. His department had just received an almost embarrassingly large supply of extra cable and electrical fittings. What no formal requests or requisitions had been able to secure, a more traditional Navy method of cutting red tape had produced in short order.

I have always thought of it as the "Daugherty method," though I suppose it has many different names. Whatever it is called, it has always worked. During World War II the Joe Daughertys of the world performed countless little miracles— and some big ones, too; without them it would have been much more difficult for the United States to win the war. Joe Daughertys are never mentioned in official histories of the war, but thank God they were there when we needed them.

Over the next few weeks the fitting out progressed smoothly, and bit by bit I began to increase the tempo of training. There were dock trials, for example, during which no lines were cast off.

The ship remained secured to the pier, fitting-out work continued, but stations would be manned just as if the ship was about to get underway. An extra boiler would be fired up, the engines warmed, and engine order telegraphs and steering gear were tested. I would even have Al Henke's men open up the throttles just a little to make sure the ship's machinery worked as it was supposed to.

Alterations and modifications on the ship continued, yet as the time for us to leave grew closer, I knew we would have to sail before some of *Laffey*'s faults were corrected. This was frustrating and it worried me. I knew perfection was impossible, but I was especially concerned about one problem in particular. Though a sea cabin and head were being added, nothing could be done with the pilothouse and open-bridge arrangement because these needed very extensive, time-consuming alterations.

The pilothouse aboard *Laffey* was a fully enclosed room with large, glass-covered portholes in its forward and side bulkheads. Located just aft and above the second forward twin five-inch-gun mount, and between that and the five-inch-gun director, this room contained the ship's controls. In it were the steering wheel, the annunciators (engine order telegraphs for signaling forward and reverse speed changes), the magnetic compass, a gyro compass repeater for the helmsman, voice radio speakers for the TBS, plus a lot of other communications equipment.

On the starboard side (facing forward, the right side of the ship) of this room was an armchair for the captain which was elevated well above the deck. One of the rules of the road a ship must observe is that ships to starboard have the right of way, and a skipper must keep a sharp lookout to starboard to maneuver his ship accordingly. When the ship is maneuvering in more crowded waters, or the skipper needs the best possible view of what is going on, he will stand on the open bridge. Yet the open bridge on *Laffey* was behind and above the pilothouse.

What this meant was that not only was the view from the open bridge partly blocked by the pilothouse forward, but, when I was on that bridge, I was not in visual contact with the helmsman. The open bridge did have a gyro compass, radar repeaters, and a rudder angle indicator, but these were poor substitutes for visual contact with the helmsman. Helmsmen are human beings. They can sometimes turn the wheel in the wrong direction by accident, or misunderstand orders they get over a voice tube or the twenty-one-megacycle squawk box which were my only means of communicating from the bridge.

Without visual contact with the helmsman, it was going to be very difficult to correct such errors in time to prevent a potential disaster. Bad as it would be on the high seas where there was room to maneuver, the situation would be a potential time bomb in a crowded harbor when docking the ship, or refueling her at sea from a tanker underway. When I had first noticed it at Bath, I had assumed there would be time to correct it at the Boston Navy Yard. Yet now it was evident this wasn't possible. To say I was displeased would be putting it mildly.

Getting a brand-new ship and a brand-new crew on a completely operational footing is much like raising a child. You do it by degrees. After the dock trials and drills, we made some very short forays out of the harbor. Perhaps "forays" isn't the best way to characterize these little trips, because they weren't bold excursions at high speeds. With a new crew that wasn't fully trained as a team, it would have been foolish to proceed very boldly. Instead, they were executed in the manner of a man handling high explosives—v-e-r-y carefully. But then as we grew more experienced, I began to put her through her paces.

These later forays matched the definition of the word much more closely. Out into the Atlantic we went with *Laffey*'s sharp bow cutting the waves, her turbines churning, her fantail dug in. We dropped depth charges. We fired our guns. And every so often there would be an extreme change in course. We weren't in battle—we just wanted to see if *Laffey* was structurally sound— but it was exhilarating.

We could find no faults with the ship as she sliced along, the white froth from her sides mingling with her wake, the chill wind tearing the wisps of smoke from her stacks. Nothing gave way when her guns where fired, and she shook off the concussions of the depth charges without the least protest. Even when the helmsman put the wheel over hard, she'd lean into the turn like a racehorse. She was a thoroughbred all right, and every man aboard soon knew it.

Though I enjoyed these forays to sea thoroughly, none of them were joyrides. If she had had any structural faults, that was the time to find out about them.

She didn't. By the time we returned to port from our last little voyage, I knew *Laffey* was sound and solid. Later on she would need further testing; but for now, she was as ready to head for the Washington Navy Yard as she ever would be.

I was a little less certain about my men, however, because the trip to Washington was to be a new experience for some. It would be our first overnight voyage, and for some officers especially it would be a brand-new challenge. As the time of our departure neared, I noticed that some of the less experienced officers had begun to look a little apprehensive when the trip was mentioned.

At first I'd thought it was the prospect of the inspection that was bothering them. They knew that officers from BuShips (Bureau of Ships), BuOrd (Bureau of Ordnance),and many other Navy Department offices would be boarding the ship. And there would be more than one admiral casting a critical eye at us. It was an unsettling prospect, but I soon realized this was not what was bothering those officers.

A few hours steaming off Boston in daylight with everyone alert and on their toes was one thing. But an overnight trip meant the possibility of some lonely hours on watch, possibly without a superior right at hand to turn to. That was the kind of full responsibility that some had never faced, and they were worried about it.

As soon as I realized what was the matter, I knew it was time for another speech. I am not fond of making speeches, but in this case one was definitely called for, and at noon on the day before we were to depart I gathered my officers together in the wardroom. If some had doubts, it was my job to reassure them.

"All of you know your jobs," I began, "and you will do them and well. I realize that most of our internal training thus far has been confined to individual departments. You have been working under the direction of Al Henke or Harry Burns, but now—all of a sudden—you realize they might not be there all the time you are on watch. You think you are going to be on your own, and you're worried about it. You shouldn't be! Your department is part of a team. You are going to have others to help you."

I hesitated for a few seconds to let that sink in, trying to think just how I could drive my point home. Then my eye lighted on a little metal statue of a water buffalo that we always kept on the wardroom table. We used it to show the stewards at meals where, around the table, they were supposed to start serving. At any given time, some of our officers had to get through a meal more quickly than others because some had to go on watch or perform duties needing immediate attention.

Jokingly, we called the statue "buck," and it was our informal way of saving time and preventing confusion. I picked it up; nodding at it, I said that from now on I wanted everyone present to remember that there was another buck aboard. It rested on my shoulders. The ship, I said, was my responsibility; and that went for everything that happened aboard her, to her, or to any of her people.

No, I did not use the words, "The buck stops here." President

66

Harry S Truman popularized that phrase some years later. But the term *buck*, meaning responsibility, did not originate with him. Skippers of U. S. Navy warships had carried the buck on their shoulders for many decades before Mr. Truman became President, and though some may have referred to their responsibilities by somewhat more colorful names, they meant the same thing.

I went on, saying, "Any time one of you is OOD [officer of the deck, the captain's representative during a watch who is in charge of the ship], never hesitate to call me if you believe a dangerous situation is developing. That means even when I am asleep. When there's a problem, my place is on the bridge."

That seemed to do it, because I noticed then that the tense looks on the faces of some of my officers began to disappear. There were also several knowing smiles from some of the more experienced people. I suppose they had tried to reassure their companions, but now, coming from the skipper, the word was official.

In the coming months it became evident that all of my officers had listened and taken this little speech to heart. I did lose some sleep, and there were even a few times when I was called when perhaps it wasn't really necessary. But that was fine with me. At sea, there were always other opportunities to catch a little rest when things were quiet, but in times of crisis there are no second chances.

The next morning the wind was up a little, though nothing like it had been when the ship left Bath. Even so, it called for careful preparation. We set the special sea details which put our most experienced men at vital stations—our senior yeoman on the annunciators, our senior quartermaster at the wheel, our chief signalman on the signal bridge aft of the pilothouse. And we had an expert quartermaster aft in the emergency steering room who could take over if the bridge lost steering control. Al Henke had our best throttlemen at the controls of the forward and after engine rooms. And to make doubly sure there would be no hitch in communications between the bridge and the various stations in the ship, I had an extra telephone talker on the sound-powered telephone stationed close to me.

When all these men were in place, I leaned out over the bridge railing on the starboard side and ran my eyes along the ship, fore and aft. Then, when all seemed correct, I gave orders to cast off, and we were on our way. But I did not call for power immediately and steam away from the pier. You can do that with a small power boat, but not with a 2,200-ton, 376-foot-long ship like the *Laffey*.

She must first be well clear and away from the pier or you risk damaging the ship's stern and propellers.

Had there been a strong onshore wind and current that morning, holding the ship against the pier, I would have had to use a spring line. A spring is a mooring line that extends from the bow back to a bollard (an iron post) on the pier. By going ahead on the outboard engine and keeping the spring taut, the ship's stern will swing clear.

Luckily, a spring wasn't needed. Weather and current conditions were such that the ship slowly drifted sideways away from the pier. Then, once we were well clear, I gave orders for "All engines ahead, two-thirds standard," (ten knots) and had the helmsman swing the bow and head us down the channel. We soon passed Boston lightship tossing at her moorings; speed was increased to standard (fifteen knots), and we secured the special sea detail. This meant the regular helmsman took over the wheel and other regulars manned the rest of the stations.

Those who have watched large ships leaving or arriving at piers may wonder why *Laffey* was not assisted by a tug when we left Boston. Certainly, other warships used tugs, and *Laffey* was quite large. But she was a destroyer, and destroyers have powerful engines. *Laffey*'s could deliver sixty thousand horsepower. With all that power at their command, destroyer skippers traditionally disdained the use of tugs for such maneuvers. Except under extreme weather conditions, or when his destroyer had suffered serious damage, a skipper's competence might be called into question if he could not maneuver his ship without the help of a tug.

By February 1944, there was relatively little danger of any German submarine activity in the coastal waters between Boston and Washington, but regardless, I had Condition III watches set as soon as we were at sea. This was our normal pattern of watches for wartime cruising, a state of readiness in which members of our crew would stand a four-hour watch every twelve hours. It meant that the ship was in a state of readiness just in case one of Hitler's more daring U-boat commanders ventured close to the coast, and it also gave everyone a chance to stand one or more watches during our overnight cruise. The sooner we all got used to it, the better.

As soon as we were well to the east of the tip of Cape Cod, I had the navigator set a course for the entrance to Chesapeake Bay. On deck, we had a big job ahead of us. The ship was in good shape, but she had just left the Navy Yard and she had an inspection coming up. Her topside needed a good cleaning and there wouldn't be time once we arrived in Washington. Those not on watch had to turn to for a "field day," and for the next thirty-six hours we scrubbed and steamed, steamed and scrubbed our way toward the nation's capital.

I suspect that some of the newer hands were something less than pleased. Here they were in a fighting ship at sea at last, and the first thing they were being ordered to do was scrub and polish. I suppose they must have thought they were leaving that sort of thing behind when we sailed. But I am certain that the experienced, ranking enlisted men—especially the chiefs—patiently explained the need for it all, and quickly set them straight.

The truth was that the ship was being cleaned up not solely to satisfy the officers who were going to inspect her. The men were doing the job for their own good. A filthy ship is not only an uncomfortable place to live, but it's also a dangerous one. Isolated and living in close quarters the way we were, cleanliness wasn't just a major defense against illness. It was a matter of pride in one's home. Men who cared enough about their ship to keep her spotless were men who would fight to defend her when things got rough.

Naturally, since I was not present, I can only assume that this is what our chiefs told those men who might have voiced some distaste for our field day. After all, the soft-voiced, quietly persuasive ways of Navy chiefs are legendary. But whatever it was that they said, it had a desired effect. By the time the first visitor stepped aboard *Laffey* in Washington, she was sparkling—and she stayed that way until mothballed after the war.

The morning after we had secured alongside a pier at the Washington Navy Yard, the parade of visitors began. Officers from the various bureaus of the Navy Department poured aboard. And if there was some part of *Laffey* they didn't inspect, it was under water. They were all over her, looking, studying, asking questions about her performance and that of her equipment. But one thing in particular almost all of them studied. It was the bridge arrangement.

Among our visitors were at least four flag officers (one of the rank of commodore or higher who is entitled to fly a personal flag). Early arrivals were Rear Admirals Braisted, Delany, and Reichmuth. And at noon, tall, dignified Rear Admiral George Rowcliff arrived.

As Admiral Rowcliff came aboard, the alarm was sounded to alert everyone of the approach of a rear admiral. When I heard the six bells, I dashed back to the stern where our brow to the pier was located. I was more than a little nervous. Rowcliff was a member of the general board, a group of admirals that passed on a new ship's characteristics—the number, size, and location of her guns; crew accommodations; and the like. What he had to say about *Laffey* would carry a great deal of weight and influence.

I welcomed him aboard in the manner that any skipper would greet an important superior. Then, at his request, I took him on a tour of the topside. I told him how much I liked the ship's twin rudders, which greatly improved her handling characteristics. I praised the interior ship-length passageway, the extra five-inch gun (six instead of five as in the Fletcher class), and other features. But I didn't need to say anything about the bridge arrangement. Admiral Rowcliff was fully aware of this problem and he mentioned it himself.

As we walked forward on the starboard side and reached the forecastle the admiral turned around and shook his head. "My God, just look at that!" he said. "She looks like the Hanging Gardens of Babylon."

He was pointing to the antiaircraft gun tubs, and I had to admit that there was a resemblance. That middle-eastern biblical city's tiers of elevated gardens had been one of the seven wonders of the ancient world, but the tone of Rowcliff's words expressed dismay, not wonderment.

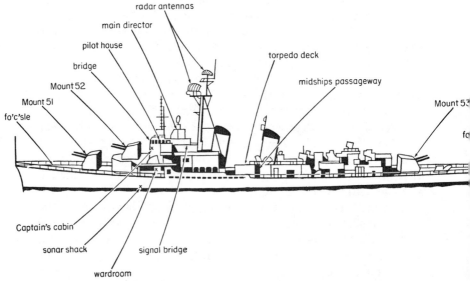

Diagram of an Allen M. Sumner-class destroyer in 1945, showing location of armament and other features. CIC and wardroom were in forward superstructure, near pilothouse and bridge.

The admiral sighed. "This isn't the ship we wanted them to build," he went on. "Every time a task group commander in from the Pacific came in with the recommendation for more guns, they'd add another. Just look at that!"

I did, but I didn't say anything. As far as I had been able to determine, none of these guns had created a stability problem. Maybe they didn't look beautiful there in the Navy Yard, but they sure would have in the South Pacific. I wasn't going to say it to Rowcliff, but I was glad we had them; and to get off the subject quickly, I invited him to have lunch aboard.

He thanked me, but declined, saying he had to get on to another appointment. We walked aft, then at the brow he turned to me and I noticed a twinkle in his eye, suggesting he'd been reading my thoughts.

"Never mind my criticism, Becton," he said. "This is a fine ship, hanging gardens and all. I'd like to be going to sea with you as your executive officer."

And with that he turned, saluted the officer of the deck and the colors, and departed before I could think of what to reply. But needless to say, I felt pretty darn good. Our inspection had been a success, and that's what mattered because now we could steam off for our shakedown training. We were ready to go.

We sailed for Bermuda on March 2, 1944, and I think everyone aboard was keyed up to a high pitch and anxious to get on with it. Both the sea and the weather cooperated, the ship ran smoothly, and there didn't seem to be a single cloud on our horizon. Unfortunately, by afternoon there was.

I had just gone down to my cabin for a few minutes and was about to return to the bridge when Lieutenant (j.g.) Matt Darnell appeared. Matt was always a cheerful sort of person with a keen wit and a ready smile, but he wasn't smiling. As the ship's medical officer, he had urgent business with me.

"Capt'n," he said in that Kentucky accent of his, "I'm afraid I've got some bad news. We have a case of spinal meningitis aboard."

The first thing I thought of was Chefoo. That had been China, 1937, the destroyer *Pope*. I was then her chief engineer, and at that time we'd had a big, powerful, healthy-looking sailor aboard who had come down with the same disease. He had eventually recovered and no one else had contracted it, but it had put the ship in quarantine for three weeks. I suddenly had visions of *Laffey* isolated at a mooring in Bermuda, dozens of men down with the illness, and our entire training schedule completely disrupted.

It wasn't a very pleasant prospect, and my face must have shown it, because Dr. Darnell quickly tried to reassure me. He said that the seaman, Dick Hyson, seemed to be doing OK, and that there wasn't any danger of an epidemic aboard. Everyone aboard, including myself and all the other officers, would have to take some sulfa pills daily until the danger of infection had passed. (There were no antibiotics like penicillin generally available in 1944, only sulfur-based anti-infection drugs.) But Darnell assured me that by the time we arrived in Bermuda, everything would be OK.

My response was, "Thank God for that," and I certainly did. I also thanked Matt, praised him for his initiative in making a correct and early diagnosis, and asked him to keep me informed about Hyson. It was a close shave, but thanks to Matt, it wasn't Chefoo all over again.

One other incident that occurred during our trip to Bermuda bears mention because it illustrates how quickly our less experienced people had already begun to learn what I expected of them. The minute we had cleared Chesapeake Bay and were out in the open ocean, I had ordered a resumption of our internal training. I wanted everyone aboard, especially the junior officers, to get as much experience as possible even before the instructors from the Bermuda Training Command boarded us.

Al Henke had given Lieutenant (j.g.) Harvey Shaw, one of his two assistant engineering officers, the responsibility of training watch standers to maintain and operate the ship's boilers. Shaw was a reliable and capable man with sound engineering experience and a talent for getting people to work well together. But like most of our junior officers, Shaw was quite young. He just hadn't had a chance as yet to learn all the little things that could go wrong with a power plant or where to look for them.

But slender, dark-haired Harvey Shaw had taken my little speech at Boston very much to heart. The minute he discovered that one of our boilers was losing feed water by some means he could not determine, he came straight to me on the bridge. That was exactly what I had asked my officers who were on watch to do, and I appreciated it.

Some might assume that, with an entire ocean around the ship, a little water leakage from a boiler would make no difference. Wasn't there plenty more where that came from? No, actually there wasn't. *Laffey*'s boilers had to have pure, distilled fresh water to operate properly. Only in a situation of extreme emergency could seawater be used, and then only for a brief time. When you boil brine you get salt and mineral residue, and both of these do terrible damage to your steam plant. It will quickly cake up, quit working, and leave you dead in the water, and the cleanup job that is necessary afterward is both long and tedious.

Like all steam-powered warships, *Laffey* carried her own distillation equipment. The production capacity of its evaporators was more than adequate to supply fresh water for the boilers, for drinking and cooking, but its operation used up some of the fuel in our tanks. Fuel was always limited on a destroyer, and wasting feed water meant wasting fuel. It reduced our margin of safety.

Having put in a lot more time in the engineering departments of destroyers than Shaw, I was able to make a good guess about the source of his problem. There were panels on the backs of the boilers which covered openings. These openings allowed inspection and work to be done when the boilers were cold. But when the boilers were in use, these panels were held in place by nuts, and these had to be very tightly secured. From experience I knew that what might seem like a well-secured panel on a cold boiler could leak like a sieve under hot pressure.

Lieutenant Shaw thanked me and left the bridge, and when he returned later, he thanked me again. It had been just what I suspected. The nuts had been tightened on the panels and we weren't losing feed water anymore.

I will admit that I was a little disturbed by this incident. I felt that young Lieutenant Shaw should have discovered the problem himself and corrected it. But I didn't reproach him. Harvey Shaw was human just like the rest of us, and he was less experienced than some of us. He had tried to locate the problem; then, when he couldn't, he'd had the guts to come to me and ask for help. That's exactly what I'd asked my officers to do, what I wanted them to do, and censuring Shaw was not the way to encourage it.

As I have said, the incident did disturb me a little. Yet in balance, it had a very positive outcome. I now knew that Shaw was an officer on whom I could depend absolutely. He was not the kind of person who might try to disguise his ignorance or an error. He had done what he could, then what he'd been told, and that was very reassuring. Furthermore, I was certain we would never have that particular problem again—and we didn't.

That same day I received a message from Bermuda from Commander, Underway Training Group. Captain Dashiell Madeira, USN, relieved any remaining worries I had about the illness aboard, which we had reported to him. He informed me that *Laffey* would indeed be quarantined on her arrival. As soon as we moored in Great Sound we were to hoist the usual yellow quarantine flag, but it was to be almost a formality. Captain Madeira's training group medical officer was aware of the measures we had been taking to prevent the spread of the infection. And as soon as Commander Gray, the staff doctor, could come aboard and confirm Matt Darnell's procedures, the quarantine would be lifted.

This meant that our quarantine would be very short-lived and there would be no interruption in our training schedule. But it also meant something else. It was time again to do what Navy skippers have to do so often—give another speech.

I had the OOD, Lieutenant Tom Addison, an assistant gunnery officer, order the boatswain's mate of the watch to pipe "All Hands." That's the traditional signal used to alert the crew. As soon as the shrill notes of the pipe died away, I took the microphone in hand and began with the usual words, "This is the captain."

I knew that everywhere in the ship the signal and those words would cause men to pause, stop what they were doing, and listen, just as sailors have ever since public-address systems became part of a warship's equipment. I suppose there are officers who get a sense of self-importance from the idea that, in a matter of seconds, they can have dozens, hundreds, or even thousands poised, waiting, straining their ears for what comes next. But I have always abhorred such conceit.

I feel that a skipper should keep his speeches to his crew to a minimum, reserving them for things that are important. I do not believe a skipper should use his public-address system to inflate his ego. And over the years, every time I commanded a ship and was tempted to broadcast something just because I wanted to, I've remembered the words of an old sea chantey which goes like this:

> The officers ride in a motorboat
> The captain—he rides in a gig.
> It won't go a damn bit faster
> But it makes the old bastard feel big.

As a skipper, a captain of a ship, I had that microphone and PA system. But that old chantey reminded me that if I used them just to "make the old bastard feel big," I was making a damn fool of myself—and I tried not to. Gaining and retaining the respect and loyalty of a crew is far more important than boosting one's ego.

On this occasion, however, what I had to say was important. I told my men that we would be in Bermuda for about three weeks. The objective was to get the ship ready for action. Training instructors would be aboard every day. Some would be gruff and not too tactful, but they were experienced professionals. The idea was not to get mad at them but to listen to them, to learn from them.

These instructors, I went on, would want to see how we handled just about anything that could come our way in combat. They would pay special attention to how we handled damage control and how we improvised ways of keeping the ship operational regardless of the type of damage she might suffer. They would be checking our gunnery, our antisubmarine work, our ability to use our torpedoes, and just about everything else we and the ship could do together. And if they found any weaknesses, they would make certain before we left that these were corrected.

It was going to be rough, I added, but we had to be attentive, cooperative, and learn just as much as we could. If we were, we would leave Bermuda a lot better trained than we were right then—and that would pay off when we finally got into action.

I concluded by saying that at the end of our training, there would be a formal personnel inspection. It would be white uniforms, the whole business, and I expected perfection.

Though *Laffey*'s public-address system was not adjusted for two-way communication, I knew that this last would produce moans and groans in many compartments. As a group, sailors are never what could be termed wildly enthusiastic about formal personnel inspections. In fact, at the very least it is safe to say that most sailors thoroughly dislike them.

With this in mind, I waited a few moments to let those groans die down to make doubly sure that everyone caught my last comment.

"But you can be sure of this," I added. "That personnel inspection is going to be perfect because it's the last one we are going to have on this ship as long as I am the skipper!"

I did not hear the cheers either, but as I put down the microphone, I was sure of one thing. My crew would do their darnedest to make that one inspection perfect if only to make sure I didn't change my mind. At the time, they could not have known that I made it a point never to go back on my word. And later, when we all got to know each other better and they did realize it, it made no difference. By that time they didn't need promises from me to make them try harder. Their pride in our ship and our record would be enough.

On the fourth of March, after more than five hundred miles of open ocean, we finally sighted the green, white, and pink of Bermuda. From a distance it looked like a mirage of paradise. Beautiful as it was, Bermuda was also an important strategic base in the Second World War.

The islands, of which Bermuda is the largest, had been laid out by nature in a curving string that on a chart resembled a giant fishhook. The lower part of that hook enclosed a huge harbor called Great Sound. This is where the modern town of Hamilton and the naval facilities were located, and I had the helmsman alter course to pick up the channel leading into it.

I also ordered a reduction in speed. Great Sound, I knew, was filled with coral shoals and outcrops, and even the channel that ran into it between Ireland Island and Spanish Point opposite it tended to be somewhat shallow. Before the war the cruise ships that docked at Hamilton had to be specially built to draw less water. Though *Laffey* wasn't a liner, I was taking no chances.

Once we were securely moored in Great Sound, I went aboard the flagship to report to Captain Madeira, and discovered my caution had been well advised. One of the first things Madeira mentioned was the hazardous navigation condition in the harbor. He told me some warships had recently run aground, and he urged reasonable caution.

Laffey now became part of the Atlantic Fleet Destroyer Force, which was officially known as DesLant (Destroyers, Atlantic Fleet) and one of five destroyers of Squadron Sixty. (Eventually there would be eight.) The squadron commander was Captain William L. Freseman. He arrived the next day in the *O'Brien*, a sister ship of *Laffey*, and as soon as possible I went aboard her to meet him and pay my respects.

Bill Freseman proved to be a professional naval officer of considerable experience and intelligence. He was forty-two, tall, with prominent, regular features and reddish-brown hair. He could easily have passed for a Hollywood leading man of that period because he was quite handsome. He could be genial and very pleasant company off duty and in social situations, but as a squadron commander, Bill could also be very demanding. If something was not handled just the way he felt it should be, he could become irascible—and this happened quite often.

Bill welcomed me warmly and I liked him the minute I met him, but my arrival in his cabin coincided with one of those situations. As I was later to learn from a friend, Stuart Cowan, who was Bill's staff communications officer, when *O'Brien* was approaching Bermuda she had received a priority message. At first Bill thought it concerned some serious war situation, and he became agitated and anxious until the entire message had been received. But then it turned out to have nothing to do with naval matters. It was a personal invitation to one of Bill's officers to dinner—and the invitation did not include Bill Freseman.

That kind of thing would have caused any squadron commander some concern because, though it came from the governor general of Bermuda, it suggested a violation of wartime secrecy regulations. Certainly, had I been in Bill's place I would have asked my subordinate how the governor general had found out he was aboard the *O'Brien*. Bill Freseman did, but apparently the whole thing was quite innocent. The wife of the governor general was an old friend of the officer. She had somehow learned he would be arriving in Bermuda aboard Bill Freseman's flagship, but she had not learned it from that officer.

The explanation may have calmed Bill's concern about a breach of wartime secrecy regulations, but it didn't do much to improve his humor. Bill was, after all, the commander of a newly arrived squadron, and the officer's superior. He was also an ambitious officer and—because of his prior assignment—I think his pride was hurt by what he thought was a slight. He had recently been in the White House in Washington as aide to Admiral William D. Leahy, President Roosevelt's naval advisor. It was the kind of job which would have brought him a lot of attention and deference even from officers who far outranked him.

Bill Freseman wasn't a self-important man, but he was human. No matter how hard he must have tried in Washington to remind himself that it was his position, not himself, that brought that attention, he could not help but be affected by it—anyone would have. Being ignored that way on his arrival in Bermuda—which was how he must have seen it—certainly must have stung him.

If Bill Freseman could have passed for a movie star, this went double for his operations officer, the man who had received that dinner invitation. He was extremely handsome, well spoken, and had a polish and manner that made him fit the role perfectly—with good reason! Robert Montgomery was a top Hollywood star who had given up his career to help defend his country.

Bob Montgomery, however, was not a typical actor and personality in uniform. He was modest and very serious about his duties. He had joined the Navy early in the war, working his way up to the rank of lieutenant commander on active combat duty assignments. He wasn't in it for the publicity, but because he loved his country; and wherever possible he shunned situations in which he could have used his fame to advance himself or make his life easier.

I got to know Bob quite well. We became fast friends and have remained friends since World War II. But what I have said about Bob's dedication is fact. Bob was to run himself ragged for Bill Freseman and the squadron in the months ahead, and he came very close to letting the job kill him. Bob may have acted the part of a hero in front of Hollywood cameras, but in real life he was a real hero, and a professional naval officer to his fingertips.

Laffey's shakedown training began the next day. As I'd expected, it was both rugged and thorough. All the exercises were designed to be as realistic as possible. Many were gunnery problems in which we fired live ammunition against surface targets at sea or those on a coastline. Others involved the use of star shells for night illumination and practice for our anti-aircraft guns against actual aerial targets.

But gunnery wasn't all of it. Our radar operators got a thorough workout. We practiced ship maneuvering and depth charging so often it became second nature. Our sonar operators got some first-class realistic antisubmarine training, though we could not use depth charges to finish off the target they locked onto. That would have been carrying realism a little too far, because our target was an actual—though friendly—submarine.

This submarine was commanded by an experienced skipper who in fact, until some months before, had been on the other side. He was an Italian; the sub was the *Vortice*, and those who manned her really knew what they were doing because they had done it in combat against Allied ships.

Despite the skill of this skipper and his crew, they were never able to shake our determined sonar operators. They tried everything—high speed, low speed, stopping, backing down— but none of it worked. *Laffey* hung right on just as if we had that submarine hooked like a shark on a line.

When the exercise was finally over and the sub came to the surface, the Italian skipper appeared on her conning-tower bridge. He clasped his hands over his head, congratulating us, acknowledging our ability to stay with him despite all his evasive tactics. I waved back our thanks, and believe me, I was happy to do it. That submarine skipper was an experienced, battle-wise professional, and his good opinion meant something.

One of our exercises was not on the schedule, and was actually the real thing. At 7:00 A.M. on Friday, March 10, we were out with the *Walke* preparing to take part in a shore-bombardment exercise when suddenly Charlie Holovak in CIC (combat information center) got a voice radio message from headquarters ashore. Holovak notified me immediately; the minute I heard the message I had the helmsman bring the ship to the course mentioned, and I called Al Henke.

We were then steaming with two boilers. With these we could make over twenty-five knots, but we were going to need full power. I rang up flank speed (twenty-five knots) on the annunciators, but I told Al to put two more boilers on line as soon as possible.

Very quickly I felt the ship shudder as we increased speed. The Pitometer log indicator, which showed our speed through the water, was at twenty knots, but soon it moved to twenty-three. Then it steadied on twenty-five.

It didn't stay there long because very quickly the engineers had the extra boilers ready and Al Henke called the bridge to say all four were on line. With that I rang up turns for twenty-six knots, then twenty-seven, twenty-eight, twenty-nine. Laffey's fantail dug in, and soon we were making over thirty knots going flat out.

Walke, to the south of us, was also making high speed. Though our mission was serious, I suddenly had a feeling of exhilaration. Like two great evenly matched thoroughbreds, Laffey and Walke were in a race. It was a race I intended my thoroughbred to win.

On and on we went that way, turbines straining, white mustaches of foam curling back from the two ships' bows. The seas were slightly rough. But the ships were now so settled down in the water, and charging ahead with such speed, they sliced right through the swells with little pitching or plunging.

This kept up for some time without either ship gaining an advantage. Then gradually Laffey began to creep ahead, improving her position, and finally she led Walke by several hundred yards. I knew then that we'd be the first to reach those downed aviators.

One of the routine duties of destroyers, and one we had practiced often, was the rescue of pilots whose aircraft had come down in the sea. But this was no drill. A Navy PBY-5A patrol amphibian, flown by Lieutenant A. H. Cowart, which had been on a routine air mission, had developed engine trouble about twenty-four hours earlier. The plane could land in water, but when it came down the seas were too rough. She had bounced three times coming in without power. Cracks had opened in the plane's hull, and the minute she was in the water she'd started to settle. She had sunk in half an hour; and there were nineteen men out there ahead of us with two inflatable rafts which could hold only fourteen.

After two hours of steaming wide open, *Laffey* did get to those aviators first. It was the best kind of race to win. The gratitude of those flyers when we pulled them aboard was better than any silver cup. At least one of them never forgot the *Laffey*. As pilot Cowart was to write me later, "Maybe it wasn't your ship's first real operation, but for me, it was certainly her best."

There was, however, more to it than that. It was excellent training for all of us, and the fact that we handled it so well brought us official praise which did a lot for morale. As soon as we had all the aviators aboard, I had informed Commander, Underway Training Group, by voice radio that the operation had been successfully completed. This brought an immediate, "Congratulations, well done!"

I passed these on to my men and used the opportunity to give special individual praise. The deck force, the engineers, the medical people, and even the cooks and bakers who had given the survivors a hearty brunch deserved it. I missed no one. We had done it as a team, and everyone deserved credit.

I believe that incident did more to teach us all to work together smoothly than any training exercise during our shakedown. After that race, it was the *Laffey* against the rest of the world. But it wasn't belligerence or cockiness. Though there was some kidding by *Laffey*'s men directed at friends in the *Walke*, it was good-natured and accepted as such. We were proud of what our ship had done, but we knew that *Walke* had done well too. Both ships were on the same team and all of us still had a great deal to learn.

This spirit was best summed up by Sonarman Charlie Bell, who had by then become my telephone talker. *Laffey* was a lucky ship, he insisted. Winning that race had proved it. He was positive she was destined for great things. *Walke* and the others were good, but *Laffey* was the best.

Our time in Bermuda was not spent entirely on one long, uninterrupted series of grueling exercises. Certainly our training schedule was very tough and thorough, and it was so tight there was never any opportunity on weekdays for the men to get ashore on liberty. It was always late when we returned to our mooring. Very often we would stay out all night, steaming in circles so as to be ready for an early-morning exercise. But weekends were another story. Most of our men really wanted to see something of Bermuda, and I made certain that liberty cards were issued to some at every opportunity.

Granting liberty is one way a skipper can reward his men, and I had no qualms about it. I knew my men by now. I was sure most would behave themselves; as for the few who might be inclined to do otherwise, I didn't have any qualms about them either. Bermuda was small, tidy, and peaceful. There were some bars, but even these maintained the traditional, orderly British attitudes about how customers should be served and should behave. Neither Hamilton nor any of the other communities had one of those gaudy recreational areas found in many of the seaports of the world. The men could enjoy themselves ashore, but they would have no opportunity to overdo it.

There were no automobiles to speak of on the islands in those days. Aside from the narrow-gauge railroad that ran from Hamilton to St. George, at the opposite end of the main island, the only transportation was by horse and carriage or by bicycle. Since the number of carriages was very limited, and a train trip had little appeal for sailors who wanted to get off the ship and move around, most of my men rented bicycles.

Bicycles were a great way to get around the narrow streets and roadways of the island, a fine method of taking in the scenery while getting some exercise. But for sailors on leave, even in well-ordered Bermuda, they weren't the best way to get home after spending some time in one of the local watering places. As a result, there were a few incidents, but none, I am pleased to report, that could be called too rowdy. They didn't involve lawbreaking, brought discredit to no one, and were mostly the result of American unfamiliarity with English-style bicycles.

Typical of such incidents was one involving a young radar-man from the *Laffey*. Having enjoyed a little liquid conviviality, this poor, unfortunate sailor mounted up on his two-wheeled steed and began to pedal. For a time everything went well, but then he came face to face with a situation in which the brakes were needed.

The problem was that this bike wasn't equipped with the familiar foot-pedal-applied coaster brakes of an old American Iver Johnson or Columbia two-wheeler. The brake levers were on the handlebars. Reversing the foot pedal didn't slow the wheels. Down a small hill went this bike, with the sailor furiously backpedaling, rapidly losing control of the direction of his machine.

Despite this, he probably would have suffered only a minor

spill had his luck been better. But suddenly, in the middle of the intersection ahead, stood a local policeman. The officer could see the sailor was having trouble with the bike. Quickly he signaled cross traffic to halt until the bicycle got through the intersection, but he misjudged the seriousness of the situation. The policeman didn't realize just how completely the sailor had lost control, and he neglected to stand aside. Instead of racing by, the bicycle with its now-confused rider homed right in on him. After all, that rider was a radarman.

Luckily for our sailor, the policeman turned out to be a tolerant individual well used to the antics of American sailors. Instead of dragging his attacker off to the station, he politely but firmly gave him a lecture which would have done justice to any chief petty officer. Then he let our sailor go with a warning: Before he got on a bicycle again in Bermuda, he was either to learn how to ride or how to hold his spirits.

Laffey, her shakedown training completed, departed Great Sound for Boston on March 31, 1944. The training had gone very well, and so had the personnel inspection. All of us were happy that the training was over, though some probably weren't so happy about leaving Bermuda. New England in the early spring may be warmer than it is in winter, but its climate just doesn't match that of those blessed islands.

Our training may have been completed when we steamed away from that paradise in the Atlantic, but we still had one more test ahead of us. Like any product made by a good company, *Laffey* was covered by a warranty. If something was found structurally wrong with her in the first six months, the contractor was supposed to correct it without further payment from the government.

Thus far we had found no evidence of weaknesses or defective construction in the ship. She seemed sound as a dollar—a 1944 dollar—even though she had been driven hard and put through her paces. That race to rescue those downed flyers, for example, had stretched her considerably. But now we had to do it again.

Just as soon as it was practical, I had Laffey's speed increased to near maximum. We were to maintain this for at least four consecutive hours. During this time, and for the rest of our trip back to Boston, we were supposed to push her hard, but it was those four hours that would be the most critical. They involved a certain amount of risk. When you put that much stress on a ship and her machinery for such a length of time, if there's a defect, something can give way. Men can get hurt.

I was confident this would not happen, but as we steamed toward Boston, there was another troubling factor. When we left Bermuda the sea was moderate, the skies blue, and the sun was shining. But soon the weather turned dirty, and I knew it was going to stay that way. We had received a report that between *Laffey* and Boston there lay hundreds of miles of stormy seas, and generally bad weather. Under usual steaming conditions this would have made life aboard the ship uncomfortable. But now, driving into the teeth of such weather at top speed, we were in for an unpleasant experience.

I ordered maximum Condition III set. This meant that our lookout and control stations, as well as all our detection apparatus, were to be fully manned. All watertight doors and hatches would be tightly closed. I had all deck gear checked to be sure it was firmly secured. The last thing I wanted was to have something come loose in a blow.

By that time the blue water had changed to a steely gray, and the sky was about the same color. The horizon where they met was rapidly disappearing and the bad weather was closing in fast. The storm was a northeaster coming down on us from off Cape Cod. In that part of the Atlantic, a northeast storm can be the worst kind, but in this case—for us at least—it would be something of an advantage.

A northeaster meant that, on our homeward-bound course, we were taking the rolling whitecaps on our starboard bow. This was a lot better than having *Laffey*'s bow plunge directly through them, lifting her screws out of the water as we cleared a wave crest. But the motion of the ship wasn't comfortable by any means. Not only was she plunging and lifting and taking solid sea over her forecastle, but she was rolling heavily as well. By then most of our men had their sea legs, but before this was over a lot of them were going to be very seasick. This little run was supposed to test the ship, but it was going to test every man aboard at the same time.

We roared and rolled, pounded and bucked our way on like this for a half hour. The ship shuddered, groaned, and thrashed her way ahead like something gone wild. Men were hanging on for dear life as the decks played corkscrew under them. Her bow would slice through a trough, then there would be a thud and vibration as she hit a new wave, hesitated, and lifted. I know that for many it was pure hell, but for me it was exhilarating. Nature was throwing the works at us, but *Laffey* was shaking it all off and continuing to challenge.

It was then that CIC reported a ship a few miles away going

east. Visibility wasn't good, but quickly our lookouts reported her ahead on the horizon. The odds were that she was friendly, but we couldn't take any chances. I had the signalmen send a challenge by searchlight and alerted our gun crews.

We waited, but there was no reply. She was big, far south of the usual Atlantic shipping lanes, and alone. CIC reported their plots showed she was making at least twenty-five knots. That was fast for a ship of her size.

Could she be a German surface raider? It seemed unlikely. But this dirty weather was perfect cover for her if she was, and she wasn't answering our challenge. We had no choice—we had to identify her; and we gave chase.

As *Laffey*'s bow came round on an interception course, I felt a tingle of excitement. Though by 1944 the Germans were confining most of their surface ship operations to European waters, one never knew. If not a raider, she could have been a U-boat supply ship or perhaps even carrying some sort of new Nazi weapons to strike at U. S. coastal cities. Hitler was always boasting about secret vengeance weapons he was going to use against us, and that ship was big enough to carry almost anything.

At the speed we were moving, the range soon closed. We came up astern of her. Every pair of glasses in *Laffey* focused on her fantail. Then, despite the fact that she still ignored our signal, we all relaxed.

Her name was *Mauretania*. She was a British Cunard liner. No wonder she was so fast. The *Mauretania* had flown the Cordon Bleu—the Blue Ribbon—from her peak for years. We'd been chasing a champion. Before larger, more powerful liners like Cunard's *Queen Mary* came along, the *Mauretania* had held the record for the fastest Atlantic crossing.

After identifying the *Mauretania*, I ordered the helmsman to bring *Laffey* back to her original heading. I was just a little sorry she hadn't been German. What a catch that liner would have made! Yet as I thought about it some more, I was glad she was British. If she had been German, she would have been armed and would have fought. We would have had to sink her.

The rest of our trip, even the remainder of our high-speed run, was something of an anticlimax. By the time we reached Boston, fast steaming through rough seas had become almost routine for the men, and the ship had shown no signs of any defects. We had come through it all—even that run-in with a "raider"—with flying colors. We weren't just ready, we were also set, and now all we needed were orders to go!

FIVE

Those who fought in World War II produced more than their share of memorable bits of wit and wisdom, but none of these more accurately defined what war meant to the average serviceman than the four words, "Hurry up and wait!" Countless times throughout the war, members of military and naval groups found themselves urged on relentlessly toward some goal. Then, almost as if by prior arrangement, just before that goal was reached, word would come down to put everything on hold.

It was frustrating, mystifying, and confusing. Yet there was always a good reason—the problem was, it was usually impossible to let everyone in on it. Often there wasn't time, but on the whole it was a matter of maintaining secrecy.

I am sure that many of my men aboard *Laffey* felt that way after we returned from Bermuda. All of them may not have been eager to rush into combat, but all of them were certainly keyed up and ready to go. Yet typically, go we did not. After a stay in Boston, we were sent to Norfolk, Virginia, to help train new destroyer crews. And after Norfolk, it was orders for New London, Connecticut, to work with the submarines stationed there.

I didn't mind, however. I knew that the more time we had for drills and added practice the better, yet I could sympathize with my men. They had worked very hard during our shakedown training to prepare themselves and the ship for combat, not for more training. When I reported to Rear Admiral Daubin, Commander, Submarine Force Atlantic Fleet, at his New London headquarters, I was happy to discover that the waiting was over.

Admiral Daubin handed me new orders; the next day we were on our way to Brooklyn, New York, to rejoin the squadron. That could mean only one thing.

We took on a full load of supplies and fuel at the Brooklyn Navy Yard. As soon as this was done, I paid a call on Bill Freseman. He told me we'd been assigned to a fast convoy as part of its escort. We were headed for England, he said, but that was all he could tell me. Even Bill hadn't been told what would happen to us after that.

I had my suspicions. By May of 1944, what was called the Battle of the Atlantic had just about been won. Superior radar equipment, high-frequency radio direction-finding gear (which the British called Huff-Duff), escort carriers and their anti-submarine aircraft, and an ample number of specially built escort warships had beaten back the German U-boat menace. The Germans had countered with the snorkel, (an air-breathing tube with a valve on top which allowed their subs to cruise submerged on diesels) and better submarines, but to no avail. Troops and supplies were reaching England in ever-increasing numbers. It was just a matter of time before the great invasion of Europe would be launched.

Laffey and her sister ships would certainly be part of that effort. They were among the most modern heavily gunned destroyers in the world. To continue to use them as convoy escorts in the Atlantic would have made no sense at all.

We sailed on Sunday, May 14, together with *Barton, Walke, O'Brien,* three smaller destroyers, and the rest of the convoy. Many of the convoy ships were tankers loaded with aviation gasoline. Our destination was Plymouth, a seaport on the south coast of Devon, and this fact too tended to confirm my suspicions. Plymouth, on the English Channel, was about 150 miles north of Brest and roughly the same distance west-northwest of Cherbourg. It was a major port of concentration from which invasion forces could be launched against the French coast. But it was not a port usually visited by convoy escorts assigned to the North Atlantic run.

Since early in the war, convoys from the U. S. had approached England from the northwest to keep as far out of range of German aircraft as possible for as long as possible. Then, once the cargo and troop ships reached the protective air cover of land-based planes in Scotland, they'd turn south. Steaming down into the protected waters of the Irish Sea, their North Atlantic escorts would be withdrawn and replaced. This freed the

North Atlantic escorts for the job for which they were best suited, but in our case, we were going the whole route. The only logical reason for that had to be that we were going on to take part in the invasion of France.

I mentioned my suspicions to no one, but on the voyage across the Atlantic I made sure we took every opportunity to hone our skills. Not only did we conduct fire, collision, and damage-control drills, but when possible, we practiced our gunnery. I also insisted that my men get plenty of training in aircraft recognition. The odds of our having to contend with the enemy in the mid-Atlantic might be slight, but the closer we got to Plymouth, the more these would change. Not only would there be the usual danger from U-boats in waters close to the British Isles, but there would be the Luftwaffe. Even in the safety of Plymouth harbor we might find ourselves the target of bombs.

We had the naval oiler (tanker) AO 56, the *Aucilla*, skippered by Captain Charles Sullivan, with us for the trip. As I've said, the convoy was a fast one—fast meant an average speed of ten to fifteen knots. Even at those speeds destroyers burn up a lot of fuel, and could have used much more in the event of a U-boat attack. In the early days of the war, some British escort vessels had almost exhausted their fuel defending convoys against U-boat attacks. There had been some bitter lessons learned; one of them was the absolute need for some way to refuel escorts at sea during the voyage across the Atlantic.

Refueling underway in the seas of the North Atlantic was a tricky and difficult operation which could also be dangerous. Escorts had to ease their way up alongside the tanker, but never so close that the ships might collide. Then, steaming at the same speed, hoses had to be passed by lines from the tanker to each escort, fixed to connections, and the three ships had to maintain their stations and speeds exactly until the escorts had filled their tanks with fuel.

The process can be likened to two automobiles speeding along a three-lane highway on either side of a tank truck in the middle lane, with hoses from the truck connected to both. But at sea, there's a difference: Highways are smooth and highway lanes well marked. The waves of the North Atlantic throw ships about, make them pitch, yaw, and roll, and there are no well-marked lanes in the ocean.

As difficult and tricky as refueling underway was, there was also the added potential danger of a sudden attack by U-boats. Though unlikely at that stage in the war, it still existed. U-boat commanders always favored tankers as targets, and one locked together with two escort vessels was even more tempting. One hit on the tanker could take out all three ships in a flaming fireball.

Under these circumstances, it was natural for Captain Sullivan of the *Aucilla* to want to move things along as fast as possible. But though Sullivan's attitude made sense, there was one instance in which haste made for waste. Three days out, as I brought *Laffey* up astern of the *Aucilla*, I could see that something had gone wrong. The destroyer *Davis* was ahead of us to port of the oiler, and the seas to starboard were covered with oil.

What had happened, I learned later, was that Captain Sullivan, intent on getting the job done, had urged the skipper of the starboard destroyer to take on oil at one-hundred-pounds pressure. Then, when the *Davis* came alongside to port, he had made the same request to her skipper, Commander William Dunn. Sullivan was the senior officer and highly experienced in techniques of refueling underway, but Dunn knew his ship. He had insisted that for the *Davis*, sixty pounds was the limit.

No sooner had Dunn said this than both hoses to the ship to starboard carried away and she got an oil bath in the process. A much-embarrassed Sullivan knew then that he was wrong, and he was the first to admit it and apologize. He called over to Dunn, "I see what you mean," and the *Davis* got her fuel at sixty pounds.

I suppose Sullivan assumed that Dunn was just being overcautious—a trait some skippers have been known to have—and he felt that increased speed was more important. In that sense he was right, but the incident illustrated something I've always felt is the key to successful naval operations: No officer, regardless of rank, has a right to assume that something is so just because it has been so under similar circumstances in the past. Neither rank nor experience are sufficient grounds for ignoring facts supplied by a subordinate who knows them. High rank and vast experience do not confer omnipotence on those who have them, and the naval officer who believes they do is steaming at high speed in shoaling waters.

For one member of *Laffey*'s crew, the linkup with the *Aucilla* meant more than just a drink of fresh fuel for our thirsty power plant. Not long after the hoses were aboard us Coxswain Andy Stash, who was standing on our forecastle, spotted a familiar face aboard the tanker up near her bow. The men were too far apart and there was too much noise for any real vocal communication. Not only that, but the refueling was nearing completion.

The two ships would soon be drawing apart, the *Aucilla* taking with her the brother Andy hadn't seen in two years. It appeared as if there would only be a shout, a grin, and a couple of waves of an arm, and then that brother would be gone.

But Andy Stash was a good sailor, and sailors know how to improvise in an emergency. He grabbed a heaving line to which was attached a covered lead ball known as a monkey fist. He scribbled a note. Then, attaching the two together and mustering his best pitching style, he tossed them over to his brother just as the two ships began to separate.

The distance between the two ships was longer than the heaving line, and the *Aucilla* ended up with the message. That wasn't exactly according to Navy regulations; in fact, it was downright contrary to them. *Laffey* was short one heaving line and Chief Boatswain's Mate Bill Keyes quickly noted it.

Keyes, however, did not chew out Andy. He could see the tears in Andy's eyes and he understood. Gear was important but men came first, and instead he just asked Andy to make up a new heaving line to replace the one then aboard the *Aucilla*. It meant extra work for Andy, but his rapid response was, "Chief, I sure will," and that ended the matter.

We reached Greenock, Scotland, without serious incident a few days later and moored for the night. Greenock was an important base for convoys on the Atlantic run. Located at a point on the west coast where the River Clyde, after passing Glasgow, turns south and widens into the Firth of Clyde, our anchorage was just across the river from the important Royal Navy base of Rosneath.

The anchorage was crammed with ships, many secured side by side with lines; and taking a hint from what I observed, I had rat guards rigged on ours. These were circular metal plates with holes in the middle through which the lines ran, and were designed to deter the movements of rodents. All ports, no matter in what part of the world, are home for such creatures, and they are especially active when waters are filled with dozens of opportunities to ship out. Like the other skippers of ships in Greenock's anchorage, I had a full complement of two-legged sailors aboard my ship and I didn't want any with four legs and a tail joining them.

The next day, in convoy with a large group of transports, we headed down the Firth, through the North Channel, and into the Irish Sea. As I've noted, these were well-protected, well-watched waters, but I did not take any chances. As we neared St. George's

Channel and began to move out into open sea, I kept the ship on a modified Condition III.

I wanted her ready just in case something happened—and something did. The day before we neared Plymouth, one of our squadron mates, the *O'Brien*, picked up a sonar contact. Since Bill Freseman had no information indicating the presence of an Allied submarine in the area, *O'Brien* and the *Laffey* were sent to run down the contact and deliver an attack.

As our sonarman picked up the same contact, I could see the looks on faces nearby tighten. This was it, at last. We weren't drilling anymore. This was the real thing.

Laffey's speed increased as our helmsman steadied her bow on the heading, and with her screws biting the water, the white foam began to increase along her flanks. Then we were over it. Whatever it was directly below got a pattern of eleven depth charges. There were bone-jarring shocks, the hull reverberated, then there was silence. The contact was gone.

The convoy steamed on, but for some time after, we continued to search with our sonar. This was routine. The idea behind it was to keep the submarine down even if you couldn't locate her exactly and destroy her. Most U-boats could only manage about five knots running submerged on electric motors. If you could keep one down long enough, both her air and batteries would be exhausted and she'd have to come up. Yet even if this did not happen, submerged, she'd lose the convoy. It was not as good as a kill, but it served the purpose. The convoy would be safe from the sub's torpedoes.

There was no further sonar contact, and later evaluation was that it had been a nonsubmarine. A whale or a pinnacle of rock was the judgment, and maybe it was. But as far as all of us aboard the *Laffey* were concerned, we had dropped depth charges as if we had been in action. Whale, pinnacle, or U-boat, we had finally been playing for keeps.

As soon as we were released from our convoy duties, we proceeded toward Plymouth harbor. Plymouth in mid-1944 was designated an advanced amphibious base. It had both military and naval headquarters. There were ship-repair facilities, and it was to be an important embarkation point for forces that were to land on the beaches of France. But at that particular time, the thing that concerned the skippers of Bill Freseman's squadron was the number of ships in the harbor.

As we approached the waters off the port, the old English Channel played one of her usual tricks. We were smothered in a thick fog. It was so thick, in fact, that without radar we would have had to postpone our arrival.

Freseman's flagship—the *O'Brien*—led our column, searching out obstacles with her radar. Or she did until that radar—in the words of her sailors—crapped out. That put us in what the British would have called a sticky wicket, but I didn't have a chance to call it anything. No sooner had it happened than Freseman was on the TBS. *Laffey* was to slip out of column, move forward, and take over.

We did, and for more than half an hour we led the squadron's column through some of the most crowded waters I have ever had the misfortune to steam. I am proud to say there were no problems. Radar used close to land can sometimes prove unreliable, but ours functioned perfectly and accurately, and everyone stayed on their toes. By the time *O'Brien*'s radar recovered from its fit our column of ships had made a safe passage for some miles without incident.

It was not a combat situation, but it was one of the most realistic "exercises" we had ever had. And in the days ahead this added "training" was to stand us in good stead. The waters off Normandy may not have been cloaked in a great deal of fog, but they were choked with even more ships than those near Plymouth.

Laffey entered Plymouth early in the morning. Charlie Holovak identified our berth; we slipped into it. But it was not until 11:00 A.M., when the fog lifted, that we finally got our first real look at the place. That settled it! There was no question now where we were headed. The concentration of ships at Plymouth would never have been so great under usual conditions. Plymouth was an important port, but it was still within range of German bombers. And the ships themselves weren't the tired, battered freighters from convoys we had seen at Greenock. Plymouth wasn't the end of the run—it was the beginning of a jump.

As I stood on the starboard wing of the bridge surveying the panorama around me, I was suddenly struck by the feeling that I was in a huge football stadium waiting for the game to begin. *Laffey* and the other battle-ready ships were the players down on the field. The hills, towering a hundred feet or so above us and all around the harbor, were the stands. And on those hills, in the houses and buildings of the town itself, were the spectators—watching, looking, and waiting. They had been waiting for years, enduring shortages and bombings, the sights of loved ones injured and killed. But now the field, that harbor, was full of their players and the waiting was almost over.

There was now no question about it. The ball was in place. Very soon, the whistle would blow. And when it did, *Laffey* and the rest of the players would sweep down the field.

I got further, though unofficial, confirmation of this later that day. That afternoon three destroyers came in and moored in the same nest. HMS *Eskimo* tied up alongside of *Laffey*, and though most of our crew were ashore on liberty, the men of our duty section soon struck up conversations with the British sailors.

Eskimo and her men were veterans. They'd been fighting the Germans for years, and some of that had been in Arctic seas off Norway in Murmansk convoy operations. Those British sailors knew their way around, and most of all, they knew the latest rumors. One of these had it that the invasion of Europe was very, very close—the time span mentioned was a week or ten days.

How very close they were! No wonder that even before *Laffey* arrived at Plymouth, Allied counterintelligence had begun its work of hermetically sealing off millions of men who were to take part in "Overlord." Earlier in May, Supreme Allied Commander, General Dwight D. Eisenhower, had set a tentative date of June 5 for the landing in France; by late May, parts of the whole vast operation were already in motion. The Germans knew there was something in the wind, but they didn't know when that wind would begin blowing, and they would have paid any price to have heard what *Eskimo*'s sailors told mine on the *Laffey*.

The Germans never did, of course, nor did they overhear what millions of others of the Allied services in England were undoubtedly saying to each other at that very time. Intelligence did its work well. Over the coming days Army troops were sealed in marshaling areas behind barbed wire and held under guard. The whole southern coastal area of England was closed to travel, and communications between it and the rest of the country were restricted and carefully monitored. Nothing was left to chance.

When you are waiting for some great test you are sure is coming soon, it is natural to feel the tension building inside you. But the worst thing you can do is to keep thinking about it. Under such conditions I had always found in the past that the best way to get through that kind of period was to spend time relaxing and talking with friends. I was happy when Bob Montgomery and Bill Dunn came aboard and suggested dinner that night in the officers' club. The idea suited me perfectly.

I was certain that neither Bob nor Bill wanted to spend an evening sitting around a table hashing over rumors, repeating gossip, and making guesses as to when D day would be. I was correct. Though the choice of food at that time in England was limited, even for service people, the company and the conversation made up for it many times over. We didn't talk war; we talked peace. We didn't talk rumor and gossip. We spent the entire time swapping funny stories, jokes, and anecdotes from our pasts.

I've always remembered one anecdote that Bill Dunn recounted to Bob, because for me it evoked memories of my earliest years in the peacetime, prewar Navy.

Bill was in the battleship *Pennsylvania* when the then Vice-President of the United States, Charles Curtis, paid a ceremonial visit to the ship. At that time the *Pennsylvania* was the fleet flagship. There was a four-star admiral aboard, and orders from him were that all officers had to assemble in frock coats, cocked (fore-an-aft) ceremonial hats, swords, and white gloves. There were to be no exceptions, and woe betide the officer who marred this scene of pomp and circumstance—which would have done justice to a Gilbert and Sullivan operetta—with some uniform irregularity.

Unfortunately for Bill, he had a problem. Circumstances delayed him. When he finally managed to don his uniform, he discovered to his horror that his white gloves were dirty. Absolute disaster threatened!

Undaunted, Bill Dunn sought to solve his problem by putting on his gloves, picking up a bar of soap, and washing his gloves and hands together. But this innovation, no matter how inspired, could not overcome the time problem completely. The wet gloves would not come off. He couldn't squeeze them dry. And he had to race up the ladder to the quarterdeck with the gloves still dripping.

Bill took his place in line seconds before Mr. Curtis and his entourage came aboard. A bugle called everyone to attention; the band boomed out "Ruffles and Flourishes." Then a gun salute followed and Mr. Curtis was welcomed aboard.

First, the Vice-President inspected the Marine Guard, rigid and perfectly decked out in their best uniforms. Then he was introduced to the senior officers. And then, much to Bill's horror, he noticed that Curtis was shaking hands with everyone. As the tallest ensign aboard, Bill was the first junior officer in the front rank, and he knew he would be the first to whom Curtis offered his hand.

Curtis did, and sheepishly Bill stuck out his dripping glove.

The moment of truth arrived with a soft, squishy sound and some drops of water fell to holystoned teakwood deck. Bill cringed inside as a sudden look of surprise shot across the Vice-President's face. Then it was over, and Curtis passed on without a word, but Bill knew there would be an explosion later.

For some reason, there never was. The only punishment Bill received was his terrible embarrassment, but that, he told Bob Montgomery, was lesson enough. I don't know if Bob, who had never served in that peacetime Navy, really understood, but I certainly did. In those days, unlike the years of World War II and those since, form was often more important than function.

The next day, May 29, a total security blackout was dropped over every ship, unit, and man involved in "Overlord." That was the day on which specific briefings were conducted for BIGOTs—those who had been designated to receive detailed information about the forthcoming landings in Normandy. Despite every effort to limit the numbers of people who were to get such information, there were hundreds of officers who had to have it. I was one of them.

Our briefing took place in an old theater in Plymouth. It was attended by destroyer squadron and division commanders, and the captains and communications officers of each of the ships. We learned that there would be a huge variety of warships, amphibious ships, and landing craft involved in "Neptune"—the naval part of "Overlord"—but despite the multitude of types of ships, I soon discovered that—in one aspect at least—this one was to be no different from my past combat experiences. As they always had been, destroyers were to be the workhorses of the naval forces.

They gave us a full explanation at that meeting, beginning with the commmand structure—from General Eisenhower on down. Admiral Sir Bertram Ramsay, RN, headed the naval units; British Field Marshal Bernard L. Montgomery, the army units. Both of these Englishmen were experienced, capable officers. Ramsay had had a long and distinguished career, and had been involved with the successful evacuation of British and French troops from Dunkirk by Royal Navy forces in 1940. Montgomery had led the British 8th Army, which helped chase Rommel out of North Africa.

Five beaches were the targets of the invasion forces, all of them located between the Normandy Peninsula in the west and the Caen Canal and River Orne to the east. The eastern beaches—Sword, Juno, and Gold—were assigned to British and Canadian troops supported by warships under Rear Admiral Sir Philip Vian, RN. The western beaches—Omaha and Utah—were the job of U. S. First Army troops led by Lieutenant General Omar Bradley. His men were to be supported by the Western Naval Task Force under Rear Admiral Alan G. Kirk.

I was pleased by this last information. Admiral Kirk was a very capable man, a natural for the assignment. Before being given this job, he had been a top-flight naval attaché in London. He personally knew just about every ranking British naval officer with whom he would be working. Many of them were his friends, and this kind of close relationship was bound to assure a smoothly functioning, cooperative effort.

As part of the Utah Beach section of the Western Naval Task Force, *Laffey* was one of the destroyers of an Escort and Reserve Fire Support Group. The ships at Utah were under overall command of Rear Admiral D. P. Moon, but those engaged in bombardment, fire support, and related screening duties were the direct responsibility of Rear Admiral Morton L. Deyo. *Laffey's* initial assignment was to protect and assist the amphibious assault ships on their trip across the Channel. But then she was to screen these and the heavy bombardment ships, and to back them up once the invasion began.

I listened carefully to every word of the briefing. But the minute I learned we were headed for Utah (the westernmost of the invasion beaches) I began to pay special attention to what was said about it. Utah was on the eastern coastline of the Cotentin Peninsula, down near its base. And its eastern flank, adjacent to Omaha Beach, was very near to the point where the Carentan Canal flowed into the sea.

To me, Utah and its approaches looked like potential hot spots. Ashore, German troops were sure to fight hard to prevent our soldiers from any attempt to cut across the base of the peninsula, and thus isolate Cherbourg, which was out on its tip. But in addition, German naval forces on the peninsula would be out along the starboard flank of the sea lanes off our beaches because the eastern shores of the peninsula almost paralleled that flank for miles.

We would, of course, have plenty of support. Thousands of Allied aircraft would batter enemy airfields, naval facilities,and military installations as our amphibious forces approached the shores of France. Our fighters would sweep the skies of German bombers, and Hitler's few remaining large warships had already been completely neutralized. But despite this powerful support and the large naval forces we had, the enemy could still hit us hard. The Nazis had powerful guns in well-protected emplacements, guns that had considerable range. They also had mines, submarines, and E-boats.

These high-speed German torpedo boats, similar in some respects to our own PT boats, mounted light automatic cannon (20-mm, 37-mm, and 40-mm) and they carried torpedoes. In darkness they could easily creep along the coast from Cherbourg to Point de Barfleur without being spotted. From there they would have only about ten miles of high-speed running in open waters to reach our waves of ungainly, slow-moving amphibious ships and landing craft. If they got in among these in the dark, the E-boats could raise hell with them; it would be up to destroyers like the *Laffey* to make sure that they didn't do so.

The original function of the destroyer was to fight torpedo boats, and as I thought about *Laffey* engaging Nazi E-boats, the prospect had a curious appeal. I was the skipper of a destroyer, a professional naval officer, and the E-boat was a traditional enemy. It was not that I hoped the E-boats would challenge us. We had enough work to do without that. But—like the skipper of a battleship who faces the possibility of slugging it out with an enemy battle line—professionally, it was a piquant idea to think about.

The briefing covered everything from beach obstacles, mines, tidal and expected weather conditions to positions of enemy gun batteries, communications, and how our forces were to be organized. Nothing was omitted. The assault on the beaches of France was perhaps the largest, most thoroughly planned amphibious operation the world will ever see. The published plans for it were a masterwork of cooperative effort by thousands of people.

Nothing, however, is perfect, and the plans for "Overlord" had one great flaw: Putting them on paper required so much paper that the final result was massive. By General Bradley's own admission, the 324 pages of the First Army Operation Plan alone contained as many words as that huge, classic Civil War novel, *Gone With the Wind*. And the operation orders that came aboard *Laffey*, stacked one atop the other, made a pile over a foot high.

With just these orders alone we would have been awash in paper, but there was more. In addition to the orders themselves, we also got a stack of corrections that also stood well over a foot high. And all of these corrections had to be integrated into the original orders in the space of a few days, a seemingly impossible task.

Still, it had to be done. Neither of these huge piles of paper could have been distributed earlier because their contents might have found their way into enemy hands. Secrecy was far more important than making things easy for those who would have to execute the orders. Yet I have to admit that when I saw what was ahead of us, I wondered whether we'd be able to cope with it. We could steam and we could shoot, and we were ready to do both. But nothing—not training, experience, or the number of people we had aboard who could do clerical work—equipped us to meet this challenge.

Fortunately for everyone—except possibly the Germans— those who were running the show were men with a good deal of common sense. When we got those huge stacks of operation orders at the Plymouth briefing, they gave us a bit of advice. This was a priority list for both reading the orders and adding corrections that directly affected our ships.

True, this list added to the paper, but it helped. We still had an awful lot of paperwork and reading to do, yet it gave us a fighting chance. Without that chance, one of two things would have happened: Either those aboard *Laffey* and every other ship would have gone into the invasion without knowing what they needed to know, or the invasion would have been delayed long enough for them to find out.

In 1864 David Glasgow Farragut had needed only six words—"Damn the torpedoes—full speed ahead"—to send his ships into battle. But eighty years later it took billions of words on millions of sheets of paper just to get things started. Is it any wonder, then, that many a Navy skipper in 1944 felt a twinge of regret that the good old days were gone?

Regret or not, I knew we had to win this battle-before-the-battle. On returning aboard the *Laffey*, I filled in Charlie Holovak on what was ahead of us. Like Ted Runk—my communications officer, who had been with me at the briefing—he was appalled. But like Ted, he gritted his teeth, made a few unkind remarks about red tape under his breath, and, damning the paperwork, went full speed ahead.

Holovak rounded up every available officer and yeoman and put them to work immediately. No one escaped. At that time we had two reserve naval officers aboard from Washington, Lieutenant Ned Turner and Lieutenant Bill Grelle. They weren't part of *Laffey*'s complement, but were visiting in connection with some study for the Bureau of Naval Personnel. Yet that didn't matter to Charlie Holovak. They were available. Study or not, Holovak had them up to their eyebrows cutting and pasting corrections into the operation orders before either of them could open their mouths.

Over the years since, every time I have thought back on that titanic battle of the paste pots, I've chuckled about Turner and Grelle. With Charlie Holovak, they didn't have a chance—nor would any other visitor have had one. It wasn't that Holovak was a blunt, overbearing type of man—far from it! He was the soul of tactfulness, with the skills of a diplomat. But when he wanted to get something done, he got it done.

As the battle of the scissors, paste pots, and orders continued, we sortied the next morning. All of the ships of Destroyer Division 119—*Laffey, Barton, O'Brien, Walke,* and *Meredith*—moved out of Plymouth harbor on May 30 for some exercises off a place called Slapston Sands.

Slapston Sands was an area of beach about due east of Plymouth, but to reach it we had to steam down around Start Point, then up past the naval base at Dartmouth. Since late 1943 Slapston Sands, whose beach and terrain closely resembled landing areas in France, had been used for amphibious training exercises. And though these were now over, the place was still used for shore-bombardment exercises by warships which were to give direct, close-in fire support to troops ashore.

Exercise or not, all of us were keyed up for this little operation. We had heard what had happened at Slapston Sands less than a month before, and we did not want it repeated. In late April, following a practice bombardment, LSTs (landing ship, tanks) had moved into a cove in preparation for landing troops. It was dark, but everything seemed to be going according to plan until the enemy opened up.

The gunfire and torpedoes came from a group of German E-boats. They had slipped through Allied patrols off Cherbourg, made a high-speed run to Slapston, and used their advantage to the fullest. Several of the cumbersome, clumsy, and fully loaded LSTs were hit. One sank, taking with her more than five hundred soldiers and sailors. And despite the intervention of some covering destroyers, all the E-boats had escaped.

This had made the exercise a little too realistic. Though nobody really expected it to happen again—especially in daylight, with an ever-increasing number of Allied aircraft and ships patrolling the Channel—we weren't taking any chances. The E-boats were tricky devils. They were manned by expert—sometimes desperate—crews who had been at it since 1940. Even if their potential targets were five destroyers, they wouldn't hesitate to attack if they got the chance. Destroyers are no more immune to torpedoes than LSTs, especially if lookouts do not keep a proper watch.

Ours did; but as it turned out, the exercise was something of an anticlimax. No E-boats showed up. Still, I suspected this had less to do with their ability to get to Slapston Sands than orders. The Germans must have suspected we were coming soon, and probably ordered their E-boats to hold themselves in readiness to repel our invasion forces. Why risk a long, dangerous journey to Slapston Sands to find targets when those targets would soon be coming to them?

Naturally, the Germans did not know where we were coming in, and they didn't know when we would be there. But despite the massive cloak of secrecy which covered preparations in England, they knew it had to be soon. The facts of nature were obvious. The landings had to be made in the next two months because of sea and weather conditions. If they were delayed beyond that, it would be a year before there was another ideal opportunity.

After firing a total of thirty-eight rounds of five-inch ammunition at targets at Slapston Sands, we made an uneventful return to Plymouth. It was a rather limited preparation for the kind of shooting that would soon be expected of us. Most of our gunnery training had been for engaging ships or enemy aircraft. We had not received a lot of training in acting as a floating battery of artillery supporting troops advancing ashore.

Regardless, I still had full confidence in our gunners. A target was just that, a point of aim. It didn't really matter whether it was a plane, a ship, or a gun position. If it was out there, we'd find it and destroy it.

From what I had heard at the briefing and had read in our orders, there were going to be plenty of targets. Most of them were going to be shooting back. According to General Bradley, the Germans had a lot of heavy, casemated guns along the coast. We were going to be very busy.

General Bradley did not have full confidence that the Army's B-17 heavy bombers could deal with these targets. High-level bombing was useful. But in 1944 it wasn't all that accurate, especially against relatively small and very well-protected targets like coastal gun emplacements. General Bradley wanted naval gunfire to back up his troops because it could be delivered with much greater accuracy.

General Bradley was correct. A five-, six-, eight-, twelve-, or fourteen-inch naval gun could register fire with rifle-bulletlike precision and do it safely over the heads of advancing ground troops. Guided by radio-equipped observers with the forward line of soldiers, naval guns could put their shells exactly where they were wanted, when they were wanted. A B-17 at eight thousand feet could only stay over a target for a short period, and the odds of its bombardier laying its bombs in exactly the right spot were not the kind Bradley—"the foot soldiers' general"—found attractive.

The Navy did its best to give General Bradley as much heavy firepower as possible, but even in June of 1944 its resources were stretched to the limit. There were only three old battleships—*Nevada, Texas,* and *Arkansas*—and three heavy (eight-inch-gun) cruisers—*Augusta, Tuscaloosa,* and *Quincy*—available. The balance of the heavy-gun support had to be supplied by England's Royal Navy. Yet even this was limited. Destroyers like the *Laffey* were going to have to do a lot of filling in.

In fact, this is the reason that *Laffey* and her sister ships had been rushed over to England almost at the last minute. With their 6, five-inch, thirty-eight-caliber guns, each of the 2,200-ton destroyers actually carried almost as much firepower as some of the British light cruisers. Though our five-inch shells didn't have the penetration power of some of the British cruisers' projectiles, we could sustain a high volume of fire. We could hit a target rapidly and repeatedly, smother it with bursting shells, and—in all but the most extreme cases—we could knock it out.

By the time we returned to Plymouth harbor, the final, most stringent security measures were in force. No one aboard the ship was allowed to go ashore. We were in quarantine, restricted to the ship just as if we carried some dread, contagious illness—and in a sense, we did. The "illness" was our knowledge about the upcoming invasion. Had it accidentally spread to the wrong ears ashore, it would have killed hundreds, perhaps thousands, just as surely as any plague.

I explained this to my men, and though I do not think all of them were happy about it, not one of them complained. In fact, not only did they take it in stride, but I sensed that some were almost eager to get on with whatever job we had to do. It was not that any were eager to get shot at—only fools wish for that, and my men were no fools. But now they were in this state of suspended animation, waiting, with nothing else but shipboard routine to keep them busy. For some, that waiting was the worst thing of all.

On Friday, June 2, I called my officers together for a final meeting in the wardroom. This was it; this was the time to make one final check to be sure that every department had what it needed and that every officer understood what would be required of him. Charlie Holovak would handle our combat information center, and he was set. Al Henke would have us steaming on a split power plant and his engineers were ready. Harry Burns had his gunners primed and they were set. And everyone else, from Communications Officer Ted Runk to Torpedo Officer "Gag" Parolini, had things right up to snuff.

Once I was satisfied that we were as ready as we would ever be, I told them the approximate time of our departure. We would leave Plymouth early in the afternoon of June 3. D day was to be June 5, I said, and everyone aboard was to be informed. The die was cast. There was no reason now for any more secrecy.

Once the news was spread throughout the ship, it had varying effects on the men. Some, who had been bothered by the previous uncertainty, actually relaxed somewhat. Others remained pretty much as they had been before. And still others, faced now with the facts, weren't quite sure what they meant.

Among the last group was a steward named Robert Long whom I overheard later talking with another, Clyde Dunson, outside my cabin. Long was puzzled about the term *D day*, and he asked Dunson about it. Dunson thought for a moment, then gave Long what I considered an accurate definition. He said, "When you hear about D day, you start shakin', but when it comes, you stop. You're too busy and you're too scared."

The time we spent at Plymouth before we finally sailed for France was not entirely taken up by serious matters. It did have its lighter moments, and a sequence of these began not long after we arrived.

Ashore, some distance from our mooring, there was a high hill with a number of bombed-out buildings on top of it. In front of these there was a level, grassy area. Farther down the slope facing us, the ground was steeper; and near the bottom there was another level area close to the water which was shielded from above by some bushes.

The level, grassy area at the top of the hill seemed to be a favorite gathering place for couples who would sit on the grass, enjoy the view, talk, and occasionally embrace, though in a very proper manner. But late one afternoon a young man and woman left their spot at the top of the hill and made their way down the slope. When they reached the bottom, those above could not see them because they were behind the bushes.

Apparently the young couple wanted to enjoy the view from a lower vantage point, because as soon as they were behind the bushes, they lay down on the grass near the shore and were soon enjoying it thoroughly. But unknown to them, so too was someone aboard the *Laffey*. Though the ship was moored a considerable distance away, and the couple was well beyond the range of unassisted vision, neither of the pair apparently realized that warships carry optical instruments.

They did not realize it the next day either, because they showed up at the same time, same place, and went through a repeat performance. And, though most of the crew was ashore on liberty that day, there was a bigger audience. There were three chief petty officers on the bridge, and all of them were equipped with telescopes or binoculars.

The following day when the couple again reappeared, they played to a much bigger audience. Since security regulations had been tightened and liberty could no longer be granted, *Laffey* had her full complement aboard, and word had begun to spread. Matt Darnell, our doctor, told me later he was almost knocked down and trampled by the rush of sailors to the bridge at the 5:30 P.M. "curtain time," and quickly every pair of binoculars and every telescope on the ship was focused on the shore. Not just on the shore, of course, but on that couple who were again making love.

The next day we had to go to sea for that shore-bombardment exercise at Slapston Sands, and we returned too late to catch that afternoon's performance. But on Wednesday and Thursday the performers ashore played to a packed bridge. And on Friday the audience was the largest ever. Not only were chief petty officers borrowing a long glass or a pair of binoculars, but at exactly 5:30 P.M. there were sounds of whirring motors as *Laffey*'s 3 five-inch-gun mounts swung around toward the Plymouth hillside. Even the gun director atop the pilot house was pressed into service just as the performance began. All, of course, had excellent optical devices which gave their users a front-row seat.

There were only two flaws in this otherwise enjoyable situation: Where the men were concerned, probably the most important was that this daily performance provided no means for audience participation "on stage"; but for a few like Signalman Bill Kelly, it was something else. That Friday he was lying on his bunk fully clothed when he heard two shipmates talking about the crowd of chiefs on the bridge.

The bridge? That was his territory. What the hell were chiefs doing on his bridge?

Kelly certainly knew what they were doing, because they had been doing it for some days, but Bill Kelly was fed up. He dropped to the deck, his legs moving before his feet touched the ground, and he raced up the ladders two steps at a time. When Kelly reached the crowded bridge he took one look and burst out with a disgusted, "What in hell is this?"

Chief Quartermaster Ryder, who was Kelly's immediate boss, turned around, lowered his glass, and said, "RHIP, Bill."

RHIP is an old service acronym for "Rank has its privileges," but it didn't satisfy Kelly. This sort of thing had gone on too long as far as he was concerned, and he looked around trying to think of some way he could end it. Then, spotting an ally, duty Signalman Ted Purrick, Kelly motioned him over.

Purrick, Kelly knew, wasn't any happier about the situation than he was. The way I got the story was that Kelly suggested they "clear these @*#%&*#+&*@ chiefs outta here," and Purrick agreed with the plan. They flipped a coin. Kelly lost the toss and he headed for the pilot house.

Kelly went in through the door on the port side, tripped and fell. Then he got up and came hobbling out onto the bridge, bent over, holding his knee, and using some rather expressive words. Meanwhile, as the "Clang! Clang! Clang!" shattered the quiet, Purrick collected the glasses and binoculars from the departing chiefs, who were anxiously hurrying to their battle stations.

As I rushed to the bridge I couldn't imagine what the emergency might be, and all sorts of things ran through my mind. Were German bombers on the way? Had E-boats or a submarine penetrated the harbor? Or had there been some terrible accident?

On reaching the bridge, I quickly found out otherwise. Signalman Kelly came to me at once. He told me what had happened, then said he was sorry, and I immediately had word passed over the public-address system that the alarm had been sounded accidentally.

I wasn't very happy, but I didn't chew Kelly out. After all, he could not help it that his knee, "injured playing high-school football," had buckled under him. It was just an "accident" that his hand had grabbed the general alarm switch when he fell. And to prove it, he certainly was limping badly. As he said, "It could have happened to anyone."

I agreed with that; but as Kelly talked on, I had a chance to think about it a little. The pilothouse was full of buttons and switches and certainly an "anyone" might grab one by accident— but not a man who knew the place by heart. A light began to dawn, and I had a great deal of difficulty to keep from chuckling.

As the skipper, I was not completely unaware of what had been taking place on my ship the last few days. Since no regulations were being broken or orders disobeyed, and it had not endangered the ship or interfered with duties, I had let it pass. We were moored in a safe harbor, restricted to the ship, and waiting to be sent into battle. Watching the shore and whatever could be seen there helped take the men's minds off their worries.

But now I could see it had also created some problems, and I really didn't want to punish Kelly for trying to solve his even if I didn't like his methods of solution. Any sailor resourceful enough to clear a bunch of chiefs off his turf was a sailor worth having in *Laffey*. The bridge was Kelly's domain. The chiefs didn't belong there.

"Kelly," I said, trying to sound as stern as possible and glad that the light was too dim for him to make out the look on my face, "next time that trick knee of yours gives way, fall clear of that switch!"

And Signalman Bill Kelly, whose face I couldn't see too well either, replied, "Aye, Aye, Captain," like the good sailor he was— and continued to be in the future.

At 1:30 P.M. on June 3, 1944, *Laffey* was underway for France. The frustrations and tensions of waiting melted away. Everyone went about his duties in a calm, matter-of-fact way. Even my youngest and least experienced men were acting like veterans.

All the ships leaving Plymouth had to steam through an opening in the torpedo nets that protected the harbor. We were next astern of the *Walke* as she reached the opening when over her loudspeaker came the announcement that she was headed for Normandy. It was a routine way of informing her crew, but it was a little premature. Down by the nets was a small boat with two men in it, and they heard that announcement.

Commander John Zahm, the *Walke*'s skipper, took no chances. There was a net tender nearby which opened and closed the nets. Since no one was sure who the men were, Zahm called to the net-tender's crew to take them into custody. Probably they were local fishermen and loyal Englishmen, but whoever they were, I have the feeling that their wives didn't see them or hear from them for quite a long time.

The seas began to build up as soon as we were clear of the harbor, and the weather didn't look too good either. I didn't like it. *Laffey* could handle bad weather easily enough, and so too could most of the ships that were now steaming along the south coast of England. We'd be fine, even after we reached that point about five miles south of Portsmouth, turned, and began the run across the Channel. But D day's H hour—the hour the troops would begin to land on the beaches—was still more than thirty-six hours ahead. The way the weather was threatening to work up, the Channel and the surf off those beaches could be a maelstrom by the time H hour was at hand.

I was just a skipper of a destroyer with some years of experience at sea, and I knew I could be wrong. In fact, I hoped I was. It would take an expert meteorologist to accurately predict the weather in the English Channel for a given day and time, and thank heaven there was one working for Eisenhower. My hope for good weather was in vain; my guess about the weather was correct. By 9:00 A.M. June 4, weather conditions were so bad and the prediction so much worse that Ike put the whole thing off twenty-four hours.

That sounds like a simple decision to make, but it wasn't. There were hundreds of ships and invasion craft already at sea. They couldn't just keep steaming on toward France because they would arrive ahead of schedule and give the whole thing away to the Germans. On the whole, they couldn't just stop and maintain station by steaming in circles, either. At the least some would founder, collide, break down, or run low on fuel. At the worst, a German submarine, plane, or E-boat might spot them. Every single one of those ships had to be turned around and headed back where they came from.

Laffey's assignment was to ride herd on a truly large formation of 175 landing ships and craft. Helping us was the Royal Netherlands gunboat *Soemba*, the fleet tug USS *Bannoch*, and YMS (motor minesweepers) 348 through 352. And among our charges was LCT (landing craft, tank) 2489.

As this armada of ungainly ships struggled to come about in the heavy seas, I suddenly noticed that LCT 2489 was slowing down. Shortly, she was dead in the water, rolling like a soaked log and signaling frantically for help. Had I been her skipper, I would have reacted exactly the same way. An LCT was nothing more than a large, powered, open-decked barge; and 2489 was loaded to her gunwales with men and heavy equipment. If that heaving continued, some of that equipment was going to break loose and start sliding around.

Flat-bottomed ships can carry proportionately heavier loads and draw much less water than a ship like a destroyer. They have great initial stability; but once they begin to roll and pitch in a seaway, they are in a lot of trouble. Even a narrow-beamed ship like *Laffey* could recover from a greater roll than an LCT. And if 2489's cargo shifted and she developed a list, that would cut her chances even more.

We came to her assistance at once. I moved *Laffey* to a position shielding the weather side of the LCT. In our lee, the force of the seas on her was reduced, her rolling lessened, and soon the *Bannoch* arrived and took her in tow. We saw them safely on their way, then caught up with the rest of the ships, and by about 1:30 A.M. June 5, we were anchored at Weymouth.

We did not stay at anchor very long. Three and a half hours later, out we went again. We rounded up our stragglers, got them in formation, and it was off to Normandy again. This time I hoped we would make it.

I didn't know it then, but this was our last chance. The meteorologist at Eisenhower's headquarters had predicted a break in the weather. No one could be absolutely sure exactly how long it would last. But if the invasion hadn't come off on June 6, it would have been delayed almost a month. It was the moon—the moon controlled the tidal conditions on the beaches, and these conditions only existed at certain times of the month.

Tidal conditions were important for a number of reasons, but perhaps the most critical of these had to do with the German beach defenses. The Germans had erected long belts of steel and wooden obstacles along many sections of the French coast and protected them with antipersonnel mines. At anything but extreme low tide these obstacles could rip the bottoms out of our landing craft or prevent them from getting in far enough to unload troops safely. But at low tide the obstacles were exposed. Our engineers could get at them, deactivate the mines, and remove the obstacles with explosive charges.

Even by early afternoon, the seas of the Channel were still quite rough. It was windy, very choppy—with waves about four or five feet high, and the men in the flat-bottomed amphibious craft were suffering terribly. For the most part these men were soldiers, not sailors, and though they had been trained for amphibious warfare, few of them had their sea legs.

The landing craft and landing ships, useful and valuable as they were, were also among the worst-riding ships used in World War II. Rolling, sliding, slipping, their blunt bows pounding into the chop, these landing craft and ships tossed those soldiers around like so many sacks of wheat. Men were soaked with spray, men were hurt, and—worst of all—men were seasick. Crammed in, weak, miserable with stomachs heaving, those soldiers had the worst of everything. To this day I am still in awe of how they were able to surge up the beaches once we reached France.

First, however, we had to reach those French beaches, and we could not have even come close without the work of the minesweepers. The Germans had laid sixteen naval mine fields in the Channel between Cherbourg and Boulogne. Even our most powerful ships dared not try to pass through them unless channels were swept.

It's ironic when you think about it. Here we and our British allies had assembled a large force of very powerful ships to support the greatest amphibious assault the world will ever see, and we had to be led in toward the beaches by some of the smallest, most lightly armed warships we had with us. As we neared the belts of mines our minesweepers moved out in the van and began to clear channels. It was a tricky operation. A minesweeper is no more immune to most mines than a mongoose is to a cobra's venom. But despite the fact that they too could be ripped apart, the sweepers had to tow torpedolike paravanes on cables. The cables were secured from each side of the bow; the paravanes at the other end cut the mine cables. The mines would then pop to the surface and be destroyed by gunfire. As I said, it was tricky.

We sighted one of these floating mines and blew it up with 20-mm fire just after racing to help LCTs 2056 and 2226, whose bow ramps had fallen down. The blast from that mine when it went off was a pointed reminder of what could happen to any of us. Naval mines pack a lot of explosive; when one blows up near a ship, all the force is directed toward the ship. One mine can break the keel of the largest ship afloat.

This is what happened to the minesweeper *Osprey*. Ripped open below the waterline, she was immobile and sinking when we reached her. Her sister ship, *Chickadee*, was alongside. But there was little *Laffey*, *Chickadee*, or the tug *Bannoch*—which arrived soon after—could do. Shortly, she capsized and went down; but like the other minesweepers, she had done her job well. There were ten marked lanes through the mine fields, and through them poured over two thousand ships.

Protecting us overhead was an almost airtight umbrella of fighter planes. But just in case, many of the LSTs (landing ship, tank) towed barrage balloons. They had been used to protect British cities during the Battle of Britain. Our planes flew at about three thousand feet. Below that an enemy aircraft would have to contend with the cables of the balloons.

I had never seen anything like this before. We had had fighter-plane protection in the South Pacific, and antiaircraft guns. But we never had them in quantities large enough to completely stop the Japanese from attacking our ships. Here in the Channel, however, it was different. German planes put in an appearance, but that was about all. Most just dropped mines and got out as fast as they could. The Luftwaffe, for practical purposes, just didn't seem to exist.

This massive air superiority was a great comfort to someone like me who was used to dodging Jap bombs in the Pacific, but it did not make me complacent. The Germans had other ways of hurting us. By now, they certainly knew where to find us, even in the dark. Darkness meant a lot of our fighters would be grounded, but it wasn't that which concerned me. Darkness meant something else—the E-boats would be out.

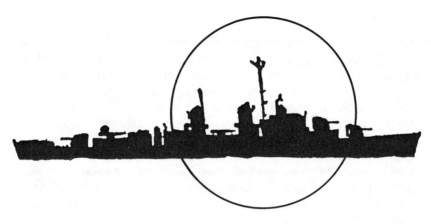

SIX

The invasion of France actually began just about twenty-four hours after *Laffey* anchored at Weymouth following our turnaround in the Channel. At around 1:30 on the morning of June 6, 1944, about thirteen thousand paratroopers were dropped at selected points inland from the invasion beaches. Their objectives were causeways connecting the beaches to the mainland, bridges, crossroads, and other key positions. And they were to hold them until our troops stormed ashore, pressed inland, and could link up with them.

As *Laffey* approached the coast of France some time later, C-47 transport planes could still be heard flying overhead. They were towing gliders filled with troops of the 82nd and 101st Airborne Divisions who had with them equipment that could not be dropped by parachute. They would land at dawn to support the paratroopers already on the ground, and there seemed to be hundreds of them.

By then I assumed that the Germans had been alerted and were taking every measure to counter our assault. Shortly, however, it became evident that some at least were not. The tall lighthouse at Point Barfleur was still brightly lit, just as it had been fourteen years earlier. Then, I had been at Cherbourg on a midshipmen's cruise. And long ago as that was, when I saw the lighthouse I remembered the taste of those strawberries dipped in sugar that I had eaten at a fine Barfleur restaurant.

The entire invasion area had been thoroughly photographed from the air, and pilots had those air maps. But it was very dark that night, and in many cases the paratroopers—and later the glider troops—were often dropped in the wrong places. Yet in spite of these mistakes, our airborne troops did their job well. The Germans, apparently lulled into a false sense of security by the recent bad weather, were stunned and confused by the air drops. Not only that, but they were not expecting the Allies to make a major landing effort in the Normandy area. Thus, not only did the scattered and frequently isolated paratroopers and glider troops have an opportunity to take their objectives, but there was at first no reaction at all when our minesweepers began to clear boat lanes and fire-support ship areas off the invasion beaches. Off Utah, for example, the destroyers *Fitch, Hobson,* and *Corry* were able to maneuver for over two hours covering the minesweepers before a shot was fired at them.

This didn't last. As it began to grow lighter, the Germans manning gun positions ashore suddenly began to wake up to what was happening. By then it was too late. Our main bombardment groups were in position and at anchor. They had missed their chance to hit us during that critical period when mines were being swept and our heavier ships were still maneuvering to get into their correct positions.

H hour at Utah Beach was to be 6:30 A.M., and the bombardment was to commence at 5:50. Spotting planes from England were expected to be over enemy batteries at 5:18 A.M. But the now-aroused Germans didn't wait. They opened fire on the British cruiser *Black Prince* at 5:30, and soon after, on the USS *Tuscaloosa.*

Commander Jerry South, Rear Admiral Morton L. Deyo's Chief of Staff in the flagship *Tuscaloosa,* saw a German battery open fire. He could see the two shells in the sky grow bigger and bigger and then they raised waterspouts uncomfortably close to the ship. That was all it took. Admiral Deyo didn't wait. At 5:36 A.M. Admiral Deyo ordered *Tuscaloosa* and *Black Prince* to commence counterbattery bombardment. And shortly the shore erupted with explosions. The battery was silenced.

Deyo had a lot of gunpower at his disposal. There were ten 14-inch guns aboard the battleship *Nevada* (BB 36), nine 8-inch guns aboard each of the heavy cruisers *Tuscaloosa* (CA 37) and *Quincy* (CA 71), and the British monitor *Erebus* mounted two 15-inch guns. There were also the guns of the British cruisers *Black Prince* and *Enterprise.* And supporting these heavy ships were eight American destroyers, two U. S. destroyer escorts, and the Dutch gunboat *Soemba.*

The naval bombardment of designated targets (as opposed to targets of necessity like that battery) began on schedule at 5:50 A.M. and lasted forty minutes. Then, as soon as our warships stopped shooting, about three hundred B-26 Martin Marauder two-engined medium bombers swept in to attack. More than four thousand bombs smothered German positions; though the bombs did not destroy many of these, they did explode many enemy land mines. So too did the rockets from seventeen LCTs which were specially equipped for this bombardment role.

At H hour—6:30 A.M.—the first wave of twenty LCVPs (Landing Craft, Vehicle, Personnel) moved in and unloaded troops on the beaches. Following came eight LCTs which put ashore four tanks each, then two battalions of infantry in thirty-two LCVPs which also carried eight Navy demolition teams. These last were to destroy the wood and metal beach obstacles, and they were followed in the third wave by combat engineers who would complete the job.

Chance has always played an important part in warfare, and on June 6, 1944, we got a lucky break at Utah. The landing areas were located on a sandy strip which was separated from the mainland by a flooded, baylike marsh. This strip of sand and dunes resembled Fire Island on the south coast of New York's Long Island, Assateague Island on the coast of Maryland, or Padre Island on the Gulf of Mexico in southern Texas, in that it had no outstanding terrain features. And, when this lack of terrain features combined with a current that ran parallel to the shore, they produced an error. Our troops landed over a mile southeast of their intended destinations, much closer to the estuary of the Carentan Canal, and at a spot on the coast which was far more lightly fortified and defended than the area that had been selected.

The *Laffey* stayed with her LCTs until they were very close to the beach, and then she moved out to a station in the defensive screen around the bombardment ships. Since the ships in the screen—like those they were guarding—had limited room for maneuver in the minesweept area, they had to anchor. And this meant that we had to remain especially alert. Though thus far there had been little sign of German aircraft, and no submarines had been spotted as yet off any of the beaches, at anchor we would have been a sitting duck for a German attack.

Despite the absence of the Luftwaffe and the subs of Germany's Kriegsmarine, Hitler's E-boats had put in an appearance. Far over on the eastern flank off the British beach Sword, three of these deadly sea wasps had attacked. Cutting through the smoke screen of the bombardment group, they had fired spreads of torpedoes, just missed the British battleships *Ramillies* and *Warspite*, and sunk the Norwegian destroyer *Svenner*.

Those three E-boats probably came from LeHavre, and they did not concern me a great deal. But those which surely were based at Cherbourg certainly did because they were much closer and there was nothing between us and them. I did not know it then, but some had already sortied in the dark hours of the early morning. More than a dozen had tried to strike our western flank as our long columns of ships had steamed toward Utah, but in this case the weather and ugly seas had been on our side. Unable to find us, they had to return to base, frustrated and empty-handed.

The Germans did have several dozen submarines ready to challenge us, but the waters off Utah were not good for submarines. To be really effective a submarine needs at least several hundred feet of water in which to operate, and to hide in when necessary, but there just wasn't that much. The *Nevada*, for example, was moored in an area where the water depth was between sixty and one hundred feet. If a submarine had tried to get near enough to her to fire a spread of torpedoes, it would have been spotted immediately by the ships of our screen or by any aircraft flying over us.

The submarine situation might have been different had the Germans' development and production of midgets been more advanced in mid-1944. The Japanese had used midget submarines at Pearl Harbor without much success. But Pearl Harbor was a protected anchorage, and our mineswept areas off Utah were not. A fifteen-ton midget like the German *Seehund* (which did not get into action until early 1945) could have operated in those shallow waters off the beaches quite successfully. Several dozen of these two-man boats, each carrying two torpedoes, might have given us a good deal of trouble.

The most troublesome thing to us—and, from the German point of view, the most effective weapons used off the beaches—were mines. The Germans had laid fields of various types of naval mines long before D day. Our minesweepers, knowing the approximate location of these contact mines, were able to sweep channels and areas in these waters. But all of the German naval mines were not the conventional contact types, nor could all of them be located before our bombardment ships and landing craft moved in. Our planes could not keep every German aircraft on the ground; and in darkness, both before and during the actual invasion, the Germans were able to drop numerous mines from planes.

A number of the German mines were a brand-new type. Resting on or near the bottom, especially in shoaling waters, their mechanisms were activated by the change in water pressure and currents created by propellers passing overhead. The Germans had tried magnetic mines earlier in the war, but these had been rendered ineffective by electrical degaussing cables. These cables—rigged inside the metal hulls of ships—neutralized a magnetic field created by the metal hull, rendering magnetic mines ineffective; but we had no equipment to counter the currents and water pressure set up by ships' propellers. Not only did these pressure-activated mines go off immediately in some instances, but in others the mines were rigged so that they would not go off until a second ship had passed over them. This meant that minesweepers could move through an area where such mines had been laid, but the mine might not actually go off until a much more valuable victim followed the minesweeper in.

The *Laffey* did not remain at anchor throughout D day nor in the days after. Our squadron commander, Captain Freseman, had ordered all his ships to stay at anchor each day only until minesweepers had swept the surrounding areas; on D day, once this was done, *Laffey* was able to move, continuing her screening operations. Every gun, every position, was manned and ready for action. Having fought in the Pacific, it seemed impossible to me that Hermann Göring's vaunted Luftwaffe wouldn't show up to do battle. True, we had numerical superiority. But it was very hard for me—and, I am sure, for other Navy men who had served out there in the days when Jap planes were so numerous—to get used to the idea that the tables had been turned. This was a different kind of war than the one I'd known. Though in its own way it was just as deadly and dangerous, it took a little getting used to.

By dusk, the situation on all of the beaches was fairly well in hand. At Utah, Sword, Juno, and Gold, troops and naval gunfire had overcome German resistance. Troops had pushed well inland to link up with our paratroopers. And even on Omaha, where just about everything that could have gone wrong did, the enemy's back had been broken.

Omaha had been a carnage. The first waves of troops were

supposed to get armored support from some Sherman M-4 medium tanks which our British allies had tricked up as quasi-amphibious armored vehicles. They were called D-D (duplex-drive) tanks, and thank God we never had to use them in the Pacific. The Sherman weighed more than thirty tons, carried a 75-mm (approximately three-inch) gun and was an excellent armored vehicle. But it had never been designed to go to sea by itself—even with a folding canvas screen that extended up above its turret, and a couple of propellers which could move it at about four miles per hour. While the British concept of swimming armored vehicles was sound, and the D-Ds probably would have been excellent for crossing rivers, they weren't really up to rough water eleven miles off the invasion beaches. Almost all of those headed for Omaha had foundered, leaving the infantry ashore without any armored support.

This led to a lot of casualties among the troops on Omaha. The landing ships carrying tanks to Omaha should have taken them closer to the beaches before launching them, but there had been a miscalculation about the D-Ds' seaworthiness. Only after it became obvious that they could not cope with the sea conditions at Omaha was this done elsewhere.

Despite all the difficulties, the Army and Navy working together did a good job. Still, I think we could have all done better had the Navy had some of its own "soldiers" at Omaha. By June 1944 our Marines in the Pacific had LVTs (landing vehicle, tracked) to invade Saipan. Some of these armored amphibious vehicles would have been very valuable at Omaha.

The LVT was an American invention. Some mounted 75-mm howitzers or 37-mm guns in armored turrets, and all of them had paddlelike extensions on their track treads. Not only were they seaworthy, and could move toward the beaches without help of propellers or a vulnerable canvas-screen flotation device, but once ashore they could climb over obstacles. Unfortunately, there just weren't enough LVTs available for the invasion of Europe.

On June 7, D day plus one, *Laffey* continued her patrolling and screening around the bombardment ships. Again, all stations were manned. But being too far off shore for our five-inchers to take part in a bombardment, we spent most of the day in a frustrating holding pattern watching the larger ships support the Army ashore.

Then it came. At 4:30 A.M. on the morning of June 8 we were on station a couple of miles off the beaches, ready to shoot. The heavier ships with their longer-range guns were now firing at targets well inland in support of VII Corps Army troops under Major General Joseph L. Collins. These were advancing up the Cotentin Peninsula toward Cherbourg. But our assignment involved a little more direct shooting. There were still a number of coastal guns and groups of enemy troops closer to the shore and numbers inland that we could reach. And all of them were giving considerable trouble to the soldiers.

We were ready. We had organized our communications between our five-inch-gun director, the CIC, and our radio room. As soon as map coordinates of a target were received from the SFCP (Shore Fire Control Party), Lieutenant (j.g.) Bob Storm or Ensign Lloyd Hull in CIC would plot the target location on our grid chart. They would send the range and bearing to Harry Burns. As our gunnery officer, Burns was in the fire-control director.

At the same time, Lieutenant Ted Runk or Ensign Jay Bahme in the radio room would hear the information sent from CIC over their earphones. They had charts that showed the time of flight of a five-inch shell for the range given. As soon as Burns pressed the trigger to fire a gun or guns, a light would flash in the radio room. Runk or Bahme would then start a stopwatch and would call out "splash" at the instant the shell(s) hit. Burns would see the dust rise in the target area and the Shore Fire Control Party would then "spot" the *Laffey* onto the target. SFCP would request that our next salvo be up or down in range (longer or shorter) by a certain number of yards, and right or left so many yards.

We got our first target at 7:57 A.M. The whole ship shook as we opened fire. From then on, for the rest of the day, the sounds reverberated through compartments with very little letup. There were a lot of the enemy out there with howitzers, field guns, machine guns, mortars—just about every weapon you could imagine—and they were playing hell with the troops of the 4th Division.

Sometimes even SFCP couldn't help us. Once, instead of range and deflection corrections, all we got back over the radio was, "We're lying on our stomachs in a ditch. Can't see! They've got us pinned down." But by then we had enough information. We gave the Germans a ten-minute barrage. And it ended with, "Right on target! You did it! Whoever was shooting at us has stopped," over the radio.

Altogether, *Laffey* got eleven calls for support on June 8; each shoot helped the 4th Division move closer to Cherbourg. June 9 brought more of the same. At 6:30 in the morning we started off on some cement pillboxes and fortifications; and, for the next hour and 20 minutes we fired over 275 rounds of 5-inch ammunition into various enemy positions.

That was a lot of shooting, and it meant an awful lot of work for the men crowded into the mounts and those below in the ammunition-handling rooms. Both locations, even in the relatively cool weather, were soon hot and stuffy; the men manning them were dripping with sweat and exhaustion. There was a certain amount of power-assisted automation like powder-and-projectile hoists in the handling rooms. But the process wasn't really automated. It operated mostly on muscle and sweat and depended on just plain stick-to-it guts to keep going. Because it was a carefully organized team operation, if one man fell out or collapsed, the rate of fire might slacken.

In that hour and 20 minutes of steady, high-speed shooting, not one mount faltered. Even Mount 52! This was our second forward 5-inch twin mount, located just forward of the bridge and the pilothouse. At some point, not long after the shoot began, there was a problem in the handling room of Mount 52. The regular hoist operator stationed there suddenly doubled up with what, in polite company, is known as an urgent call of nature.

There was no question about the urgency of the situation, nor what might have happened had the man not gone to the head. The last thing you need in a place full of gunpowder and explosives is a human being stumbling around in agony. One little slip and you have real trouble.

With the hoist operator out of action for a while, Mount 52's rate of fire should have slackened. But it didn't! Down in that handling room was a steward named Henry Teague, and Teague took up the slack. He handled over half the shells fired by the mount before the regular man was able to get back to his station. And he did it without anybody in the rest of the ship even being aware that anything was wrong.

On the face of it, the situation may not seem all that unusual. Teague was a husky fellow. He was agile and he was intelligent. He was also a hard worker. But Teague, a black man from Mississippi, could neither read nor write. He had never been trained to handle both hoists at the same time, much less trained to handle them at high speed. It was an amazing performance, one that a lot of other men couldn't have managed. But Henry Teague did it; and when I heard about it later, I made darn sure he knew I appreciated it.

116

Henry Teague may have held the rating of steward. But as far as I was concerned, he was something else too. He was a gunner, and off the Cotentin Peninsula on June 9, 1944, he proved it.

Exactly one month to the day after that bombardment, when we were back in Boston, I found out just how much that opportunity had meant to Henry Teague. I was told by Lieutenant (j.g.) Harvey Shaw that Teague always carried the Letter of Commendation I'd given him in his pocket. Teague knew what was in it because I had told him. But, not being able to read it himself, he had asked Shaw to read it to him again later on. And when Shaw had finished, Teague had thanked him, carefully put the letter away, and said something to Shaw which almost brought tears to my eyes when Shaw repeated it to me.

Teague said, "In the years to come when I'm back down in Mississippi, and someone tells me I'm no damn good—as a lot of 'em do—I'll tell 'em maybe not, but one time I was. Then I'll pull out this letter and prove it."

I've always hoped he did. Henry Teague was not "no damn good"; he was damn good, and he had proved it. Some men with a lot more chances in life than he had ever had, never do.

All of that high-speed, uninterrupted fire had by then used up a lot of our ammunition. We had shot almost seventy percent of our five-inch shells; I reported this to Rear Admiral Deyo, the head of the bombardment group. But low on ammunition or not, Admiral Deyo needed us, and during the rest of the morning we were called on a dozen times to pound enemy coastal positions.

By early afternoon we were down to twenty percent of our five-inch ammunition capacity, and Admiral Deyo radioed us to withdraw. Twenty percent was cutting it rather fine, and the admiral knew it. But rather than have us haul all our few remaining shells across the Channel, he suggested we send "a few farewell salvos to targets 88 through 100 so they won't forget you." We were happy to comply.

I have probably given the impression that the Navy's warships got off scot-free during the first days of the assault on Hitler's Festung Europe. I would have been happy if this had proved true. But it did not. Even off Utah, where resistance was somewhat less than at other beaches, the enemy got in some licks. And some of these were on American destroyers (DDs) and destroyer escorts (DEs).

On D day, at about 6:30 A.M., the USS *Corry* (DD 463) was stationed in a forward fire support area about two miles off the shore. *Corry*, skippered by Lieutenant Commander George D.

Hoffman, was not covered by the smoke screen put down by our planes, and she had to maneuver frantically to avoid being hit by German batteries. Unfortunately, she did not have much room in the relatively narrow area cleared by our minesweepers, and a few minutes later a mine exploded under her.

Her bottom was ripped open. Her keel was broken. And, to add to her misery, German gunners ashore already had her range.

Destroyers *Hobson* (DD 464) and *Fitch* (DD 462) rushed to her aid, blasting the enemy with their five-inchers and doing what they could for her survivors. But there wasn't much they could do for the ship or about five percent of her men. *Corry* cracked in two and sank, taking those men with her even before her rescuers could reach the spot.

On June 8, two more destroyers and destroyer escort *Rich* (DE 695) got it as well. (Destroyer escorts were smaller ships built for convoy escort duties, but they lacked the speed and firepower of destroyers.) At about 8:00 A.M. a mine, later thought to be one of the new German pressure-activated mines, shattered the USS *Glennon's* (DD 620) stern. Her skipper, Commander C. A. Johnson, at first thought the destroyer could manage. But eventually her torn stern went aground. *Rich* came to her aid, was shortly ripped apart by several mines, and went down with almost ninety men. And some time after, the helpless *Glennon*, hit by a number of German shells, followed her.

Another U. S. destroyer, the *Meredith* (DD 726), had been hit during the dark hours earlier that morning. Like *Laffey*, she was a 2,200-tonner built at Bath, and one of the ships of Bill Freseman's Destroyer Division 60. *Meredith* apparently hit a mine, which may have been laid by the Luftwaffe during the night; but whatever caused the explosion resulted in her loss the next day.

By that time the Luftwaffe had begun to appear every so often, especially during the hours of darkness. Its activities were restricted mostly to dropping mines, but at the time there was concern about other weapons the German Air Force might employ. Hitler had been boasting for months about a whole series of new and terrifying secret weapons which would win the war for Germany. And though some of these boasts were just propaganda, we took them quite seriously. The Germans were clever inventors and good engineers, and they had already proved it.

For example, in the Mediterranean in 1943 they had introduced a winged, radio-controlled bomb which, though primitive, had proved very accurate, and it carried a ton of explosives. They also had a winged, rocket-assisted, antiship bomb. Though it carried a much smaller warhead, it too was radio controlled, quite accurate, and had a much longer range. It had been used with considerable effect against Allied ships in the Mediterranean earlier in the war.

Both of these were examples of the kinds of new weapons the Germans had in their arsenal. We had developed radio-jamming techniques to disrupt the guidance systems of these weapons, rendering them ineffective, yet there was no way of knowing if the Germans had come up with something better. They had done it before.

The *Laffey* left the waters off Utah early on the morning of June 10, and steamed for Plymouth. We were low on fuel and low on ammunition, and it made a lot more sense to send us back to England than to have those supplies hauled across the Channel to us. Transport and supply ships were needed to carry supplies to the troops ashore, and we could make the trip over and back much faster than they could.

Steaming at twenty-five knots, the trip to Plymouth took us about four and a half hours. The trip was uneventful, the only incident being an encounter with a floating aircraft torpedo which we exploded with our 20-mm guns. By 2:30 P.M. we were alongside an oiler in Plymouth. As soon as our tanks were filled with fuel, we began to stock our almost-empty magazines from an ammunition ship.

Taking on ammunition is a laborious job, and the sailors of our ammunition detail were tired, happy to have the help of some men from the Royal Navy. Quite naturally, there was a good deal of conversation about Normandy and questions about what had been happening across the Channel.

Among the men from *Laffey* assigned to the ammunition detail was a seaman named Mark Anderson. At one point, as Anderson told me later, when he was passing on some information about the Royal Navy's part in the Normandy operation to some Britishers, he referred to it as "the English Navy." There was a moment of silence, a couple of frowns, a chuckle or two. And then came the good-natured reply.

"English Navy? It ain't no English Navy. Don't you Yanks know the ruddy Royal Navy has more Scots, Irish, and Welsh sailors in it than English?"

Anderson was somewhat taken aback by this corrective

statement. No, Anderson didn't, and even if he had, he probably would have considered them all English anyway. He'd never been to England before. He didn't realize that the people from various parts of the British Isles—the United Kingdom—had as much regional pride as a Virginian, a Texan, or someone from Maine. He didn't call it the English Navy after that.

Knowing that our fuel and ammunition replenishment would take some time, we'd been ordered to remain at Plymouth overnight rather than to return to the assault area across the Channel in darkness. It was a chance for a short break, and gave us time for some solid food. When a ship is at battle stations for as long as we had been in recent days, meals especially have to be rather limited.

While the ammunition loading was in progress, I called Charlie Holovak in and asked him to check on the dinner menu. I wanted to know if it was too late to change it. It wasn't. There would be a half-hour delay getting dinner, but everyone aboard would get a steak.

The men deserved it. Tired as they were, they'd worked like the devil, and so too had the British sailors with them. As much as I know Laffey's men enjoyed that dinner, those Britishers relished it more. None of them had seen a steak for months.

The Dixie line was a screening line three to five miles off the coast of Normandy. This was manned by a line of destroyers whose duties were to keep the Germans away from the transports, amphibious ships, and bombardment ships off Utah and Omaha beaches. But the Germans kept trying with everything they had, and more often than not, what they had were torpedo boats.

These E-boats (a British designation which actually included a number of kinds of high-speed motorboats) were a constant threat until Cherbourg in the west, and Le Havre in the east, were neutralized. Beginning with that first sally by three E-boats on D day itself, they kept at us with constant forays.

But it was not until June 12 that Laffey's gunners had a chance to engage them. During our first period off the invasion beaches we had been stationed in areas that put a lot of other ships between us and E-boats that sallied from Cherbourg. Unlike the E-boats at Le Havre, those from Cherbourg had a long trip to get near the beaches. If they came by Cape Barfleur on the northeast coast of the peninsula, they had to turn southeasterly and move down the entire length of the peninsula to make contact with the ships off the western beaches. The only times

Laffey had been on the westernmost flank at Utah were the daylight hours, when she'd been giving fire support to troops ashore. The E-boats didn't move much in daytime—there were too many planes overhead.

The early morning of June 12 was a different story. Instead of trying to slip down the coast of the peninsula, the E-boats took a more easterly course after passing Cape Barfleur. Despite the heavy ship traffic across the Channel, they slipped through it, and came in behind the invasion ships just about at the point where the Omaha and Utah sectors met. When they arrived in the area about 1:00 A.M., *Laffey* was in position on the Dixie screening line and right across their path.

To the west-northwest of us, some 1,700 yards away across the calm water, was the destroyer *Nelson* (DD 623), skippered by Lieutenant Commander T. D. McGrath. And to the east was the USS *Somers* ((DD 381), under Commander W. C. Hughes. We could just barely make out both of them. It was very dark. There were thick clouds overhead. And there was no horizon at all. There was nothing in the immediate vicinity except the three of us and blackness.

We knew these were perfect conditions for a torpedo-boat attack. We'd been on alert for hours, but at 1:00 A.M. we didn't have to wait much longer. Our radar had picked up a very faint, fuzzy contact about 8,000 to 9,000 yards away.

I sensed this contact might be E-boats, but my past experience with surface radar had taught me caution. No matter how wonderful that electronic marvel could be at times, it could also be fickle. *Laffey* was ready for E-boats if they came, and I was certain the other destroyers were too. But that fuzz wasn't enough to act on.

Destroyers on the Dixie line had standing orders to challenge contacts by signal light before they opened fire. If that had been just an electronic ghost out there we would have given away our position for nothing. And, if it proved to be enemy E-boats, we would have given it away too soon. We did not challenge at once because either situation would have been a misstep that could have ended in disaster.

The *Somers* picked up the same contact very shortly after. And, as the *Nelson*'s radar recorded this contact as solid blips on its screen, she challenged by signal light and opened fire. As I maneuvered *Laffey*'s bow on toward the targets and our five-inchers opened up, the blips suddenly slowed. Then, quickly, there followed a muffled explosion from the direction of the

Nelson. The blips reversed course and fled, and the *Nelson* reported she had been hit with a torpedo.

At that time we admittedly needed every destroyer we had, but the *Nelson* went into action with two strikes against her. The standing orders requiring Dixie-line picket ships to signal first put them all at a disadvantage. (The orders were later changed to require ships approaching the line to signal first.) But also, the *Nelson* was a cripple.

I found out later that *Nelson* had lost one of her propeller shafts in an accident at Plymouth just before she sailed for France. Though she could steam and maneuver, that picket line was no place for her. She wasn't playing with a full deck, and the cards were stacked against her. A destroyer without agility in a situation like that is a destroyer in trouble, and *Nelson* soon was. Unable to maneuver quickly, the E-boat's torpedo had caught her in the stern, blowing off a large section and killing a number of her men.

The *Somer*'s radar lost contact with the E-boats about fifteen minutes after they had been spotted. That left the job to us. It was a job I wanted to do, especially after hearing the *Nelson* had been hit; and everyone aboard my ship felt the same.

When I called for more boilers to be put on line, Al Henke had us working up to top speed in jig time. But fast as *Laffey* was, she was chasing a very fast and elusive foe. The official German designation for E-boats was *S-boote* for *Schnellboote*. That meant "fast boat," and fast meant up to forty-two knots. Unless we got them with our guns, they'd outrun us.

The targets we were chasing were very small, low in the water, and could turn on a dime. A direct hit wasn't very likely, and our gunners tried for air bursts over the targets. The shrapnel from a five-inch shell exploding over one of those E-boats could tear it apart.

We used our two forward five-inch twin mounts, 51 and 52. Mount 51 fired star shells to illuminate the targets; Mount 52 fired high-explosive rounds to destroy them. Our gunners kept up a fast rate of fire, and some of our rounds seemed to come fairly close, but spotting them was very difficult. The powder we had ready at the guns and in our magazines was for day bombardment. Every time a pair of guns went off, we were blinded by the flashes.

As time passed, the range increased, and slowly it became apparent that we had a long stern chase ahead of us. But we kept at it. *Laffey* roared through the water like an express train, her guns blasting, our eyes blinking, trying to regain their night vision. Then our own ships did us in.

The E-boats were racing northwest, trying to reach their rat holes at Cherbourg, when suddenly our radar screen was full of blips. These weren't more E-boats; they were Allied ships moving across our bow on their way from England to the beachheads in France. The skippers of those E-boats had spotted them too, and before we knew it, they split into two groups. These dove in among those ships like rabbits diving into a briar patch to escape a dog; and the minute this happened, we had to cease fire. We were unable to tell friend from foe; the E-boats had finally escaped. It was a disappointing end to what had had a painful beginning.

Generally, I avoid using bad language. But there are times when it does serve a purpose. Later, in the privacy of my cabin, a few well-chosen words helped—not much, but some; though frankly not enough to overcome my disappointment. I had wanted very much to get those E-boats.

During the next seven days American troops pushed well inland, far beyond the range of *Laffey's* guns. But we still had plenty to do. The larger ships, whose guns could still support our troops cutting across the Cotentin Peninsula, had to be screened and protected.

We had knocked the Germans back on their haunches, but they were far from beaten. Our troops had not yet captured a major port; and until they did, German E-boats, submarines, and the Luftwaffe posed serious threats. Not only could they attack our bombardment ships, which had to remain relatively immobile in open waters, supporting our troops; but they had a continuing opportunity to disrupt the flow of supplies to those troops.

With the large number of troops then ashore, the supply situation—even without German interference—was beginning to grow critical. The invasion plan had included the creation of two artificial harbors. These "mulberries," formed of huge concrete caissons and old ships which were towed over from England and sunk off the beaches, had pontoon-supported, floating roadways or docks on which supplies were off-loaded. Conceived by President Roosevelt and Prime Minister Churchill at Quebec in 1943, the mulberries had shortened the unloading time of a supply ship from twelve hours over the beaches to sixty-four minutes. But the one serving more than six U. S. Army divisions then ashore was destroyed by a storm on June 16.

Laffey rode out that storm safely, but though we managed to avoid collisions, we came very close to losing Chief Boatswain's Mate Herbert Lewis. He was on the forecastle when a huge wave came up over the side and sent him slipping, spinning, and falling through a mass of foam and water. He would have gone over the side had it not been for a lifeline netting rigged all around our forecastle. Off Normandy, the Germans were not the only enemy. There was also that ever-present, traditional enemy —the sea.

That storm changed everything. The next day, while it was still raging, Admiral Deyo got orders to plan for a naval bombardment of Cherbourg. General Bradley's troops were going to move west up the peninsula and take on an estimated forty thousand Germans who held the port, and they needed the Navy's help to do it. The whole place was a thicket of heavy gun emplacements which neither bombers nor Army artillery could handle.

But orders were one thing, and facts were something else. The storm had scattered many of our ships. Not only was it still raging on June 20, but some of our warships—their fuel low, their ammunition almost exhausted—would have to go to England for replenishment before they could take part in such an operation. The assault on Cherbourg was going to take some time to prepare for, and the bombardment date was set for June 25.

On the evening of the twenty-first, I received orders to take the *Laffey* to Portland, England. Like many another ship, we were again low on fuel. At 9:35 P.M. we hauled up our anchor, and were getting underway when once again we were reminded—as if anyone aboard needed reminding—that the Germans could still hurt us badly. The destroyer *Davis* (DD 359), another Bath-built ship, had been heavily damaged by a mine.

At Portland, we filled our tanks from the *Elderol*. After this we moored alongside the battleship *Nevada*. I paid my respects to her skipper, Captain P. M. Rhea, then I returned to the *Laffey* to take care of some rather unpleasant business. I had to discipline a member of my crew—a duty I have never relished.

The skipper of a warship holds a considerable amount of power over those in his charge. In the old days, this included the power of life or death, because in those times ships were often isolated from land for months. A ship could not put into port every time a sailor had to be disciplined, and the safety of a ship depends on her men following orders to the letter. The skipper, then, was the prosecutor, jury, and judge all rolled into one. And, though in 1944 my power to discipline my crew was nowhere near as absolute, I still had the responsibility and the duty to exercise it when necessary.

In this case, it was necessary. One of our crewmen had been charged with disrespectful responses to a superior. The name for this trial was "disciplining at mast." This man had come to us from another destroyer. He had a poor record and apparently the change of surroundings had done nothing to change his attitudes. He was surly, almost belligerent, when I questioned him. And no matter how hard I tried to break through his shell, I just couldn't reach him.

This was frustrating. Whatever was eating at the man couldn't be dug out and eliminated. I told him such behavior would not be tolerated, but still he showed no regret. I sentenced him to three days on bread and water in the chain locker. *Laffey* had no brig.

The chain locker was up near the bow of the ship. There wasn't much room inside it because this was the place where the anchor chain was stored when the ship was underway. It was a pretty miserable place, but it was all we had, and the alternative for the crewman would have been much worse. Had he been sent ashore, he would have had to face the certain possibility of a much more severe and longer sentence, and a permanent black mark on his record.

I didn't want that for him. It was far better to take care of our dirty linen aboard with a brief sentence at mast. That would give him another chance.

The Germans stopped the advance of General Collins' VII Corps about four miles south of Cherbourg on June 23. There had been some hope that the Army might break through their defensive positions without the help of the Navy's guns. But the German soldiers under General Karl von Schleiben were dug in, well supplied with firepower, and had orders from Hitler to hold out to the last man. The naval bombardment would have to go forward as planned regardless of the consequences, and Admiral Kirk wasn't very happy about the decision.

Admiral Kirk was worried. In mid-August the Allies were going to launch a second invasion in southern France along the Mediterranean coast to capture the ports of Toulon and Marseilles. From there, the idea was to sweep north, trapping large numbers of German troops by joining up with the forces in

Normandy. But for that invasion, the Army would need heavy naval gunfire support, and our guns had already had a great deal of use.

All ships' cannon have twisting ridges running along the inside of their barrels. These ridges or lands are called rifling, thus the technically correct name for a naval cannon or gun is a naval rifle. (*Gun* and *cannon* are general terms for weapons with barrels that shoot projectiles, but both can be smooth-bore without rifling.)

When a shell is fired by a naval rifle, a rotating band—a band of soft metal that surrounds the base of the projectile—engages the barrel's rifling. The rifling gives the shell a twisting motion as it moves up the barrel. This twisting motion acts much like a gyroscope's spinning wheel: It stabilizes the shell and prevents it from wobbling in flight as old cannonballs did when they were fired from smooth-bore cannon aboard sailing ships of an earlier day. The shell's twist keeps it on a true course to its target; this is what makes a naval rifle an accurate weapon.

Rifling, however, can be a problem. In high-powered naval rifles, especially in those of larger size, it wears down very quickly when many shells are fired. We had done a lot of firing. What was worrying Admiral Kirk was that a bombardment of Cherbourg would increase that wear so much that our guns wouldn't be available for operations in southern France. With smaller guns like those aboard the *Laffey*, the whole gun barrel could be replaced fairly quickly. But the fourteen-inchers aboard the *Nevada* had rifled liners in their barrels, and to replace these was a major, time-consuming operation.

As I understand it, Admiral Kirk put this to General Bradley rather directly, then asked him if the Navy's firepower was really needed at Cherbourg. Bradley didn't mince any words. The answer was yes, and that was all Kirk needed. The naval bombardment of Cherbourg would take place as planned.

Admiral Kirk's decision was certainly based on more than just a yes from General Bradley. The admiral knew the Army had to have that port soon if it was to advance across France quickly; and by the time he consulted with General Bradley, speed had become of paramount importance. On June 13, 1944, Hitler had finally unleashed his first *Vergeltungswaffen* (vengeance weapon)—the V-1 (FZG 76) unmanned flying bomb—against England from launching sites in France. Though very inaccurate, this terror weapon carried almost a ton of explosives. No one could then be sure that its accuracy might not shortly be improved, and if that had happened, ports like Southampton, Plymouth, and Bristol—on which we depended—might have been completely disrupted.

Allied bombers were trying to knock out all V-1 launching sites, but these were well hidden and many would escape damage. This meant that the only sure way to stop the V-1's was to overrun their sites with troops—and soon. But until the Allies had a port like Cherbourg through which we could supply those troops, our advances across France would be slowed and hindered. No wonder that yes from General Bradley to Admiral Kirk was all that Kirk needed.

The shoreline of the tip of the Cotentin Peninsula is U shaped. Cherbourg is at the base in the middle between two extended bulges of land. The one in the east, tipped by Cape Barfleur, was nearest to Utah beach; the one in the west by Cap de la Hague. But most of the heavy German batteries were located on a 15,000-yard strip on either side of the city of Cherbourg, and sighted to protect it. Thus at 3:30 A.M. Sunday, June 25, 1944, *Laffey* and the other bombardment ships left Portland harbor and steamed toward these two heavily fortified areas with orders to reduce them to rubble.

Our ships were divided into two groups. Admiral Deyo, in overall command and flying his flag in the heavy cruiser *Tuscaloosa* (CA 37), led Group One. The rest of the group included the heavy cruiser *Quincy* (CA 71), Royal Navy cruisers *Glasgow* and *Enterprise*, six American destroyers, and the battleship *Nevada* (BB 36). Group Two—led by Rear Admiral Carleton Bryant in the battleship *Texas* (BB 35)—was made up of the battleship *Arkansas* (BB 33); and destroyers *Barton* (DD 722), *O'Brien* (DD 725), *Hobson* (DD 464), *Plunkett* (DD 431), and *Laffey* (DD 724). British and American minesweepers would clear approach lanes and bombardment areas for us. And overhead, fighters of the U. S. 9th Army Air Force would keep the Luftwaffe off us.

The bombardment plan was well worked out. Group One would move in on the western bulge of the coast from the northeast, and Group Two from the north and slightly to the northeast toward a point about twenty thousand yards off Cape Barfleur. At that point, Group Two would turn west-southwest and join up with Group One off Cherbourg, the object being to delay the arrival of Group Two ever so slightly. It would come in on the blind side of a particular German battery just about the time the fourteen-inch guns of the *Nevada* took the battery under fire. The huge eleven-inch guns of Battery Hamburg, located several thousand yards inland from Cape Levi (a small coastal projection east of Cherbourg) outranged the twelve- and fourteen-inch guns of the *Arkansas* and *Texas.*

Both of these battleships were elderly. The *Texas* was commissioned in 1912, the *Arkansas* in 1911, and their main battery weapons did not match the ten 14-inch guns of the *Nevada.* But Admiral Deyo figured if they could get in range before Battery Hamburg could zero in on them, their guns could do the job. Yet, as often happens in battle, things didn't go quite according to plan.

As we were following our minesweepers in at five knots—their maximum speed when they were rigged for sweeping—the German guns around Cherbourg opened up on Deyo's ships in Group One. The fat was in the fire. The first targets of Battery Hamburg were Group One's minesweepers, and soon shells were raising waterspouts around them. HMS *Glasgow* replied. Then HMS *Enterprise* joined her, and the two ships went to work on the battery. At 12:30 P.M. Deyo ordered the minesweepers to pull out. They had done their job, and now they got away free. But as fire intensified, *Glasgow* wasn't so lucky. She took two hits, and though her teammate, *Enterprise*, kept trying, it was two hours later before *Glasgow* was finally avenged.

The *Nevada* never did get over to help Group Two. Apparently, Major General Collins' troops had broken through some of the German defense lines, and there was concern that long-range gunfire from *Nevada* might fall on them. Bryant's group had to go it alone. The minute we got into the arc of Battery Hamburg's guns, all hell broke loose. Yet it wasn't just from the guns of that battery. There were others; and the closer we got to Cherbourg, the more of them there seemed to be.

At that time we still had our minesweepers from U. S. Squadron 7 with us, and the *O'Brien*—skippered by Commander W. W. ("Bill") Outerbridge—was closest to them. He was ordered to go to their aid, support them with gunfire, and cover them with a smoke screen. But *O'Brien* couldn't handle the job alone. Very shortly, Commander Ed Dexter's *Barton*, Bill Freseman's flagship, and *Laffey* were sent up to help.

This is what we had been waiting for. *Laffey*'s crew had been at battle stations for some time—a maximum Condition I of absolute readiness. Our five-inch-gun director had our mounts trained on the point ashore where Battery Hamburg was

DD 459 was the first World War II destroyer named *Laffey*. Launched October 30, 1941, she went down fighting the Japanese battleship *Hiei* in the Battle of Guadalcanal on November 13, 1942, near Cape Esperance. Admiral Becton witnessed her gallant struggle.

Japanese Mitsubishi G4M torpedo bombers, code-named Betty, executing a torpedo attack on U.S. ships off Guadalcanal in the Solomon Islands, November 12, 1942, about twelve hours before the night battle in which the first *Laffey* (DD 459) was sunk.

DD 724 was the second World War II destroyer named *Laffey*, and the ship that Admiral Becton commanded. Launched at Bath, Maine, November 21, 1943, she is seen here on her shakedown cruise in Bermuda. She was one of the first Allen M. Sumner-class warships.

The *Laffey* (DD 724) steaming through Philippine waters under enemy air attack on December 15, 1944, during the American assault on the island of Mindoro. The dense pattern of smoke puffs from shell explosions attests to the advanced proficiency of her gunners.

Pilots at an airfield in Japan in 1945 prepare for a mission as a Betty (Mitsubishi G4M bomber) waits in the background. This Japanese bomber had a range of over 2,000 miles and could carry more than 1,700 pounds of bombs or a heavy torpedo.

A Japanese Mitsubishi A6M fighter aircraft takes off on a mission. Also known as a Zeke Zero, later versions—which became so familiar to *Laffey*'s gunners—could also carry a load of bombs. Agile and a difficult target, the Zero was outclassed by 1945.

Three Japanese Aichi D3A carrier-type dive-bombers, winging their way toward a target, display their characteristic fixed landing gear and wheel pants. The Val played a major role in Kamikaze attacks of the *Laffey* (DD 724) off Okinawa.

A Japanese Yokosuka D4Y dive-bomber—the Judy—heads for a formation of American ships. Judys also executed attacks on the *Laffey* (DD 724). Although not really a successful aircraft, with a suicide pilot at the controls it could be deadly.

The Nakajima Ki-43 fighter, code-named Oscar, was used by the Japanese throughout the war. A late model, bomb-carrying Oscar, pursued by an American F4U Corsair fighter, clipped the *Laffey*'s yardarm off Okinawa on April 16, 1945.

The *Laffey* (DD 724) was photographed after the Okinawa action from
the medical rescue ship PCER 851. Here—down by the stern and with
heavy damage aft quite visible—she waits for Lieutenant Commander
Frank Bayley to bring his ship alongside and take off casualties.

Laffey's starboard side—as seen from PCER 851, from the after funnel
looking toward the battered fantail—is proof of the ferocity of the
Japanese attacks off Okinawa. This section of the ship took the greatest
number of hits.

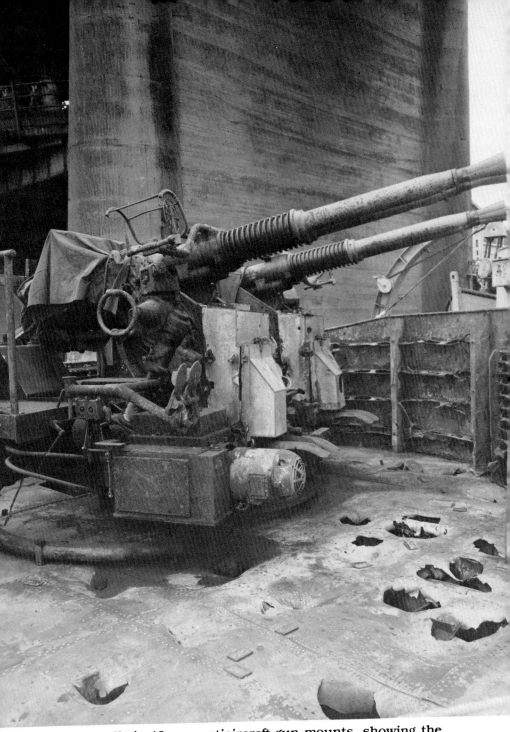

One of *Laffey*'s 40-mm antiaircraft gun mounts, showing the destruction caused by burning gasoline and shell explosions. The rack inside the mount's shield held ammunition. Some was tossed over the side by her men, but some exploded, making holes in the deck.

The deck near *Laffey*'s fantail was punctured by explosions and flying shrapnel during the Okinawa action. Even with temporary repairs, it was so weakened that a catwalk had to be installed at Seattle, Washington, for use by crowds of visitors to the ship.

The ship's after five-inch twin Mount 53 was hit by two bomb-laden Kamikazes and was torn open. One gun was upended and canted skyward. The mount's shield was not armor plate but thin metal, which was never designed to resist such impacts.

A Kamikaze ripped through the thin waist-level shield around the three 20-mm guns on *Laffey*'s fantail, killing and wounding many, destroying the guns, and wrecking the mount before it continued on to impact against five-inch twin Mount 53.

Survivors of the Okinawa assault (left to right), Boatswain's Mate Art Baumhart, Gunner's Mate Warren Walker, Sonarman Louis Nordstrom, and Ship's Cooks Jerry Pinkoff and Dan Essig stand on the port side next to battered Mount 53, aft.

Machinist's Mate John Michel stands in one of the charred and burned-out after berthing compartments following the Okinawa action. Although Michel looks like a schoolboy in this photo, he was by then an experienced and able crewman.

Home safe at last in Seattle, the battered *Laffey* (DD 724) prepares to display her battle scars to an American public for whom she fought so hard. Black area to the left of gun is the after deckhouse where two Kamikazes crashed in rapid succession.

Laffey at Seattle showed ugly black battle scars that were in sharp contrast to the blue paint on her hull and the gray of her superstructure. Blotch at masthead is from censor's pencil covering what remained of air-search radar.

A sign on *Laffey*'s starboard side and the empty base on which a 20-mm mount was once bolted is mute testimony to the courage and sacrifices of her men off Okinawa. It was here that a bomb hit the ship, destroying the gun and killing three.

The fury of attacking Kamikazes is brought home to the 93,000 civilians who visited the ship on her arrival on the West Coast. The Kamikaze threat was minimized during the war but emphasized in connection with *Laffey*, in order to spur efforts of shipyard workers who assumed the war would soon be over.

In January 1946 Admiral Becton (far right) was awarded the Navy Cross and his fourth Silver Star Medal during a ceremony in the office of the Secretary of the Navy. Among those present were Fleet Admiral Chester W. Nimitz, just to the left of Becton, and Secretary Forrestal to the left of Nimitz. Rear Admiral Morton L. Deyo is on the far left.

Some of the *Laffey*'s officers in bomb-damaged wardroom. Left to right: Dr. Matthew Darnell, Lieutenant (j.g.) G.A. Parolini, Lieutenant Paul Smith, Lieutenant (j.g.) Harvey Shaw, and Lieutenant Tom Addison.

F. Julian Becton, USN, skipper of the destroyer *Laffey* (DD 724), in a picture taken during the war. Like many of his men, he looked hardly old enough to vote, but he was then an experienced naval officer who was to guide his ship and men through their greatest trial.

Imogen Carpenter, whose letters helped sustain then Commander Becton's spirits through many months of difficult wartime service. Although a Broadway star with a demanding career, she kept up a morale-building correspondence with him throughout the war. Both had grown up in the same hometown.
(Courtesy F. Julian Becton)

The USS *Laffey*, DD 724, shown still serving her country in the post-WW I period. By then her superstructure had been greatly modified, her equipment modernized, and her armament much changed to meet new challenges. Although *Laffey* is now retired, some Allen M. Sumner-class destroyers still serve with the U.S. Navy.

supposed to be. I say *supposed* because it was hazy in that area and we really couldn't make out the target. It was maddeningly frustrating. Being shot at is a lot easier to take when you can see who is shooting and you can shoot back at them.

The first German shells had been aimed at the minesweepers, but as bigger game came into the Germans' sights, they switched to it very quickly. There was a splash in the water near the *Barton*. It was a hit. The shell tore into her, cut through some bulkheads, and then just came to rest. Thankfully, it did not explode, but it was enough of a hint for all of us.

"Right full rudder," I gave the helmsman; then, "All engines ahead flank."

Al Henke's boys had been ready. They poured it on and we surged ahead. They had been ready when we needed them and, for just a second, I thought of the disciplined crewman. He'd been let out of the chain locker some hours before, and no matter how he must have felt about his job, when that order came, he must have done it without argument. The crewman was not stupid. He knew that in a situation like that, speed was the only thing that could save our skin.

We were up to twenty-five knots when it happened. Just as if a giant's hand had smacked the water, there was a huge splash off our port bow. That was all, just the splash. There was no explosion, no flying chunks of jagged metal, no smoke or fire, nothing except water raining down on the deck. It was a very near miss.

We kept dodging around, pouring out a smoke screen to cover the battleships, our helm going from port to starboard to port as we steered for the latest shell splashes. The guns of the old *Texas*—the ship on which I had served as a young officer—would roar, then those of the *Arkansas*. Between the roars you could hear the almost machine-gunlike series of cracks of five-inchers.

As at Utah, there were Shore Fire Control Parties with our troops at Cherbourg. But the situation at Cherbourg was somewhat different. We were not behind our troops shooting over them or to one side. Most of the time the Germans were between our ships and soldiers ashore, and this made things rough. Very often it was a case of having to fire at the flashes of enemy guns located in areas we were sure the Germans occupied.

At 12:40 P.M., for example, we saw some flashes in the vicinity of the Battery Hamburg. Naturally, we threw everything we had at them; but it's impossible to say whether we connected.

129

There was so much stuff coming our way, and so much going back at the Germans, that pinpointing explosions of specific shells was very difficult.

For some reason that has never been fully explained, the Germans at Cherbourg concentrated a lot of the fire of their heavier guns on the minesweepers, then on the destroyers of Group Two. Possibly they may have felt that by eliminating these, they would force the battleships to retire. But whatever the reason, the results were both impressive and unsettling, because Bill Freseman's destroyers attracted a lot of attention.

At about 12:53 P.M., a minute or two after *Laffey* had ceased firing at the flashes of Battery Hamburg, the *O'Brien* staggered. We were just astern of her and could see the explosion. A heavy shell struck her signal bridge. The blast damaged her CIC below, killed thirteen of her men, and disabled her radar.

This wasn't a mortal wound, but it certainly was a critical one. The CIC was the nerve center of the ship. *O'Brien* could continue to fire her guns independently, and she could maneuver; but her centralized control and information capability was gone. Her guns continued to fire, but she was like a person who had received a stunning blow to the head.

Barton and *Laffey* now turned north and began to lay a smoke screen astern of the minesweepers. These little ships, their job done, had been ordered to retire. *O'Brien* went with them. With her CIC wiped out, the ship was almost blind; and if she had stayed in the open, the German batteries might have finished her.

The rest of our destroyers kept maneuvering, laying smoke, and shooting whenever their five-inchers were in range of the enemy. Smoke from *Laffey* and the others gave the battleships cover as their heavy guns pounded enemy positions. But it couldn't hide them completely. Every so often a gust of wind made them visible targets, and at one point the German gunners got the range of the *Texas*.

The *Texas* had been working over Battery Hamburg with her fourteen-inch guns when a gust of wind suddenly parted the smoke. Seconds later, there were geysers from shells all around her. Though her helm was put hard over, one of them connected. The huge eleven-inch projectile exploded. It wrecked her navigation bridge, killed her helmsman, and killed or wounded a number of others.

But the *Texas* kept right on firing, and in time she extracted revenge. Her gunners put a fourteen-inch shell squarely on the mantlet of one of Battery Hamburg's guns. Though this mantlet —a movable shield attached to the barrel, which covered the opening through which the barrel extended—was thick steel, that gun was finished for good.

At 3:01 P.M., Admiral Deyo contacted Admiral Bryant on the TBS, informed him that our work was finished and ordered Bryant to take Group Two back to England. General Collins's troops were now well into Cherbourg. Many of its batteries had been overrun and taken, and it was the Army's show from then on. The soldiers didn't need us anymore, but they were darn glad we had been along. A large number of German guns could have been trained around to fire on the advancing G.I.'s if we hadn't been there to hold their attention and to knock them out.

When I received word that we were to retire, I ordered *Laffey*'s damage-control parties to make a thorough inspection of the ship. She was operating perfectly and there didn't seem to be any damage. But we'd had some near misses, and I could remember what near misses had done to the *Aaron Ward*. There was always the chance she had hull damage below the waterline. We could be taking on seawater slowly without even knowing it. The time to check her out was right then so we could take emergency measures that would see her safely back to port in England.

One man aboard, Electrician's Mate Gene Miller, was sure something wasn't quite as it should be. When that shell had splashed in the water near *Laffey*'s bow at 12:32 P.M., Miller was at his battle station on the switchboard in the forward engine room watching the meters for our degaussing cable. One had gone dead and dropped to zero, and "Round Eye"—as Miller was nicknamed—immediately called Al Csiszar, our leading electrician's mate.

Csiszar did not know about the shell that had splashed near our bow. But certain that there was a break in the cable, he started inspecting it, beginning with the after part of the ship and working forward. This wasn't something he could do quickly. The degaussing cable ran completely around the inside of the hull. But throughout the action, Csiszar kept at it, and by the time it was over he had finally reached the forecastle.

Just ahead of one of the damage-control parties, Csiszar climbed down to the door of a small storeroom in the bow known as the boatswain's locker. The deck of this forward storeroom was about on the level of the waterline of the hull, and the degaussing cable ran along its sides. Flipping the dogs that held the door shut, Csiszar pulled it open. It came a lot easier than he'd expected, and behind it there was a surprise waiting for him.

In fact, there were several surprises. Al found the break in the degaussing cable, all right—once the water which hit him in the face had receded. But he also found a gaping hole in the port bulkhead of the locker just above the waterline, and he found something else. There, sitting on its nose, its base upright, was one of the biggest shells he had ever seen.

SEVEN

There was not much room in *Laffey's* boatswain's locker. A small compartment in the forward part of the ship, it was a storage room filled with tools and gear for rigging and cargo movement. The shell itself took up quite a lot of space. It was a 240-mm (approximately 9.6 inches in diameter), about 3 feet long, and it weighed well in excess of 400 pounds. Getting it out would be a tough, dangerous job. And, if it happened to go off, some of our 5-inch ammunition might go with it, probably taking the whole bow of the ship.

As soon as I got word of what we were carrying, I called Lieutenant Sam Humphries. He was our damage-control officer, and my orders to him were simple and direct: "Sam, get it the hell off the ship as soon as you can."

Sam, together with Chief Boatswain's Mate Herbert Lewis and their damage-control party, didn't waste any time. They crowded into the locker and began to rig the hoisting gear at once. No sooner had the shell been shifted, and there was enough room in the place, when in came Al Csiszar. Al and two electrician's mates, Claude Scott and Claude Brockett, went to work on the degaussing equipment even as the shell was being hoisted up to the deck.

Slowly, carefully, but working as fast as possible, Sam Humphries, Lewis, and their men shifted the heavy menace up through the hatches. It was difficult, nervous, and exhausting work. One little slip, one little jar could have set the thing off, and no one dared breathe until that monster finally stood on the main deck.

While this was going on I cut *Laffey*'s speed and kept our course changes to a minimum. I didn't want more seawater coming through the hole in her side. Luckily, the sea was fairly calm, the compartment remained relatively dry, and best of all, the ship wasn't rolling or plunging. If she had been, anything could have happened. Even if the shell had not gone off, a sudden, violent movement of the ship could have put too much strain on the hoisting gear, made the shell break loose, and sent it rolling around in confined quarters below.

Actually, no one really relaxed until the monster finally splashed over the side, sank to the bottom without exploding, and we had steamed well clear of the spot. The very same defect that had made it a dud could have made it go off when it hit the water. And an explosion in the water so close to our hull might well have torn the hull open below the waterline.

Sam Humphries got a close look at the shell before we got rid of it, and he reported that the markings on it were Czech. When the Germans marched into Czechoslovakia in 1938, one of the prizes they took over was the giant Skoda munitions works. Skoda was recognized as one of the leading munitions makers of the time, and the Germans put Czech productive capacity to good use. But the Germans made one mistake. The Czechs didn't make very good slave laborers. They hated the Germans, and every chance they got, they did what they could to cause them trouble.

That Czech shell that came to rest in *Laffey*'s boatswain's locker—and many others the Germans fired at us at Cherbourg —must have been sabotaged. It's my understanding that three out of four that scored hits on Admiral Bryant's ships never went off. The men aboard the *Texas*, for example, found a similar dud resting quietly in the cabin of the ship's clerk after the bombardment. It was still in one piece despite the constant concussions from the ship's guns during the action.

For *Laffey* and other bombardment ships the Normandy operation was now over. Thanks in no small measure to our bombardment, General Collins's troops had taken Cherbourg. Army forces under General Eisenhower were now well inland. As we headed back to Portland, we knew our job was done. From now on it would be up to Army guns and our planes to blast a way for our infantry and tanks in the sweep across France.

Despite this, I think the Army would have liked to have taken us with them if it had been possible. Our artillery was good. Our planes dominated the skies. But from every quarter, high and low, we got unstinting praise for the way our naval guns had chopped up the Germans.

Former Corporal Hitler—and many of his generals—just didn't understand naval power. As landsmen, they had clung to the old theory that warships could not win gun duels with well-protected land batteries. They had assumed—incorrectly, and perhaps because of their own navy's previous experience in Norwegian waters—that naval guns on ships were no match for those on dry land.

Hitler apparently had never forgotten what happened to the German heavy cruiser *Blücher* on April 9, 1940, in Oslo Fjord, but he had not learned from it either. Unlike the *Blücher*, the *Laffey* and other bombardment ships had not been in completely restricted waters at Normandy. Our ships had had to anchor for a time, but on the whole, they were moving targets. And they also knew where their targets were. We took some hits, but before German coastal-defense guns could really do much damage, we plastered them—and we kept it up. Not only could we shoot, we could steam—and that made all the difference.

The shell hole in our bow was patched at Portland by men from the destroyer tender *Melville*. Then, along with the other destroyers of our squadron, and the *Tuscaloosa*, *Nevada*, *Arkansas*, and *Quincy*, we headed for Belfast in Northern Ireland. For *Laffey*, it was a false start. Three hours out on June 28, our oil service pumps, which supplied oil to the turbine bearings, developed trouble, and Admiral Deyo ordered us to return to port.

By 10:00 P.M. we had the trouble cleared up, thanks to Al Henke and his men, but by then there was other work for us to do. Instead of going to Belfast, we were assigned to escort the amphibious command ship *Ancon* to Plymouth. And for a while, I was a little concerned. Were we going to be separated from the squadron on detached duty? Were we going to stay in Europe?

I don't think I was the only one on the ship who asked himself those questions. Destroyers were maids of all work, and detaching one from its parent organization wasn't all that uncommon. By now, all of Freseman's ships were well on their way to Belfast—and that meant only one thing. Belfast was the takeoff point for the trip back to the States. If the squadron sailed for home, I wanted *Laffey* to be with it.

Home meant more than just some time off and a chance to get the ship's bridge and pilothouse problems corrected. Home meant that Freseman's ships would probably be sent out to the Pacific. I had already seen too much of war to have any great craving for more of it. But the Navy's job in Europe was about finished. I didn't want *Laffey*'s men to miss out on some time at home. And I didn't want the ship spending the rest of the war doing odd jobs. Neither deserved that. It would have been a waste.

We finally got to Belfast on June 30, much to my relief. By then, of course, the grapevine had it that we were returning to Boston—which is exactly what everyone aboard wanted. The men had had enough of Europe, had done what they had come to do, and they didn't want to hang around. They knew that Boston meant battle again in the Pacific, but they preferred that to boredom.

We cleared Belfast harbor outward bound at 7:00 A.M., July 3, 1944; our destination, Boston. And as soon as we were clear of the land and on our way, I picked up the microphone to announce it to the crew over the public-address system. But something got into me that morning. Maybe I was just plain happy to be going home. Or maybe I just wanted to have a few seconds of fun to heighten the crews' eventual pleasure. But whatever it was, I started out by announcing, "The *Laffey* is en route to Cherbourg."

I hesitated a moment to let the groans die down, then I quickly added, "Belay that! The *Laffey* is en route to Boston, Massachusetts, U.S.A." The groans, I hadn't heard. But the wild shouts and cheers that swept through the ship were clearly audible. We were going home, and everybody was happy.

I learned something that day about the dangers of practical jokes. When I had said Cherbourg over the public-address system, one of our stewards, Clyde Dunson, dropped three of our breakfast eggs. That wasn't so funny. Fresh eggs weren't all that plentiful in the World War II Navy. We had some aboard, but not enough to waste on practical jokes, and powdered eggs were not an amusing replacement.

On the whole, our trip back to Boston was a welcome respite. Nothing much happened. The weather wasn't very good; the *Walke* suffered some structural damage. *Laffey* had some minor engineering difficulties. One crewman got into some trouble and he had to be disciplined and given a lecture. And on the Fourth of July we celebrated with some gunnery practice. But essentially, the voyage was quiet, routine, unmarked by any major incidents.

At the same time, however, it was quite a special voyage. *Laffey* had always been a happy ship. But on that trip she was an exuberant ship, a ship full of self-confident combat veterans, and a ship with a crew looking forward to some leave at home. That voyage wasn't a pleasure cruise for any of us, but it certainly was much more of a pleasure than anything we'd experienced in the past—or would in the future.

About the only thing out of the ordinary that took place aboard was a little ceremony we held on July 6. The fact that we could hold such a ceremony on a destroyer in the mid-Atlantic at that time suggests how close the naval part of the war against Hitler was to ending. A few months before, assembling a large group of officers and crewmen on an open deck aft of the bridge of a destroyer would have been courting disaster. But the battle of the Atlantic had been won; Europe had been successfully invaded. Whatever remained of Hitler's navy was either bottled up or far too busy trying to survive to devote any attention to ships that far from Europe. And that was especially true of a group of ships that included a lot of destroyers.

Had an enemy U-boat appeared, we could have handled the situation. Just because we had many of our people assembled didn't mean the duty watch wasn't alert. But there were no sightings or contacts because there were no U-boats.

It pleased me to be able to commend so many of my men individually at that time. As a group, everyone aboard had received a lot of recognition for what we had done in the waters off France. But a Letter of Commendation was a personal recognition of good service. It went in a man's personal file, influenced his chances of promotion in the Navy, and has been known to have a positive effect on a man's future in civilian life.

I had a large group of commendations to award because there were so many of *Laffey*'s men who I felt deserved one. From Al Csiszar and Henry Teague to Harry Burns and Charlie Holovak, they represented every department, every area of the ship, men of all ranks and ratings, regulars and civilians in uniform. I had heard of cases of officers in the Navy who played favorites when it came time for awards for merit, but that is not the way to run a ship or anything else. If you heap all the praise on the running quarterbacks and ignore deserving linemen, you don't have a winning team very long. Radio Technician George Osman, Chief Gunner's Mate Norman Fitzgerald, and a lot of other enlisted men deserved commendations just as much as Chief Engineer Al Henke and Lieutenant Sam Humphries—and I made sure that they got them.

Laffey entered Boston Harbor early in the afternoon of July 9, and it was some time after this that I discovered how close we had come to staying in Europe. Apparently, had it not been for the ill-designed bridge structures of our Allen M. Sumner 2,200-ton destroyers, we might have been kept there. But Fleet Admiral Ernest King had become so disturbed by the barrage of complaints from prospective skippers of 2,200-ton destroyers that he had brought the whole situation to a head, and this brought us home.

King—the Navy's top officer—was Commander in Chief, Unites States Fleet (Cominch). He had threatened to convene a court of inquiry to investigate the situation. That had done it. A court of inquiry was a very serious step.

A court of inquiry in the Navy might best be compared to the appointment of a special federal grand jury in civilian life. One is not convened unless there is some very serious matter such as a ship running aground or a collision. The design defect in the bridges of our destroyers was serious, but not that serious, and a court of inquiry took time. Thus it was probably best for all concerned that King's staff talked him out of it. Instead, he had the Navy's Inspector General, Admiral Charles P. Snyder, conduct an investigation. This produced the needed results—and it produced them much more quickly.

Admiral Snyder's investigation and recommendations meant that *Laffey* would be tied up undergoing modification of her bridge structure for a period of five weeks—plenty of time for each of two leave parties to take off for ten days to see their families. Everyone aboard had hoped for some leave when we got home. But when word spread that it was to be ten days, you can imagine the reaction. Men like Howard Leary, John Branka, and Herbert Remsen rushed to phones the first chance they got to pass the news on to their families. And from then on, the almost universal subjects of conversation aboard *Laffey* were either how leave was going to be spent, or how leave had been spent.

I say *almost* universal because at least in one case there was a disturbing and depressing problem. About 1:15 P.M. the day we arrived in Boston, a serious-faced Charlie Holovak came to the bridge. A problem sailor was on report again. He was charged with disrespect toward a superior and disobedience of orders.

This was a sour note in what was otherwise a joyous and happy time on the ship. I had hoped that the crewman would straighten out after a couple of brief periods on bread and water. But he was apparently as recalcitrant as ever, and I couldn't let it go on. Sooner or later some of our more impressionable men would note how easy this crewman got off and might start copying him. Lack of discipline was a dangerous, infectious disease. It could spread throughout the ship and would eventually endanger the lives of everyone aboard. It had to be stopped, either by removing the source of the infection or by curing it.

I told Holovak to have the crewman brought to the bridge and held there. And I added that Holovak was to convene a summary court martial as soon as possible. When the crewman was brought to the bridge, I heard his side of the story and that of the petty officer who had reported him. Then I sentenced him to be tried by the summary court.

Within thirty minutes the three summary court officers returned a verdict. The crewman had pleaded guilty. He was to be fined and given a bad-conduct discharge, and he was to be sent to the Navy Yard brig pending completion of the necessary papers.

After the crewman had gone, I began to think about him and the sentence. The fine was one thing, but frankly, I was of two minds about discharging him. Money a man can recover, but not a reputation. In effect, that bad-conduct discharge was a life sentence.

By the time the papers arrived, I had made up my mind. I had the crewman brought back to my cabin; the minute he came in I was about as sure as I could be that I had made the right decision. He looked worried, unsure of himself, almost frightened. And from the tone of his voice, it appeared evident he regretted his actions.

Still, sure as I was that what I intended to do was correct, I wanted to make certain that the change in the crewman's attitude was permanent. In the past, I had explained to him what a bad-conduct discharge would mean to his future, but it had had no effect. This was the last time I intended to do it. He was on the edge of the cliff, I told him; one false move and it would be all over. And, if he made that plunge, I said, he could never come back.

That may sound harsh. In recent years, there's been a tendency in American society to take a more lenient view of people who have been thrown out of the military services. But in 1944 no such view prevailed. The country was fighting for its life. Even those whose religious beliefs forbade killing a human being were expected to pitch in and serve in some useful capacity— something all of them did, many with great bravery and distinction. In 1944 Americans had no patience with anyone who evaded duty willfully. Once this crewman had that bad-conduct discharge on his record, he'd be an outcast, and many would view him as a criminal.

I concluded the interview by telling the crewman I was giving him one more chance. He would have to pay the fine. But I remitted the bad-conduct discharge pending good behavior on his part for a year. A year would be enough—by the end of that time, he'd either have proved himself worthy of trust, or have ruined the rest of his life.

He thanked me and promised me he'd never get in trouble again. He was as good as his word: He never did. He developed into one of the most solid, dependable men aboard the ship, and I was glad to have him with us in the months ahead. He'd fought the hardest battle any man can face, and he'd won a victory over himself. A man like that wasn't going to have any trouble handling whatever the Japanese could dish out.

Monday morning, July 10, Bob Montgomery came aboard. Bob said he wanted me to have dinner with him that night. He had a room at the Ritz Carlton Hotel and he asked me to meet him there about 5:30 that afternoon.

Naturally, I accepted his invitation. Bob was now a close friend, and I thoroughly enjoyed his company. But somehow I sensed there was something more than relaxation on Bob's mind. He didn't look well. I suspected there was a problem and that Bob wanted to talk it over.

My suspicions were confirmed when I arrived at his room that afternoon. Bob ordered a drink for me but not for himself. He excused himself, saying that his stomach was upset, but this didn't make much sense to me. If he wasn't feeling up to par, he could have just called off the dinner engagement.

Knowing something was wrong, I pressed him to tell me what was bothering him. It wasn't like Bob not to have a drink before a good dinner. He finally came out with it. He said he had lost twenty pounds during the Normandy operation. He had thirty days leave and was going to California to see his family. He intended to go into a hospital there to find out what was wrong with him so he could get it straightened out and return to duty.

I was fairly sure I knew what was wrong. Bob Montgomery was one of the most conscientious naval officers I've ever known. He was just plain worn out, exhausted, and the reasons for this were obvious.

Bob got into the war right at the beginning. In the spring of

1940 he was in England making a movie. Then the Germans attacked France and the Low Countries, and Bob gave up his five-thousand-dollar-per-week job to drive an ambulance. When Paris fell and France collapsed, Bob had to make his way across France to Spain in order to get home. As soon as he got home, he went after a commission in the U. S. Navy.

Bob had been sent back to London to the naval attaché's office. Since he was never one to talk about his experiences, to this day I still don't know all the details of his service during that period. Yet I know well enough that Bob didn't spend his time at posh social gatherings. According to the late Joseph Driscoll, the then-war correspondent for the old New York *Herald Tribune*, Bob saw active service in the North Sea and the Mediterranean.

After that, when the U.S. was in the war, he went to the South Pacific. Again, he did not spend his time at any base headquarters. Bob was in the thick of it in those same Solomon Island waters where I had served, and where the first *Laffey* was sunk. He had combat duty in destroyers; he had been out with PT boats; and he even had time aboard a cruiser. He'd gone days in combat without sleep, had contracted malaria, and had also been laid low by dengue (breakbone) fever.

After going through all of that, Bob came back to the States and became Bill Freseman's squadron operations officer. He'd been through the Normandy operation, and the strain of that was added to the rest. A friend of mine who bunked with Bob aboard Freseman's flagship told me that by then, Bob couldn't even sleep half the nights.

Combat wears any man down after a while, but as I looked at Bob that evening, I knew it was more than just that. Bob was suffering from Freseman. Bob never uttered one word of criticism of Bill Freseman, but he didn't need to. I knew what Bill was like and the situation was obvious.

Bill Freseman was a fine naval officer who could be very genial and a lot of fun to be around at an off-duty social affair. But he was a very ambitious man, driving, demanding, hovering, and fussy. He also had a considerable amount of ego, and the combination of all these traits made him a difficult person to work for. Much as I liked and respected him, I think even I would have felt a considerable strain being with him constantly.

For Bob Montgomery, this physical strain was even worse because he had already had to endure so much of it long before he joined the squadron. Also, it never let up. One very disturbing thing that Bob did mention was that he couldn't even relax at

141

meals. Freseman insisted Bob have all his meals with him in his cabin instead of in the wardroom with the other officers. That wasn't right!

I told Bob that he had done more than his share already. The Navy was proud of him. He had turned himself into a really professional naval officer and had not just become a celebrity in uniform. I said I did not think he should continue in his present job. I finally got him to agree, but there was a problem. Freseman wouldn't let him go unless transfer orders came from some higher authority. Not only was Bob doing a very good job for Freseman, but Bill enjoyed having a famous film star on his staff.

I thought about the problem, then I remembered that Bob had once told me he'd become a good friend of Captain Robert Briscoe. Briscoe had had a squadron of destroyers in the Guadalcanal area when Bob was there. I was sure that Briscoe had been promoted to rear admiral by then, and he could be the key to helping Bob.

"Bob," I said, "please, on your way to California, stop off in Washington and have a talk with Briscoe. He will know what to do."

As it turned out, Bob did; Briscoe knew what to do, and he did it. Not long after, Bob got orders to report to a new job in southern California. I was sorry to see him go because he was a good friend whom I enjoyed being with. But I'm glad he did.

I don't know how Bill Freseman reacted to Bob's leaving. I suspect that at first he was upset, but then, after some time passed, he probably realized it had to be. Bill could be tough to work for, but he wasn't a monster. He was rough on his subordinates, but he cared about them and worried about them, even as he drove them. Yet because Bill carried a heavy responsibility, there were times when he just did not see what was happening to some of them.

As for Bob Montgomery, though he did not get another wartime combat assignment, he certainly continued to serve his country. One of the first films he made when he went back to acting was about the Navy in combat. In 1945 Bob starred in *They Were Expendable*, with John Wayne and Ward Bond. It was the story of the PT boats under Commander John Bulkley in the Philippines early in the war, and Bob didn't need anyone to coach him. He knew what war was like. He'd been in it.

Even after the war, Bob continued to serve his country. Some years later, despite his heavy television schedule, Bob—a commander by then—completed the necessary requirements for promotion. He was to retire as a captain in the Naval Reserve.

At Boston, the squadron lost Bob Montgomery, but *Laffey* got a new officer. While I was visiting the headquarters of Captain George Menocal, the representative of the Atlantic Fleet Destroyer Commander in Boston, I talked with some of Menocal's staff. And one of these staff officers was Lieutenant (j.g.) Frank A. Manson, USNR.

Manson—a wiry, intelligent Oklahoman—was desk-bound, but he desperately wanted to go to sea. I'd met him before, liked him, judged him to be a good officer, and sympathized with his plight. Few good young naval officers like Manson enjoy running a desk and spending their time shuffling through piles of forms and correspondence.

"Is there room for me in the *Laffey*?" Manson wanted to know.

I had to say no, that every berth was filled. But when I saw the disappointment on his face, I hurriedly told him we'd make room—if he could get a transfer. We could use another good officer where we were going.

Manson filed the proper request for transfer with Bupers (Bureau of Naval Personnel) in Washington, but nothing happened. Days turned into a week, then two, then three, but still there were no orders. Finally, one afternoon, Manson came up to me, desperation written on his face. Giving me a handful of change, he asked me to call a friend in Washington—any friend I thought might be able to help.

Naturally, I told young Manson again that his request had to go through proper channels, but I said I'd think about it. Then, after thinking about it for at least five seconds, I went to the phone.

"Julie," the senior destroyer detail officer asked on the phone after I told him why I was calling, "do you really want this officer?"

This put it squarely up to me, and I couldn't lie to an old friend. Did I really want a highly articulate, intelligent, well-trained, hard-working, personable young officer with us in the Pacific? Again, I thought about it—this time for two seconds. You're darn right I did, and I said so.

"OK, I'll get his orders out this afternoon," was the reply, and they arrived in Boston very soon after. Captain Menocal wasn't too pleased. For the moment, he had no one to replace Manson. But Menocal was an officer with a good heart and a lot of common sense. He knew Manson wasn't a Regular but a Reserve officer, and that he wasn't trying to get to sea just to enhance his career. Any young man who was that highly motivated about getting a crack at the enemy deserved a chance to do it. Menocal said he'd find some way for his office to take up the slack, and Manson became one of *Laffey*'s officers.

Not long after we arrived in Boston, members of the Navy Inspector General's staff arrived, gathered Bill Freseman and the skippers of 2,200-ton destroyers together, and went over changes the ships required. As soon as these officers made sure what was needed, the changes were made—especially those in the bridges —and then we went out into the Atlantic to test the ships for possible structural failure. And with us we took yard technicians who were still working on the ship.

At sea we fired 2 four-gun salvos from our forward gun mounts to make certain there were no problems with the new members which had been added to the ship. All went well, and as soon as we'd completed firing, I sent Quartermaster Charles Weygandt down to my cabin on an errand. Weygandt returned at once, quite agitated. Apparently, all had not gone well. He had found a crowd of yard technicians in and near my cabin gathered around a junction box. While there was no fire or damage, Weygandt reported the box had a huge, hand-lettered sign on it reading "DON'T TOUCH."

I knew my friend Electrician Joe Daugherty was aboard, and I asked Weygandt to find him at once and send him to me. Whatever the problem was, I was sure Joe would have the answer.

Joe did! The problem was serious, though not quite the way I had feared it might be. Joe had just found out that the electrician who had been working on that junction box was color-blind. All electrical leads in that box were color-coded, just like those in other parts of *Laffey*'s wiring on which the man had been working for almost two weeks. They'd all have to be checked.

"But what about the sign?" I asked Joe, and then he grinned.

Apparently, just as the color-blind electrician was testing his work on that junction box by throwing a switch, *Laffey*'s five-inchers had roared. They scared the living daylights out of that man. Aware that he was color-blind, he thought he'd made some incorrect hookup with the wires and set off the guns. And, fearful that it would happen again, he'd put up that sign.

Our routine structural tests were a success. We did not uncover any structural weaknesses in the new work that had been done, but we uncovered something just as important. God only knows what that color-blind electrician might have hooked up to what somewhere along the line. And not just in *Laffey*.

144

Sure, it was amusing, right out of an old Marx Brothers movie. But antics like that are for comedy films, not for ships going into combat. That color-blind electrician had chosen the wrong career.

During our stay in Boston, I had several chances to get down to New York to see Imogen again. Nothing seemed to have changed between us. As far as I could tell, she still was as fond of me as I was of her. When it came time for *Laffey* to leave Boston, and I could not get away, she took a plane up to spend a last Sunday with me.

This time both of us sensed that when *Laffey* sailed, we might be separated for a long time. Even though I hadn't known our work would be so quickly over when we had left for England, I'd been fairly sure the ship would get back to the States on a visit within a reasonable amount of time. But the Pacific was another story. Though things out there had been going our way, there was still a long way to go. The Japanese had a large navy and air force; their army was as powerful as ever. It could take a year, even two, to defeat them. I'd be thousands of miles away with little chance of getting home on leave, if I even got leave, and that was unlikely. No, that Sunday was going to be it, and the fact that Imogen was coming to spend it with me made me even more sure of her affection.

When Imogen came up to Boston, I asked her to bring me another picture of herself. She seemed pleased, but as I think back on it now, I think perhaps I may have hurt her feelings a little when I told her why I wanted it. I suppose she thought I wanted another picture of her for my cabin. But then when I asked her to inscribe it so that it could be put in a scrapbook full of complimentary messages that we kept in the wardroom, perhaps she wasn't so pleased. She wrote on the picture: "To the Officers and Crew of my favorite ship—the *Laffey*. God bless you and keep you. . . . Imogen Carpenter." Though I know she meant those words sincerely, I realize now that she probably would have preferred a more personal inscription directed solely to me.

As I have mentioned before, Imogen was not so much interested in the war as in my war, and the same applied to the ship. After we had a late but leisurely lunch aboard in my cabin, her first request was to see the place I would be in battle. I had told her my station was on the bridge, and this is what really interested her.

The steep ladders of a WW II destroyer were never designed to be used by women in skirts and high-heeled shoes, but Imogen—

145

perhaps because of her active theatrical training—negotiated the one to the pilothouse as easily as anyone aboard. Once we reached there, I began explaining the equipment; but though she was attentive, her main interest seemed to be focused on the captain's chair and on the spot out on the starboard bridge where the skipper usually stood. Then, when I showed her my sea cabin, she was really taken aback. I guess she found it hard to believe that anyone could get much rest or relaxation in such a confined space.

After our visit to the bridge, we walked over to the Officers' Club, sat and talked for some time, had a cocktail, and then dinner. Then I took her to Boston's South Station. I saw her to her train, told her I'd call her from wherever the ship was before she left the States, then I kissed her goodbye.

Her kiss was warm and affectionate; but as we drew apart she smiled, a little sadly, I think. I got off the train just before it started to move. I was happy, but I too felt a little sad as I watched it pull out. The afternoon had gone so quickly. I wouldn't see Imogen again for a very long time and, though I would not forget her, another sweetheart of mine, the *Laffey*, would now demand most of my attention.

Laffey left Boston in early August, the first of Freseman's ships to sail, but we did not head straight for the Pacific. We went to Norfolk; to Chesapeake Bay near North Beach, Maryland; and even cruised around the Atlantic off Cape Cod for a while. Our radars needed to be thoroughly tested and calibrated, and this took time. We didn't actually sail from Norfolk for Panama, in company with an LSD (landing ship dock), until August 26. And it was September before we reached Balboa, at the Pacific end of the Panama Canal.

Up to that point the journey was uneventful, but at Balboa, and on the way north to San Diego, there was one casualty among *Laffey*'s crew. No one was injured. It was a casualty of the heart.

For obvious reasons, I won't identify the man. But I will tell you what happened to him, because his case was a perfect example of how war can mess up human relationships. At Balboa I gave liberty to those of the crew who wanted it. Our hero went ashore—like others—to look for some romantic adventure. But romance in a foreign port like Balboa had its dangers. As soon as the man returned aboard, he sought out the ship's doctor to get a prophylaxis.

146

In this he was very sensible, but in his correspondence he was not. En route to San Diego he wrote to his girl friend. He wanted to tell her he'd been in Panama, but that was forbidden by wartime security regulations. So instead he kept raving to her about how plentiful bananas were where he'd been. All he wrote about was bananas, how wonderful it was to get some and how much he had enjoyed them.

This was a dead giveaway where the ship was, and the censor could not let it go through. The censor in this case happened to be the ship's doctor, and he crossed out "bananas" wherever it appeared in the letter. Unfortunately, these blanks gave an entirely different meaning to many sentences in the letter. Thus for weeks this young man was complaining to his buddies that, after Panama, his girl never wrote to him.

Laffey arrived at Pearl Harbor on September 18, 1944. By then, events in the Pacific had begun to move more and more rapidly. Our forces had taken Guam and Saipan in the Marianas. New Guinea had been just about cleared of Japanese troops. And we had won a major battle against the Japanese fleet in the waters of the Philippines. Pearl Harbor was no longer on the front line. Though it still was the major headquarters base in the Central Pacific, it now served as a rear staging area where forces were trained and built up for future campaigns.

Still, the Japanese were by no means hanging on the ropes, and the ferocity of their air attacks on our ships was actually increasing. We had many more carriers and much better planes than we had had when I had been in the South Pacific. But that made little difference. Jap pilots' determination to stop us had become almost suicidal, and that put an even greater premium on antiaircraft gunnery.

As a result, before *Laffey* was allowed to steam farther west to join Admiral William F. Halsey's Third Fleet, we were given several more weeks of intensive training by the training groups based in Hawaii. This I approved of completely. We were good and we had proved it off Normandy. But that had been almost two months before. Not only did our gunners need to hone their skills firing at land targets on Kahoolawe Island and at simulated torpedo-boat (PT-boat) targets at sea. But we definitely needed more antiaircraft practice. In Europe we hadn't had that many German aircraft to shoot at, but out there it was going to be an entirely different story.

Other ships of Freseman's Squadron Sixty soon began arriving in Pearl Harbor, and as they did, they too joined in the training exercises. But at these, *Laffey*'s gunners seemed to excel. For example, one day, Captain Joseph H. "Gus" Wellings, Commander Destroyer Division 120 in our squadron, led five destroyers, one of them the *Laffey*, out to shoot at target sleeves towed by aircraft. The plane would come in from the port side, then approach from the starboard. When it came *Laffey*'s turn, our gunners had a field day.

By that time, *Laffey*'s gunners had really worked out the rust and reached a pinnacle of prowess. We were at the rear of the column and the first time the plane came in, towing the sleeve, we riddled the target. Down it went, its cone shape no longer able to trap air and keep it aloft.

The pilot rigged a new sleeve and came back again, but again the sleeve never made it across the ship. Again and again the pilot went through the same routine, and again and again the results were the same. Not one sleeve got by our gunners.

It was training, an exercise, but I was proud of my men. This was a truly superb performance and Wellings let us know it. Coming from Gus Wellings, that meant something. He was a battle-wise naval officer. He'd been a U. S. naval observer aboard HMS *Hood* when she was sunk in the Atlantic by the German battleship *Bismarck*. And his own destroyer, the *Strong*, had been sunk at Kula Gulf in the Solomons on July 6, 1943. Wellings knew good shooting when he saw it.

Soon after, *Laffey*, her new black-and-white camouflage paint design making her look like a confused zebra, left Pearl Harbor. She steamed off toward Eniwetok Atoll in the Marshall Islands in company with other destroyers and the battleship *North Carolina*. Though en route we continued to have gunnery exercises—and get compliments for our performance—I knew that soon we would be shooting in earnest. The farther west we steamed, the closer we would get to skies filled with enemy planes intent on destroying us. Yet I felt confident. With gunners like those we had aboard, that was much less likely to happen. Perhaps we would take some hits. But the Japs were going to pay very dearly to score them.

Even before *Laffey* and the other destroyers of Freseman's squadron left Pearl Harbor, an intense debate had been taking place at the topmost levels of command. American forces had reached a fork in the road to victory with the capture of the Marianas in the Central Pacific and General MacArthur's advances up from Australia. MacArthur, wanting to fulfill his pledge to the people of the Philippines as quickly as possible, argued for an invasion of Mindanao, one of the southernmost of the Philippine Islands. But Admiral King and Admiral Nimitz, Central Pacific Commander in Chief, favored an assault on Formosa off the coast of China.

In both cases the objectives were the same—cutting off Japanese supplies from the Dutch East Indies. Japan had no oil of her own. Without that from the Indies, her war machine would grind to a halt once her storage supplies were exhausted. In addition, either the Philippines or Formosa—once they were secured—could be used as a staging area for the final assault on the Japanese home islands.

By the time *Laffey* was halfway to Eniwetok Atoll, this debate had been resolved in favor of the Philippine approach—but not in exactly the form in which it was first put forth by MacArthur. Instead of a series of shorter, island-hopping jumps culminating in the invasion of Mindanao, we were going to take one big jump and invade Leyte, several hundred miles to the north and east of Mindanao and beyond the range of most of our land-based aircraft.

It was a daring and dangerous move. Not only did the Japanese have strong forces on the island, and aircraft based on nearby islands, but the soil of Leyte itself wasn't very good for airstrips. It would take us time to build them; meanwhile, the troops ashore would have to depend on carrier planes for air support.

As a mere skipper of a destroyer at the time, I had no knowledge of any of this as we steamed westward. But on October 20, when Ted Runk—*Laffey*'s communications officer—came to me on the bridge, I began to find out. Runk's men had intercepted a series of messages, and the gist of them was that General MacArthur had returned to the Philippines. At that very moment the U. S. battleships *Mississippi*, *Maryland*, and *West Virginia*, supported and screened by destroyers, were pounding the east coast of Leyte from stations in Leyte Gulf.

They'd started without us, and I felt just the slightest touch of regret. But it didn't last long. Leyte was a key Japanese bastion of their defenses in the Philippines, and hitting it was like touching a raw nerve of the Japanese war machine. *Laffey* might still be a long way from the fighting, but the fighting was going to last quite a while. We'd have more than our share when we finally got there.

The enemy did react, violently and swiftly, to the invasion of the Philippines. Even before we crossed the International Date Line on October 26—which immediately became October 27, and was U. S. Navy Day—a massive force of Japanese ships had steamed toward ours in the Philippines. For the Japanese, this was an all-or-nothing gamble. They threw everything they had left at us in the hope of winning one final, crushing naval victory. And they put up a good fight.

One Japanese force steamed south from the home islands. This included 4 aircraft carriers with about 108 planes and 2 converted battleships, *Ise* and *Hyuga*, which could launch planes from abbreviated flight decks, but had no planes aboard. It was led by Vice Admiral Jisaburo Ozawa.

Though the Japanese had plenty of planes and a lot of good army pilots, they were short of trained naval aviators and were holding back those they had. Ozawa's carriers and battleship-carriers were intended as bait. They were supposed to lure American carriers away from Leyte.

With the bulk of American naval air power absent from the Leyte area, two other forces of Japanese warships, under overall command of Vice Admiral Takeo Kurita, were to execute a pincers movement on the American transports in Leyte Gulf. These Japanese forces had no planes or carriers, but their formations included a number of battleships, some heavy and light cruisers, and a strong screen of supporting destroyers. One force was to transit southern Philippine waters north of Mindanao, then pass through Surigao Strait between Mindanao and Leyte. There it would join another force coming down along the east coast of Samar.

It was a well-thought-out—if somewhat complicated—plan, but it didn't work. Halsey's fast carriers were lured north and shattered Ozawa's carrier group. But the Japanese southernmost thrust through Surigao never had a chance. Part of it was knocked to pieces by U. S. planes, but the bulk of it ran head on into Rear Admiral Jesse B. Oldendorf's battle line. Battleships *Mississippi* (BB 41), *Maryland* (BB 46), *West Virginia* (BB 48), *Tennessee* (BB 43), *California* (BB 44), and *Pennsylvania* (BB 38)—most victims of the Pearl Harbor attack—extracted terrible revenge. Hit from port and starboard by American destroyer and PT-boat torpedo attacks, the oncoming van of the Japanese force found its T crossed by Oldendorf's ships. That meant that every gun in every main battery turret of every American battleship could be brought to bear on the Japanese while they could only return fire with their forward turrets. The Japanese ships were pummeled unmercifully into junk.

The only Japanese thrust that had any success at all was the one that came through San Bernardino Strait. This Japanese force had been hit by American aircraft and had suffered heavy losses that included the battleship *Musashi*, a sister ship of the super-powerful *Yamato*. But, on October 25, as this still-powerful force steamed southeast along the east coast of Samar, it ran headlong into a force of American escort carriers (CVEs) and their destroyer and destroyer-escort screen.

These escort carriers were little more than merchant ships and tankers converted with a flight deck. Their job was to supply air cover for troops ashore. They were slow. The *White Plains* (CVE 66), for example, could only do about nineteen knots. They were never intended to challenge battleships, but challenge they did.

The American escort carriers were in three groups—Taffy 1, 2, and 3—and each had its own escort of destroyers and destroyer-escorts. Taffy 3—composed of six CVEs, three DDs, and four DEs—was commanded by Rear Admiral Clifton Sprague; and it was on this group that the Japanese first stumbled. Another Taffy, under Rear Admiral Felix Stump, was thirty miles to the south; and a third, commanded by Rear Admiral Thomas Sprague (no relation to Clifton Sprague), was seventy miles south.

The minute the Japs made contact with Taffy 3, Clifton Sprague sent out a call for help, and Stump's carriers launched planes to support him. Help also came from Thomas Sprague's ships, but because his carriers were under attack by Jap planes, those of Admiral Stump were the only ones which were able to launch and recover planes continuously during the battle. The Taffies stopped the Japs cold. Their destroyers made repeated torpedo attacks on Admiral Kurita's warships, covered the carriers with smoke screens. And the carriers themselves launched everything that would fly against the enemy.

Kurita thought he'd caught a group of large American fleet carriers, protected by cruisers and screened by a massive force of destroyers. His armor-piercing, large-caliber shells did not seem to be having much effect. (They were, of course, but what Kurita did not know was that these heavy shells were going right through the thin-skinned American ships.) American planes kept diving on his ships—many kept it up even after they ran out of bombs and ammunition. And the American "cruisers" kept shooting and scoring hits. (The "cruisers," of course, were destroyers.)

By about 8:15 A.M., Kurita had had enough. He broke off the action and reversed course to the north. He had sunk four American ships—the destroyers *Johnston* (DD 557) and *Hoel* (DD 533), destroyer-escort *Samuel B. Roberts* (DE 413), and the escort carrier *Gambier Bay* (CVE 73)—and damaged other American warships. But he had not accomplished his purpose. He never got to the transports off the beachhead. He never got a shot at Halsey's carriers. And, after he cut back through San Bernardino Strait, Halsey's planes found his ships and continued to make Kurita's life miserable.

After Kurita broke off the action and Japanese air attacks on the CVEs ceased, the men of the Taffies breathed a sigh of relief and a prayer of thanks. Praise for their gallantry began to pour in. Those men deserved it. The planes from those little carriers, their screening destroyers, and destroyer escorts, had taken the worst that the Japs could dish out and sent them home beaten. It had been David versus Goliath—and again, David had won.

These naval defeats in the Philippines were the swan song of Japanese naval power, but they did not bring an end to the war. Neither *Laffey* nor any of the other ships that were with her got orders to reverse course and head for home. The Japanese had taken some terrible beatings, but they were a long way from finished. If anything, the losses they suffered between the twenty-fourth and twenty-sixth of October, 1944, only made them fight harder. After the twenty-sixth, bit by bit and with ever-increasing tempo, their tactics became more desperate, their resolve more fanatical. For us, the worst was still ahead.

We stopped at Eniwetok only briefly, arriving on October 30 and departing the next morning for Ulithi in the Caroline Islands. For months Eniwetok Atoll had served as a major forward naval base in the Central Pacific, but as our forces had advanced, they had left it too far behind the areas in which we had to fight. As a result, on September 23, troops of the Army's 81st Division had been put ashore on the islands of Ulithi Atoll more than fifteen hundred miles to the west of Eniwetok. And by the time *Laffey* reached Ulithi in November 1944, its lagoon had already become a major anchorage for our fleet.

Ulithi was ideal for this purpose. Falalop Island, on the northeastern side of Dowarugui Channel, was big enough for an airstrip. Ascor, to the west, could hold a headquarters complex. And Sorlen was excellent for an advanced base hospital. There were even enough roomy islands for recreation areas, the main one being on the curiously named island of Mog Mog.

But what really made Ulithi Atoll such an ideal base was the size of its lagoon, the depth of its waters, and the barrier reef which surrounded them. The lagoon could—and later did—hold more than seven hundred naval ships from the largest carriers and battleships to the smallest auxiliary craft. And, because there were a limited number of channels through the reef, the anchorage was relatively safe.

I use the word relatively because the Japs never quit trying to get at our ships there. Some Japanese had been on the atoll before we occupied it. When they left, not long before our troops went ashore, they left us some little welcoming presents. They planted mines in various locations, and these damaged some of our ships. In subsequent months they tried torpedo attacks, bombing, and they probably would have tried naval bombardment if they had had any ships to spare and throw away. The bright, translucent waters of Ulithi's lagoon were safe, but until near the end of the war they were still a target for the enemy.

Laffey and the rest of Bill Freseman's destroyers arrived in Ulithi at 6:00 A.M. on November 5, but as part of the Third Fleet, I knew we would not stay anchored there for any length of time. The Army on Leyte was still having trouble getting aircraft landing strips in shape for its planes because constant rains had turned the soil into liquid mud. Yet the Japanese planes based on Luzon and elsewhere in the Philippines were able to operate without difficulty. The Army needed help, a lot more help than the battered and exhausted pilots of the escort carriers could give it, and that help was coming from Halsey's carriers. *Laffey* would be going out soon with a task group.

The afternoon of the fifth, I got my officers together in the wardroom. I had had both training and battle experience working with carriers, and I wanted to make sure they knew what to do. Aircraft carriers could not operate like other warships of the fleet. Their primary reason for existence is to act as a mobile airfield for their planes, and the needs of their aircraft dictate many of their maneuvers.

I explained that the fast carriers of the task group usually had a screen of destroyers and other warships surrounding them. Except under conditions of an enemy air attack, when the destroyers would close in to give extra antiaircraft fire support, this screen stayed at a considerable distance from the carriers to ward off enemy submarines.

"But keep an eye on the carriers every second," I emphasized. "Sometimes they have to maneuver independently, move out of formation to recover an aircraft in some emergency. The moment you see that fox flag [a red square, its points against the inner sides of a larger white square, meaning F for *flight operations*] be prepared to maneuver. And maneuver according to what that carrier does, not just its maneuvering signals. If the one we are screening turns out of formation, go ahead of her and make sure there's no sub waiting to launch a spread of torpedoes at her."

I came down hard on the idea of visual observation of carriers. I had seen a carrier once signal a turn to port, then change course to starboard. Another had impaled a destroyer on her bow. Destroyers with carriers had to be like foxhounds at a hunt—they had to stay out in front, cover the ground, and look for the fox (in this case a sub); but it was up to them to keep out of the way of the horses.

I ended with a few comments about antiaircraft gunnery. All planes approaching were to be tracked by the gun directors, and the crews were to stay on them as long as they remained in the guns' arc of fire. If an officer on OOD watch spotted something and it was obvious the gunnery officers hadn't, that officer was to alert them at once.

"Don't wait!" I said. "Don't assume anything! Act! Get orders to the director, quick! And if there's any argument later, tell 'em the skipper is the SOB who wants it done!"

I think I made my points. There were only a couple of questions after I'd finished, and they weren't about anything basic. We'd played for keeps off Normandy, but this was a much more complex ball game as far as *Laffey* was concerned. In a naval sense, we were now in the big leagues, and everyone in the wardroom knew it.

Laffey was part of Task Group 38.4. The fast carriers of the Pacific Fleet were designated Task Force 38; and the whole fleet was the Third Fleet when Admiral Halsey was in command. (They became, respectively, Task Force 58 and the Fifth Fleet when Admiral Raymond Spruance was in charge during other periods, but were the same group of ships.) Task Group 38.4 was one of four such groups which kept up unending daylight bombing and strafing attacks on the Japanese in the Philippines, and we were never idle for long.

On November 11 (Armistice Day, the day in 1918 that WW I ended), at about 5:00 P.M. our carriers were just recovering the planes from our final air strike of the day when our TBS squawked. The words, "Large bogey approaching from the west," were all that we needed. Hurriedly, we manned battle stations, increased our speed, and closed in on the carriers. They were what the bogeys would be after.

Every ship in the screening force was soon ready to repel air attack, and extra fighters were launched by the carriers to augment the Combat Air Patrol. The planes were vectored by radar out toward the oncoming Japs. Then we waited, the ships steaming on, but prepared at any moment to open fire and execute radical evasive maneuvers.

To say that all of us aboard the *Laffey* were just a little bit tense would be putting it mildly. Our men had been in combat and under fire, but the Japanese were not the Germans. By that time Jap air tactics had begun to show signs of unusual change. Japanese pilots sometimes seemed to ignore the conventional methods of delivering air attacks and, even if our CAPs got eighty percent of them and our guns knocked off fifteen percent more, the other five percent would ride their planes right in for a kill. We were no longer facing ordinary bombers. We were by then dealing with missiles guided by pilots intent on suicide.

Suddenly, we heard a strained voice on our TBS from one of our picket destroyers on station far out from the main body. "Three Jap planes diving at me . . . got one . . . out!" I never did learn what happened to the other two, because at that moment the sky over us was filled with others. Every gun in the task group opened up.

Within seconds *Laffey*'s hull began to reverberate with that mixture of sounds I had heard so often. Our 20's chattered, spitting out streams of lethal slugs. Our 40's thudded with a steady *whump, whump, whump,* punctuated by the booming cracks of our five-inchers. Rapidly the sky was filled with black puffs of smoke, deadly round polka dots of shrapnel which every so often turned a plane into a sheet of flame.

Those Jap planes that managed to get through our CAPs kept on coming, and it was quickly clear that some were bent on crashing into our ships. But our shooting was so good, our barrage of antiaircraft fire so concentrated, that even those enemy pilots failed to penetrate our formation. None of the Japs got through.

The raid ended almost as abruptly as it had begun—and with

the same kind of audio accompaniment. Our TBS blared again. Two parachutes had been sighted coming down about ten miles to the north, and the task group commander wanted the nearest destroyer to go after them.

That was us! That was the *Laffey*, and as I had done so often in the past, I called Al Henke for speed. Black puffs of smoke popped out of our funnels. Our bow wave began to increase. Shortly, we were slicing through the water at twenty-five, then more than thirty knots.

Those flyers were out there ahead of us. They were enemy pilots, but they needed our help. With all the planes that had gone down, there was bound to be blood, and blood usually attracted sharks.

Not long after, we sighted something off our starboard bow. It was a man; and carefully, I brought *Laffey* as close to him as I could without running him under. Bill Keyes, our chief boatswain's mate, threw him a heaving line (a cotton-fiber rope about three eighths of an inch in diameter). He grabbed it. And then we began to haul him in.

We got him no farther than the foot of the sea ladder. He hung there, making no attempt to climb. A seaman and our First Lieutenant Sam Humphries had to go down and hoist him up. But unlike many Japs who had refused rescue, this one wasn't bent on suicide. He did not pull a pistol and try to shoot Humphries. He was ready to give up, but he just couldn't climb. He had a bullet hole in his right hand and his lower arm was broken.

We searched the area for the second pilot but never found him. Either he was too badly wounded and his life jacket did not keep him afloat, or he just did not want to be captured. But either way, he must have gone under, taking his parachute with him.

Our prisoner was a naval aviator, and except for his wounds he looked healthy and in good shape. He was about five feet six, weighed about 150 pounds, and he wore a green cloth flying suit and had on a long, white silk scarf. His ID tag showed his name to be Yoshuio; whether he was a Kamikaze pilot or not, I just don't know.

One thing I was absolutely sure of, however. Yoshuio was very frightened, but he wanted to live. Perhaps he was a Kamikaze who had changed his mind about dying for the emperor. If so, I couldn't blame him. Yoshuio appeared to be only about sixteen years old.

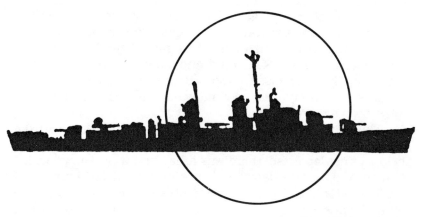

EIGHT

Our long jump to Leyte, well beyond the range of the Army's land-based fighter and tactical bomber support, had been a bold gamble; and by early November, we had won most of the throws. We had inflicted three crushing defeats on the Imperial Japanese Navy, defeats from which it could never recover. We had sunk thousands of tons of Japanese shipping, almost completely choking off their supplies of oil from the Dutch East Indies. We had destroyed hundreds of their planes and many of their airfields in the Philippines. And we had secured a firm foothold on Leyte itself.

Despite all of this, the Japanese were far from licked. They still had planes and pilots. They still had ships. And Lieutenant General Sasaku Suzuki's 35th Army on Leyte was continuing to make things very tough for our troops ashore. The liberation of Leyte was taking much too long.

Besides the weather, which continued to be terrible, the basic problem was the configuration of Leyte itself. The island is about one hundred miles long and averages between twenty and forty miles wide. The lower third of jungle-covered mountains held few Japanese in 1944 because it had little in it of military value and a lot of Filipino guerrillas held it. But north of this area, Leyte is divided down its middle by a long spine of mountains. This separates two valleylike areas—one in the east, one in the west—and it was these that contained most of the towns, roads, and developed areas that the Japanese had occupied early in the war.

General Kruger's troops had landed on the eastern shores of Leyte in October. By early November they had captured the eastern valley areas, advanced to the mid-island mountain spine, and had begun to fight their way across them. But Japanese resistance was bitter. Rain, mud, and impossible terrain complicated supply problems. And no matter how many victories our soldiers won, no matter how many Japanese they killed, there were always more.

The problem was similar to the one we had faced in the Solomons earlier in the war. At the southern end of the valley still held by the Japanese, there was a bay and a port town called Ormoc. And to it the Japanese kept running the 1944 version of the Tokyo Express. We hit these troop and supply convoys from other Japanese-held islands whenever we could find them, but many of them got through. And, as at Guadalcanal, the troops they put ashore enabled General Suzuki to beef up his defense lines.

It had taken us almost seven months of fighting in the Solomons to finally put a stop to the Tokyo Express. But at Guadalcanal we had essentially been on the defensive, fighting for time. At Leyte the situation was different. We had the Japs on the run in 1944, and we couldn't afford to slow up and let them get their breath. Both General MacArthur and Admiral Halsey agreed that something had to be done, and it had to be done soon. We had to get on with the war and hit the Japanese home islands before those crazy Kamikaze tactics caused us too many losses.

By November 12 *Laffey*'s fuel tanks needed to be refilled. We had been steaming constantly at high speeds with the carriers. Our fuel was getting low and, like any destroyer skipper, I was darn glad to get my ship alongside the oiler *Taluga*.

As the fuel lines were being rigged I had our prisoner, Yoshuio, brought up on deck. We had been ordered to transfer him to the *Taluga* by boatswain's chair—a seat suspended on a pulley block on a line secured to both ships which would be hauled over to the oiler by a second line. On Yoshuio's back, Frank Manson taped the information he'd gotten from the Japanese flyer during their conversations, as well as a chart we had recovered with him. The *Taluga* would transfer him to the carrier *Enterprise*, fueling opposite. She had combat intelligence officers. Good as Frank Manson was at asking questions and getting answers, those specialists could learn a lot more from the young fellow without his even realizing he was telling them anything.

158

Just as we got ready to launch our young prisoner on his chairborne journey, a CAP of Wildcat fighters flew over us. Yoshuio looked up and surprise spread across his face. I guess he'd been told the Americans had lost so many planes we were very short of them, and those Wildcats came as a shock.

I never did find out whether young Yoshuio was a member of the recently formed Japanese Special Attack Force. Certainly he hadn't acted like a Kamikaze pilot when we picked him up. Thus far our experience had been that a Kamikaze pilot wouldn't allow himself to be rescued. We had even heard that a few had actually fired pistols at American sailors trying to haul them aboard. Our prisoner had not and, to our way of thinking, if Yoshuio was a Kamikaze pilot he was one of the smart ones.

I say to our way of thinking because at that time in the war most Americans had a great deal of difficulty making sense of this new Japanese tactic. We could understand impulsive bravery, the kind of heroic self-sacrifice a man might make in the heat of battle. Nor was the concept of volunteering for an extremely dangerous mission beyond our ken. But for Americans, implicit in any such act was the idea that the man who took such a risk did so believing he had at least some chance of survival.

With the Kamikaze, no such idea seemed to govern his attitude. The men who piloted those diving planes seemed determined to commit deliberate, preplanned self-murder. How could any sane human being, no matter how patriotic, ride a burning fireball of a plane all the way in until it hit a ship?

I think the best way to show how little most of us in the Pacific in 1944 really understood the concept of the Kamikaze is to illustrate the point with this wry American joke of the time. It's the story about an instructor of Japanese Kamikaze pilots who had just finished lecturing his group on their duties. And, having told them how they would crash their planes into American ships, the instructor then asked if there were any questions.

There was a brief silence, then from the back of the room came a voice. "Just one, honorable leader. . . . Are you out of your honorable mind?"

That's exactly the kind of question a World War II American pilot would have been likely to ask a superior who insisted it was the pilot's duty to commit suicide. The American wouldn't have questioned a very dangerous mission, but suicide—that would have been nuts. However, in the case of the World War II Japanese Kamikaze pilot, what the American called suicide would have been seen by the Japanese as a sacred duty to his emperor.

The whole idea of Kamikaze, the Japanese Special Attack Force, had its roots in Japanese history and the Japanese belief that their emperor was a god, the soil of their homeland sacred. In 1281 an armada of Mongol ships, headed for a conquest of Japan, had been destroyed by a typhoon. The Japanese took this as a Divine Wind (which is what Kamikaze means), a wind sent by heaven to save a people who must be the anointed of heaven. This belief persisted down through the centuries.

Then, in 1944, when the war leaders of Japan became desperate for some means of stopping our advances, they conceived the idea of creating a human Divine Wind. With their fleet decimated, their armies reeling, and many of their best-trained airmen gone, the Japanese decided their only hope lay in using what we would call suicide units. Young volunteers would be indoctrinated with the idea that they had a sacred duty to become human guidance systems. Even a half-trained man could guide a plane, a winged bomb, a torpedo, or a speedboat full of explosives to a target if he were willing to commit suicide to get it there. And if enough Japanese did that, Japan might still win the war.

When the Divine Wind first appeared during attacks in the Philippines, there were only a few of them; I, like many others, just assumed they were a handful of crazies. But bit by bit, with each succeeding action, their numbers grew. By the time I received orders to take *Laffey* back to Ulithi on November 21, it had slowly begun to dawn on me that we were up against something entirely new. We had taken the measure of the skilled Japanese professionals and knew how to handle them. But these Kamikaze fellows were fanatics, religious fanatics, and that was beginning to worry me.

As I have already mentioned, Ulithi Atoll wasn't exactly a tropical paradise, nor was it entirely safe either. In fact, about thirty-six hours before we arrived, one of those Japanese *kaiten* (man-guided) torpedoes hit the oiler *Mississinewa* in the lagoon. Loaded to the gunwales, mostly with gasoline, she took more than four dozen men with her when she blew up.

With the arrival of the *Laffey* and the rest of the task force, that lagoon had taken on the appearance of a nautical version of a huge shopping center parking lot at rush hour. The place was mobbed with ships of almost every type. Most of the ships were in individual berths with ample room between them so they could swing at anchor without danger of collisions, and many destroyers were given berths close to destroyer tenders. Others, however

—and *Laffey* was one—were moored close alongside tenders either for repairs or to facilitate taking aboard much-needed supplies.

By late afternoon, November 22, the *Laffey* was tied up inboard of another destroyer, between it and our tender, and almost all of the crew was allowed to go ashore. Recreational facilities at Ulithi were then very limited—though they were improved later on. But even the prospects of standing on dry land, drinking a few cans of 3.2 beer, were inviting. We had been at sea a long time.

As a general rule, U. S. Navy regulations—unlike those of the British Royal Navy—forbade keeping alcoholic beverages aboard its ships. But regulations or not, in World War II there were some situations where rules had to be honored in breach. Ulithi was a long distance from anywhere, had only been a naval anchorage a short time, and couldn't yet supply the entire fleet with beverages. Each ship had to carry its own.

The beer aboard *Laffey* was stored in a locked storeroom in the bow of the ship, and when our officers went ashore about 4:00 P.M., they were allowed to take some of it with them. Since warm beer is worse than no beer at all, they had stored the cases on ice in a couple of empty aluminum 40-mm ammunition cans to make sure it arrived ashore chilled. It was a typical naval improvisation, one in use throughout the fleet.

Cold beer at Ulithi, and in the Pacific in general, was more precious than gold. As those officers carried the two ammunition cans full of chilled beer across the deck of the destroyer tied up outboard of us to the waiting motorboat, their thirst must have got the better of them. They were fine, disciplined men; yet the sight of another unguarded, unwatched ammunition can right next to the destroyer's gangway was just too much. Down into the motorboat it went, along with the other two, and off that boat sped to the beach before anyone knew what was happening.

However, I am proud to say that those officers of mine came to their senses and returned that aluminum can unemptied. They had been sorely tempted, and had given way to temptation; but once ashore, they had realized the error of their ways. Cold beer was great, but who wanted 40-mm ammunition?

I was able to get ashore myself several times while we were still anchored at Ulithi, but I'm afraid most of my recreation was shop talk with other officers. Just about everyone I spoke to was concerned about the shift in Japanese tactics and how to counter them. By then every skipper in Freseman's squadron

161

knew we were slated to become part of the Seventh Fleet and would probably be involved in another landing on Leyte. No longer would our ships be protected by the thick CAP's of Wildcat fighters from the Fast Carrier Task Groups. Our air cover would be provided by fewer planes from some little escort carriers, or P-38's of the Army Air Force.

They would do the best they could. But there wouldn't be enough of them to beat off all the suicidal Kamikaze attacks. Nor were the Army planes, based on half-finished airstrips miles from the beachhead, going to be able to stay with us constantly. The Army pilots were good, but if they didn't happen to be around when the Japs came in, *Laffey* would have to depend on her own resources to survive. She would have to steam and shoot as she had never done before.

I had every confidence in my ship and my men. I knew we could do it, but we were going to be up against some difficult odds. The Kamikazes were going to keep coming at us. Unless we could shoot them out of the skies or managed to dodge them, we'd be in trouble. The proof of this was overwhelming. Even big carriers like the *Intrepid, Essex, Cabot,* and *Hancock,* protected by heavy CAPs of fighters, had been hit by the enemy during their most recent operations. But I knew that we weren't going to have all those fighters.

I don't want to give the impression that I, and other officers at Ulithi, spent all our time going around with long faces, worrying and exchanging grim comments on what was ahead. I heard more than my share of stories that made light of what was ahead and what we'd been through. For example, I was aboard the destroyer tender *Piedmont* one day when an old friend, Vince Mullins, introduced me to a chaplain of one of the carriers, and that padre was full of stories.

The best concerned a formation of Japanese planes—a very big formation—that approached his carrier one afternoon. The chaplain was summoned to the bridge by the skipper. He apparently felt the ship needed a little extra help.

"Padre," the skipper said, "if you have any influence with that Man Upstairs, *use it now.*" He was pointing at the heavens, and it was a direct order.

The chaplain told me that on his way back to his station, he'd said some prayers. And at that very moment, the dark clouds of a rain squall suddenly appeared in the sky between the carrier and the Japs. They turned tail without attacking and headed for home.

162

Chuckling, the chaplain said the skipper had called him to the bridge the next day and thanked him for his help in a way that suggested he was convinced it was all the padre's doing. The chaplain allowed as how he wasn't so sure of that, but in a way, maybe it was a miracle. Word had gotten around the ship, and a lot more men had suddenly become much more interested in religion. His prestige aboard had risen sky-high.

Bill Freseman's ships departed Ulithi on November 27. We still weren't absolutely sure of our ultimate destination. We knew we were headed for San Pedro Bay, off the northeast shores of Leyte, but that would be only a stopping-off point. By ultimate destination I mean the beachhead I was certain we were bound for. We were going to be part of Vice Admiral Thomas C. Kinkaid's Seventh Fleet. Admiral Kinkaid's Seventh Fleet was not composed of big carriers and fast battleships. In the Philippines, it was the fleet that delivered the troops to the beaches, covered their advances with gunfire from our older battleships, and kept the troops ashore supplied.

To me, all of this meant only one thing. The *Laffey* wasn't going to be steaming at high speeds with lots of air cover and plenty of room to maneuver. No matter what her assignment, she'd be in relatively confined and crowded waters. The Japanese would have an accurate fix on where those waters were, and whatever planes the Japanese still had that could fly and carry bombs would head right for them.

Under the circumstances, I was more than happy that Bill Freseman ordered his destroyers to conduct gunnery exercises on the trip to San Pedro. Our gunners were good, but they'd been away from action for a while. They had probably lost some of their edge. A little practice would chip off the rust, put them on their toes, make them a hundred percent once again—and that's exactly what we were going to need.

By the twenty-ninth the *Laffey* was anchored in San Pedro Bay, her fuel tanks topped off from an oiler, ready to go. But even before I was told where we were going, the high proportion of amphibious ships anchored in the area confirmed my belief about what we were headed for. There were APDs (destroyers like the old *Ward*, converted to high-speed transports), LSM's (landing ship, medium), LST's (landing ship, tank), and LCI's (landing craft, infantry). There were also some AM's (minesweepers), and of course our destroyers. Had it not been for swarms of outrigger canoelike native bancas, whose occupants were trying to trade with the *Laffey*'s sailors, it could have been Plymouth or a dozen other British harbors all over again. We were headed for another D day.

Matt Darnell, our ship's doctor, had some business aboard one of our neighbors. The hospital ship *Hope* was in port, and Matt had Boat Coxswain Ramon Pressburger run him over to her in our motorboat. Providing such nautical taxi service was one of Pressburger's jobs, but had the rest of our men known what else the motorboat would be carrying that night, many would have volunteered to replace him.

When Matt Darnell boarded the *Hope*, he told Pressburger to stand by, that he'd be about thirty minutes. When the *Hope*'s officer of the deck heard that, he asked Pressburger to run in to the beach on a brief errand. Pressburger was cooperative and the beach was only five minutes away. He'd have plenty of time, and his reply was "Yes, sir."

On arrival at the pier, there were complications. There was a four-foot drop from the pier to the boat. There wasn't a lot of light, and the doctors that Pressburger was picking up were a little concerned about jumping.

So was Pressburger. He didn't want to be blamed if one of the doctors went in the drink or broke a leg, or maybe his neck. And, since he was husky and powerful, in addition to being good-natured, he offered to catch each under the arms as they landed.

Everything went according to plan until the last doctor jumped. As before, Pressburger reached up, groping for a good grip. But the jumper landed unsteadily, and to keep the doctor from falling, Pressburger hugged. Then he froze. The two remained locked together in this emergency embrace for some moments. Not until a decidedly unmanly voice said, "Thank you very much . . . now will you *please* put me down!" did Pressburger let go.

As Pressburger later put it to his shipmates, he'd been paralyzed with embarrassment, all shook up, when he'd realized the doctor was really a very pretty Navy nurse. He even claimed he blushed and wanted to crawl into the boat's bilges after it was over. Whether his shipmates believed him or not, I can't say.

At 11:30 A.M., December 6, *Laffey* hoisted her anchor and steamed south as part of Rear Admiral A. D. Struble's Ormoc assault force. Its mission was to put ashore the Army's 77th Division on two beaches about five miles down the coast from Ormoc, and to support the Army drive north to seal off the end of the Ormoc Valley. By the first week of December 1944, we had pushed the Japanese on Leyte into a large pocket in the northwestern section of the island. As long as the Japanese held Ormoc, they could keep feeding in supplies and reinforcements.

Despite the weather and the terrain—and the fierce Japanese resistance—the Army had done very well. In the north, our 1st Cavalry and the 24th Infantry Divisions were approaching the top of Ormoc Valley, and in the center the 96th Infantry and 11th Airborne were pressing across the mountains toward it. But in the south, the 7th Infantry Division (with elements of the 96th) was finding the going increasingly tough. The 7th had executed a wide sweep on our left flank, had reached the shores of the Campotes Sea on the western side of Leyte, and had pushed its way up the coastal road to a town called Baybay. Though it was now only twenty-five miles south of Ormoc, its advance had been slowed to a crawl.

The reason for this was obvious. The Japanese had plugged the coastal road area between the sea and the mountains with a constant stream of reinforcements, and there was no way the 7th could outflank their positions. No way, that is, unless it got help; and on December 7, 1944—three years to the day after Pearl Harbor—it got that help.

At 6:30 A.M. *Laffey* and other destroyers were on station off the beaches on the eastern side of Ormoc Bay. The two landing areas we had selected were just south of a small place called Desposito, and, like the actual landing areas at Utah, they weren't as strongly held as other parts of the coastline. Most of the Japanese troops were to the south fighting the oncoming 7th Division, and our landing was going to come in behind them.

Not that it was peaches and cream, a walkover. The Japs had fortified some caves overlooking the beaches. Even as our rocket-firing LSMs launched their barrages and we got ready to begin our bombardment, they opened up on us with some three-inch guns. *Wooosh . . . boom, wooosh . . . boom*, the battery's shells came in, raising waterspouts, straddling the *Laffey*—much too close for comfort.

That was all we needed. "Knock hell out of 'em," Harry Burns yelled when he'd fed the target information to our mounts. But our gunners didn't need any urging, especially one named Ed Zebro. Ed was captain of our Mount 51, our forward pair of five-inchers. Not only did Ed know that three-inch battery could do us a lot of damage, but Ed had a brother in the Army aboard one of the landing ships.

Harry Burns hardly had time to finish what he was saying over the telephone before every five-incher we had that would bear opened up. *Wham-Wham, Wham-Wham, Wham-Wham,* brought some very satisfying blossoms of orange fire and clouds of smoke ashore, right on target. In the words of Harry Burns, we sure did knock hell out of 'em. I suspect those Japanese gunners regretted their impudence. Very soon, no more Japanese battery, and—by the time we finished about twenty minutes of bombardment—not many Japanese soldiers either. Ed Zebro and all our other gunners did their work well. Ed's brother and the rest of our troops went ashore in a rush and rolled over the opposition.

Up to that point, everything had moved as smoothly as a destroyer steaming at full speed in a dead calm. But not very long after that, the calm changed into a storm. Out of the skies and down on all of us roared the Divine Wind. Though it didn't keep the Army from taking Ormoc and joining up with the 7th Division, it sure played hell with our ships.

At that particular point, the destroyers with Admiral Struble's force were positioned to bring maximum firepower on the Japanese ashore. Some 2,200-ton destroyers like the *Laffey,* with 6 five-inch guns, were near the eastern coast of Ormoc Bay or well up into the northern part of the bay. Other destroyers and some minesweepers, most of which mounted fewer or smaller main battery guns, were to the west and southwest of us, acting as an antisubmarine screen, performing radar picket duty and fighter-director functions as the assault took place. But, though this was a sound and logical disposition of ships, it led to some problems, when the Divine Wind finally began to blow. When the Japanese planes came, they came in from a northwesterly direction, and this meant that many of our older, less heavily gunned ships took the brunt of their initial attack.

Our Combat Air Patrol fighters, P-38 Lockheed Lightnings of the Fifth Army Air Force, tried very hard to stop them. But, as I've noted before, weather and soil conditions on Leyte had delayed the building of many airstrips, and there just weren't enough P-38's available. Those overworked pilots, flying from muddy, hastily improvised fields, did their best—and their best was awe-inspiring to many of our sailors. Yet in the end, there were just too many Japs for them to handle alone, and between 9:40 and 9:50 A.M. some of the enemy planes broke through.

At that time *Laffey* was up at the northern end of Ormoc Bay in very confined waters. Like the rest of the ships in that area, we didn't have much room to maneuver. All we could do was steam in circles in our assigned support area, man our guns, and wait until the Japs came closer. We had to stay put until we got orders to do otherwise; it was one of the most difficult things I have ever had to do.

I think the *Mahan* (DD 364) was one of the first to get it. Commissioned in 1935—1,450 tons—she at least mounted 5 five-inch guns and could steam at more than thirty knots. (She was a sister ship of *Flusser* and *Lamson*, which were also present.) But she was on a fighter-director station, way out by herself some fifteen miles to the west-southwest of us. And though we couldn't see her because the mountains of Calunangan Point were in the way, we knew she was getting it. We could see the planes in the sky, the puffs of smoke, the tracers, and hear the radio chatter.

The P-38's followed the Jap planes right in, and splashed some of them, but three of those suicide pilots got through. They came in low, apparently carrying bombs which were not released, and all three of the Japs plowed into her. There were a series of explosions in the forward part of the ship. There was burning gasoline everywhere.

Her skipper, Commander E. G. Campbell, poured on the power, tried to get his flaming, exploding ship closer to some of our other ships on the antisub picket line to get some help in fighting the fires. But the *Mahan* had taken a death blow. The fires and explosions had knocked out fire mains used to flood the ship's ammunition magazines; the high speed was fanning and spreading the flames, and she was finished. The *Walke*, which had been sent to her aid, along with the *Lamson*, could do little for her except take off her survivors. Later, on Admiral Struble's orders, *Walke* sank her with a torpedo and gunfire.

The *Mahan* was a relatively modern ship, with enough firepower to fight back with some chance of winning. But it was the poor old *Ward* that really got to me. The *Ward* (APD 16) had been commissioned in 1918. She'd been one of our 1,090-ton flush-deck, 4-stack destroyers (DD 139) before she'd been converted to a fast transport; and she had fired the first shot against the Japanese on December 7, 1941.

On that infamous day, the *Ward* had been skippered by Commander Bill Outerbridge. He had gone on to become captain of the *O'Brien*, one of the 2,200-tonners of Freseman's squadron. Outerbridge was bringing the *Ward* back to Pearl Harbor that morning, after some exercises, and on her way in the destroyer made contact with a submarine. Since there were no American submarines in that area, the old destroyer had manned battle stations and eliminated one of the three midget submarines the Japanese had sent against our fleet.

That had been a glorious day for the *Ward,* but now—three years later—she was up against odds that were just too great. She was only four or five miles to the west of us, and we could see her twisting and turning, trying to avoid the oncoming Japs. All she had to fight back with were a few 3-inch guns, some fifty-caliber (half-inch) machine guns, and some 20-mm mounts they'd welded to her ancient hull. They just weren't enough. Her skipper, Lieutenant R. E. Farwell, and his men were doing their best, but *Ward* was overmatched. There were too many Japs.

I gripped the edge of the bridge railing, hating everything I saw, wishing like the devil that our guns could reach those Kamikazes. I knew it wouldn't be long before they got to us too, but at least we had heavy stuff to fight back with—*Ward* didn't. She was a very old lady, and it made me mad as hell to have to stand by and watch a bunch of toughs pummel her.

The fight didn't last very long. One of those Kamikazes roared in on her, locked her in his sights, and went into her port side just about where her boilers were situated. The entire central area of the ship erupted in flames and an explosion. Three or four minutes later she stopped moving, dead in the water. But the old lady wasn't going to give up. Half the ship was in flames. There was a towering cloud of black smoke coming out of her. But her gunners kept shooting until ordered to stop and help with the fires.

The *Ward* was hit about 9:54 A.M. For almost twenty minutes her men struggled to control the fires, but by 10:15 A.M. they knew they'd lost their fight. They were ordered to abandon ship and Bill Outerbridge with the *O'Brien* stood by to pick them up.

There wasn't any question of taking her in tow and trying to salvage her. By the time all of her men got off her, the *Ward* was a mass of burning, twisted, exploding metal. Outerbridge was ordered to sink what remained of his former command with gunfire.

For Outerbridge and his gunnery officer, Lieutenant Paul Smith, it must have been an extremely painful duty. Smith, on loan to the *O'Brien* from the *Laffey,* had once served in a destroyer exactly like the *Ward.* Though this was an advantage because he knew exactly where to have his gunners place their shells to get it over with quickly, I suspect he felt like he was putting an old friend out of her misery. Warships may be nothing

168

but steel, guns, and machinery, but those who serve in them get attached to them.

I know. I had never forgotten the *Aaron Ward*, and by then, that's exactly the way I felt about the *Laffey*. I still do.

By the time both the *Ward* and the *Mahan* had disappeared forever, we had landed the 77th Division and all its equipment on the beaches, and the Army had a firm foothold and was advancing. Our end run had worked. The Army still had some hard fighting ahead, but as far as Leyte was concerned, the Japanese had lost the ball game. There would be no more Tokyo Express carrying reinforcements to Ormoc. What remained of General Suzuki's 35th Army would soon be sliced up into smaller and smaller pockets of resistance, then eliminated completely.

The Japanese certainly knew this, but even after they had lost their battle to break up our landings, they kept on coming. They were like hornets whose nest we had invaded. They were determined to make us pay for it. Time and again, some slashed through our CAP of P-38's and dived on our ships.

One of them tried it with the *Laffey* about 12:30 P.M. on D day. But that pilot quickly discovered we weren't an easy mark like the poor old *Ward*. Harry Burns had our five-inchers on him even before he got into range. For a while he continued to come on, but then the sky around him began to erupt with explosions, our tracers began to lick out toward him, and he apparently thought better of it. If he was a Kamikaze, he was one of the smart ones, because he reversed his course and roared off as fast as he could.

Not long after, Admiral Struble ordered the task group to withdraw. *Laffey* and the other ships had done what we had come to Ormoc Bay to do, and it was time to get the empty transports away. Resupply convoys would be run to Ormoc Bay the next day. But for the moment, keeping the empty transports and most of the destroyers there served no useful purpose.

The Japanese planes continued to follow us. At 12:37 P.M. one of them came within range of *Laffey*'s guns and we opened fire. It made a bombing run on a nearby destroyer, but the antiaircraft fire was too much for the pilot. He missed and went into the water.

Still the Japs kept at it. Destroyer escort *Liddle* was hit, and the destroyer *Lamson* came under attack by an especially tricky Jap pilot. Bobbing, weaving from side to side like a prizefighter, he swooped in low with machine guns blazing and rammed the destroyer midships. There were explosions in *Lamson*'s firerooms, gasoline fires. And she soon looked as if she were finished.

But *Lamson* wasn't. Commander T. R. Vogeley, skipper of *Flusser* (the flagship of Captain William Cole, commander of Destroyer Squadron Five) stood by *Lamson* until she could be taken in tow. *Lamson* survived but *Flusser* had to exhaust every bit of her ammunition to save her.

Other ships had some very close calls, the *Barton* being among them. Skippered by Commander E. B. Dexter, the *Barton* was Bill Freseman's flagship and, about 3:26 P.M., a Jap Judy dived for her. At that particular time she was leading our formation in restricted waters, unable to do much maneuvering.

Somehow, Ed Dexter managed it. Using what little space he had, Ed put *Barton* into a series of rapid course changes better suited to a PT boat than a destroyer. But in this case, they did the trick. And Bill Freseman, never a man who was lavish with praise, let Dexter know exactly how he felt about them. In that somewhat laconic manner of his, Freseman told Dexter he liked the way he maneuvered his ship.

Coming from Bill Freseman, those few words were the equivalent of an hour of fulsome praise from a toastmaster at an awards banquet.

The Kamikazes kept after us until about 6:40 P.M. when it was too dark for them to see us. I breathed a sigh of relief as everything outside the pilothouse disappeared in the blackness. It had been a long, tough day.

Sonarman Charlie Bell, who was my bridge telephone talker (the man who relayed my messages), apparently agreed. He pulled off his earphones after passing on my order to stand down from battle stations and start feeding the crew supper, ran his hand over his forehead, and shook his head.

"Captain," he said, "I've never seen anything like what we've had today in my life, except in a war movie. I hope we don't have to go through that again."

I certainly agreed with Charlie's sentiments, and I told him so. In all my months in combat in the war, I'd never seen anything like it either. But by then I'd become fairly certain that what happened at Ormoc Bay was just part of a growing pattern of Japanese frenzy. We were pushing them back, and the harder we pushed from now on, the more desperate they'd become. Soon every plane they sent against us would probably be a Kamikaze.

But there wasn't any point in my mentioning any of this to Charlie Bell right then. I didn't want the ship's grapevine spreading it around that "the old man's worried about Kami-

170

kazes." That wouldn't help morale any, and besides, I wasn't really worried. I was concerned, just like every skipper in the fleet was concerned, but that was part of my job. There was a great deal of difference between thinking about a challenge and the best ways to meet it, and letting it get to you. I didn't want my men confusing the two.

My feelings about the ferocity of the Japanese attacks at Ormoc Bay, and what they meant, were confirmed by two conversations I had not long after we returned to San Pedro Bay.

After *Laffey* had refueled, I went over to the *Barton* to talk to Bill Freseman. When I entered his cabin I found Bill sitting on a bunk, his back against a bulkhead, legs crossed, his fingers intertwined behind his head as if he had been meditating on some great problem. This pose wasn't very characteristic for Bill, and it was obvious he had something on his mind. After he waved me to a chair on the opposite side of the cabin, I quickly discovered he'd been thinking about the same things I had.

"Julie," he said, "they damn near got us yesterday. If it hadn't been for Ed Dexter [skipper of the *Barton*], they would have finished us. Julie, these Japs are crazy, absolutely crazy."

Bill leaned forward, elbows resting on his knees, his long, handsome face very serious. Like all of us, he had a tan by then, but in the light of the cabin he looked almost pale.

As we talked, I began to realize that the events of the last day or so had done something to Bill Freseman. He was still the same man he'd always been, but there was a difference. Bill had always been direct, outspoken; some even called him arrogant. He'd never minced words about our work, about how it should be done, and what the results would be if we did it as ordered. But at that moment, sitting in his cabin facing him, I suddenly was aware that Bill Freseman had come face to face with something he just couldn't understand.

I don't know exactly how to define the change that had come over Bill except to say that his tone was reflective, thoughtful. He didn't make statements. He asked questions—or maybe I should say, he raised them. Bill knew I couldn't answer them any more than he could, but it was obvious he wanted to discuss them. That whole Kamikaze business was something for which he had no frame of reference.

Not long after I returned to the *Laffey*, Al Henke told me that one of his men, a machinist's mate named Arthur Hogan, had said something to him about Ormoc. And when I found out what it was, I asked Henke to send Hogan to me. Hogan, it seemed, had been at Pearl Harbor on December 7 in a net tender that opened and closed the submarine-barrier net.

Hogan's comments about the Kamikazes at Ormoc—comments that I knew must be circulating through the ship among our crew—were even more disturbing. Pearl Harbor had been a holocaust of attacking Japs, bombs, torpedoes, fires, and explosions. But according to Hogan, Ormoc had been much worse. Not in losses of ships and men, but the way the Japanese had executed their attacks. Like Bill Freseman, Art Hogan just couldn't make any sense out of them, and he was certain there would be more attacks like those.

If Hogan had left it at that, I would right then have begun to have serious concerns about morale. But Hogan didn't. No sooner had he finished this than he started talking about Cherbourg. In his opinion, we were the best, and he added that he felt *Laffey* was a lucky ship.

This put a different face on it. If that was what Hogan was spreading around among his shipmates, there wouldn't be a morale problem. Far from it. Praise from a man like Hogan, who had seen a lot of battle, would just give our men more self-confidence.

As for *Laffey* being lucky, I wasn't so sure. I've always been one who believed that what a crew *could* do, and what they *did* do, was what made a ship lucky. And I told Hogan I'd do everything I could to make it so. But I didn't go too far or press the point. Sailors, since the beginning of time, have believed in luck. I did not quarrel with success.

We didn't stay put very long. By December 10 we were well at sea again as part of the screen for the cruisers *Boise* and *Phoenix*. At that particular time, a Sims-class destroyer—the Bath Iron Works-built *Hughes* (DD 410), skippered by Commander E. B. Rittenhouse—was on picket duty down near Surigao Strait and Dinagat Island. Soon we were going to be involved with her. The *Hughes*, out by herself with no air cover, was to be one of a number of ships hit that day in a renewed assault by the Kamikazes.

Not all of the Japanese pilots who fixed the 1,570-ton *Hughes* in their sights were suicidal. Some of the planes just roared in, dropped bombs, and pulled out of their dives. But one didn't. Instead of yanking his bomb release, the pilot homed his plane right in on the ship and kept on coming.

The *Hughes* had good gunners. They fired away at the Jap

with everything they had. They scored hits and continued to do so until their guns wouldn't bear. But they couldn't deflect his aim.

The Kamikaze headed right for the destroyer's midships section and blew up on impact. The force of the explosion made *Hughes* stagger, heeling her to starboard. Boiler and engine rooms were ripped open, chunks of metal tossed in the air. Men— their clothes on fire, or badly scalded from escaping live steam— were thrown around like so many sacks of flour. And flaming gasoline from the plane poured into her compartments, turning her midsection into a mass of fire.

Other Japanese planes flew over the *Hughes*, watching the pall of heavy black smoke climb up from her. But even as they concluded she was finished, damage-control parties were beginning to win their battle to save her. Bit by flaming, bitter bit, they beat back the fires. They rescued the injured, and by the time American fighters arrived on the scene, the fires were under control.

But *Hughes* had been terribly punished. Eighteen men had been killed, more than twenty badly injured, and the ship was a derelict. She couldn't steam by herself because her propulsion plant was a mass of hot wreckage, and her skipper called for help.

By then the weather was beginning to worsen, the wind was growing stronger, and it had started to rain. Since the tug *Quapaw* couldn't reach the *Hughes* for some hours, *Laffey* was ordered to go to her aid. We were to stand by her, take off her casualties, and take her in tow until the slower-moving fleet tug could arrive.

The minute I received word over the TBS, I pulled *Laffey* out of her position in the screen. I rang up Al Henke for all the power he could give me. And I then set a course in the direction of Dinagat Island.

The *Hughes* had already started to drift in that direction. Unless we reached her in time I knew that an enemy far more powerful than the Japanese, one every sailor has battled since men first went to sea, might claim her. The weather was worsening, the sky growing darker, and the seas were getting steeper with every passing minute. Like a square-rigged sailing ship dismasted in a storm, the *Hughes* was adrift and helpless. She was being carried toward the coastline. If we did not get to her soon she'd be driven ashore, battered to pieces by wind-whipped breakers, and many of her surviving crew might be drowned.

As Henke poured it on and *Laffey*'s fantail dug in with each increase in our speed, I alerted Matt Darnell—the ship's doctor—to get ready to receive casualties. I also had Sam Humphries ready some of our damage-control parties. These would be sent aboard the *Hughes* to assist her men and help them get their wounded over to the *Laffey*.

By the time we picked up the *Hughes* on our radar it was dark as a coal mine. Except for the radar, we couldn't see anything as we approached the wounded destroyer, until I had Jerry Sheets turn on a couple of our floodlights. Under usual conditions, we didn't use these in a battle zone at sea because they would make us a perfect target for a lurking enemy sub. But these conditions weren't usual. After racing to her rescue, I didn't want us to ram the *Hughes*, and we had to have light to safely transfer her casualties and rig a tow.

Slowly, carefully, I brought *Laffey* alongside the *Hughes*. Then, as the beams of our floodlights cut through the torrents of rain, all of us were stunned. The entire middle section of the *Hughes* was little more than a blackened hole filled with twisted metal.

But it wasn't just the damage. Most of us had seen battle damage before. It was what had caused that damage that gave us all pause for thought. That mess, all those casualties, had been caused by one lone suicide-bent Kamikaze.

There were more shocks to come. Many of the *Hughes*'s casualties had suffered horrible wounds and burns. Getting them across safely to the *Laffey* in the driving rain and the rough seas, and down to our sick bay, was an experience our sailors could never forget. They had seen ships blown up; they had seen men in the water. But all of this had been at a distance. Close up it was an entirely different story.

Some of our men were frightened. Some were ill. But the general effect of the experience was to make most of them just plain mad. One, who fainted twice, kept coming back, swearing quietly until the job was done. No longer were the Japs just someone we were fighting. Now they were the enemy, to be hated.

As the wounded were brought across from the *Hughes*, we also sent men and salvage equipment over to her. There wasn't any time to waste. The wind and sea were getting worse all the time, and both ships were being swept toward the shores of Dinagat. By the time we had finished, got a towline rigged, and our screws were pushing us upwind, we didn't have very much room to spare.

174

Laffey fought her way through the seas, dragging *Hughes* behind for about two hours. Then the tug *Quapaw* arrived and took over. As far as I was concerned, it wasn't too soon. She was much better equipped and suited to the job than we were. *Laffey* had power, but she wasn't a draft horse. She was a racehorse with power for speed.

By midafternoon of December 11, we had seen *Hughes* and *Quapaw* safely to port, off-loaded the wounded, topped off our fuel tanks, and had dropped our hook in San Pedro Harbor. But there wasn't much rest for the *Laffey*'s weary sailors. The very next day we became part of a large task group whose principal mission was to put troops ashore on Mindoro.

The island of Mindoro actually had few important military installations. Occupied by the Japanese in February 1942, they had subsequently paid it little heed because it had no major population centers, and seemed strategically unimportant. And even in December 1944, after we had taken Leyte, the Japanese still felt the same way. They had only about 1,500 troops on the island.

But for the Americans Mindoro, which was about 150 miles west of the southern tip of Luzon, was to be a key stepping-stone in the liberation of the Philippine Islands. November and December comprised the typhoon season on the eastern islands of the Philippine archipelago. But those in the west, like Mindoro, were bone dry. Our rain-soaked, waterlogged airstrips on Leyte could not supply air cover for an invasion of Luzon, and we needed to establish others that could.

The key to our success with Mindoro was an elaborate scheme of deception. When *Laffey* and the task group left San Pedro, we steamed south down through Leyte Gulf to give Japanese reconnaissance planes the impression we were headed elsewhere. But as soon as darkness fell, we turned west through the Surigao Strait and into the Mindanao Sea.

That too was part of the ruse. Ahead of Admiral Struble's transports, and the covering screen which included the *Laffey*, was another force of ships that included escort carriers, battleships, cruisers, and destroyers. Commanded by Rear Admiral Theodore D. Ruddock, Jr., its primary mission was to give us air cover. But as soon as it passed the southern tip of Negros at the western entrance of the Mindanao Sea, it was to make a feint toward Palawan.

That long, narrow island, about two hundred miles southwest of Mindoro, was an important Japanese base. The object of the feint was to deceive the enemy into thinking that's where we were headed, and it worked. Not until the transports and landing ships and their screen reached the southern tip of Negros, sometime later, did the Japanese finally react.

It was then about 3:00 P.M., December 13, and *Laffey* was steaming on station about five hundred yards to port of the light (six-inch gun) cruiser *Nashville*. The *Nashville* was Admiral Arthur Struble's flagship and, in addition to this officer and his staff, she had Brigadier General William C. Dunckel and his staff aboard. Though that Japanese pilot couldn't have known it, he had picked the prime target in our whole formation.

At that particular time our radar, and that aboard the cruiser, was masked by the land behind which the Val approached. That Jap was a clever fellow. Flying low, following the terrain until he reached the shoreline, he was over and passed us before our gunners could get him in their sights. Then he went into a crash dive and rammed the *Nashville* on her port side just below the bridge. He was after the bridge itself, but he was close enough. Both Struble's and Dunckel's chiefs of staff and many other officers on both staffs were killed outright, and burning gasoline enveloped that part of the ship.

The next Jap wasn't quite so successful. He came in just a few minutes after as I was trying to get *Laffey* alongside the cruiser to help her men fight the fires. Even as some of the *Nashville*'s ammunition was exploding and zipping over us, the *Laffey*'s gunners opened up on the Jap. He kept on coming, but only for a few seconds, and then he apparently decided he did not want to be a Kamikaze. As our bursts and tracers closed in on him, he went into a quick, banking turn, reversed his course, and hightailed it out of there.

Exploding ammunition made it impossible for us to get close to the *Nashville*, but even without our help her men finally got her fires under control. Despite the heroic work of her damage-control parties, *Nashville*'s time as the flagship for the operation was over. Her radars were out. Her communications gear was inoperable. And Struble and his staff had to transfer to the destroyer *Dashiell*. The battered cruiser was sent back to San Pedro in company with a destroyer, one more example for us all of what a single Kamikaze could do.

We spent December 14 steaming north toward Mindoro. We had a fighter-director unit on board, and our assignment was to direct Combat Air Patrols over the formation. Six of the seven

CAPs came from our CVEs, the escort carriers of Admiral Ruddock's force, and one from the Army. But as usual, it was raining on Leyte, Army airstrips were bogged down in mud, and not until late in the afternoon could the P-38's give us any air cover.

We needed Mindoro and we needed it badly. On December 15 we took it.

Again, as far as the air was concerned, it was more of the same. The bombardment and landing went off smoothly. Resistance by Japanese defenders was light, and by noon we had captured San Jose, the only major town on the island. But in the air, the Japs kept right on coming.

Some of these enemy pilots duplicated the tactics of that single Kamikaze which had hit *Nashville.* They approached at low levels, then swung in over the land and disappeared. But minutes later they'd reappear, hugging the terrain, and pour on the speed in an attack.

Our CAPs did a great job of breaking up these attacks. But neither they nor antiaircraft fire could get all of the Japs. Some crashed through, going into LSTs and other ships near the beach.

Obviously, the best tactic was to get our landing craft away as fast as possible, and that's what we did. As soon as they had disgorged their cargo or unloaded their vehicles and troops, they were pulled off the beaches and formed into a group for a return trip to Leyte. And, since *Laffey* had a fighter-director team aboard for controlling CAPs, we were assigned to shepherd many of them.

About two and a half hours after the initial landings, *Laffey* left Mindoro with thirty-one LCTs (landing craft, tank) and twelve LSMs (landing ship medium). The landing-craft commander, in APD (fast transport) 63, the *Lloyd,* and destroyers *Hopewell* and *Pringle,* were with us. And overhead three groups of carrier-based fighters flew CAP.

We had no trouble at all that day. Apparently the Japs weren't interested in empty ships, or maybe they just didn't have enough planes. But the next day, December 16, at 4:42 P.M., a bogey appeared on our radar screen. He was twenty-five miles away, too far for our guns, but we vectored some CAP fighters in on him. Six minutes later over voice radio we heard, "Tallyho." Within four minutes the Japanese had one less plane and pilot.

At sunset the same day, after the CAPs had left us, sharp-eyed range-finder operator Bob Ray spotted another bogey to the north. But this Jap was cagey. He stayed well out of range until it got dark, and then he made his move. We'd been watching and we were ready. With radar feeding the gunners range, altitude, and bearing, our five-inchers opened up. That was enough; and one more potential Kamikaze pilot suddenly decided he wasn't. He never came near the formation again.

After that, no more Japanese bothered us. Most, I suspect, were too busy trying to get our CVEs (escort carriers) and other, larger ships. But, whatever the reason, *Laffey* and her charges reached San Pedro safely a few days later without even having to fire a gun. Once we had arrived at San Pedro, taken on fuel, and then anchored, we finally got a brief breather.

Christmas Day, 1944, *Laffey* spent quietly at anchor. We put away a sumptuous turkey dinner and, at least for a time, there was a feeling aboard of peace on earth, good will toward men. There was no winter landscape, no snow softly dropping from the skies. But there weren't any Japs, either!

Early on the morning of December 26, with the memory of that Christmas dinner still fresh in our minds, we were ordered to get underway and run over alongside the heavy cruiser *Louisville*. So too was the *Walke*. As I have noted before, destroyers in World War II were maids of all work, but on this occasion our job was a little unusual. At sea larger ships often refueled destroyers, but at San Pedro we were to do the reverse and top off Rear Admiral Ted Chandler's flagship.

When we pulled away from *Louisville*, we had just about enough fuel in our tanks to reach the stationary oiler. But it made a lot more sense for us to steam to that oiler than for the cruiser to do it. We could move faster, get it over with more quickly, and meanwhile, the *Louisville* would be ready to go if her big six-inch guns were needed.

As it turned out, they were, and very soon. *Laffey* got to the stationary oiler at dusk, and no sooner had we finished filling our tanks than in came a flash radio report. The Japs were out. A Japanese naval task force was headed for the beaches of Mindoro. *Louisville*, with her fuel tanks full, had been able to sail to meet the enemy in company with the light cruisers *Phoenix*, *Boise*, and *Minneapolis*, and some destroyers, without any delay. But the radio report was more than a report. We were ordered to chase after them.

It was going to be a long night!

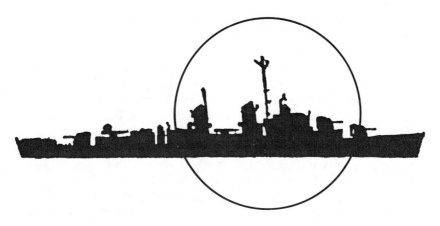

NINE

As soon as we finished refueling, we lost no time in getting underway. We slipped out into the growing darkness, then, when we were clear of other shipping, I increased our speed to twenty-five knots. Rear Admiral T. E. Chandler's task group had sailed hours before. If we were going to catch up by morning, we'd have to run at that speed all night.

By December 26, 1944, even the most optimistic of the Japanese leaders knew they were going to lose the Philippines. But, as so often in the past, Army leaders in Tokyo refused to recognize reality. There was very little left of the Imperial Navy, but they insisted that reinforcements ought to be sent to Mindoro—and that the Navy should transport them there.

In this instance, however, the Japanese Army had to compromise. General Yamashita—commander of the Japanese troops in the Philippines—opposed the idea of a counter-landing. Also there just wasn't any transport shipping available. Too much of it had been sunk by our planes. As a result, a naval force under Rear Admiral Masanori Kimura was sent from Camranh Bay (in what is now called Vietnam) to execute a hit-and-run bombardment of American beachheads on Mindoro.

Admiral Kimura's task group sailed on December 24 to execute one of the last sorties by Japanese surface ships in World War II. It consisted of the flagship, heavy cruiser *Ashigara* (ten 8-inch guns); light cruiser *Oyodo* (six 6.1-inch guns); and seven destroyers. It was a considerable force, but one without any naval air cover. Yet Kimura had one piece of luck: The weather was bad.

The heavy, low clouds covered him until the midafternoon of December 26, when he was less than two hundred miles from the San Jose beachhead.

Then, between 3:00 and 4:00 that afternoon, a Navy-manned Liberator (a four-engined Army B-24 heavy bomber converted for long-range patrol work to a Navy PB4-Y1) was returning from a mission when its crew spotted Kimura's ships. Radio messages were sent at once, giving their course, speed, and numbers. But exact identification of ship types was impossible. The original reports received on Mindoro and at fleet headquarters, San Pedro, indicated the *Ashigara* was the battleship *Yamato*.

At that time we had no strong naval forces either at Mindoro nor in adjacent waters. The Army was well established ashore, had its own air cover, and needed no naval gunfire to support its operations. Except for resupply convoy escorts, our warships had been withdrawn for work elsewhere or for badly needed repairs and overhauls. It was a calculated risk, but with Mindoro virtually secured and the assault on Luzon imminent, it was one we felt it necessary to take.

The sea on the night of the twenty-sixth was reasonably moderate. Our radars were operating at peak efficiency and we had good charts. But as far as I was concerned, there wasn't any question about where I'd be spending the night. The skipper of a destroyer that is racing through relatively confined waters doesn't go to bed. Watches would be changed, crewmen relieved, but my place was on that bridge or in the pilothouse.

Not long after *Laffey* was settled on her course, I went out onto the starboard wing of the open bridge railing, squinting my eyes, trying to see what might lie ahead out there beyond our forward mounts and the bow, I suddenly yawned and realized just how tired I was. I had had some rest on Christmas Day, but the twenty-sixth had begun early, been busy, and was far from over. I ran my hand over my forehead and eyes, then sighed. It was going to be a long, tough night.

With that, I turned to go back inside the pilothouse and saw Steward Roscoe Wilson standing at the door. "Cuppa coffee, Captain?" he asked in a concerned voice. Yes, I sure did want a cup of coffee, and I thanked him.

Wilson waited until I was finished, took back the cup, then asked me where we were going. When I told him, he looked at me and nodded understandingly. He knew I was tired.

"Don't worry, Captain," he said, " I'll keep you awake if I have to bring you a cup of this stuff every fifteen minutes all night long."

I laughed, thanked him again, and said it wouldn't be necessary. But somehow I don't think Roscoe Wilson believed me. Every once in a while during that long night I'd look around and catch a glimpse of him at the entrance to the pilothouse. He always had another cup of coffee in his hand.

We caught up with Admiral Chandler about 6:00 the next morning, took our assigned station in his formation, and pressed on toward Mindoro. Racing against time, we finally arrived off Mindoro in the early afternoon. But we were too late. Kimura had stolen a jump on us. About 10:00 the night before, he'd made his move, bombarding San Jose for about half an hour. Then he had moved on, thrown a few more shells at the island farther down the coast, and disappeared.

Kimura's effort had been a far cry from the kinds of operations the Japs had conducted in the Solomons, and it certainly showed how little strength and resolve the Imperial Navy had left. Kimura had been very cautious, had done little damage, and our planes and PT boats had driven him off. These had managed to sink the destroyer *Kiyoshimo* and damage some other ships. If he had stayed around, we would have finished him—and Kimura knew it. Admiral Kimura's sortie was the last real Tokyo Express of the war, a feeble shadow of what it had once been. For three years we had been trying to derail it. Now, we finally had.

December 26, 1944, was the date on which the Imperial Japanese Navy made its final, organized, conventional effort to stop our advances in the Pacific. From that date on, their naval, air, and many of their ground forces were to devote their main energies to Kamikaze tactics. (The final sortie of the Japanese Navy in April 1945, led by the battleship *Yamato*, was to be a one-way suicide run.)

Laffey was back at anchor in San Pedro December 30, fueled and ready for the next advance. She had plenty of company. By then the place was filled with ships and more kept arriving each hour. Yet for some reason, the Japs ignored this concentration of ships until near midnight on December 31, and even then only one plane appeared. That was puzzling, but it was also infuriating. I think the little devils did it on purpose. That one bogey, which may have been all they had available, forced us to celebrate New Year's Eve at our guns.

After lunch on New Year's Day I decided to go up to the bridge and have another look around the harbor. But when I got there, I found others ahead of me. Four of our chief petty officers were standing by the rail talking. Chief Radioman Jack Najork, Chief Machinist's Mate Carl Dubbs, Chief Water Tender Roy Woods, and Chief Commissary Steward Clarence McIntyre were the kind of men who were considered the backbone of the Navy. Yet it was obvious to me they had come up to the bridge to talk privately about something that was bothering them. Their discussion was heated, but they weren't angry. They seemed worried

After we had chatted briefly, Woods turned to me and let me in on it. "Captain," he said, "at lunch we started talking about those damn Jap flyers. Carl and Jack here claim they are volunteers. Do you think so, Captain? Why, they'd have to be nuts!"

At the time, I just did not know the answer to that one, and I said so. But I quickly added that I believed the Japs must be hurting badly. They had to be desperate men driven by fear of defeat. Sure, some of those pilots probably were volunteers, I told them. But not all. A lot of those pilots, I added, were certainly being forced into what they were doing by a group of fanatics. And, once we had polished those off, the rest would probably change their minds.

I was not being entirely candid, because by then I had a lot of doubts myself. But I was the skipper of the *Laffey* and these were some of her best senior enlisted men. I knew they weren't cowed or frightened, but they certainly were concerned. If I had let them go off believing that every Jap plane was piloted by a volunteer bent on destroying himself, the ship's morale might have been affected. That would have hurt our performance, something we could not have afforded. To win and survive, we had to have full confidence in ourselves and one-hundred-percent efficiency.

Laffey left San Pedro for the last time on January 2, 1945, one of 164 ships under the command of Vice Admiral J. B. Oldendorf which were bound for the beaches of Lingayen Gulf. Lingayen is on the western side of Luzon, not quite a hundred miles northwest of Manila, and its beaches were among the best on Luzon for an amphibious landing. South of them, a wide valley runs between two rugged, jungle-covered mountain ranges all the way down to Manila Bay. It was a classic invasion route, and those beaches and that valley had been used by the Japanese early in the war.

The enemy knew we would have to use Lingayen Gulf as a major landing area at some point in the Luzon campaign, and we knew that they knew we would use it. We believed they would not only fortify the beaches,but there was little chance of surprise because they could spot us long before we arrived. In addition, and in spite of our attacks on their airfields, they had lots of operational planes on the island. Not only would we need plenty of air cover, but General MacArthur insisted his troops would have to have massive naval gunfire support when they landed.

What we did not know at the time our task group sailed was that General Yamashita had never deceived himself into believing he could hold on to the beaches of Lingayen Gulf, nor had he any intention of holding Manila. Luzon is a large island full of rugged terrain. In 1945 its population was actively hostile to the Japanese. Yamashita had a considerable army, but knowing he could expect no reinforcements, he adopted tactics far different from those the Japanese had used earlier in the war.

Yamashita devised a clever plan for the defense of Luzon. Unlike some high Japanese Army officers, this general fully understood the meaning of sea power and the best way to counter it. In his view, Luzon might be held—and our advance toward Tokyo itself delayed for months—if our Navy was crippled. And that wasn't a job for his foot soldiers. He planned to commit just enough troops to Lingayen's beaches to delay us while his Kamikazes went to work on our ships.

Bill Freseman's Squadron Sixty (*Laffey, Walke, O'Brien, Allen M. Sumner, Moale, Ingraham, Lowry,* and flagship *Barton*) sailed as part of the protective screen for the heavy bombardment ships. With us were the battleships *California* 1(BB 44), *West Virginia* (BB 48), *Pennsylvania* (BB 38), and *New Mexico* (BB 40); plus heavy cruisers *Louisville* (CA 28), *Minneapolis* (CA 36), HMAS *Australia,* and HMAS *Shropshire.* But our formation also included six escort carriers (CVEs), some fast transports (APDs) and just about every type of ship imaginable, with the exception of large fleet carriers and fast battleships. These last were in the Fast Carrier Task Groups of the Third (later Fifth) Fleet.

It was a huge formation, and once we had passed through Surigao Strait and headed west toward the Sulu Sea, it was strung out over miles of open water. From *Laffey's* position I could observe only a fraction of the ships that were with us. Fore and aft, they stretched well beyond the horizon—a huge assembly the Japanese surely could not fail to spot.

In spite of this, there were no attacks on any ships in our part of the formation for almost thirty-six hours. I guess the Japanese were holding back, waiting until we got closer. But on the evening of January 3 we were apparently close enough. Suddenly a single Jap appeared out of nowhere and made straight for the Australian cruiser *Shropshire.*

The sky soon began to blossom with puffs of smoke, the tracers weaving a pattern among them, but the Jap kept on. Then, his aim spoiled by the antiaircraft fire, his mission suddenly terminated. He missed the cruiser completely and ended up with an explosive splash in the sea.

Although this lone plane was not followed by others for almost twenty-four hours, his appearance struck an ominous note. It meant that we had been spotted, no question about it. We had more than three hundred miles of steaming still ahead of us. And some of that would have to be done less than one hundred miles from Jap air bases on Luzon.

I guess the best way to describe our situation is to compare it to one often used in movies about the settling of the American West. *Laffey* was an outrider, a guard for a wagon train that was just about to enter a pass held by hostile Indians. We knew those Indians were waiting for us up there ahead, that we'd have to run their gauntlet, and there was no way for us to turn back. No one doubted that the wagon train would make it—it always did. But some of the wagons and the settlers wouldn't, and that's what was on everyone's mind. Once we got through the pass we had a job to do and enough of us had to get through to make sure that job was done.

The next attack came at 5:16 P.M. on January 4. At that moment our TBS was busy reporting to all nearby ships that there was a Jap plane well into a dive over the van of our formation. Somehow, this clever Kamikaze had sneaked into a position just aft of one of our Combat Air Patrols. And before he could be stopped, he went for the escort carrier *Lunga Point* (CVE 94). Yet clever as that Jap was at deception, his aim wasn't so good. *Lunga Point* went into a series of radical maneuvers and the Japanese emperor lost one more plane and pilot in the drink.

That was a good beginning, but unfortunately this soon changed. Four minutes later, as our TBS crackled with orders for a series of fast turns and course reversals, another Jap arrived. His aim was much better. He went into a roaring power dive straight toward the 7,800-ton escort carrier *Ommaney Bay* (CVE 79). She tried to avoid him, but she couldn't. The Jap plane

184

bounced off her island superstructure, hit her flight deck, and the bombs kept going. They blew up deep inside the ship.

Captain H. L. Young and his men did what they could, but damage, fires, and subsequent explosions made their job impossible. With her fire mains knocked out, flames turning her plates white-hot, and her ammunition exploding, the ship finally had to be abandoned at about 8:00 P.M. As soon as her survivors were clear, Commander Jacob Bullen—whose destroyer, *Burns* (DD 588), rescued many of *Ommaney Bay*'s crew—was ordered to torpedo the carrier.

Ommaney Bay went down in the Sulu Sea about fifty miles south of Mindoro Strait. During the night we steamed on through that strait without further incident. But on January 5, when we reached the South China Sea west of Luzon, there were no more free rides. From airfields like Clark, Nielson, and Nicholas on Luzon, Jap planes began to take off for a short flight to our formation.

Since the war, I have heard people say that many Kamikaze pilots were inexperienced flyers who knew little about navigation. Perhaps that was true, but in this case it didn't matter. All those Japanese zealots had to do was fly west to find us, and an awful lot of them did.

January 5, 1945, was much like the first day of a duck-hunting season—turned upside down. Sure, we had hundreds of "hunters" standing at their guns pouring fusillades into the sky, but those "ducks" weren't ducks—they were hawks. Before the day was over, a number of our ships felt their talons.

For *Laffey*, the season opened about 2:30 A.M. Our radar picked up a bogey, began tracking him, and we went to battle stations. But this hawk wasn't overanxious. He wanted to play with us for a while. He closed in, then turned away, then he closed in again. He kept it up for almost an hour before he finally made his move.

The *O'Brien* was nearby, and when the range finally closed down to five miles and steadied, both of us opened up. Of course we couldn't see him because he was only a spot on our radar screen, but we kept firing. Then, at two miles, he suddenly disappeared from our radar screen.

At dawn, *O'Brien* blinked us a message by signal lamp. One of our "hunters" had found the mark. A shell had clipped that hawk. He'd lost control and gone into the water just ahead of the *O'Brien*'s bow.

Other ships in our formation did not make out quite so well.

At 5:49 P.M. the destroyer escort *Stafford* (DE 411) had a hole torn in her side by a Kamikaze. It knocked out her power, flooded her firerooms, and she had to be taken in tow. The Aussie cruiser *Australia* took a bad hit midships about the same time. And the escort carrier *Manila Bay* (CVE 61) was forced to take aboard an unwanted aircraft. It was a Jap Zeke, and it came in nose down, directly into her flight deck.

The Australian destroyer *Arunta* was also attacked. But she was too agile. The Kamikaze missed. The cruiser *Louisville* was not quite so lucky. At more than nine thousand tons and six hundred feet long, the heavy cruiser didn't have the agility of the Aussie destroyer. A Kamikaze came at her, bow on, from a position that masked many of her antiaircraft guns.

Louisville maintained her course. Even had she been able to make a fast turn to port or starboard, this would have done little good and perhaps would have done more harm. By turning, she would have given the Jap a bigger target to aim for. The Kamikaze went into her number two (second forward eight-inch gun) turret. Although this was heavily armored, the Jap plane exploded in a fireball, scattering flaming gasoline everywhere. More than fifty of the ship's men were wounded, and among them was her skipper, Captain R. L. Hicks.

If January 5 was bad, it was only a foretaste of what was to come on the sixth. In the early hours of that morning we had reached the entrance of Lingayen Gulf and split up into groups, each with a particular assignment, and prelanding operations had begun. For *Laffey*, that meant steaming along as part of the screen of heavy bombardment ships which were going to blast a way for our troops. But for some destroyers of Bill Freseman's squadron, that meant moving right in near the beaches to support Commander W. R. "Rosy" Loud's minesweepers. *Barton*, with Freseman aboard; *Walke*; and two destroyers from other squadrons got the job of taking care of any Jap artillery that might open fire on Loud's ships.

None did. Intelligence estimates had indicated that the Japs had a lot of heavy guns sited along the beaches at the southern end of Lingayen Gulf. We had assumed that the Japanese would defend those beaches to the last, just as they had on islands like Tarawa. But, in a scene reminiscent of the early hours off Normandy, not one gun ashore opened up on the minesweepers.

It seemed impossible to me that we caught the Japs napping. Yet there were Loud's minesweepers out there ahead of us, paravanes streaming, groping for the three chains of mine fields that the Japs had supposedly moored off the beaches, and the enemy wasn't bothering them at all. Nor, as it grew lighter, did this situation change. It was puzzling. Surely the enemy had spotted us!

Then, as time passed, we began to get what I thought might be the answer to this puzzle. Commander Loud's ships reported that there didn't seem to be any actual belts of mines, only a few floaters. No wonder the Japanese didn't open up on Loud. His minesweepers were no threat to enemy defenses. The Japanese were being cagey, holding their fire so as not to give away their gun positions to our destroyers. They were apparently waiting until our bombardment was over. It was the landing craft that they wanted.

At that time neither I nor anyone else, from our commanding officers on down, could have guessed what Yamashita planned to do. Up to that point in the war, the Japanese had always been consistent in their defensive tactics. On Guam, Saipan, and countless other islands in the Pacific, they had fortified the beaches, emplaced heavy guns, and done their damnedest to stop us at the water's edge. At that time, conventional military wisdom had it that the moment to strike an invasion force and defeat it was when that force was approaching the beaches in landing craft. And, though it had never worked any better for the Japs in the Pacific than it had for the Germans in Europe, there appeared to be no viable alternative. Surely, I thought, there had to be gun emplacements ahead of Loud's minesweepers. But their crews were just biding their time.

For most of that morning, it also appeared as if Japanese aerial defense forces were doing the same. For hours, the only planes overhead were those of our own CAPs, our attack bombers, or planes which were supposed to help spot the fall of shot from the guns of our bombardment group. But suddenly, late in the morning, all this changed. The first ten Kamikazes showed up.

Our CAP got half of them and drove the others off, but it was just the beginning. Now, the worst kinds of things began to happen, things that would etch January 6, 1945, in the memory of thousands as one of the worst days of the Pacific war. At noon, the old battleship *New Mexico*, (BB 40) commissioned in 1917, was lobbing some of her fourteen-inch shells shoreward, when one of the Japanese planes broke through and went straight for her. *Laffey*, and the other destroyers of her screen, did their best to help this grand old matron's gunners knock down the aircraft.

But he kept on coming. We hit him and hit him again. His plane turned into a fireball of a comet; but he kept coming.

The plane ripped into the port navigation bridge of the *New Mexico* and exploded in a shower of flaming gasoline and flying metal. The bridge wing—unlike other areas of the battleship, which were protected with heavy armor plate—was only shielded by thin metal. It was torn apart, and the casualties were heavy. Her skipper, Captain Robert W. Fleming; British Royal Marine General Herbert Lumsden; his aide, Sub Lieutenant Brian Morton; and *Time* magazine correspondent William Chickering; along with more than two dozen sailors, were killed. Rear Admiral G. L. Weyler, in charge of the bombardment group, and Admiral Sir Bruce Fraser, who was to lead a Royal Navy Fast Carrier Task Group in the Pacific, escaped death by inches.

Laffey stayed with the *New Mexico* and saw her clear of nearby ships even as another Kamikaze came in. But both of us were ready for this one. He was splashed.

Though *Laffey* was ready to render any assistance the battleship might need, *New Mexico* didn't require any. She was elderly but she was tough. Under direction of Commander John Warren, her crew soon had the fires out. She was back in the fight, lobbing fourteen-inch shells toward the shore very soon after.

This was just the beginning; but as time went on, I began to think that maybe the Japanese had some kind of special grudge against Destroyer Squadron Sixty. At 12:02 P.M., one of their planes rammed into *Allen M. Sumner* (DD 629). More than a dozen men were killed; part of her superstructure was wrecked, and one of her torpedo mounts was battered into scrap. At 12:26 P.M., the *Lowry* (DD 770) was damaged when a Kamikaze just missed and blew up in the water alongside her. Then, at 12:41 P.M. *Laffey*'s longtime squadronmate, the *Walke*, really got it— and I lost a friend.

Four of those devils right in a row went after the *Walke* (DD 723). Her gunners were good. They knocked down one, knocked down another, but a third got through. He ripped deep into her bridge and pilothouse—a favorite target of Kamikazes— and wrecked the port side completely. His gas tanks burst open on impact and the gas ignited.

The *Walke*'s skipper, Commander George P. Davis, was turned into a living torch, and was horribly burned before his men managed to put out the flames. But Davis, despite his condition, refused to leave the bridge. He stayed at his station until his executive officer, Lieutenant John Burns, managed to make his way to the bridge and take over the job of controlling the ship and fighting the fires. And then, even as Davis was carried below, a fourth Kamikaze came in.

Thanks to Davis, *Walke*'s gunners were ready for that one. They hit him and he went straight into the water.

Commander Davis's heroic refusal to leave his bridge may well have cost him his life. He died soon after, but he was not forgotten. He was awarded the Medal of Honor posthumously, and a room in Bancroft Hall—a huge dormitory for midshipmen at Annapolis—bears his name.

Davis was a superb officer, the kind of man who should have had the best of chances to survive in the stress of battle. But in the heat of action, fate can sometimes be fickle. Who survives and who does not can depend on accidental circumstance.

The case of John Burns, another fine officer, illustrates this perfectly. Burns, the *Walke*'s executive officer, could have been killed by that same Kamikaze. In fact, he would have, had he not been a smoker.

Just before that obsessed Jap rammed his plane into the *Walke*, Burns was at his station in charge of the CIC, one deck below the bridge. The ship's radar operators were tracking the Kamikaze as he came streaking in, and Burns told everyone when the range dropped to one thousand yards that they were to hit the deck. There was a mad scramble in the crowded room to find some free deck space, but Burns—wanting to make sure everyone was down—remained standing for a moment, cigarette in his mouth. Then, for some reason Burns was never able to explain, the cigarette slipped from his lips.

What followed, Burns later told me, was a sequence of events that film critics would have rejected as pure and impossible fantasy in a Hollywood war film. Reflexively, Burns stooped down and reached for his cigarette. He was groping for it in the half darkness among the men pressed close to the deck just as the plane rammed into the ship.

At that moment, a bomb from the Jap plane—fortunately a dud—tore through one side of CIC, sailed over Burns, and exited through the other bulkhead. It missed Burns completely and came to rest in another room. Smoking may be dangerous to health, but in this instance it proved to be very healthy for John Burns. It saved his life—and he had witnesses to prove it.

About 2:30 P.M. the fourth ship of Bill Freseman's squadron was hit. The *O'Brien*, together with the *Barton*, was then working with a group of Loud's minesweepers when two planes with meatball (red circle) insignias suddenly appeared over them and began to dive. *Barton* avoided one. But the other caught *O'Brien* squarely on her fantail. It tore open some of her plates, flooding several compartments. Although she could still steam, she had to be withdrawn; and Freseman's flagship, *Barton*, had to carry on alone.

In addition to the ships of Squadron Sixty and others I have mentioned, there were more victims of Kamikaze tactics that same day. The light cruiser *Columbia* (CL 56) sustained serious damage aft on her port side near one of her six-inch gun turrets. She lost power, and magazines had to be flooded. The minesweeper *Long* (DMS 12), a converted destroyer, was hit by two planes and sunk. The *Southard* (DMS 10) had a fireroom ripped open. And the battleship *California* (BB 44) had her after fire-control director smashed and burning gasoline spread across her decks.

Two ships of Vice Admiral Oldendorf's shore bombardment groups which had been hit on the fifth, were battered again on January 6. The HMAS *Australia*, whose three smokestacks and high freeboard (height from her waterline to her main deck) made the Japs think she was a troop transport, took a second hit. (She was crashed by four Kamikazes during the Lingayen operation.) And the *Louisville* (CA 28), flagship of Rear Admiral Theodore E. Chandler, whose skipper had been badly burned in an earlier attack, got another bath of blazing gasoline.

The *Louisville* was attacked by several Kamikazes about 5:30 P.M. Two Japs were knocked down at once with the help of the cruiser *Portland* (CA 33); a third was torn apart by 20-mm slugs less than 100 yards from his intended target. But while this fight was taking place, another Jap had sneaked in from starboard. Before *Louisville*'s gunners could get on him, he hit the ship like a pile driver.

Again, the hit was forward; and again, flames leapt high up toward the ship's bridge. A bomb exploded in an open gun tub, vaporizing the gun and crew. Another bomb ripped through the skipper's sea cabin. Instantly, the whole starboard area of the bridge was engulfed in a roaring gasoline fire.

What happened next was one more example of the kind of courage shown by men like Davis of the *Walke* and Captain Hicks of the *Louisville* on previous occasions. Admiral Chandler was horribly burned over most of his body, but he insisted on joining his men manning hoses to fight the fires. He would not accept medical attention until it was his turn.

But no first aid, or even blood plasma, could save Admiral Chandler's life. He had inhaled some of the searing heat of the burning gasoline and he died not long after in the ship's sick bay. He was a third-generation Navy man, a hero who insisted to the end that no price was too great to pay for his country's final victory.

Following that pounding on January 6, Admiral Oldendorf realized we needed more air support, and he contacted Admiral Kinkaid. Although it had been planned that our Fast Carrier Task Groups were to be sent on a strike against Formosa while the Lingayen operation was in progress, Kinkaid agreed that too many Kamikazes were getting through to our ships. Instead of hitting Formosa, the planes of the task groups were sent to batter Japanese airfields on Luzon, and on the seventh the situation was eased considerably.

Early that morning the *Laffey*, what remained of Destroyer Squadron Sixty, and the other ships of the bombardment group were right back on station off the beaches of Lingayen. We moved in slowly in two columns to take up those stations in areas that had been cleared by the minesweepers. But this time, few Japanese planes appeared in the sky overhead. The aircraft from our Fast Carrier Task Groups had done their work well. There were some harassing attacks and the minesweeper, *Palmer* (DMS 5)—a converted destroyer which had originally been commissioned DD 161 in 1918—was hit by a Kamikaze. But compared to the day before, January 7 was relatively quiet.

Lingayen Gulf is about twenty to twenty-five miles wide and approximately thirty to forty miles long. Its shores form a deep U, the bottom of that U being somewhat flattened, and it was at targets on and behind the beaches at the base of the gulf where our fire was concentrated. Both visual and radar ranging were difficult, especially in the western areas over near the town of Lingayen where the ground was low and swampy. Had it not been for the Japanese we could have had some navigation problems. But the day before, some Jap shipping had been spotted and sunk. The *Laffey* was able to use the hulks and their masts as radar beacons to plot our positions.

We began firing about 10:30 A.M., much of our shooting in the form of area-covering barrages, or at specific spots where we believed the Japanese had constructed gun emplacements. Even with aircraft spotting for us, the only specific targets we could positively identify were things like an airstrip the Japanese had built close to the shore just in front of Lingayen village. The airstrip was right behind Orange and Green beaches, the westernmost of those on which our troops would land, and it was given a thorough pounding.

Then, in the early afternoon the bombardment ships moved their barrage farther inland in a creeping advance so that our UDTs (underwater demoliton teams) could begin work. Such frogmen had been used in Normandy to clear paths through mined obstacles set between high and low tidelines by the Germans. We had expected the Japanese to have similar obstacles at Lingayen, but they didn't. A very few mines were found, but no obstructions, and the only opposition the frogmen encountered was some scattered machine-gun and rifle fire. This was dealt with firmly and quickly by some five-inch shells. The UDT frogmen returned safely with all the beach and surf information our troops would need when they landed.

January 8 was pretty much like the seventh, though a few Kamikaze and conventional aircraft attacks were made on our ships in the Gulf. But except for a third and fourth hit on the gallant Aussie cruiser, *Australia,* none of these did much damage. The Japanese, their air strength greatly depleted by our carrier air strikes on their fields on Luzon, had other fish to fry on the eighth. They concentrated most of their efforts on our approaching attack transports, loaded with troops and equipment, which were then nearing a rendezvous at Lingayen Gulf with Oldendorf's bombardment ships.

Like Oldendorf's ships, both Task Force 78 under Vice Admiral D. E. Barbey, and Task Force 79 under Vice Admiral T. S. Wilkinson, had had to run the gauntlet of Japanese Kamikaze attacks. Ships had been hit. There had been casualties. But, until about the seventh, it was our bombardment ships in Lingayen Gulf that had attracted the most attention. *Laffey* and the other ships of Admiral Oldendorf's bombardment group had been sent out to pound enemy beach defenses to rubble. But what we actually did was to act as a lightning rod, drawing many of the Kamikazes to us.

This had not been part of our plan, or at least part of the Navy's plan. Whether it was part of General MacArthur's strategy, I just don't know. After the war I heard that one of the American officers commanding Filipino guerrillas on Luzon had sent a preinvasion report to MacArthur's headquarters which indicated there were few Japanese defenses at Lingayen. That report turned out to be essentially correct. General Yamashita put less than two dozen large-caliber artillery pieces in position at Lingayen. It was no Omaha or Utah. Though some naval gunfire support was certainly needed by our troops when they went ashore early on January 9, the opposition they faced suggested that we had been sent in days earlier to swat a fly with a baseball bat. And that, we had never been told.

Our amphibious landings on the ninth were an unqualified success. After being pounded by everything from fourteen-inch naval guns to barrages of rockets from specially equipped LCIs, what few Japs there were left gave our troops little trouble. Only over on the easternmost flank was there any real opposition. There, near the village of Mabilo which was backed by the Zambales Mountains, some dug-in Japanese had to be rooted out of their holes with extra applications of bombs and naval gunfire before our advance could continue. But that was the exception. Before the day was over, it was obvious to many that the Navy's baseball bat would not be needed much longer.

If the Japanese troops ashore seemed to be caving in without much fight, the same could not be said for those Japanese who were members of their suicide units. On the night of the ninth, some of these hopped into their speedboats, raced out into the gulf, and began to execute a series of seaborne Kamikaze attacks on our ships. These tiny craft, less than twenty feet long, had nothing in common with the E-boats *Laffey* had faced off Normandy. The Jap boats mounted no torpedoes. They toted a heavy explosive depth charge, and their targets were our cargo ships and transports. Since many of these were in shallow water, a depth charge dropped right next to one would exert most of its force upward—blowing out the ship's bottom, or breaking her back.

Though manned by soldiers, not sailors, these suicide speedboats did manage to damage some of our transports and LSTs seriously. But they had little success against any of our destroyers. Those that tried were spotted by sharp-eyed American lookouts and sunk with gunfire long before they could get close enough to do any damage.

The Japanese also tried another type of seagoing Kamikaze against our ships. On January 10, as *Laffey* was screening the cruiser *Minneapolis* (CA 36), our TBS crackled with a request that we go and investigate some objects in the water not far from her. They appeared to be khaki-colored Japanese ponchos. There were a number of them quite close together, and they seemed to be moving toward the heavy cruiser.

That request was all I needed. Carefully, I conned *Laffey* closer to the ponchos and ordered some of the M-1 .30-caliber rifles we carried brought up from below. Not many hours before, a report had been circulated through the group of ships off the beaches. Some Japanese had been sighted in the water swimming near one of our ships. Orders had been issued to rescue these supposed survivors, but as they came closer, it soon became obvious that they were anything but. No lifelines were heaved. No boats were launched. Instead, the swimmers—with the explosives they carried—got a good dose of gunfire.

I knew the Japs were tricky. Since some had been spotted in daylight swimming toward one of our ships with limpet mines, this bunch apparently had decided to disguise themselves as floating debris. With ponchos covering them, they might get close enough to attach mines to a ship's hull with magnets, then swim away undiscovered. It had been done by Italian frogmen in the Mediterranean with considerable success, and obviously the Japanese intended to duplicate it.

Target practice began at once and, as usual, *Laffey*'s gunners zeroed in quickly. Bullet after bullet found its target in a superb demonstration of small-arms marksmanship that made me proud of my sailors' shooting. A bullet would go into a poncho, and then it would begin to sink. We never did see any swimmers, but we didn't need to. A piece of waterproof canvas will usually float even if you poke a hole in it—unless it's tied to a swimmer loaded down with a weight. We believed those ponchos were!

After the initial landings on the ninth, *Laffey* remained at Lingayen Gulf, providing antisubmarine and antiaircraft screen protection for the larger bombardment ships. But with each passing day, it was becoming increasingly evident that General MacArthur's troops were doing fine without much help from us. On our right (western) flank, troops that had landed near the village of Lingayen had pushed more than thirty miles south— well beyond the range of even a fourteen-inch gun. In the center, the G.I.'s had passed Malasiqui, about fifteen miles inland, and were relying mostly on their own artillery and air support.

Only over on our left (eastern) flank was there any holdup. There, troops advancing through rugged, mountainous terrain toward Rosario had met heavy concentrations of Japanese entrenched well inland at Baguio. And there they called on the Navy for gunfire. Yet by January 16 even these troops no longer

194

needed our help. As long as supply convoys continued to reach the beaches, that was enough, and General MacArthur released some of the battered ships of the heavy bombardment group. With them *Laffey* left Lingayen for Ulithi.

We reached Ulithi on the afternoon of January 27, with what remained of Squadron Sixty: *Laffey* plus *Barton* (DD 722), *Moale* (DD 693), and *Ingraham* (DD 694), escorting the battleships *West Virginia* (BB 48) and *California* (BB 44) into the busy lagoon anchorage. As before, it was crowded with ships, but it had become more than just a staging area. During the time we had been absent, not only had shore facilities been greatly developed, but the place had been turned into a real base with facilities for repairing ships and servicing those needing overhaul. It was now one of those instant but complete major bases created almost from scratch which, in World War II, made our fast advance possible in the Pacific.

Thanks to our gunnery and our ability to steam and maneuver, my ship had suffered no battle damage, but she did need some work. The sea is a harsh mistress. No matter how thoroughly and efficiently seamen maintain a ship; no matter how much chipping, painting, and repair work they do while she is on active service; the sea alone will take a toll. Any ship that has steamed thousands of miles, often at high speeds and under great stresses, will have some damage.

In the weeks before we returned to Ulithi, I had begun to notice that, increasingly, *Laffey* was responding to her helm sluggishly. Since we had been steaming at high speeds most of the time, I knew this could not be caused solely by barnacles and seaweed. I was sure we had collected some of both, despite the antifouling paint below her waterline, because we had been in warmer waters which promote their growth. All underwater parts of the ship would need a thorough scraping. But something else was definitely wrong with her.

As soon as possible, I took *Laffey* over alongside the destroyer tender *Piedmont* (AD 17), and requested a diver. I had him go down into the water off the stern to inspect our rudders and screws, and what he found confirmed my suspicions. *Laffey*'s rudders weren't solid steel slabs. These would have made her stern-heavy. The rudders were hollow. They were made of rectangular steel plates which formed a skin over an interior steel framework, and some of these plates were missing. What made the ship sluggish in responding to her helm was water which was flowing through these openings like a sieve, creating unwanted drag. If the plates were not replaced at once, we would soon lose more and eventually would lose complete control of the ship.

Earlier in the war this situation might have meant a return to a place like Pearl Harbor where *Laffey* could be put into a drydock. But by 1945 bases like Ulithi had their own drydocks. They weren't on land and they weren't permanent installations. As with many other servicing and repair and refueling facilities in the Pacific, these drydocks were mobile. They were Landing Ship Docks (LSD's) which were self-propelled and could steam forward to each new base we had to establish as we advanced ever closer to Japan. And, like the mobile repair facilities of the Army's tank divisions used during our rapid advances across Europe and elsewhere, these mobile drydocks helped keep our ships operational just as well as any permanent facilities.

I made arrangements for the *Laffey* to go into an LSD anchored in our vicinity just as soon as possible. And, as the welders repaired her rudders, I planned to take the opportunity to have our own men clean off seaweed and barnacles and give her bottom a new coat of antifouling paint. I knew the prospect would not make them happy, but sometime in the future it might save their lives. With a clean bottom, the *Laffey* would pick up an extra knot or two of speed—and in a clutch, that might make all the difference.

The floating drydock (LSD) was rectangular in shape, with a huge watertight gate at its stern. As we approached this stern, ballast tanks on each side of the dock were flooded with enough seawater to make the dock's interior bottom sink to a level just below *Laffey*'s keel when the open interior of the dock was flooded. Then, with the stern gate open, I could move *Laffey* carefully forward until she was inside the dock.

Once this was done, *Laffey* was secured in place and properly centered over the wooden chocks on the bottom of the dock's interior. The dock's stern gate was closed and her ballast tanks and her open interior were pumped out. As this happened, *Laffey* settled solidly on the chocks—much to my satisfaction and relief. Although I had done it before in Boston, it was a tricky job, and one I did not particularly relish.

As soon as the interior of the dock was dry, I issued orders to rig the stages and begin the scraping. A stage held two sailors. It was made of two 10-foot boards, each a foot wide and two inches thick, and it was suspended by lines running over the side from the main deck above. As work progressed, a party of sailors on the deck above hoisted, lowered, or moved the stage. The men working on the stage had separate lifelines secured on deck just in case of a fall. The whole arrangement closely resembled that used by window washers who work on the outside of nonopening windows of modern glass-and-steel city skyscrapers—except of course for the men above.

The long-handled scraping tools had straight-edged blades, and resembled choppers used to clean ice off sidewalks. Since a barnacle fastens itself to a ship with one of nature's strongest glues, operating a scraper took a lot of sweat and muscle power. The men on the stages had to be changed fairly often; to provide enough manpower, each of the ship's divisions was assigned a section of the hull. In modern terminology, it was a labor-intensive job, and that was the only way it could be done in a single day.

Even so, despite the frequent changes, men on the stages got tired and a little sloppy as the day progressed. Ted Runk, for example, found some unpainted spots just as it was getting dark. He had his men go back over them, and this produced some griping. One of Runk's signalmen complained that he was a signalman, not a painter. I heard him outside my sea cabin, and so did Runk. The man was sadly mistaken. He was a painter until Ted Runk was satisfied the job was done and done right.

It was well into February by the time *Laffey*'s maintenance and repair work was completed and the ship had her new coat of gray-and-blue camouflage paint. By then, I think all of us would have welcomed some rest. But there was no rest scheduled for *Laffey* and her men. We were, instead, scheduled to leave Ulithi on February 10.

Admiral Halsey's carrier groups had returned to Ulithi on January 25, and Halsey had turned them over to Admiral Raymond A. Spruance. Task Force 38, the Third Fleet, became Task Force 58, the Fifth Fleet, and *Laffey* was assigned to it. We were to be part of Task Group 58.4, one of five such groups under Spruance's command, and when I found out about it, I was glad *Laffey* had had a good scraping and painting. TG 58.4 was fast company, and we would need every extra knot of speed we had to keep up with and screen it.

TG 58.4 had seventeen destroyers, the carriers *Yorktown* and *Randolph* (CVs 10 and 15), and light carriers *Langley* and *Cabot* (CVLs 27 and 28). It also had two modern, fast battleships, *North*

Carolina and *Washington* (BBs 55 and 56); and the light cruisers *San Diego, Sante Fe,* and *Biloxi* (CLs 53, 60, and 80), making it by itself more powerful than what remained of the Japanese fleet. But though the Japanese still had some powerful warships, they were not our primary target. We were going to Japan to knock out as much as we could of Japanese air power.

The reason was Iwo Jima. That island in the Bonins chain, about halfway between Tokyo and our bombers based in the Marianas, was going to be invaded by our Marines on February 19. We needed Iwo as a base for fighters to escort our B-29 bombers over Japan—and also as an emergency landing area for crippled bombers that couldn't make it back to Saipan.

Iwo, however, was close to Japanese air bases. We believed the enemy would launch masses of Kamikazes against ships of our invasion force if we did not neutralize those air bases first. We had learned that lesson at Lingayen and now we intended to put the knowledge to good use.

On the morning of the ninth, the day before we were scheduled to depart, I went up to the bridge to take another look around the anchorage. As I swept my binoculars from ship to ship, I suddenly focused on a DE (destroyer escort) moving up Mugai Channel. I studied her for a few moments, then was just about to turn away when the TBS crackled.

"This is Blood-Thirsty! This is Blood-Thirsty! Request drinking assignment!" was the message to the officer in charge of refueling assignments, and the voice sounded very familiar. I put my binoculars on her again and told the signalman to look up DE 415 and her skipper. Sure enough, I was right! She was the *Lawrence C. Taylor,* and that jocular voice belonged to Lieutenant Commander Ralph Cullinan. He was one of my Annapolis classmates, an old friend I hadn't seen for a very long time.

That afternoon, when I finally got a chance to go ashore on Feitabul Island (another like Mog Mog, used for recreation), I tried to find Ralph, but I had no luck. That was typical out there in the Pacific in World War II. There were literally dozens of times when I would hear the voice of an old friend I hadn't seen in years coming from a nearby ship, but I never would get to renew that old acquaintance. That man Longfellow was right when he said, "Only a look and a voice, then darkness again and a silence...." But in the Pacific in World War II it wasn't true only of "Ships that pass in the night..."—out there it could happen any time, night or day.

In terms of renewing old acquaintances, however, my visit to

Feitabul wasn't a total washout. Among those I talked to were Les Woods, skipper of the destroyer *Laws* (DD 558), and Captains H. B. "Beanie" Jarrett and Roland Smoot. Jarrett and Smoot were both destroyer squadron commanders who had seen a great deal of action in the Pacific.

Everyone I spoke to was cheerful and eager to get on with the forthcoming operation—everyone, that is, except Jarrett. He was eager enough to get on with it, but he wasn't as jovial as usual.

I found out why when I mentioned our operation order. The order called for a picket line of destroyers to be stationed about fifty miles ahead of the fleet. Their job was to give the main body advance warning of incoming Japanese aircraft, to direct our CAPs as they flew to intercept, and to destroy any surface craft they might encounter. Jarrett's destroyers had been given the responsibility, and Jarrett did not seem very elated about it, despite its importance.

Beanie made no bones about his feelings. He wasn't afraid— he knew the job had to be done by someone and he was all set to do it. But he didn't like it one bit. If the Japs decided to get really nasty, there would be a lot of casualties. No officer welcomes that prospect.

If that had been all, I wouldn't have said anything. But when he added, "Maybe this time I'll get a new medal—the permanent Purple Heart," that bothered me. I did not want Beanie going out feeling he wouldn't survive, because that state of mind might make the thought a reality. I did what I could to make light of it, and I insisted we would see each other again soon, right there on Feitabul, perhaps in three weeks.

Beanie looked at me quizzically for a moment, and then he laughed. He knew darn well I was just trying to cheer him up, but what made him laugh was the tone of my voice as I'd gone about it. The very idea of Julie Becton taking on the role of chaplain was just too much for him to accept with a straight face. He knew that on occasion I could be a little irreverent, but he surely knew that a Reverend I certainly was not.

I am not sure if my feeble little attempt to reassure Jarrett had any influence on future events. But as it turned out, I made a pretty good guess. About three weeks later, back on Feitabul Island, I ran into Beanie again. But that time he was as jovial as ever—hale, hearty, and in the best of spirits. His gloomy predictions had not come true and he had recently received word that Admiral Mitscher was highly pleased with his performance throughout the operation.

After talking with Jarrett and some others, I then got into a conversation with my classmate Les Woods and another friend from my Annapolis days, Lot Ensey. But as we chatted, a curious thing happened. Les was right in the middle of some story or other when I heard a voice—and what it was saying made me turn around immediately. I suppose that wasn't very polite, but I guess Les understood because he stopped talking. Or maybe he too just wanted to hear the joke an officer nearby was telling to a group of others.

I did not know the voice, and the joke wasn't told exactly as I had heard it, but I sure knew the punch line. The last time I had heard it was in New York at the 21 Club. When Les and I looked to see who was talking, I was also certain I knew the man. He looked very familiar, yet I just couldn't place him.

I asked Les, and he laughed. "No, Julie," he said, "he wasn't at the Academy. That's Eddy Duchin!"

That solved the mystery. Duchin—a famous pianist, orchestra leader, and musician—was a sonar officer on one of our destroyers, and he had come ashore for a little relaxation. Musicians like Duchin were prized by the Navy. Their hearing was far more acute and sensitive than that of the average person. Their ears could quickly spot the difference between sounds made by a whale, a school of fish, or an enemy submarine.

Les's answer also explained how a story that Imogen had told me months before in New York could be known to a naval officer who might have been out there in the Pacific for a considerable time. Duchin and Imogen were both artists of the entertainment world. Undoubtedly they did not know each other, but both moved in the same professional circles. The world of professional entertainers was just like the professional Navy. If a good joke got loose in the group, it would run through the whole crowd very quickly.

I spent a couple of pleasant hours ashore on Feitabul, but I returned to *Laffey* shortly before dark. I wanted to make sure she was shipshape and ready to go in the morning. But more than that, I felt that might be the last night of peaceful, uninterrupted sleep I'd get for some time. We had a long, dangerous journey with a lot of high-speed steaming ahead of us; and once we sailed, sleep would be at a premium.

By the time I had checked everything out, had something to eat, and headed for my cabin, I was beginning to feel pretty tired. Yet somehow I wasn't sleepy. Hearing Duchin tell that joke had reminded me of Imogen. I hadn't heard from her in a while, and it bothered me. Although I suspected her letters just had not caught up with us because we had been on the move pretty steadily, I was concerned. Maybe, I thought, she really hadn't written recently.

I went to the drawer in my cabin and took out her picture. To protect it, I always put it there—wrapped in a bath towel— whenever the ship was in a battle zone or just about to enter one. Everything on a destroyer got bounced, jounced, and thrown around when the ship went into action. And since the picture was by then in a new silver frame I had received from Imogen as a Christmas present some weeks before, this safety measure seemed even more important.

I put the picture up on my desk, sat down opposite, and studied it. Somehow that made me feel better. I could almost hear her voice explaining why she hadn't written recently. There had been other times in the past when I didn't hear from her for a while, and on one occasion—when I chided her about it—she had told me why.

I suppose I should have kept quiet, because she had either been hurt or annoyed. Maybe both, because she remarked that my letters to her had become mixed up with a lot of other papers and correspondence. She hadn't, she said, found them until much later—too late to answer them.

That had hurt me a little until I realized she was telling me the truth and trying to tell me something more. Imogen was a professional entertainer, a star. She didn't have much free time for personal matters. She had professional responsibilities just as I did. She could no more ignore them to sit down and write a letter whenever she chose than I could leave the bridge while *Laffey* was at battle stations to do the same thing.

I sat there for a time—exactly how long, I'm not sure; then suddenly I realized something. I hadn't heard from Imogen in some time—but I hadn't written her recently either. Tomorrow we'd be off and away. There might not be time for weeks. It was late, but at least I could get a letter started. . . .

TEN

On the afternoon of February 10, *Laffey* and the rest of Bill Freseman's destroyers left Ulithi with the carriers of Task Force 58 and headed for Japan. On February 19, our Marines would be landing on the beaches of Iwo Jima. We had learned some bitter lessons at Lingayen, and TF 58 was being sent to Honshu to deal a staggering blow to Japanese air power before those landings on Iwo began. We now knew that the best place to take care of Kamikazes was on the ground before they could take off—and that is exactly what our task force commander, Vice Admiral Marc A. Mitscher, had in mind.

Under most circumstances, the best way to reach an objective is to steam directly toward it, but this case was an exception. We had to reach a point about sixty miles off the coastline of Honshu and launch our planes without being discovered, and that called for both secrecy and deception. We left Ulithi on a northeasterly heading just in case the skipper of a Jap picket submarine was observing our departure. It was to be several days before the bows of our ships were aimed at Honshu, well over a thousand miles to the northwest. Like a boxer, we threw a long, powerful right hook at the enemy's jaw which we hoped he wouldn't see coming until it was too late to stop it.

To make sure that the Japanese were thrown off the track, our aircraft conducted exercises with Marines based in the Marianas on the twelfth. Although this was also a necessary dress rehearsal for the assault on Iwo Jima, it provided one more way of disguising TF 58's ultimate destination. The Japs expected us to invade Iwo fairly soon, and when TF 58 disappeared right after the exercise, they would assume that it was headed for Iwo Jima.

Earlier in the war it would have been impossible for a huge carrier task force which included a lot of destroyers to stay at sea for a long period of time and fight a number of actions without returning to base. But by 1945 the U. S. Navy had developed a means of sustaining an entire fleet like TF 58 at sea for weeks on end. It was, in this case, Rear Admiral D. B. Beary's Service Squadron Six. This included everything from oilers, aviation gas tankers, reefers (supply ships), ammunition ships, and even escort carriers; these made our long-range strikes against the Japanese home islands possible. Not only could Service Squadron Six replenish our fuel, ammunition, and stores while we were underway, but the escort carriers could deliver replacement planes and pilots directly to the flight decks of the larger carriers.

TF 58 refueled twice while underway between Ulithi and Honshu and still far out of range of any Japanese picket ships or Jap occupied islands. The second refueling was on the fourteenth, about five hundred miles due east of Iwo Jima. But from that time on, *Laffey* and the other destroyers would have to depend on fuel from the larger ships of the task force. There was a limit to how close Admiral Beary's service squadron could come to the shores of Japan. Task Force 58 would need every plane it had for its primary mission, and—without proper air cover— Service Squadron Six would have been a sitting duck and an inviting target for the Kamikazes.

At 7:00 P.M. on February 15, we were ordered to increase our speed to twenty knots for that final run-in to the point where our planes would be launched. Despite the worsening weather, which had helped cover our approach, and the precautions we had taken to avoid discovery, Admiral Mitscher wasn't taking any chances. He intended to reach that position about sixty miles off Honshu before he had to launch those planes; if he did not, the aircraft would have to use up too much gas just reaching their targets.

That was a burden Mitscher did not want to put on his pilots; as the skipper of a destroyer, I could easily understand and sympathize with his determination. Like aircraft, destroyers carry a limited amount of fuel. And, like aircraft pilots, destroyer skippers know how battle odds against them increase if fuel has to be stretched too far. Mitscher, who graduated from the Naval Academy in 1910, had been one of our early naval aviators. Like a former destroyer skipper, he knew his men would be up against it if they had to take off too far from their targets, because early in the war Mitscher had had such an experience.

On April 18, 1942, the then Captain Mitscher was skipper of the carrier *Hornet* (CV 8) which, with the carrier *Enterprise* (CV 6), was steaming toward the coast of Japan. The task group, commanded by Vice Admiral William F. Halsey, was on a secret and unusual mission. Aboard *Hornet* was Lieutenant Colonel Jimmy Doolittle with sixteen Army Air Force B-25 medium bombers and specially trained crews. The plan was to launch these bombers against Tokyo from a range of five hundred miles. Although the bombers had not been designed to fly off carriers, they had been picked because they could fly those five hundred miles and then go on and safely reach the coast of China afterward.

Up to 2:00 A.M., everything had gone well. But then radar began to pick up Japanese picket ships. By 7:00 A.M. it seemed certain that the Japs had spotted the carriers, and this created a crisis. At that point in the war the U. S. had very few carriers, and loss of *Enterprise* and *Hornet* would have been a major disaster. Yet the mission was of vital importance. The only option was to launch the planes immediately and retire—and this is exactly what was done. The sixteen bombers got off *Hornet* safely despite high winds and heavy seas. But, beginning with their 7:30 A.M. launch, Doolittle's flyers had to fly more than 650 miles to reach their targets. Only part of them made it safely to the coast of China.

It had to be done, but I know it was something that Admiral Mitscher did not like doing—and would do anything he could to avoid in the future. If it was humanly possible, I knew Adm. Mitscher was going to get us to that launch point off Honshu on February 16, 1945, before he sent off any planes. And frankly, I intended to do anything I could to help him. As skipper of a short-legged (fuel-limited) destroyer, how could I have felt otherwise?

At dawn the next morning the weather was terrible. There was a cold, damp wind blowing out of the northeast. The sea was an ugly, dirty, lead-gray-green of rollers topped with white foam. And when it wasn't raining, flurries of snow swept across *Laffey*'s wet, plunging, and rolling forecastle.

As I stood on the starboard wing of the bridge, hanging onto the rail, staring up at the sky, I wondered if the strikes were going to be called off. This wasn't good bombing weather. The ceiling was very low. Those pilots were going to have one devil of a time finding their targets and hitting them.

My question was quickly answered. Not long after it became completely light—or as completely light as it was going to get—the carriers started to launch their planes. Visibility was so bad I couldn't really see them. But I didn't have to, because wave on wave of roaring motors were soon passing overhead.

Most of these must have been fighters—F6F Grumman Hellcats—because our operational plan called for our fighters to clamp a lid on Jap air activity before our bombers went in for their strikes. By early 1945, the activities of the Kamikazes had forced us to increase the numbers of fighter planes aboard our carriers at the expense of other types, thus my assumption could not have been far off the mark. But, if it was part of the Japanese plan to limit our bombing capability by forcing us to increase the numbers of our fighters, it just didn't work. The Hellcats were fighters all right, and good ones. But by then they had become multipurpose planes: They could mount machine guns and cannon but, when needed, they could carry rockets and even a thousand pounds of bombs, and still could outfly anything the Japs could put up against them. We had come a long way in aircraft development from those old clumsy F2A Brewster Buffalo fighters the Japs had slaughtered in 1941-42, just as we had in surface ships with our new destroyers.

As our planes began their sweeps over Honshu, *Laffey*'s crew went to battle stations; and we maintained that state of readiness throughout the day. It was not a comfortable condition. None of us were used to that drizzling misery nor the numbing cold after so many months in warmer latitudes. It was probably the first time in months that those of our crew who were manning guns and other stations on open decks envied the men in our engineering department below. In that kind of bone-chilling weather, a boiler or fireroom station had some advantages.

I spent most of the daylight hours of February 16 out on the open starboard wing of the bridge, looking, so Seaman Emile Mallette told OOD, Lieutenant (j.g.) Ernie Saenz, like a man from Mars. On that occasion, it was probably true. Having warned all men stationed topside in the open, and those of our damage-control parties, to use the new burn-prevention materials we'd received, I had to set an example. Since I too was out in the open, I put on the stuff myself.

As Kamikaze attacks on our ships had increased, so too had the numbers of our men who were seriously burned, and the Navy had developed some protective materials to help reduce such casualties. These consisted of some kind of paint or cream which was supposed to be smeared on exposed skin surfaces like the face, and pairs of long-sleeved knit gloves to protect bare hands and arms. I am sure both were scientifically designed and tested. But the trouble with them was that they weren't very practical for men trying to handle a ship in combat. The creamlike paint got all over everything, and into places it didn't belong, like the eyes. And the knit gloves, which would have been fine for a Victorian matron with dozens of servants to take care of her needs, made it almost impossible to use your hands.

By the end of the day, I was very glad to get that creamlike paint and those long knit gloves off, put away, and forgotten. I had set an example, and that was enough. From then on I intended to take my chances on the bridge without whatever burn-prevention protection the cream and gloves might afford. I didn't mind looking foolish, or like a man from Mars, but I had a job to do. Since I could not do it with all that gunk smeared on my face and those knit gloves making me fumble anything I picked up, I was damned if I was going to wear them. And if my men couldn't do their jobs wearing them either, well, there was a solution to that one too. If the great British Admiral, Lord Nelson, could turn his blind eye toward something he chose to ignore, the skipper of the *Laffey* could at least wink once in a while.

At dusk, after recovering our aircraft, we retired eastward. We had been little bothered by Japanese planes and, on the whole, our own had had a reasonably successful day. But the next, we hoped, we'd do even better.

After steaming east for some hours, we came about 180 degrees and settled down on a westerly course straight back toward Japan. This was to put us in the same launching area in the early hours of February 17 so that our carriers could fly off more air strikes against Japanese targets. Or that, at least, was the plan. But by the time we had turned around and all ships were on their proper station, the weather had really fallen apart. We were plunging like flying fish reentering the water, bucking like broncos, and even with SG surface-detection radar, it was difficult to make out where nearby ships were located. Were such conditions to continue, launching planes at daylight might well be impossible.

Laffey was then one of a number of destroyers forming a large circular screen around the rest of the ships of our task group. We were in no great danger. Although maintaining station wasn't easy, there was plenty of room between the destroyers of the screen; we weren't in a typhoon and we had plenty of fuel. If those on watch kept a sharp lookout and stayed alert, we would have no problems. In fact, if anything, the weather was an advantage—or would be until morning. With that kind of murk, the only thing that might have given us any trouble would have been an enemy submarine.

About 10:00 P.M. I was in my sea cabin trying to catch a couple hours rest when I had a call from the officer of the deck. Two of our screening destroyers had collided. They'd merged on our radar scope to the west of us and left a huge gap in our formation. I grabbed my robe and slippers, and rushed to the pilothouse. After studying the radar for some moments, I had the officer of the deck shift our position about five hundred yards to the west.

I knew that the bad weather could cause an enemy submarine just as much trouble as our destroyers. But there was always the possibility that there was one out there in the murk. The Japs knew we were somewhere off the eastern coast of Honshu, and one of the emperor's I-boat skippers might be shadowing us, waiting for a chance to strike. By shifting the *Laffey* from her original position, our sonarmen would have a larger search arc which would cover the gap in our destroyer screen. If the enemy sub tried to slip through it into our formation, we'd be there to get him.

By this time our TBS was squawking and crackling again with more information about the collision; and as it came through, I had a sudden mental picture of Bill Freseman exploding in anger. The two ships that had collided were the *Ingraham* and the *Barton*. Both were part of Bill Freseman's squadron, and the latter was Bill's flagship. Bill was not the type of man to suffer mistakes by his subordinates in silence. The collision would surely make him go up like a rocket and bellow like a bull stung by a bumblebee. I could just imagine what Bill was saying aboard the *Barton* at that moment, and exactly how loud he'd be saying it. I suspected that Ed Dexter's ears were ringing, and that shortly, so would those of Commander John Harper of the *Ingraham*.

Actually, the collision caused only minor damage to each of the destroyers. And, though they had to be detached for repairs and escorted south by the *Moale*, apparently Bill Freseman surprised both their skippers. Bill did not explode with anger and produce his usual torrent of reprimands. He quietly took the blame himself.

Bill Freseman contended that his own staff officer in the *Barton*'s combat information center should have been more alert and called attention to the dangerous developing situation. He stated further, that since his staff officer in CIC was representing him, he—Freseman—should bear the responsibility for the collision.

I know that there were some officers in our ships who were puzzled by this development, and even more puzzled when the Navy accepted Freseman's point of view. But I do not think these officers knew Bill as well as I did. Freseman, for all his other faults, was extremely loyal to his skippers. He had always protected their interests. If a ship of his squadron was short of officers or men, for example, Bill wouldn't rest until the destroyer-force commander did something to fill the gaps.

Although Bill sometimes drove his subordinates crazy with nit-picking, he also may have made himself even more unpopular with his own superiors in his efforts to help those subordinates. Bill would not let go of something until it was just the way he felt it should be. Having made up his mind that he was responsible for that collision, he must have pressed this view on his superiors until they finally had to agree with him.

In doing this Bill Freseman certainly protected his two destroyer skippers. One later told me he never received any derogatory disciplinary correspondence with regard to the collision. But the other side of that coin was that Bill most surely hurt his own professional standing by taking all the blame on himself. Though he was to eventually retire a rear admiral, the assignments he was given between the time he left the squadron in April of 1945 and that retirement were probably not what he might otherwise have hoped to get. Bill, who could be a tough man to work for, was a damn good man to have working for you. He never went halfway with anything—even when it threatened his own future.

By dawn on the seventeenth, the weather had moderated a little and air strikes against Japan could be renewed. Our crew, manning battle stations, watched the planes take off, get into formation, then head away west into the gloom. But I think all of us who watched did so with a sense of foreboding. The clouds were still low and thick. The targets would be difficult to find. And the predictions were for things to get much worse.

They did. When the first of our planes began returning about 10:30 A.M., the pilots reported freezing weather that jammed guns, targets that could not be located because of the thick clouds, and difficulties engaging enemy aircraft which rose to challenge them. By the time our ships changed course to head for a position from which we planned to launch strikes against the industrial city of Nagoya, it was evident the weather wasn't going to cooperate at all. The Nagoya operation had to be cancelled, and *Laffey*—like the rest of the ships of Task Force 58—turned her bow southward. Time had run out. Further attacks on the enemy's home islands would have to wait because on the nineteenth we were needed off Iwo Jima.

On a map, the island of Iwo Jima looks like a leg of roast lamb; but there was nothing inviting about that pile of volcanic rock and dust. Iwo is about 4½ miles long, and at the butt end, about 2½ miles wide. The butt end of the island is an elevated but relatively flat plateau; opposite, at the much narrower shank end, sits the 550-foot high, semiactive volcano, Mt. Suribachi. The mountain dominates all the low ground between itself and the plateau. It was on the beaches of that low ground where our Marines would be forced to land, because there were just no others which were suitable anywhere on the shoreline.

Iwo Jima was held by about 23,000 Japanese soldiers under the command of Lieutenant General Tadamichi Kuribayashi. He turned the island into a Gibraltar of the Pacific. It was honey-combed with deep tunnels; concrete blockhouses; machine-gun pillboxes; and carefully positioned, heavily protected artillery positions. And Suribachi itself got more than its share of these defenses. When our Marines came ashore, they would have very little cover and would be forced to advance against an enemy who held the high ground, would often be hidden, and occupied positions which would be very difficult to smash.

We did not have much choice in the Bonins. There were only two islands in the chain large enough for airfields, and we had to have one of them. We could not outflank the defenders. We had to go head on in and take Iwo Jima. There was no other option.

What we could and did do was to pound the daylights out of the place. For ten weeks prior to February 19, both our planes and our ships pulverized those several square miles of volcanic rock and sand with bombs and shells. As the time for the landing grew closer, the intensity of that bombardment was increased. In addition to the guns of battleships, cruisers, and destroyers of the bombardment force, and planes from about twelve escort carriers, Task Force 58 was to bring its massive striking power to bear just as the Marines started to go ashore.

We arrived off Iwo from the coasts of Japan on February 18, and for the next three days, our carriers launched wave after wave of planes against the island. We smothered it with bombs, shot at it with aircraft machine guns and cannon. But unfortunately, even this added heavy battering did not really do the job. The Japs were so well dug in, their positions so well protected, nothing but a direct hit could knock many of them out.

At Iwo Jima, bombs from the air may have helped the Marines ashore, but it was naval gunfire on which the Marines really had to depend to take out many enemy strong points. A near miss with a bomb did little good. The position had to be pinpointed exactly, often by spotter planes, and the information radioed to a fire-support ship. Then the spotter-plane pilot would have to direct and coach the heavy naval guns directly onto the target.

This put a considerable responsibility on the shoulders of those spotter-plane pilots; and after a few hours of such duty, many of them minced no words if they thought something was wrong. I recall hearing a pilot's voice on the radio one morning when *Laffey* was stationed off the beaches screening some of the heavier warships. Like that pilot, we'd been on line—meaning at battle stations—for some time. We were beginning to feel the strain, but what came over the radio broke all of us up.

The spotter-plane pilot apparently had some kind of fire-support plan up there with him and was trying to make sense out of it so he could give "spots" to one of our bombardment ships. Up to that point, his voice had been rather even—a monotone—but then something must have got to him.

"What dumb son of a bitch made up this fire-support plan?" he yelled. "This is the most screwed-up thing I've ever seen!"

That brought an immediate response from the flagship of the admiral in command. "Who made that last transmission? State your name, rank, and serial number!"

There was a second or two of silence, then the reply, "Forget it, buddy! I'm not *that* confused! Out!"

After three days of bouncing around in the rough seas off Iwo Jima which, for *Laffey*, included one rather long and difficult refueling from a carrier, we went north again. Contrary to what had been expected at Iwo, there had not been a great deal of Japanese air activity against our ships. Though the planes of TF 58 had knocked down or destroyed an estimated five hundred enemy aircraft during the strikes of February 16-17, and thrown the Japs off stride, we knew the situation would not continue. The enemy had at least several thousand more planes they could send against us. With our invasion of Okinawa only about five weeks away, we wanted to eliminate as many of them as possible. If our assault on Iwo hadn't stirred up a hornet's nest of Kamikazes, our landings on Okinawa surely would.

As before, our task groups were preceded by a number of picket destroyers stationed well ahead of the destroyer screens and the main formations. We expected the Japanese to have their own picket boats out to intercept us and that they would send planes to attack us. Yet, as it turned out, though there were some Japanese picket ships, the skies overhead remained clear of Japanese planes.

This I—and I think many others with the task group—found puzzling. Surely the enemy knew we were again headed for the sacred soil of the Japanese home islands, but for some reason they just did not challenge us. The only logical explanation seemed to be the weather. It was absolutely terrible. It was bitter cold; the wind was blowing like the devil; and the seas were so wild one of our destroyers, the *Moale*, had her bow caved in. After that incident, Admiral Radford had all ships of the task group reduce speed. Enemy action posed enough of a threat of damage, and there was no point in driving ships and risking further losses from the sea when it wasn't necessary.

Actually, the absence of the Japanese was due to the weather. To begin with, it hid us almost completely until the morning of February 25. But not only did the Japanese not see us coming, they also couldn't believe that we would send our carriers north to launch air strikes in such weather. When they finally realized their mistake, they compounded it by assuming it would be impossible for us to get our planes airborne.

Frankly, I couldn't blame them. For a while that morning the weather was so terrible, I didn't think so either.

As before, I spent most of my time out on the starboard wing of the bridge. My teeth were chattering, my eyes watering; my half-frozen hands gripped the railing for dear life. Visibility from inside the pilot house was always limited in bad weather; and the SG radar, though useful, could play tricks under those kinds of conditions. As a skipper of a destroyer operating with carriers, I had to keep a very sharp lookout. As I've noted before, carriers exist solely for their planes and their moves are dictated by what they must do to launch and recover them. *Laffey* had to keep out of their way any time she was with them—and this went double in that kind of weather.

Years after that run we made up toward the coasts of Japan, Lloyd Hull—who had been a Lieutenant (j.g.) in our CIC at the time—told me how impressed he was when he saw me rigid, immobile with concentration and a determination to bring the ship through safely. It was very nice of Lloyd and I appreciated the comment. But I'm afraid it wasn't completely accurate. Of course I was rigid, immobile with concentration and a determination to see *Laffey* safely through it, and I felt it was my duty to stay out there on that open bridge. But my rigidity and immobility wasn't all due to concentration and determination. I was also frozen stiff and almost unable to move.

Uncomfortable as it was on that bridge, staying there was the kind of thing the Navy expects of the skippers of its ships. Though it was and is a duty, there were compensations. One of my crew, Machinist's Mate Buford Thompson, a huge six-footer, told me after that he'd been feeling a little shaky that day, but that seeing me up there on the wing of the bridge gave him renewed confidence and reassurance.

At 7:00 A.M. on February 25, we did manage to launch the first groups of planes, but by the time they returned there was no possibility of sending off more. Then, during that night, the weather deteriorated so much that we had to reduce speed even further. This ruined our plans for the twenty-sixth. We had turned toward Nagoya, but we made such slow progress during the night that no strikes could be launched at all that day. And on the next, our chance was gone. The task force had to head south because it had a job to do at Okinawa.

Laffey, however, did not go on with the other ships. On February 28, when we reached the vicinity of Iwo Jima, we received a radio message with new orders. We were told to pick up some photographs from one of the carriers and rush them to Guam for delivery to Admiral Nimitz's advance headquarters. They were needed in a hurry, and to get them there, the Navy did what it did so often in World War II. It called on one of its destroyers to carry the mail like a modern, seagoing version of the old pony express.

I am sure it will come as no surprise that none of us aboard the *Laffey* uttered a word of complaint about this assignment. By that time we were all very happy with the idea of returning to some place where the air was warm, the sun shone brightly all day, and the waters were blue-green instead of an icy gray-green. We had had more than enough of sleet, leaden skies, and pounding through heavy seas. And, as they used to say in the old movie travelogues, we were delighted to sail off into the sun, all by ourselves. It wasn't a pleasure cruise, but it most decidedly was a pleasure.

We made a fast, uneventful run to Guam. The photographs were delivered; then we hoisted anchor and pressed on to Ulithi. The farther south we steamed, the more our men seemed to lose that kind of strained look so typical of the faces of fighting men in a combat zone. I don't mean that anyone became lax. Some antiaircraft gunnery drills with our 20's, for example, produced a perfect score of balloons shot down. But the unpleasant pressures under which we'd been operating were somewhat relieved, and the dispositions of almost everyone aboard seemed to improve.

Unfortunately, this change was not universal. About 12:15 P.M. on the day after we departed from Guam, members of our crew were standing in chow line when there was a minor explosion of tempers. One of the men invited another to settle it with fists on the fantail. This would not have been overly serious if that had been all, but more than a hundred others forgot their food and followed the pair. Shortly, the two men were hard at it, cheered on by these shipmates, and the slugging match continued until officers and some senior enlisted men waded in and broke it up.

The situation had to be dealt with promptly. Despite several days of sun and warmth, I knew my men were still under a certain amount of strain. Sailors who had withstood the shocks of months of combat and remained on friendly, cooperative terms with their shipmates could be split into two opposing factions. And, with each faction supporting one of the contestants, our crew might become divided against itself. That would place us in jeopardy.

The next day I had both men brought to mast, charged with fighting. Witnesses identified the man who had suggested things be settled with fists, so I dismissed the other, but I did not punish the remaining man. I knew that were I to sentence either man to punishment, the rift between their supporters might grow. Instead, I had a quiet talk with the fellow who had started it.

Up to then, he had had a clean record and had always done his duty. I told him I wanted it to stay that way. And, though I did not use these exact words, I indicated that next time he got hotheaded, he was to stick his head in a bucket of cold seawater to cool it off instead of getting into another fistfight.

That seemed to settle the matter. He was not in any more fights. The whole incident, much to my relief, was quickly forgotten. And *Laffey* arrived in Ulithi on March 2 with her crew once again a united team.

The team, unfortunately, did not stay united, but this was the Navy's doing. Up to that point it had been the policy of the Navy to keep wartime transfers of officers from a new ship to an absolute minimum for at least a year after she joined the fleet. Although I realized that a year had passed since our commissioning, it still disturbed me when I learned that we were going to lose a number of our key people at Ulithi.

This policy of the Navy Department's Bureau of Naval Personnel, disturbing as its effects were to me, was logical. Experienced people were needed on the growing numbers of new ships joining the fleet, and the only place to get them was from other ships. Still, I had hoped to keep our team together for the pending operation. Okinawa was upcoming—Okinawa and a renewed surge of Kamikazes. And for it, I knew we'd need every bit of edge we could possibly get.

On the other hand, I had to take a fair-minded view of these changes. Harry Burns, the gunnery officer who had welded our gunners into a top-notch team, certainly deserved promotion. So too did out executive officer, Charlie Holovak. If they had remained aboard *Laffey*, Burns could hardly have become an executive officer of a new destroyer, and Charlie could not have been made skipper of a destroyer of his own.

Perhaps, I would not have felt so sanguine about the loss of these two key members of *Laffey*'s team if I had not known the quality of their replacements. The Navy was taking away two very good men, but it was giving us the best as their replacements. Lieutenant Paul Smith, our former assistant gunnery officer, who had been on loan to the *O'Brien* as her gunnery officer, took over from Harry. And Lieutenant Challen McCune, an expert gunnery officer who had been on a destroyer assigned to the Third/Fifth Fleets carriers, stepped into Charlie's shoes. Both were thoroughly experienced, capable men who knew what we might be up against in the future, and who were prepared to handle it.

Others left us also. There were a number of our senior petty officers and some other enlisted men whose experience and

214

expertise were needed on the new ships which were pouring from the shipyards. And there was even one instance of a man being granted emergency leave.

Under usual circumstances, men on active duty in combat zones in World War II were not granted leave to return home on visits unless there were serious medical reasons or some extreme family situations that required their presence. The latter, which might include things like a grave illness of a family member or the death of a parent who was the only remaining breadwinner for that family, was called emergency leave. And I had to recommend this for one of our enlisted men.

This sailor was a good man who had become engaged to a young woman just before we departed for the Pacific. Though engagements and the desire to marry were not considered serious reasons for granting leave, the facts in this case seemed to warrant it. The young couple had been somewhat indiscreet. With no time to formalize things, but in the belief that there would be time to do so, the pair had gone ahead and laid down a keel. Time, however, was running out by the time we reached Ulithi. With a launching imminent, and a new arrival on the seas of life needing a name, this young sailor had become desperate.

Getting approval for emergency leave had taken a lot of doing. Although the young man's request was quite legitimate and its approval was warranted, there were problems. No sooner would the request be sent from *Laffey* to the fleet commander than the ship would be switched from one fleet to another. And, no sooner would the request get to the new flagship, then back *Laffey* would go to the other fleet. The Navy was moving so fast in the Pacific that the trail of requests behind each of its ships just couldn't keep up. Only when *Laffey* got to Ulithi again, in March of 1945, did that approval finally catch up to us. It came just in the nick of time.

By early 1945, we had gained so much momentum in the Pacific that even serious, unexpected delays in one operation could not really disrupt our forward movement elsewhere. We had hoped to complete the capture of Iwo Jima by the end of February. But even as *Laffey* and hundreds of other ships concentrated at Ulithi for the invasion of Okinawa, the battle still continued to rage for that miserable chunk of volcanic rock and sand the Marines assaulted on February 19. Although the Japanese on Iwo held on until almost the end of March, they fought what can only be called a strategically useless fight. Our

Marines suffered heavy casualties taking the island from them, but the delay had no impact on our ability to launch Operation Iceberg.

By the time *Laffey* had been anchored in the ship-crowded Ulithi lagoon for about a week, we had received our operation orders for Iceberg—the assault on Okinawa. We would no longer be operating directly with the big, fast carriers of Task Force 58. Again, we had been transferred. Our job as part of the bombardment group under Rear Admiral William H. P. Blandy was to provide gunfire support for the 10th Army ashore. As she so often had in previous months, *Laffey* was once again going to be working near a beachhead, screening battleships and cruisers. We would be limited to certain areas in which we could steam, and the Japs, I knew, would have no trouble finding us. That, of course, meant more Kamikazes.

Not that the enemy waited quietly until we reached Okinawa before they struck. By March 1945 Ulithi, which was more than eight hundred miles from the nearest Jap airstrip, could still be reached on a one-way flight. And some Japs made such flights. For example, on March 11, about dusk, when a happy hour was in progress on *Laffey*'s forecastle, two of those little devils showed up.

At that time we were moored not far from some of the carriers. One, the *Randolph*, suddenly erupted with an explosion and flames. The carrier had been taking on ammunition and turned on a cargo light to facilitate the operation. The Kamikazes had spotted the light. One came in fast and crashed into her starboard quarter. The other, who also tried for a hit, wasn't so accurate. He missed and went into the ground on Mog Mog Island.

Just before these Japs arrived, three of our sailors had been doing a skit on the forecastle. Dressed in hula skirts, they didn't look exactly like Dorothy Lamour, nor did they have her talent, but the entertainment was going well. They were drawing a lot of laughs until *whoom*, that Jap hit the *Randolph*. And then two things happened. All hands raced to battle stations; and the three would-be Dorothy Lamours quickly concluded their act by going over our bow into the water. They had to swim around for some time until lines could be thrown and they could be hauled in.

I have no way of knowing exactly what those two Jap suicide pilots hoped to accomplish with their attack at Ulithi, but one thing they certainly did do. The waters of that lagoon were dark when the Kamikazes came in, and *Laffey*'s three performers spent some anxious minutes in them wondering exactly what else might be swimming nearby. By the time our star-struck actors were again on the ship's solid deck, I know that all of them had decided a career in show business wasn't for them. Kamikazes they could handle. But swimming in grass skirts in waters that might contain a shark was too much to ask.

That attack on the *Randolph* reminded everyone—if they needed reminding—of what we would be facing shortly off Okinawa. I was thinking about it the next morning when suddenly I realized that L day (landing day) on Okinawa would be something more than April 1 and April Fool's Day. April 1 of 1945 was also Easter Sunday. There would be an Easter parade, a parade of landing craft to the beaches; and everyone in this parade would be wearing an Easter bonnet—a nice steel helmet. But before that parade there would not be any time for divine services. We were going to need His blessing on our endeavor.

With that thought in mind I called Frank Manson and Al Henke to my cabin immediately. We had one more Sunday in Ulithi, I told them—Sunday March 18. After that we'd be on the high seas headed toward what probably would be one of the toughest operations of the war. The closer we had come to Japan, the more desperate the enemy had become.

"Look at that attack yesterday," I said. "If eight hundred miles of ocean won't stop them from trying, we are going to need help. No matter how many times Admiral Spruance's carriers hit their airfields, or how bad the weather is, they will keep coming. Maybe a little praying will help."

Frank and Al both agreed. And when I told them we ought to arrange an Easter service for the eighteenth, a service we could not hold on Easter, both of them were more than enthusiastic. Al offered to say the necessary prayers if Frank would take care of the sermon, and Frank was agreeable. He said he knew that one of our men, Quartermaster Ernest Belk, had been conducting lay services. Frank told me he would get some material from Belk and put together a short sermon.

Frank Manson did even better. After he left my cabin, he went to the radio room and sent for Larry Kelley. We had no means aboard of producing the proper music for a religious service, but Kelley, Frank knew, had a beautiful tenor voice. Kelley was always being asked by his shipmates to sing for them and, when Frank asked him, he was more than willing to help out with the service.

I suppose there have been many grander and more impressive religious services held to celebrate Easter and to invoke the Almighty's blessing. But I doubt if any has ever been more sincerely touching than the one we had aboard the *Laffey* about two weeks before we sailed into hell. Kelley sang several religious hymns and songs. But—fittingly, I think, for the time and the place—he also added a popular tune which was a favorite of many aboard. Its lyrics began with, "I'll be seeing you . . .," and I think the Almighty understood and approved.

I had given Al Henke a copy of *The Prayer of a Navy Man*, which Al added to those others he spoke at the service. For those men who stood and listened that Sunday, heads bowed and uncovered in the bright sunshine that lit the blue-green waters all around us, some of the words were soon to have a special meaning. "Almighty Father . . ." the prayer begins. And then it goes on to ask help with certain things, among which is the request, ". . . if I should miss the mark, give me courage to try again. . . ." The Almighty must have been listening because, when it came time, *Laffey*'s men never did quit trying.

On March 21, *Laffey* steamed away from Ulithi as part of one of the most massive naval gunfire units that would ever back up a troop landing in World War II. Including the flagship *Tennessee* (BB 43), there were ten old battleships, seven heavy cruisers, three light cruisers, plus destroyers and destroyer escorts. The gun power packed by our formation was awesome. The weight of metal it could throw in a single broadside was probably equal to that of a freight train. And, when combined with the rockets from more than fifty landing craft plus the bombs our planes would be dropping, it seemed impossible that the Japanese on Okinawa would survive to resist our landings.

For *Laffey*, the trip to Okinawa was relatively uneventful, in part, I suppose, because Japanese attention was focused on our other ships that had already arrived off Okinawa. For example, on the twenty-third, as Task Force 58 was launching strikes against Okinawa and a group of tiny islands not far to the west of it, we refueled from the battleship *Tennessee* without incident. We then spent part of the day picking up mail from eleven other ships in our unit without even sighting an enemy plane.

The islands to the west of Okinawa were collectively known as Kerama Retto. We intended to seize them on March 26, before the invasion of Okinawa itself. They were too small to hold airstrips, but they would provide us with a large, safe anchorage from which our ships could operate. And we were to need such an anchorage before the operation was over.

March 24 was equally quiet for us. We arrived in the general area of Okinawa late in the day. But neither then nor on the twenty-fifth, when some of our cruisers and destroyers went to give Kerama Retto a working over, did we see any Japanese aircraft. Our own carrier planes had given the airfields on Okinawa such a pounding, the enemy was unable to launch any serious attacks from them then—or later on.

I found this unexpected quiet a little disturbing; the lack of Kamikazes ominous. It wasn't that I was eager for the enemy to appear; in fact, I would have been happy if he had stayed away completely. But to me, this absence of enemy planes seemed to suggest that he was setting some kind of trap for us.

Okinawa's beaches were only about 350 miles south of airfields on Kyushu, the southernmost of the Japanese home islands. I could not believe they would just sit by and let us land on those beaches without hitting us heavily from the air. It looked to me as if they were waiting until we were fully committed before they went for *Laffey* and other ships off the beaches.

I do not want to give the impression that the Japanese air forces were completely passive. Although they did not, at that time, bother the ships of the Okinawa expeditionary forces, which included our bombardment groups, they did strike at Task Force 58. And, as usual, they pressed home their attacks with suicidal vigor. Even before we had sailed from Ulithi, the carriers *Franklin* (CV 13), *Yorktown* (CV 10), and *Enterprise* (CV 6) had all been hit during operations against Japan itself. The *Franklin* suffered such terrible damage it was a miracle she survived.

What I did not know then was that the Japanese air attacks on Task Force 58, and the strikes by the planes of Task Force 58 against enemy airfields, had cost the Japs heavy losses. So many Japanese planes had been destroyed that enemy plans to also hit our Okinawa expeditionary force—including the bombardment ships of Task Force 54—had been thrown out of joint. But the Japs were also misled by the reports of their own pilots. Indeed, it was later to come out that they actually assumed they had dealt us such severe blows that the whole Okinawa operation was to be called off. Our bombing of Okinawa and Kerama Retto on March 23, for example, was apparently viewed by Japanese leaders as sort of a rear-guard action to cover the withdrawal of our naval forces.

By March 26, the Japanese had discovered their error, and they began to send planes against us. At 6:20 A.M. the *Kimberly* (DD 521), one of the destroyers of TF 54 on forward radar picket duty, became the first of a long line of picket ships at Okinawa to feel the fury of the Divine Wind. Steaming on station some miles west of Kerama Retto, the *Kimberly* was jumped by two enemy planes. One hit her, crashing into a gun mount. Although damage and casualties were not severe, this attack was a nasty hint of what was to come.

Up until then, *Laffey* and the armada of ships of which she was a part had been in the unnatural calm of the eye of a typhoon of Kamikazes. The Divine Wind had been whirling all around us, smashing into Task Force 58, but leaving us untouched. Now that typhoon of Kamikazes began to shift. No longer were we ignored. The calm center shifted, and quickly we were battling the raging cyclonic force of the Divine Wind, which blew directly on us.

At 6:55 A.M. on March 27, a Kamikaze dived into the fantail of the light cruiser *Biloxi* (CL 80). A few minutes later another crashed the same location on the battleship *Nevada* (BB 36). Almost simultaneously, the high-speed minesweeper *Dorsey* (DMS 1) was hit only a few miles to the southeast of the *Laffey*. Then, ten minutes later, another of those suicide planes headed directly for the *Laffey*. But he was splashed two miles short of his target.

This pattern of attacks was to continue for the next ten days; but, though each was pressed home, the attacks were individual, sporadic. We had expected the enemy to come at us in massive waves, like the pellets from a shotgun, his planes filling the skies. But instead, the Japanese seemed to be sending out only single aircraft, each aimed like a rifle bullet at one of our ships. The attacks weren't unexpected, but their form was puzzling, and we wondered where the masses of Kamikazes promised by their radio propaganda really were.

The first few days off Okinawa, *Laffey*'s primary job was to help protect the larger ships of the bombardment force, not only against air attacks, but anything else the Japanese might come up with. During the day, our ships would close Okinawa's beaches and bombard known or suspected enemy positions. But when darkness fell, we would draw off and away, either out to sea or to the safety of the net-protected anchorage of Kerama Retto.

We executed this maneuver at night, not because there was much danger from enemy planes or gunfire from the shore, but because the Japanese at Okinawa were known to have a quantity of seagoing suicide weapons. As at Lingayen, they were equipped with dozens of explosive-packed speed boats. More than a hundred had been captured on the islands of Kerama Retto. We also knew they had increased their production of midget submarines. (Dozens were found at Kure shipyards after the war.) And, of course, they also had *kaiten*, those man-guided suicide torpedoes which could be launched from the deck of a larger submarine. Under the circumstances, the best place for our heavy battleships and cruisers during darkness was where they could maneuver freely—and where destroyers like the *Laffey* could screen them completely.

The landings on Okinawa took place on schedule on Easter Sunday, April 1, 1945, on the Hagushi beaches in the southwestern part of the island. Marines of the 1st and 6th Divisions and soldiers of the Army's 7th and 96th Infantry Divisions expected bitter Japanese resistance of the same sort that had made Iwo Jima a hell. This is why we had brought with us one of the largest forces of heavy bombardment ships ever used in the Pacific, and why that force bombarded suspected targets in the landing areas for more than a week before the actual landings. But Japanese Lieutenant General Mitsuru Ushijima had a surprise in store for us. As at Lingayen, Japanese resistance to our landings was extremely light.

Like General Yamashita on Luzon, General Ushijima had been told he could expect no reinforcements, and he knew that the one hundred thousand troops of his 32nd Army could not hold all the island. Okinawa was no Iwo Jima. It was more than sixty miles long and up to eighteen miles wide, and its shoreline had at least forty miles of beaches suitable for landings. It was just too much territory to defend against an enemy he knew would support landings with a massive naval bombardment. As a result, like General Yamashita, General Ushijima decided to concentrate his forces in only one heavily fortified part of the island.

South from the Hagushi area to Kiyamu on the southernmost tip of Okinawa, that quarter of the island's terrain is filled with ridges and high, flat-topped plateaus or escarpments. The clifflike faces of these plateaus resemble those of the Palisades of New York's Hudson River Valley. Almost vertical, they rise from the surrounding terrain sometimes as much as a hundred feet. And in these escarpments, as well as under the hills and ridges and vegetation below them, Ushijima cut tunnels, constructed gun emplacements, and dug in his army. Safe from all but a direct hit by the largest naval shell or heaviest bomb, Ushijima's troops waited like spiders to pounce on our troops once they were ashore. It was to be Iwo Jima all over again but an Iwo Jimalike campaign that was to cost us almost forty thousand casualties. Still, we had no choice. Like Iwo, we needed Okinawa as a base to support our attacks on the Japanese home islands.

Once ashore, the two Marine divisions turned north, the two Army divisions south. Meeting light resistance, the Marines secured most of the northern two thirds of Okinawa in less than three weeks. But in the south during that same period, the Army ran headlong into Ushijima's Shuri line, and got nowhere. That was exactly what Ushijima and his superiors in Tokyo had planned. It tied our bombardment and landing ships to the beaches and the seas around Okinawa—fat, ready targets for assaults by the Divine Wind.

On April 6 the sky was somewhat overcast. The wind was blowing from the northeast, whipping up white froth on the tops of the waves with its chill gusts. All that morning *Laffey* had gone about her job of screening the bombardment ships, but there had been little enemy air activity. In fact, considering where we were, it had been a rather routine day.

This situation continued through the midday meal and well into the afternoon, but then all hell broke loose. Late in the day on April 6, the Japanese finally decided to unleash the full fury of the Divine Wind on our ships in those waters directly off Okinawa's shores. They didn't come singly. They did not come in twos. They came in flocks like flights of birds headed south in the fall, and they pounced on everything they could find or thought they could reach. Transports, supply ships, LSTs took a battering. And among the ships that were hit were seven destroyers and one destroyer escort. Our CAPs got some of them; the guns in our ships got more of them. But we couldn't get them all. And those that got through inflicted more damage than we had suffered since we had arrived off Okinawa.

During those hours of the sixth when the Divine Wind swept over our ships, *Laffey*'s men remained constantly at battle stations. Our guns were manned. We stayed alert, watching for any opportunity to open fire on an oncoming Kamikaze. Though many of us aboard had been through this kind of thing before, none of us had ever experienced attacks of such magnitude and intensity.

A number of our men watched these developments unfold with some apprehension; among these were two signalmen, Luther McBryde and Ted Purrick. Both were near me on the bridge, and when I noticed how things were affecting them, I tried to reassure them. I suggested that, should some plane bore in on us, they dive for the hollow base of the five-inch-gun director.

I'm afraid that this was one instance where my words of advice did little to enhance my future credibility. Later, when McBryde and Purrick got a close look at the *Howorth* (DD 592), which had made it back from her radar picket station after being hit by a Kamikaze, I think their trust in my judgment was considerably diminished. Pointing to the five-inch-gun director on *Howorth*, Purrick looked askance at me and shook his head. Her gun director was a shattered mass of twisted metal hanging over her side, and I was forced then to agree with Ted Purrick. As he said, there was no safe place on the ship.

Just about the time our ships off Okinawa's beaches were trying to deal with these Kamikaze attacks, the Japanese were launching another of an entirely different kind. The Japanese had very little oil and very few warships left. But at 4:00 P.M. on April 6, the ships they had departed from Tokuyama. These steamed through Bungo Strait between Kyushu and Shikoku, and headed directly for the beachheads of Okinawa.

The massive, powerful 73,000-ton battleship *Yamato*, with nine 18.1-inch and twelve 6.1-inch guns; the light cruiser *Yahagi*, with six 6.1-inch guns; and eight destroyers only had enough fuel for a one-way trip. But their sortie, called Ten-Go, was planned that way. The officers and sailors of the Imperial Japanese Navy who were manning these ships knew they would not be coming back. They hoped to reach our transports and other ships supporting our troops ashore on Okinawa. Even if they didn't, they believed that they would attract planes from our carriers to themselves, leaving the sky open for the Divine Wind.

This final sortie was a futile, tragic gesture. Not long after the Japanese warships passed through Bungo Strait, they were spotted by the American submarines *Threadfin* and *Hackleback*. And with that, their doom was already sealed.

Admiral Mitscher intercepted the messages from the submarines and immediately started to move his task groups into position to intercept them. But, though Admiral Spruance approved of Mitscher's action, he took no chances. He also directed Rear Admiral Morton Deyo at Okinawa to form a surface attack force and prepare it for action.

West of Okinawa, *Laffey* joined nineteen other destroyers, seven cruisers, and six battleships under Admiral Deyo. We maneuvered for several hours to prepare for the expected surface action, then we steamed north to meet the Japanese ships.

While *Laffey* moved on through the darkness, my thoughts once again returned to that night of Friday the thirteenth, November 1942, when I had been aboard the *Aaron Ward.* I knew that *Yamato*'s 18.1-inch guns could shoot 22.5 miles, outranging the 16-inchers of our battleships which could only hit targets 21 miles away. But Admiral Deyo was not up against the kind of odds that had faced Admiral Callaghan. The Japanese commander, Vice Admiral Ito, faced a force superior in every respect except maximum range of some of his guns. The tide had turned, and for the Japanese it was at its lowest ebb. They might inflict some damage and some casualties on us, but they would never make it past us to the beachheads.

By dawn on the seventh the end was nearing, as three U. S. carrier task groups were moving into position to intercept the Japanese force. About 8:30 A.M., the pilot of one of TF 58's search planes sighted them. He gave their position, course, and speed, and at midmorning there were more than 200 planes in the sky heading toward Admiral Ito's ships.

Our carrier planes found Ito's ships around noon. They were steaming along without air cover because the Japanese high command in Tokyo was saving its aircraft for Kamikaze attacks elsewhere. Two and a half hours later, our planes had written finis to what had been left of the Imperial Navy.

The sortie accomplished nothing. It did not even divert a critical number of our planes from their main job of suppressing the Kamikazes. By late afternoon Mitscher's carrier task groups were back at their job, and Admiral Deyo could disperse his task group so his ships could resume their scheduled duties.

As *Laffey* steamed back to her assigned station, I stood on the starboard wing of the bridge feeling just a little touch of sadness. I wasn't sorry for that Jap admiral, nor the fact that we had never had a chance to engage his ships in a surface action. There were plenty more Japs where he came from, and as far as battle was concerned, I knew there would likely be more of that too. But what did make me feel slightly regretful was that I knew I had just witnessed the passing of an era of naval history. I had grown from boy to man during that era. I had studied naval tactics during its later heyday. And I had steamed into battle more than once before that era was over. But now it had ended.

With the sinking of the great *Yamato* the era in which the battleship was queen of the oceans and undisputed ruler of the waves was gone. Although the battleship was still without equal in bombardment missions in support of amphibious landings, the aircraft carrier with her planes had emerged as the major ship of our fleet. It was, of course, inevitable. No weapon or type of warship can retain absolute supremacy forever. Yet for a naval officer like myself, this final confirmation was just a little sad. The passing of an old friend always is, even when you know it is coming.

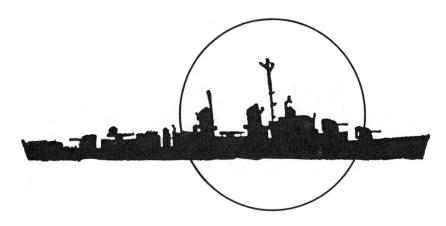

ELEVEN

By April 12, 1945, Lieutenant General Mitsuru Ushijima's troops on Okinawa were completely cut off from the Japanese home islands. Ushijima was trapped on the southernmost end of the island, surrounded on three sides by waters controlled by our fleet, and in the north by our advancing troops. We had him just where he wanted us. The daily advance of our soldiers against the outer defenses of his Shuri line was measured in yards. And our warships, transports, and supply ships were tied to Okinawa, where the Jap Kamikazes could easily find them.

But we had not come to Okinawa unprepared for this kind of situation. We had pounded Japanese airfields on their home islands. We had brought with us hundreds of aircraft on dozens of carriers and enough bombardment gunpower to destroy a major city in a couple of days. We had seized a large, protected anchorage at Kerama Retto for our ships. And perhaps most important of all, our Navy had perfected radar picket techniques that could give early warning of an oncoming force of Japanese Kamikazes.

So effective were these radar picket ships, and the Combat Air Patrols that worked with them, that the soldiers and Marines ashore saw relatively few Japanese planes. The Jap aircraft that broke through concentrated their reduced numbers to attack ships in the waters around the island. The Army leaders who dominated the Japanese high command had finally awakened to the importance of sea power. If they could get enough of our ships—and they got quite a few—they could isolate our troops ashore and perhaps eventually defeat them. But our radar picket ships and their CAPs were making this impossible.

The result was that the Japanese began to concentrate many of their Kamikaze attacks on the isolated groups of pickets stationed forty to seventy miles from Okinawa and encircling it. Most of these stations were in a half-circular arc running from the southwest to the northeast; of these, those to the north got most of the enemy's attention.

Massed Kamikaze attacks on the radar picket ships presented the Navy with a problem. The picket locations were limited, fixed areas, and under other circumstances it might have been more efficient to use ships other than destroyers for such work. With their great speed, destroyers were better fitted for duty as pickets with a fast-moving naval task force, or as close-support bombardment ships at beachheads where there was air cover. But the smaller LCS (landing craft, support), while quite capable of maintaining a limited, boxlike course in one area and protecting itself with artificial smoke generators and guns, could not mount a high mast with air-search radar. The radar of a destroyer could pick up enemy bogies sixty to sixty-five miles away.

This added range reduced the number of picket stations (and ships) needed, because each destroyer's radar covered a wider arc; yet I think every destroyer skipper at Okinawa dreaded the assignment. Not the danger, because danger was part of a destroyer's job. But all destroyer men are imbued with a tradition of aggressive offense, and waiting for an enemy to come to them was not much to their liking. Also, it seemed a waste. As Admiral Richmond Kelly Turner told me later, "If the Army would get off its ass and erect an air-search radar on the north end of the island [Okinawa], we could pull you boys in." What he meant was, pull us in for other assignments that would have made far better use of our ships' capabilities.

On the night of April 12, about 8:30, *Laffey* was screening the battleship *New York* (BB 34) off Okinawa. *New York* was lobbing 14-inch shells into Japanese positions, and we were on the alert for suicide speedboats, submarines, and enemy aircraft. It had been a long, busy day. The Kamikazes had been out in force again. Three destroyers, *Purdy* (DD 734), *Zellars* (DD 777), and *Cassin Young* (DD 793) had been damaged. Destroyer minelayer *Lindsey* (DM 32—a converted 2,200-tonner) and four destroyer escorts, *Rall* (DE 304), *Riddle* (DE 185), *Whitehurst* (DE 634), and *Walter C. Wann* (DE 412) had been battered. And the

1,630-ton *Jeffers*, a destroyer minesweeper (DMS 27, formerly DD 621) had been punished. But the *Laffey*, and many other ships off Okinawa, had steamed on without a scratch, carrying out their assignments, because of the sacrifices of ships on the radar picket stations.

At that hour there was a poker game going on in our after berthing compartment where some of the off-duty men were relaxing. In the wardroom, Ensigns Jim Townsley and Bob Thomsen were playing cribbage at one end of the table, and Dr. Matt Darnell, Lieutenant Tom Addison, and Lieutenant (j. g.) Lloyd Hull were drinking coffee and chatting at the other. The ship was relatively quiet. The duty watch and those who knew they might be called on at any moment were alert and ready to go. But—like the veterans most of them were—those of my officers and crew who could were catching their breath until all hell broke loose again.

Lieutenant Ted Runk, our communications officer, had just caught his breath for another reason. Runk had just finished decoding a message, and what he had in front of him caused him to inhale deeply and suddenly. He closed and locked the door to the coding room, climbed the steep ladder to the bridge, and sought out the officer of the deck. Lieutenant (j. g.) "Gag" Parolini answered his question: The skipper was in his sea cabin.

Runk was a calm sort of person, not easily excited, but as he knocked on the door, the rap of his knuckles was quite insistent. I opened it, plunging the cabin into blackness as the automatic blackout switch cut the light. I could hardly make out Runk, but from the sound of his voice when he told me he had a message for me, I knew something was up.

"Captain," he said, "this is one I'd rather not give you."

When the lights came on after Runk closed the door behind him, I read it, then looked at him. I had kind of a tingling sensation up my back and across my scalp. It had come at last, just as I knew it would sooner or later. I looked at Runk and nodded.

"Yes, Ted," I said, "I see what you mean." And I could, not just on the paper, but on Ted's face. He told me later that that one really shook him up. But he didn't have to tell me. I could see it, and I felt the same.

The message directed me to take the *Laffey* to Kerama Retto, go alongside the destroyer *Cassin Young*, and pick up her fighter-director (FIDO) team. That meant only one thing: *Laffey* was being assigned to a station on the radar picket line. The gates of hell awaited us.

I sat down on my bunk again for a minute or two, staring at the sheet of paper; the longer I looked at it, the more angry I became. I wasn't mad at Commodore Fred Moosbrugger, who had the nasty job of assigning ships to the picket line. Moosbrugger knew what battle was. He'd led a squadron of destroyers in the South Pacific which had torpedoed and sunk three Jap destroyers in a hot action. Nor was I angry at Moosbrugger's Chief of Staff at Oki, Captain H. T. "Dutch" Deutermann, an old destroyer man. I'd known Dutch for years and he'd had to do what he'd had to do. What made me angry was a sudden recollection of a tired old lady being kicked to death by a bunch of bullies roaring down on her from the sky.

I knew those same bullies might hit my *Laffey* just as they had hit the old *Ward.* But this time they were in for a surprise. My ship was not going to play the part of a defenseless prey for those hawks. Damn it, we had guns and the best gunners around. We were going out there hunting.

We steamed into the anchorage at Kerama Retto not long after daylight on the thirteenth. The roadstead was crowded with ships, just like the lagoon at Ulithi had been, but there the resemblance ended. Assistant Gunnery Officer, Lieutenant (j. g.) Ernie Saenz, said it looked like a place he had read or heard about where old elephants all go to die. But in this case it wasn't an elephant's graveyard. There were no elephants, but there were plenty of battered destroyers and destroyer escorts, ships that had been up on radar picket stations.

It was depressing as the devil and a little frightening, too; yet the more I looked, the more angry I became. There was the destroyer minelayer *Lindsey* (DM 32) with her bow sheared off clear back to the bridge. The *Zellars* (DD 777) had a huge, blackened hole in the side of her wardroom. It went on and on until you felt you were moving down the aisle in the middle of a hospital ward full of mangled and crippled casualties. And with each ship we passed there were some men aboard the *Laffey* who would be stunned or shaken because a place on one, which was a man's battle station on *Laffey*, would be nothing but charred and twisted metal.

For example, Matt Darnell, our doctor, was shaken when he saw the wreck made of the *Zellar*'s wardroom, and came out with, "My God! That's where my battle station is!" But a veteran

229

quartermaster said he had a different reaction. No one noticed it, but he later told some shipmates he had to go below to change his underwear. That was his story, but frankly, I think he was having a little fun and kidding his friends. He was a veteran.

After running the gauntlet of this sequence of horrifying sights, *Laffey* finally slid alongside the destroyer *Cassin Young* and moored. Immediately a fighter-director team of two officers and three enlisted men came aboard. The FIDO officers were Lieutenants E.L. Molpus and J. Vance Porlier, and their enlisted assistants were Slavomir J. Vodenhal, John Cronin, and Joseph F. Siegrist. Vodenhal put his seabag by the bunk assigned to him in one of the berthing compartments, then went to the combat information center. He stayed there, or in that general part of the ship, for the next three days. No one touched his seabag, but he was never to see it and most of its contents again.

We also took on three hundred rounds of five-inch ammunition. We wanted full magazines when we went out to the picket line. We were going out to hunt Kamikazes and we would need every round we could pack in. At Normandy, *Laffey*'s gunners had fired more five-inch shells than any other destroyer off the beaches. We expected to equal that at Okinawa. How wrong we were! We ended up firing twice that number.

As veterans of the picket line, *Cassin Young*'s sailors did what veterans occasionally do—they tried to scare the new boys on the block, meaning *Laffey*'s sailors, with dire warnings of what was ahead. It didn't work—all they got for their trouble were comments like "We saw plenty of the bastards in the Philippines!" or "Our gunners will take care of 'em; they don't mean a damn thing to us!" Maybe my men were not really all that confident, but it was very reassuring to know that they were confident enough not to let some sailors from another ship throw a scare into them.

Not everyone aboard the *Cassin Young* spent their time trying to throw the fear of Kamikazes into us. Some, like the skipper, Commander J. W. "Red" Ailes, gave us some good advice. Just before we backed away from his ship, he called over to me with some of the best: "Keep moving and keep shooting. Steam as fast as you can and shoot as fast as you can." I called back my thanks, and waved good-bye. It was just what I had been planning to do, but hearing it from Red Ailes, whose ship had just come back from the edge of hell, was reassuring.

From *Cassin Young* we moved over and anchored near the command ship *Eldorado* (AGC 11), in which Admiral Richmond

Kelly Turner flew his flag. Admiral Turner was Commander, Amphibious Forces in the Pacific Fleet and under Admiral Spruance, Commander of Task Force 51, the expeditionary force, with responsibility for operations in the immediate Okinawa area. Electronic technicians from the flagship came aboard at once to check out our radar and communications equipment. This had to be in top-notch order. *Laffey* was going to be one of Turner's "eyes" up there on that picket station, as well as a communications nerve center from which the FIDO team would direct the CAPs. Even the slightest malfunction of that equipment might result in serious losses off the beaches of Okinawa.

Not long after we anchored, I received another stunning message. President Franklin D. Roosevelt had died. The country had lost a great wartime leader, and the Navy had lost a longtime friend. Roosevelt, who had been Assistant Secretary of the Navy in the First World War, had always understood naval power. After becoming President, and long before Pearl Harbor, he had begun to modernize the Navy. Now he was gone, but that Navy would carry on. It would win this one for the Chief and the country he had led and loved, because what that Chief had done made victory possible.

At that time, *Laffey* had received no mail for several weeks, and mail meant a great deal to everyone aboard. Since there was an LST anchored nearby which was assigned to handle U. S. mail, I had one of our signalmen flash her a message. Was there any mail for the *Laffey?*

We were leaving soon and were headed for a very dangerous station. I wanted my men to have those letters from home before we left, but the answer that came back from the LST was "Wait!" I could understand why. There were more than a dozen small boats from various ships near her, and all were there for the same reason. With all those boats, it was probably sheer bedlam aboard that LST trying to get that mail sorted out. Mail sorting took time; but *Laffey* had no time. We needed priority attention and I intended to see that we got it.

On February 8, 1944, in Boston, Pay Youngquist (then an ensign, and still *Laffey*'s supply officer and paymaster) had brought me some welcome news. Pay had told me the ice cream machine was aboard; in the months since then it had done much for our morale. Now, it was going to do more. I had the signalman send a message, "Five gallons of ice cream for immediate delivery of any mail for the *Laffey.*"

I have never thought of ice cream as a lubricant, but in that case it sure greased the wheels of the mail-sorting process. The immediate reply was, "Send boat!," and our immediate reaction was to get it on its way as fast as possible. It returned shortly with seven bags of mail, and *Laffey*'s mail orderly, Sonarman Roland Letourneau, reported there was pandemonium aboard the LST. Without lubricant, it might have taken days to come up with those seven sacks of mail.

On the whole, that mail was a great morale booster. But in one case, at least, it wasn't. After our first good night's sleep in weeks, we went alongside the oiler *Taluga* the next morning, and it was as we were refueling that my executive officer, Lieutenant McCune, told me about one of our men.

I knew him quite well. A highly proficient technician, he was often on the bridge. He kept our radar tuned to perfection. It was so sharp we could often pick up distant bogeys long before other destroyers nearby were able to spot them.

I felt badly about what had happened to this fine sailor, and I called him to the bridge for a little private talk. I wanted to console him if I could. Not only did I like him, but I didn't want one of our best men facing what we would have to face in a depressed state of mind. That could be deadly for him.

Many men who served on the fighting fronts in WW II got Dear John letters from sweethearts and wives, because absence did not always make hearts grow fonder. Such letters breaking engagements to marry or announcing that wives were seeking divorces were bombshells that wrecked morale. But the letter this Navy man received was especially cruel. In civilian life he had run a store; when he entered service, he put the store in his wife's name. He signed an agreement giving her sole authority over the business in his absence. And she had sold the business and moved away from their home.

It was a one-two punch, but he was a brave man with a lot of guts. It hit him hard, yet by the time we finished talking, I knew he had the shock under control. I don't think the wife was a very good judge of people, because her husband was one of the best.

My own mail was not depressing. I had a letter from Imogen and that was always a morale builder. True, there was only one, the first in quite a time, and a year earlier there would have been several for the same period. But as always, she was concerned for my safety, and as usual, the tone of her words was warm. Other letters might have been sitting in a mail sack somewhere along the route from the States to Okinawa. And even if they weren't, it was obvious from what she wrote that her work was making increasing demands on her time. I could hardly blame her for either.

It would have been nice to have received several letters from Imogen right then. But my major concern wasn't quantity. As long as she felt the same way about me as I did about her, that was enough. When the war was over and I came home, there would be plenty of time to make up for our separation . . . unless something happened!

Under clear skies, *Laffey* steamed north through calm seas on the fourteenth of April, 1945. Arriving at a point about 30 miles north of the northern tip of Okinawa, we took up our position on radar-picket-station number 1 without sighting any bogeys. We relieved the destroyer minelayer *J. William Ditter* (DM 31), a 2,200-tonner commanded by my old friend Commander Roy Sampson. With the disappearance of the Jap fleet, there was little demand for mine laying, and ships like Sampson's—minus mines—were used on picket duty. The *J. William Ditter* was a converted Allen M. Sumner-class destroyer (originally DD 751) with the same main battery and speed as the *Laffey.*

As Sampson's ship steamed past on an opposite course, I talked with him on the TBS. Roy and his men had had some luck. During her time on station, no Kamikazes had appeared, nor had any bogeys been picked up by her radar.

I was happy for Roy and his men, but this information seemed ominous. I knew the Japs were not running out of planes, pilots, nor those rocket-propelled flying bombs. These were like German rocket bombs except they were guided by a suicide pilot instead of radio and were somewhat larger. We called them *baka,* the Japanese word for idiot. Roy's ship had luckily been in the calm eye of the Divine Wind, but if the Japs followed their usual pattern, that eye would soon pass. Roy was leaving just in time to escape the full cyclonic force of that Divine Wind.

As the *J. William Ditter* steamed out of sight over the horizon, I told the officer of the deck I wanted to speak to the crew. When the last boatswain's pipe notes of "All Hands" died away, I pressed the button on the microphone and began with, "This is the Captain. . . ."

Using the most confident voice I could muster, I pointed out that *Laffey* could not expect to have the same luck as the ship she had just relieved. No, we would see plenty of Japs; I was sure of that. They would be men driven by desperation, but they were still men, I said.

"You have tangled with this kind before and come out on top," I added. "We're going to outmaneuver and outshoot them. They are going to go down, but we aren't."

I concluded by saying I had the utmost confidence in them all, and I asked them to keep in mind that old saying about the tough getting going when the going got tough. If we did that, I assured them, the enemy would end up wishing they had never heard of the U.S.S. *Laffey*.

That was all, and I hoped it would be enough. Some of my men, I knew, were nervous and worried. It was understandable. Though the previous night had been one of uninterrupted sleep, many were exhausted from days of strain and effort, and from constantly being on the alert even when off duty. Now, after that one night of sleep, it was starting all over again on an even higher level of strain. Reassurance from the skipper could only go so far.

Yet I knew these men of mine would do exactly what I said we would do once things got started. Like all good fighting men from the beginning of time, it wasn't battle that set their teeth on edge. It was that damn unearthly waiting for the thing to get started.

Within an hour, it did start. Three bogeys appeared on our air-search (SC) radar screen, and the range-finder operator, Bob Ray, could also see them. At that time we did not have a CAP of fighters, but the *Bryant* (DD 665)—on picket station 3, about fifty miles east of us—was controlling a group of fighter planes. We requested them; and as our men manned their battle stations, the *Bryant*'s skipper, Commander George Seay, sent them on their way toward us.

The planes missed the interception, but Bob Ray and our FIDO team coached them toward the Japs. By then we could see the so-and-sos, but not for long. Very soon after, "Tallyho" came over the radio, and down went the first. A second Jap soon followed in flames; seconds after the fighter pilots reported the third Jap destroyed. It was a good beginning.

Not long after that, George Osman, our air-search radar operator, picked up eight more bogeys. We were the only ship that had radar contact, and again, *Bryant* sent her fighters. The FIDO team, working like a blind full of hunters with the people in our CIC, vectored our eagles in for the kill. We could see the fighters closing in on the Japs on our air-search radar screen, and the closer they got, the more excited everyone became. We had no visual contact with either group of planes. It was like watching one of those present-day electronic combat games that are played on a television screen—but this was no game. It was deadly serious business, with emphasis on the deadly.

234

Just how deadly it was soon became apparent. Again that ancient British fox-hunting call, used by their fighter pilots and adopted by our own, sounded over the radio. The hunters had found their prey, thanks to our FIDO team, and cries of "Tallyho" filled the airwaves.

War is nasty business, but grim as all this was, the sounds on the radio suddenly reminded me of that old children's poem about the ten little Indians. In this case, of course, the Indians were Japs, and there were only eight, not ten. But the sequence of it all was just about the same as fighter after fighter scored.

> There were eight little Nipponese
> Flying through the heavens
> But a Corsair found one
> And then there were seven . . .

And then there were only six, five, four, three, two, and finally: . . .

> There was one little Nipponese
> Flying in the sun
> But the fighters hit him
> And then there were none . . .

He went down in flames, and all we could see on our radar were those friendlies of our CAP. It was almost unreal. For two days, ever since Ted Runk had brought me that message, every man aboard had struggled with a growing tension. And now this. The concern was still there—it wasn't over by a long shot—but not one of *Laffey's* guns had had to fire a shot in this, our first encounter on the picket line. Nor did we have to open fire for the rest of that day and the night that followed. The "Indians" stayed away. Apparently, they had had enough—for the moment!

Sunday dawned—beautiful, the sky empty, the seas calm. At breakfast, both officers and crew enjoyed their food in peace and read our mimeographed newspaper, prepared by the ship's radiomen. As usual, it contained a digest of news broadcast by Armed Forces Radio, and editorial comments about our own situation. On April 15, the lead editorial alluded to a current popular tune, "Blues in the Night":

Do you sleep well at night? Do you keep hearing bells ringing? Do you keep seeing things flying around in the dark and flashes before your eyes? You do? Don't worry. You aren't sick and it isn't Pinkoff's coffee. It's the General Alarm, "Bogies in the Night." But if you stop hearing bells and seeing flashes and things flying, that's when something is the matter with you—You is daid!

Gallows humor, of course, but given our situation at the time, I was glad to see it. We were all under a certain amount of stress, yet if my men could still laugh at that kind of thing, I knew we'd be all right. When sailors on a ship in a combat zone quit griping and quit making jokes about the dangers they face, that's when a ship is in trouble.

Gallows humor aside, my men still took their situation very seriously. When our "chaplain", who wasn't really a reverend but Quartermaster Ernest "Preacher" Belk, conducted church services that morning on the fantail, the crowd attending was rather large. Belk was a good lay preacher who knew his Bible and knew his shipmates. He did his best to allay their anxiety and fears with just the right biblical quotations, and he succeeded. When the services ended, a number of men came up and told him, "Preacher, you did real good." And those were the sentiments of everyone.

Sunday morning was so quiet and peaceful the hours passed very slowly, and to keep us on our toes, I had our five-inch-gun crews track every friendly plane that came in sight. It wasn't a new exercise. I'd had our crews doing it frequently in recent weeks. It kept them from becoming bored and inattentive on their four-hour watches, and boredom and inattention was not something we could afford. In the Philippines and elsewhere, Jap planes sometimes attached themselves to the rear of a friendly formation, or even followed a single U. S. plane, just to get at our ships without drawing fire. But it was not going to happen if we tracked our friendlies and watched for those of the enemy.

On Sunday afternoon our routine was broken by a report from one of our patrol planes. It reported that there was a Jap plane in the water a few miles east and asked us to investigate. We steamed to the area, found the plane, and put a boat in the water, but the boat crew took no prisoners. They brought back an aircraft code book and other items which would be valuable for our intelligence people, and the decomposed remains of the Jap pilot. Dr. Darnell examined the corpse briefly; then we put it over the side, and the plane was sunk by gunfire.

This incident helped break the routine of what turned out to be a completely quiet day. Except for that plane in the water, we saw no enemy aircraft on Sunday. Nor was the night any different. All was quiet on radar-picket-station 1 until early the next morning. But at 4:50 A.M. it began.

It did not begin with a bang, but with a look. At almost 5:00 on the morning of April 16, 1945, an unidentified plane flew into our airspace less than twenty miles away. We went to battle stations, but the intruder had no interest in tangling with us. He stayed well out of range of our guns, buzzing around up there, making a nuisance of himself for some time before flying away. I know now he must have been a scout sent out to pinpoint our general location, and not just a typical Jap heckler—a "Washing-machine Charlie." The Japs often sent out such heckler planes at night to disrupt the rest of our soldiers and sailors and keep them on edge. But washing-machine Charlies weren't usually followed by masses of others. This one was.

Even after he left, we stayed at battle stations. The usual routine was for the ship to go to battle stations an hour before sunrise, and as sunrise that day was at 6:07 A.M., it made sense for us to stay on the alert. As soon as our cooks had breakfast ready, a few men from each station were released in rotation until everyone was fed.

I'll say one thing for the Japs. That day, no matter what else they did, they at least delayed their attack long enough so every man could go into battle with a good meal in his stomach. By the time that first Val (an Aichi D3A dive-bomber) appeared at 7:44 A.M., everyone had been fed; and that Navy chow probably did a lot to reduce the quiver many aboard felt in their midsections. No one ever accused *Laffey's* cooks of being master chefs, but their food did have heft to it.

The Val came in on our port bow, our guns tracking him all the way. When he got within six miles, we opened fire with our five-inchers. He kept coming and we kept shooting. At three miles he had a change of heart. He dropped his bomb and turned away. But as Jim Brown—a gunner on a 40-mm (Mount 42) just aft of and below the bridge on the port side—put it, he felt he'd "be back with friends."

Right and wrong! The friends showed up, but on the way home, that Val met some of our CAP fighters. He never got home.

At 8:20 A.M. I was on the bridge when Radarman Philip Nulf, on the SC radar in CIC, reported a large formation of bogeys closing fast from the north. I had the general-alarm signal sounded just in case there might still be some men eating breakfast. With engine-order telegraphs and telephone, I ordered maximum speed. Then I told the helmsman, Quartermaster Jack Doran, that I'd call out orders to him over the voice tube just above his head. I knew we'd have to maneuver like we had never done before, and fast. The only way to fight off those fanatics was to keep them broad on the beam where the maximum numbers of our guns could bear.

Lieutenants Molpus and Porlier of our FIDO team contacted

Delegate base at once. That was the *Eldorado*, Admiral Turner's flagship. She would send fighters to intercept the huge oncoming bogey formation. And it was huge. Between it and our fighters flying to intercept, that screen had so many dots on it that it looked at times like an advanced case of chicken pox.

While this was going on, down in Mount 51—our first, forward five-inch mount—Seaman Herbert Oyer and Gunner's Mate Stanley Ketron were looking at each other, shaking their heads. "Stan!" Oyer said. "Let's pray!" Ketron nodded. He already was.

A short time before, Bill Welch—who baked bread, pies, and cakes for the ship's crew—had gone to his battle station in the lower handling room of Mount 53, our after five-inch mount. Bill's job was to keep the fifty-four-pound shells and the brass cases of powder moving up to the guns above on electric-powered hoists. In a handling room, cleanliness and order were absolute necessities for safe operation. A little grease or dirt might cause an accident and, since the washroom was close by and Bill needed a shower, he decided he could take a quick one before the shooting started.

At 8:29 A.M., Seaman Ramon Pressburger—a loader on 40-mm Mount 43—looked up. Pressburger's fingers gripped the clip of 40-mm shells he was holding so hard his hands shook. "Just look at those bastards!" he yelled. And, then, as the dots grew larger and larger in the clear blue skies, he added, "Here they come! Here they come!"

They were coming all right. At 8:30 we could see that the first four were Vals, because of their fixed landing gear. They split into pairs, two heading for our starboard bow.

"Left twenty-five degrees rudder," from me put Helmsman Doran to work. But when the nearest Vals swung to their right to avoid our broadside, I yelled, "Hard left rudder." Doran threw the helm over to thirty degrees, the maximum, and we were still broadside to those planes.

I had told Paul Smith, our gunnery officer, to open up on any bogey in range without waiting orders, and Lieutenant Smith did just that. There were two quick warning buzzers, and all five-inch guns opened up.

Laffey shuddered and, as usual, the noise was deafening. Below decks, light bulbs not yet removed from their sockets or already broken, shattered. Desk drawers that someone had forgotten to lock or tie shut, flew open and crashed to the decks. *Whoom-whoom, whoom-whoom,* and black deadly puffballs

238

appeared near the planes. The forward mounts sounded like king-sized machine guns. Down went one Val, pieces flying from it, and it disintegrated in a splash. The second Val staggered. He was hit. His nose went down, down, and into the water.

Seaman Felipe Salcido was standing next to me, and I heard him shout a warning. Salcido, the bridge lookout, had spotted the other Vals coming in from astern toward our beam. But before our forward mounts (51 and 52) could swing around to lend a hand, Mount 53's two 5-inchers opened up and gave the Japs the full treatment. A third Val began shaking itself like a bird dog after a swim, shedding chunks of its wings and fuselage. Lower and lower it sank in a glide, then the landing gear caught the water and it went in astern of the ship.

As *Laffey* had turned, the fourth Kamikaze Val had done the same, trying to close in for a kill. Concentrating on *Laffey*, the pilot ignored our consorts. We had two LCSs (landing craft support) with us on the picket station. LCS 51, Lieutenant H.H. Chickering commanding, and LCS 116, skippered by Lieutenant A. J. Wierzbicki, opened up on this fourth Val. Their tracers converged and that Val found itself in the water. The left wing hit first. The plane cartwheeled across the flat surface of the sea, then it settled and sank.

When the ship started shaking from the roars and recoils of the five-inchers, Bill Welch had been under the shower. It was the shortest shower Welch ever took. Hopping on one foot,then the other, as he pulled on his pants, Bill arrived at his battle station in seconds, soaking wet. He kept the shells and powder moving up to the guns, but it wasn't easy. His bare feet were wet, and wet feet on a steel deck didn't provide the surest of footings.

While the forward mounts were smashing the first two Vals, some unburned powder in one of the guns of Mount 51, nearest the bow, singed the eyebrows of a loader. This kind of thing could happen on occasion, but in that confined space, with fresh rounds coming up the hoist, it made the man jittery and frightened. And that, Mount Captain Ed Zebro knew, could be dangerous. Zebro had a rawhide maul which was used in emergencies to coax an obstinate gun to fire. He shook it under the youngster's nose and yelled, "Settle down!" The man took the hint. Zebro with that maul was a lot more fearsome than a little powder.

When the fourth of those Vals went into the water, there were cheers from many of our topside men. But Lieutenant Paul Smith wasn't cheering. He was too busy encouraging his gunners to "Keep it up, just like that!" During the action the forward five-inch mounts (51 and 52) were kept under control of our five-inch director, where Paul was stationed. But Mount 53— near the fantail—had operated in local control, and it had worked. Paul did not have a clear view of Japs coming in on us from astern or quarter to port or starboard. Mount 53, working independently, had been able to react much more quickly to the danger. Under the circumstances, and considering the results thus far, Paul was more than happy to have Mount 53 "keep it up, just like that!" And so was I.

My account of these incidents, which took place during or just after the first four Kamikazes pounced on us, takes longer to relate than it did for more of the flock to go for us. I think I was able to take in and exhale only one deep breath of relief before a Judy (a Yokosuka D4Y dive-bomber) was spotted in a dive broad on *Laffey's* starboard beam. Coming in at a right angle to the ship's right side, this Jap required no maneuvering to let our full broadside of guns come to bear on him. But he was already relatively close, and he was a job for our 20's and 40's. The 20-mm guns could spit out tracers and other rounds at about 450 per minute, out to an effective range of 2 miles. The 40-mm was capable of 160 rounds per minute under ideal conditions and effective out to a mile. I don't think that Kamikaze knew what hit him. A torrent of red and white tracers converged on him and tore the Judy to pieces as it dived into the drink.

Almost at the same instant another Judy whistled in toward our port bow. It was "Hard right rudder" and Doran spun the wheel 30 degrees. This time it was the gunners on our port 20's and 40's who got a workout.

The ship heeled into her turn, the steady thumping booms of the 40's mixing with the loud, stuttering chatter of the 20's. We were getting to him, I could see it; but he was getting to us, too. The Nip was strafing as he came in, the steady flashes of his gun muzzles winking brightly, their slugs chopping at *Laffey's* superstructure. Our 20's and 40's finished him before he could get us, but Dr. Matt Darnell in the wardroom had some work. A number of our men were hit by slugs or shrapnel.

Their shoes were filled immediately. Signalmen and radiomen who were nearby with no immediate duties, were pressed into service to keep the ammunition ready at the guns. At a time like that, an emergency job that needed doing became the job of anybody who was available.

We got that Judy, all right, but we had to pay a price to do it.

240

When the 20's and 40's splashed him, he was close aboard. He was carrying a heavy bomb, which exploded in the water and sent shrapnel everywhere. Men were hit; but bad as that was, the hits on *Laffey's* SG radar were even more serious. The SG radar was our surface target-detection radar. Though there were no Jap warships out there around us, we needed it to detect low-flying planes. The Judy had blinded one of *Laffey's* eyes.

There was no time to think about that, however, because immediately a Val streaked in on *Laffey's* port beam. All 3 five-inch mounts began coughing out shells at this seventh attacker, and as he came into range, 20's and 40's joined them. He was hit hard and began to lose altitude, but he kept getting closer and closer. As Jim Brown on Mount 42 (one of our 40's) had just remarked, the bees were getting mean and nasty. And this one didn't look as if he was going to take a dive before he reached us.

The Val was by then only about 20 to 30 feet above the water, but he wasn't losing altitude fast enough. We were moving fast, yet he kept correcting his aim somehow, and it looked as if he was trying to crash Mount 53. He probably would have preferred to crash the bridge and pilothouse but, unable to alter his course enough to get them, he'd picked the mount as the next best target.

As that Val rocketed unsteadily in a shallow dive toward Mount 53, the guns of the mount spit out shells as fast as they could be loaded. Inside the steel box, men like Calvin Cloer and Jim LaPointe worked feverishly, urged on by Mount Captain Larry Delewski. Then suddenly, instead of both guns going off, only one fired. The other had picked the worst of all times to get stubborn.

Delewski was an experienced gunner who knew all the tricks of his trade. Aware that at times a gun could act up just like an obstinate coin machine that refuses to give up a paid-for candy bar, and that convincing it to do so called for similar techniques, Delewski acted. Kicking the gun was too rough on the toes, but Delewski had one of those rawhide mauls. He used it. The gun roared; the maul went flying across the chamber and the shell out the muzzle toward that Val.

Was it that particular shell that caused the Val's pilot to flinch and ruin his aim? Frankly, I don't know, and I doubt that anyone else ever will. But what I do know is that instead of hitting the mount broadside, the Val grazed its top and went into the water off our starboard side.

More than likely that contrary gun saved Delewski's life. Atop and to the rear of that five-inch mount there was an oval hatch like a manhole cover on hinges. It was used by Delewski to spot enemy planes not visible to the crew of the gun director forward, and that hatch cover was open when the plane sheared across the top of the mount. Had that contrary gun not required Delewski's attention when it did, he might well have been half out of that hatch.

As it was, the plane did hit and wreck that open hatch cover. Some burning gasoline from the Val's wing tank splashed into the mount, and Jim LaPointe and Calvin Cloer were wounded by flying fragments. But the gasoline fire was quickly extinguished; LaPointe said he was OK, and only Cloer was sent to the wardroom for treatment. The mount was quickly back in action, though thereafter Delewski had to watch for planes from one of the two open doors at the back of it because the hatch above was jammed.

The eighth attacker was a Judy which came zooming in on our starboard beam in a purposeful dive. Its pilot was determined, but his determination did him little good because he was soon flying without a plane. Lines of tracers from our 20's and shells from our 40's disintegrated the plane in midair; what was left went into the sea with that Kamikaze pilot.

By then it felt as if we had been at it for hours, but it was only 8:42 A.M., about twelve minutes since the attacks had begun. Our gunners had performed magnificently, and our casualties and damage had been relatively limited. I looked up at the sky. It was still filled with planes. I knew our good fortune couldn't last forever, but we'd make it last as long as we could. I stepped back inside the pilothouse, and seconds later another Val—its engine whining as it came closer—raced in low from the port bow. It was 8:45 A.M. and plane number nine was on its way.

This Jap had stayed down on the deck close to the calm surface of the water as he made his approach, and he was very near when he banked slightly and headed directly for the ship. The port 20-mm guns beside the forward superstructure opened up on him as soon as he was spotted, and were quickly joined by others farther aft. Their tracers licked out and bathed the plane with slugs. It seemed to shudder but it kept coming despite the gasoline pouring from one wing tank. Nearer and nearer it came, its propeller chopping the air, pulling it faster and faster, until it zoomed over the port side.

The Jap just cleared Mount 42, the twin 40-mm mount on the port side about opposite our forward stack, and as it shot over the gunners' heads it climbed ever so slightly. How it managed to clear our stacks, I don't know, but it ripped into the 20-mm mounts amidships on the starboard side. Its landing gear and part of its wing demolished the two 20's. The wing came off and the plane hurtled over the side, leaving three of our gunners dead.

Gasoline was everywhere. It flooded across the twenty-six-foot width of the superstructure deck, eight feet above the main deck, and it ignited. Seaman Joe Matthews was soaked with it. In flames, he jumped over the side and was later rescued. On the bridge, OOD Lieutenant (j. g.) Ernie Saenz grabbed the microphone.

"Fire amidships! Fire amidships!" Saenz announced. The voice was even, measured, almost as if it were just another drill. But Assistant Engineer Officer, Lieutenant (j. g.) Jim Fravel, and the firefighters of his amidships repair party who rushed to the scene didn't have to be told it was no drill. The whole area was a mass of flames and wreckage. Choking smoke was billowing up into the clear air and being wafted aft as *Laffey* raced through the water. The heat was intense, searing.

That ninth Kamikaze bandit not only knocked out the pair of 20's, but his exploding plane and its gasoline also disabled two of our 40-mm mounts. Mount 43, just aft of the 20's on the starboard side, was wrecked. And Mount 44, less than 40 feet opposite on the port side, was a mess.

Yet bad as this was, it wasn't all. The metal sides of the tubs were intact. But around the interiors were racks filled with spare four-shell clips of 40-mm ammunition. The cases were brass, an excellent heat conductor, and when those shells got hot, they were sure to cook off.

Lieutenant (j.g.) Joel "Pay" Youngquist led a party of men to the tubs to get that ammunition overboard, but by the time they were able to get to work the cases were too hot to handle. They had to wrap rags around their hands just to get hold of the clips of ammunitions, yet even then there were some blistered hands and fingers.

Youngquist and the others moved as fast as possible, but the heat was so intense that some of the shells of Mount 44 began to explode. The explosions blew holes in the deck—not large holes, but large enough for burning gasoline to flow down through into an ammunition magazine below. Fortunately, that ammunition was packed in metal cases.

Back at Ulithi, when *Laffey* was in drydock and being painted, there had been a case of one man complaining he was not a painter but a signalman. But out on radar-picket-station 1 on April 16, 1945, there wasn't a single complaint from anyone about having to tackle any job that needed doing. When Lieutenant Ted Runk saw the black clouds of smoke pouring from that magazine, and led some signalmen and sonarmen who were not needed for other work to haul a hose there, he could hardly keep up with them. Sonarmen like Red Yeagley and Louis Nordstrom hauled that hose down the port side in jig time. They and some signalmen stood there at the entrance of that burning magazine with Ted Runk and played water on the hot ammunition just as if they had been doing it every day since they joined the ship.

Titles weren't important that day—it was the job that counted. That and teamwork.

The men down in our engine and fire rooms couldn't see what was going on topside, but the telephone talkers in these spaces could hear it on their headphones. That Kamikaze knocked out some of our communications, and one talker in the forward engine room reported to Al Henke that his phone was dead. Though another telephone circuit and the engine-order telegraph was still working, Engineer Officer Henke knew his division had to be prepared to operate without communications if it came to that. He called Lieutenant Harvey Shaw, the assistant engineer officer who was in the after engine room.

"If everything goes out," he told Shaw, "we will adjust our speed depending on the gunfire. Watch your tachometer [an instrument showing propeller-shaft revolutions] and try to match your revolutions with ours."

After an "OK, will do!" from Shaw, Henke contacted the two firerooms. He told Chief Water Tender Bob Campbell (forward fireroom) and Water Tender Dick Brusoe (after fireroom) the plan.

"Keep your steam pressure normal [600 pounds per square inch] and your superheater temperature up to 850 degrees," he instructed each of them.

Lieutenant Al Henke knew his job, and knew his team. He didn't need me to tell him how to do it or how to prepare his team to continue efficient operation of our power plant even if all communications between the bridge and the engineer areas were cut. Henke put a naval twist on that old saying about "riding toward the sound of the guns." He was ready to have *Laffey* steaming by the sound of her guns.

As our men fought the flames and tossed hot ammunition overboard, burning gasoline and smoke were sucked into the ventilators that supplied air to the after engine room. The

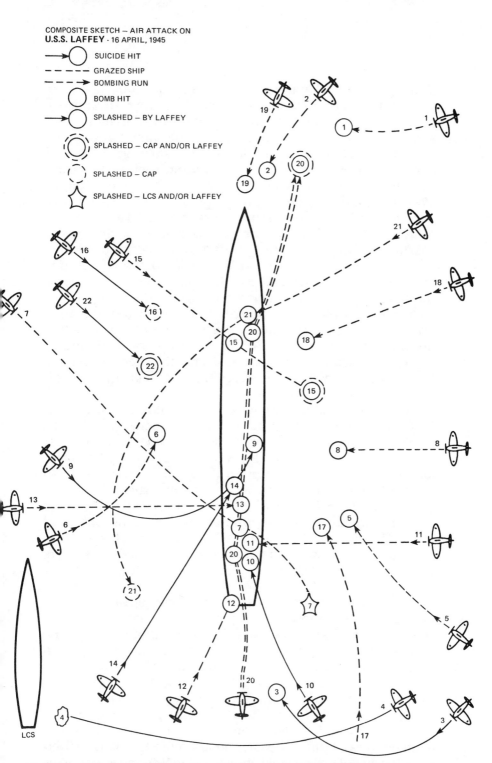

Overhead diagram illustrating the courses followed by the twenty-two Kamikazes that attacked the *Laffey* at radar picket station number 1 north of Okinawa on April 16, 1945. Overall, about fifty Japanese planes were in her area on that terrible morning.

choking smoke and fumes became so thick men could hardly see and breathe. The fans pulling in the smoke along with air had to be shut down. But that made the temperature in the engine room soar, and it was soon 130 degrees and still climbing.

Machinist's Mate John Michel was a stalwart of the after engine room. He practically lived there, and knew the place like the palm of his hand. After crawling across the smoke-clogged place and shutting down the supply fans, Michel—by then working only by feel and instinct—was able to find and work the control of the exhaust fans. He put these up to maximum, and shortly the temperature dropped and the air began to clear.

Yet that wasn't the end of it. When some of the ammunition boxes in one magazine exploded, the explosion took place above the after engine room. Some shells drilled through into the engine room below. They ruptured the turbine oil reservoir and a fire started. But a few minutes and five 15-pound carbon dioxide fire extinguishers later, Michel and some others had it out.

As I've noted, John Michel considered the after engine room his preserve, his home. He wasn't going to let the Japanese take it away from him.

The flames and damage were serious, and the black smoke that billowed up into the clear sky did not disperse. I had had the ship's speed reduced so as not to fan the flames, and with that smoke pouring out of her, I knew she'd attract every Kamikaze for miles around us. Yet crippled though we were, we still had guns. When the hawks came again, we'd give them a fight.

It didn't take them very long. From directly astern, number ten—another damn Val—shot toward us, flying just above the water. The Val came in so fast and low, the wash of his propeller seemed to make a wake on the smooth surface of the sea. There was no time to maneuver enough to avoid him. It was up to our gunners.

The three 20-mm guns in the fantail group opened up with a barrage of slugs. Tracers tore off parts of the plane, but it kept on coming. Soon it was down to one hundred yards, then fifty; and then with a terrible, wrenching, grinding crash, it plowed through the group, sending men and parts of guns flying.

The impact killed Gunner's Mate Frank Lehtonen, who was in charge of the fantail 20's. He had been wounded earlier by flying fragments, but had refused medical treatment and stayed with his men. It also killed Edmund Brown, Bernard Edwards, John Johnson, Francis Hallas, and Lawrence Kelley. The silver-smooth voice of Kelley would never again soothe and entertain us with its melodic tones.

After shearing through the mount on the fantail, the Val surged forward. It rammed the starboard part of Mount 53. Its bomb went off and the plane disintegrated. The blast ripped off some of the steel shield on the front and side of the mount, tore gaping holes in the main deck, and set gasoline fires on the fantail and around the mount. And it blew Bill Adams overboard. (He and Joe Matthews were rescued by LCS 51).

The captain of Mount 53, Larry Delewski, was in the open door of the mount when the plane hit. He was lifted bodily in the air and thrown fifteen feet. He came to rest unhurt against the port K-gun depth-charge thrower abreast of the after deckhouse. Picking himself up, he raced back to see what he could do for his men.

Delewski reached Chester Flint first. Flint and Delewski were good friends. Flint—who was in love with a Virginia girl—had, on one occasion, given Delewski some money to send home so Delewski's mother could choose a present and forward it to the girl. They were that close. Flint, horribly wounded, called out, "Ski, please help me." Delewski tried, but this time he couldn't do anything for his friend. Flint died seconds later in his arms.

While this was happening, Bill Welch got through to the bridge and reported that the fires were threatening the ammunition magazine below the mount. Permission was immediately given to flood them with salt water, and Welch turned the valve. It was just in time. In another few seconds the heat would have set off the powder-filled cartridge cases, and the resulting explosion could have ripped off the after part of the ship.

The plane had cut the fire hoses from the plugs on the stern, and Lieutenant (j.g.) Jerry Sheets sent men running to the forecastle for more hose. No sooner were they gone than Kamakaze eleven hit the ship.

It was then about 8:47 A.M. and another Val or Judy—no one ever was sure which—made a run at our starboard side, directly at Mount 53—or what was left of it. The bomb and plane blew up on impact. Jerry Sheets was killed instantly. The engine lodged in the after part of the mount, whose starboard five-incher now canted crazily skyward. More holes were torn in the main deck. The blast dished out the side of the ship and also deflected downward into the berthing compartment below. Six of Mount 53's men were killed, one of them Jim LaPointe, who had been injured earlier but refused treatment and stayed at his station. Several others were seriously wounded.

With fires roaring and smoke and broken men everywhere, Machinist's Mate Art Hogan, below decks, discovered another threat to our survival. A fire main was broken and had to be shut off. Hogan told Damage Control Officer Humphries he knew where to do it. He went into the after engine room and, with Chief Machinist's Mate Carl Dubbs, managed to close off the proper valve. Considering the beating we had taken thus far, we were fortunate that valve worked. The fire and explosions were causing enough trouble, but too much water from that broken main might have made our job almost impossible.

About two minutes later another Val, taking advantage of the lack of guns aft, flew in toward our stern. He wasn't a Kamikaze—or at least he was one who had thought better of it. Instead of crashing the ship, he dropped a bomb on the torn deck just above *Laffey*'s propeller. The flying fragments and explosion cut the electrical cables and broke the hydraulic pipes that controlled the ship's rudder mechanism. The rudder jammed. And this twelfth Jap got away scot-free.

"Captain, rudder jammed at twenty-six degrees left. No answer from steering aft," was what Quartermaster Doran reported to me. That meant we could not directly control steering from the pilothouse, and the quartermaster stationed in the steering engine room could not be contacted because his telephone line was out. Quartermaster Andy Martinis at that after station was actually doing his best despite the lack of communication, but nothing was responding properly.

Chief Quartermaster Bill Ryder raced aft to the steering engine room, picking up Chief Machinist's Mate Marcellus Hungerpiller on the way. The two climbed down into the small space to inspect the damage. But the bomb had ripped a seven-foot hole in the deck and set off 20-mm ammunition in the magazine below. Ryder and Hungerpiller tried, but the rudder just wouldn't move. It was locked firmly in place, jammed tight. Unless we could do something quick, we'd be steaming in circles.

At that moment, bridge lookout Felipe Salcido sighted two Japs approaching our port side. Though greater speed would fan the flames, I had no choice. I shouted "Flank speed!" through the voice tube, then held up two fingers. This meant, shove the engine-order telegraph pointer to flank speed and repeat the action. In other words, "Hit it, boys, give us everything we've got!"

I turned from the rail of the starboard bridge wing and looked into the pilothouse. Chief Yeoman Pierce Doyle on the telegraphs held up two fingers. He'd gotten the message, and so had Al Henke's two throttlemen. We were wide open and running as fast as we could. Not away, but just to get the devil out of the way of those oncoming Japs.

Every gun we had left that would bear—5-inchers, 40's, and 20's—were pouring a hail of steel and fire at those planes. But the Japs came on, now headed for our port quarter. As *Laffey* surged through the sea, ugly black smoke trailing from her wounds, those Japs roared at us through a sky dotted with black puffs and slashed with lines of tracers.

At that moment, in the crew's berthing compartment aft of the after engine room, George Logan and Steve Waite— machinist's mates—were starting to put out a small fire. And above, near the after deckhouse, Ensign Robert Thomsen was leading a hose party down a hatch to fight fires in the after berthing compartment. Thomsen, who had no longer been needed in CIC, had come aft of his own volition to fight fires; nearby him were Lieutenant (j.g.) Jim Fravel, Electrician's Mate Ross Peterson, and Shipfitter Medoc Irish.

Somehow, some way, those Jap planes got through that wall of fire put up by our guns. The pilot of the first, *Laffey*'s thirteenth assailant, put his hands over his face and crashed into the after deckhouse in a huge ball of flame. Seconds later, number fourteen followed him in, hitting the ship in almost the same spot. Thomsen, Fravel, Peterson, and Irish were killed immediately; and the gasoline from both planes turned the after deckhouse, or what was left of it, into a flaming inferno.

Put bluntly, *Laffey* was by then in one hell of a lot of trouble. Her rudder was jammed. She had wounds and fires in most of her after spaces. She had an engine from a plane in her after five-inch mount, and another in the washroom in the after deckhouse, and both were red-hot metal. A lot of her 20's had been smashed and some of her 40's were out of action. There was a twelve-inch incendiary shell from one of the last two planes in a urinal in a head, its cover peeled back like a banana, exposing the very flammable phosphorus. There was an unexploded bomb from the last plane lodged nearby. There was wreckage everywhere, including an aircraft wing and landing gear lodged in the K-gun depth charges. And the watertight hatches above two of the ship's three remaining after berthing compartments had been smashed, and those compartments were flooded with blazing gasoline.

I looked along her starboard side, then up at the sky again. There were more of those hawks of hell coming, but they weren't going to get her. We could still steam in a circle and we could still shoot and we were fighting mad.

No, damn it, she wasn't licked and she wasn't going to be. Not my *Laffey*, by God!

TWELVE

Even as I was swearing that silent oath, two of my men—fire fighters Logan and Waite—were trapped by flames in one of the ship's after berthing compartments. When those two Japs had rammed into the ship, they had smashed watertight hatches above two after berthing compartments and flooded both with blazing gasoline. Logan and Waite were forced to retreat into the after emergency diesel-generator room nearby, slamming the door behind them—but there was no way out. There was only a telephone.

Luckily for both men, this still was working, and they called to the after engine room. Machinist's Mate John Michel went to work with a hammer and chisel to cut a hole in the bulkhead at once, and Lieutenant Harvey Shaw informed the amidships repair party that the two men were trapped. Cutting torches were needed at once. The only way to get Logan and Waite out was through a hole in the deck above, and it had to done quickly. Machinist's Mates Elton Peeler and Art Hogan rushed topside with the torches and went to work.

Meanwhile Michel, with the help of Buford Thompson, whose place Lieutenant Shaw had taken at the throttle, finally managed to chisel a small hole through the bulkhead. Smoke poured out of it; and knowing that Logan and Waite were probably choking from lack of air, Thompson and Michel rigged an air hose with a small pipe and shoved it through the hole. Logan pulled it through, took out his false teeth, and got some air, then passed it to Waite. It was just in time. Both men were close to passing out from the smoke and fumes that filled the room where they were trapped. And with a wrench, Waite pounded out their thanks on the bulkhead to Michel and Thompson.

By this time the paint on the door and bulkheads of the emergency diesel-generator room was badly scorched and throwing off even greater amounts of smoke and fumes, and the heat in the room was becoming almost unbearable. But by then Art Hogan and Elton Peeler had a small square hole cut through the deck above. Unfortunately, it was just above some pipes, but with fresh air in his lungs Waite was able to direct the two men to move about two feet aft to an area that was clear.

Hogan and Peeler worked fast and soon had a two-foot-square hole cut in the deck. It wasn't a minute too soon. As smoke, fumes, and heat poured out of the opening, they reached down and pulled their two shipmates to safety on the open deck.

Peeler wasn't exactly what I would call the handsomest member of *Laffey*'s crew, but he had always taken his shipmates' kidding about his looks with easy good nature, and this had included remarks from Logan. But once Logan and Waite were standing safely on the main deck and Logan got his breath, he looked at Peeler and said, "Elt, you may not be very pretty, but you sure look good to me. Thanks!"

Peeler roared with laughter. Without his false teeth Logan didn't look exactly handsome either. Quickly, he reached in his pocket, then popped the teeth back in place in his mouth and laughed too. Moments later, all of them were back on the job.

While this rescue was in progress, Lieutenant Ted Runk had come to the bridge. Runk thought he might be able to free our rudder. I told him, "OK, see what you can do."

Runk disappeared and headed aft. He had to make his way through a pile of shattered airplane wings and rubble on the port side abreast of the K-guns, and in doing so he saw an unexploded bomb on the deck. He picked it up and threw it over the side, then continued on his way. But there was so much debris on deck he had to step outside the lifelines and walk along the rail, holding tight to the lifeline to keep from falling over the side. It was like walking along the top of a fence between a crowded junkyard and a cliff next to it.

On his trip to the stern, Runk came on Chief Hungerpiller and Art Hogan and took them along. By the time they got to the steering-gear room, the place was half flooded with water that had come through holes blown in the hull by explosions. The place was a mess, but working as best they could up to their waists in water, they examined the damage. It was no use: The smashed electrical leads and broken pipes would need major repairs. Runk started forward to tell me, then he saw Signalman Robert Karr, gave him the message that the rudder could not be freed, and sent him instead.

About that time the fifteenth Jap plane, which appeared to be an Oscar, (a Nakajima Ki-43 fighter which could carry bombs) came in with a whining roar from our port bow—but this one wasn't alone. He had one of our Corsairs on his tail, flying at a slightly higher altitude, and both of them were moving like proverbial bats out of hell. Our port side 20's and 40's opened up on the Nip but they had to be careful not to hit the Corsair, and their rounds probably were a little low because of this. Whatever the reason, this Jap did not drop down and ram into the pilothouse and bridge as he probably intended.

Instead, the two aircraft—first the Jap and then the American Corsair—zipped over the top of the five-inch gun director, just missing it. Death passed only a few feet above all of us, but the Jap sheared off the port yardarm on *Laffey*'s mast and sent our colors—the red, white, and blue American flag—fluttering to the deck below. And the Corsair, hot on the Jap's tail, clipped the huge "bedspring" air-search radar antenna. Like the colors, this went too, but faster. It landed with a crash on the main deck.

Once over the ship, the now wounded Oscar staggered, lost altitude, and hit the water with an explosive crash. The Corsair pilot, despite his plane's contact with our huge metal radar antenna, managed to pull up a little. The Corsair gained altitude and stayed in the air long enough for its pilot to bail out. He survived and later joined *Laffey*'s wounded in the same hospital.

When the Jap hit our yardarm and cut the halyards holding the colors, Signalman Tom McCarthy saw our flag come fluttering down. Shouting something about getting them back up there, he then went and did it. He grabbed a new flag from a locker, shinnied up that high mast like a kid going up a tall tree for some green apples, and secured the new colors in place with a section of line. After that, his self-appointed duty done, he went back to his regular duties.

Signalman Bill Kelly was on the main deck as the Corsair flew over. But he wasn't thinking about clearing any chiefs off the bridge when that massive air-search antenna was knocked loose and fell. It missed him by only a couple of feet before it landed, and it crossed Kelly's mind that he probably could have caught it.

Since he hadn't been foolish enough to try, he figured he would at least pull it out of the way later. Kelly knew better on both counts, but in the heat of battle men sometimes get capricious, illogical thoughts. That huge, bedspringlike mesh of metal probably weighed as much as a five-inch gun.

With the arrival of that last Jap plane with the Corsair on his tail, I suddenly realized that our Combat Air Patrols, which at the start had been lured out of position, were now in close support. That didn't mean we were out of trouble by a long shot, however. As if to make the point, suddenly another Jap—a Judy, the sixteenth Kamikaze—roared in toward our port beam. And he too was being chased by a Corsair.

Our 20's and 40's that would bear opened up, but the Jap was already in trouble and was losing altitude fast. Our gunners briefly punched holes in him while he went into the water; the Corsair banked left and away—which was great, except for one small thing. This Judy hit the drink only about fifty yards from *Laffey*'s port beam, just about even with Mount 52, and the heavy bomb he carried exploded. Fifty yards was very close, and flying shrapnel swept across the ship.

One large chunk of metal ripped through the three-sixteenths-inch-thick steel door of Mount 52, demolishing an electrical panel and knocking out all electrical power to the mount. Three gunners mates were wounded, among them Joe Mele, who had another piece of shrapnel rip through his body. Mele was helped outside, blood gushing from his wounds, but the interior of the mount was already drenched with it. Mele was taken to the wardroom, and Donald Carter, an old friend, held the plasma bottle as the wounds were bandaged.

The same bomb shredded the telephone leads from the control stations on the bridge, cutting our communications. But Ensign Jim Townsley quickly thought of a substitute. He hooked up the microphone to the ship's loudspeaker system around his neck and climbed atop the pilothouse, where he could direct the guns and see oncoming Japs. One soon arrived, boring in on the starboard side, and Townsley coached the starboard 20's and 40's on to him. The seventeenth gust of the Divine Wind ceased to blow and exploded in the water.

Before we sailed, I'd vowed silently to myself we were going hunting. Townsley and those gunners must have read my mind. They'd just scratched another vulture.

A minute—or maybe it was seconds—later, Mount Captain Warren Walker of Mount 52 spotted the eighteenth attacker far out on our starboard beam, heading toward the forward super-structure. This one was low, very low on the water, but the director was on it immediately. Mount 52 trainer, Seaman Raymond Faginski, trained the mount to starboard as fast as he could. The Jap came into Faginski's view and the pointer, Seaman Kenneth Pitta, opened fire.

To Faginski, who had been wounded in the thigh and back by shrapnel which had sliced through Mount 52, the Jap looked so low he figured he would be almost impossible to hit. Faginski blessed himself and muttered, "This is it!" But he kept his gun sight right on the Jap's face, which he could see very plainly, and the guns kept firing.

Gunnery Officer Paul Smith had a better vantage point and could see that the shell bursts were below the plane. He quickly cranked in an up-fifty-yards spot. *WOOM*, a five-incher recoiled, and that was it. The shell hit the enemy plane right on the propeller, and the engine and that Kamikaze went up in a flaming explosion.

Mount Captain Warren Walker was shaking with excitement as he shouted, "We got the son of a bitch! What a beautiful sight!" Paul Smith, looking down from the five-inch director, could see Walker's head sticking out of the mount's top hatch. Walker's face was a mass of blood. He'd been hit with some of the shrapnel that sliced through Mount 52 not long before. Smith spotted Larry Delewski, captain of our wrecked Mount 53, on deck and had him take over Mount 52 and send Walker to Dr. Matt Darnell to be patched up. With him went Raymond Faginski, but on a stretcher, because by the time the attack was over, Faginski had lost a lot of blood from his wounds in the thigh and back.

As Mount 52 had opened fire, the guns of Mount 51, below and forward, were elevated upward nearly thirty degrees. Mount Captain Ed Zebro told Coxswain (Boatswain's Mate Third Class) Andy Stash, the trainer, to swing the guns around to the starboard beam toward the same aircraft. But as Stash did so, another enemy plane appeared in his sights. This Val was then about two or three thousand yards away and diving toward the starboard bow of the ship.

Stash stopped training. When he stopped, Zebro looked up in the direction the guns were pointing. He saw the plane and called to Gunner's Mate Welles Meier, the pointer, to depress the guns slightly. He coached Meier and Stash onto the Jap. But Meier's electrical controls would not work. He had to use manual controls to depress and fire. He kicked viciously at the foot pedal. Then, *WOOM-WOOM*.

The shells were on the way, and the next thing Meier heard was Andy Stash shouting in glee, "We got him! We got him! Good work, Welles! Did you see that bastard explode?"

Meier's reply was, "I sure did!" And so had everyone else topside in the forward part of the ship. It was damned impressive shooting. Thank God it was.

Whether the Japs were momentarily wary of us because of this double demonstration of shooting, or our Combat Air Patrols had slowed them up for a second, I don't know, but there was a brief lull right after. And at that point, our assistant communications officer, Lieutenant Frank Manson, appeared on the bridge. I was sweeping the sky with my binoculars when Manson came up to report something to me. When he finished, he hesitated a second and asked, "Captain, we're in pretty bad shape aft. Do you think we'll have to abandon ship?"

It was a question, not a suggestion, but just for a second I felt a flush of anger. Of course we were in trouble, but couldn't Frank Manson see we were still dishing it out to the enemy? Then, as I looked at the concern in Frank's face, I realized I had no right to be angry. This young officer just wanted to know how I planned to deal with our situation, and I told him.

"Hell, *no*, Frank," I said, trying to keep my voice calm. "We still have guns that can shoot. I'll never abandon ship as long as a gun will fire!"

The concern on Frank's face faded into a look of relief. That's all he had wanted to know and it was enough. Now that he knew what I intended, he knew what he had to do to help me. And he did.

Welles Meier and Andy Stash of Mount 51 had splashed the nineteenth plane that came in to attack the *Laffey* some five hundred yards off our starboard bow. That Jap aircraft was a Val, and so was the one that now dove directly toward our fantail. The pilot of number twenty was not an inexperienced Kamikaze to judge from his tactics. He approached from almost dead astern, aiming at our port quarter and using both the sun and the clouds of thick smoke to hide his dive-bomber until he was almost ready to release his bomb. He did not ram his Val into the ship, but instead took careful aim; his bomb tore a hole eight feet long and ten feet wide in the already-battered fantail. Then he zoomed low over the ship, shearing off our starboard yardarm, and staggered away for home.

He didn't get far. He hit us; but a Corsair got him, and he went into the drink several hundred yards off our port bow. That at least was some compensation for our added damage. A smart one like that would have come back with another bomb for another ship in a repeat performance.

Seconds later, bridge lookout Felipe Salcido spotted our twenty-first assailant to starboard. Though I'd been watching to port because I thought I saw another Jap far out on our bow, I had seen the one to starboard—which was closer—but Salcido didn't think I had. In a way Felipe was right. I'd noticed the starboard plane but I didn't see him open up with his machine guns. The Val was strafing as he came in.

Suddenly, I felt Salcido's hand on the back of my neck and heard him shout, "Down, Captain, Down!" And then Felipe and I were crouched on the deck as the dive-bomber zoomed overhead, and a violent explosion shook the bridge.

The minute this Val was sighted, our starboard 40-mm and 20-mm guns and our two forward five-inch mounts opened up on him. There were two 20-mm guns just below the starboard wing of the bridge. There were four-man crews on each; and on one the gunner, George Falotico, waved to his pal Ramon Pressburger, several yards aft on 40-mm Mount 41, just as he opened up. Falotico's mother often sent him Italian food which he shared with Pressburger. He had often told Pressburger and others that no Kamikaze would ever drive him from his gun, and his wave signaled that he was going to follow the same resolve with this one.

The Val to starboard that put Felipe Salcido and me in a crouch with its heavy, determined strafing of machine-gun slugs—which had also hit other parts of *Laffey's* forward superstructure—didn't deter Falotico. He did exactly what he had always done. He kept on firing, his gun's tracers licking out toward the oncoming Jap, apparently aimed right at the bomb the Val was carrying. Falotico and the other 20-mm gunner chopped away, but when the Nip got close, he let go his bomb and it landed right at Falotico's feet. Its blast killed George Falotico, and Jack Ondracek, wrecked the gun, and killed or wounded others nearby. But George Falotico must have got a good piece of that Val before its bomb killed him. The pilot tried to climb after he went over the ship, but he didn't manage much altitude before a Corsair came down and pounced on him like an owl on a rat. The Corsair finished what Falotico had begun, shredding that Val like paper.

Seaman Calvin Cloer was in the wardroom at that time. Cloer, from Mount 53, had been wounded earlier, been patched up, had returned to the mount, been burned and sent back to the wardroom. Cloer was lying on the transom, a leather-covered couch on the starboard side of the wardroom, as Dr. Matt Darnell dressed his burns. But halfway through the job, Stewardsman Roscoe Wilson appeared from the forward passageway. Wilson had been struck by flying shrapnel and had a compound fracture of the arm. This was a serious injury, and Darnell turned Cloer over to Pharmacist's Mate Earl Waters and took Wilson into a nearby stateroom to give him some plasma. It was then that the bomb from that twenty-first Jap plane exploded outside the wardroom, ripping a hole five feet high and a foot wide in the bulkhead.

Pharmacist's Mate Waters was killed instantly by flying shrapnel. Cloer was badly hit and did not live out the day. Fragments of metal cut the tips of two of Dr. Darnell's fingers, but they were bandaged, and he kept going.

Matt Darnell was badly needed. Fred Burgess, a fireman and loader on Morris Miller's 20-mm mount, had lost one of his legs. As he was being carried below to Darnell, he saw Bill Kelly with the flag that had been knocked down earlier by a Jap plane. Burgess asked for it and Kelly gave it to him. As Matt Darnell worked on him, he clutched the flag to his chest with all his remaining strength. Darnell did his best, but even though a tourniquet had been applied to Burgess' leg, it was no use. Burgess died, still clutching the flag to his breast.

Another fatally injured man, Stan Wismer, lay quietly on a stretcher on the deck; Red Yeagley, who was helping, saw that Wismer was in shock and needed a blanket. Yeagley remembered there was one in my cabin nearby, rushed there, and snatched it from my bunk. There was a still-warm piece of shrapnel embedded in it, and Yeagley then noticed others. The clock on the bulkhead was stopped, its hands showing 9:48.

Just before lookout Felipe Salcido had pushed me into a crouching position, I had thought I saw a Jap plane far out on our port bow. I'd been right. Now that twenty-second Kamikaze, a Judy, was close, flying directly toward the port side of the pilothouse. The port 40's and 20's were putting up a hail of metal, and he was strafing back, his slugs splattering against the gun shield of Mount 42, the nearest 40-mm twin mount on the port side. The Judy got closer and closer, and so did his slugs, until finally Gunner's Mate Francis Gebhart dived for the deck to avoid being hit, and so did some others. Then the strafing suddenly stopped, a courtesy provided by one of the Corsair pilots of Major Robert O. White's Marine Fighter Squadron (VMF-441) up from Okinawa to provide CAP.

Shaken, Gebhart and others got to their feet, grateful to be alive. Then Gebhart felt something warm and liquid running down his cheek and chin. "Jim," he said to his fellow gunner, Jim Brown, "I've been hit. I'm bleeding."

Brown looked him over, then replied, "Gebby, if it's your blood, it's green."

Gebhart rubbed his chin and looked at his wet fingers. The liquid sure was green. "But how. . .?" he thought. Then he realized what it was. The Judy's slugs hadn't hit him—they had gone through the holding tank under which he'd ducked, and it was full of antifreeze coolant for the gun mount.

When the Corsair put that Judy into the drink, a bomb that the Jap plane carried exploded not far from *Laffey*, and we again got a dose of flying shrapnel. One of our men, Donald Carter, had at that moment stepped out on the deck from the wardroom. He flattened himself against the bulkhead. Jagged metal whizzed all around him, clanging against the bulkhead and cutting fire hoses on both sides of him. But as far as Carter was concerned, he believed he had emerged unscathed. He moved from the bulkhead and began to walk aft, then he fainted. He was carrying thirty-seven pieces of shrapnel in his body and he had lost some front teeth, yet he hadn't felt a thing.

Our situation was by then beginning to reach an extremely critical stage. *Laffey*, her after spaces flooded, was well down by the stern. Her fires were still burning, the rudder—still jammed—kept us on a circular course, and many of our guns were smashed or inoperable. But we could still fight back, and we intended to keep on doing so as long as humanly possible.

Thank God we didn't have to. At that moment our consorts, whose radar still worked, reported that the screens were clear of bogeys. I couldn't believe it. Why just then, when they were so close, had they let up? Then I heard the excited voice of my telephone talker, Charlie Bell. "Captain, look what's up there!"

Charlie was pointing at the sky. I tilted my head back, fully expecting to see half a dozen Kamikazes plummeting down to finish us off. But there weren't any Vals or Judys or any other of those buzzards. Instead, over us flew twenty-four Marine Corsairs and Navy Wildcat fighters riding shotgun for *Laffey*, and there wasn't a bandit in sight.

I breathed a deep sigh of relief. For the moment we were safe. Now maybe we'd get enough breathing time to rig for another attack; but it had been close, very close.

How close I wouldn't know for sure until I made a quick tour of the ship myself. But Charlie Bell, his voice suddenly very serious, gave one bit of evidence right then. Pointing to the glass port a few feet in back of where I usually stood at the voice tube, he said, "My God, Captain, look!" I did, and thanked the good Lord for one more favor, a personal favor. There were at least a dozen bullet holes in that glass.

Knowing the Corsairs and Wildcats would give us some time, I left the bridge quickly and went to the fantail to inspect the damage. The damage-control parties were still struggling to put out our fires, and they were winning that battle. But the hull aft was holed below the surface of the water and at least one after berthing compartment was flooded. Thus far the two metal doors that led into the adjacent living compartments remained water-tight, and our pumps seemed to be keeping abreast of the flooding. But if the leverlike dogs that held those doors shut began to give and leakage developed around those doors, the flooding would spread and the ship would settle even deeper than she already was.

I told Lieutenant Humphries to put a man on watch at each door and to equip them both with telephones. They were to report the condition of the doors to the officer of the deck every fifteen minutes. And if any leakage developed, they were to report it to me and the OOD immediately.

Lieutenant Chickering of LCS 51 had brought his ship alongside *Laffey* to help our damage-control parties fight our fires. But there wasn't much else Chickering could do to help us. His own ship had been hit, and she couldn't back her engines. Although by the time I returned to the bridge our fires were well under control, there was no question of Chickering's ship taking *Laffey* under tow.

I knew we had only one option—to get help from Delegate base, Admiral Richmond Kelly Turner's command ship, *Eldorado*, as quickly as possible. But we didn't have to ask. They knew what had been happening and informed our CIC talkers that two tugs were on the way. We were to be withdrawn from the picket station. With our radar out, and our communications gear battered, no purpose could be served by our staying there longer. And even had these been in working order, Delegate base knew it would be suicide to keep us on station. We had little left to fight with, and the Corsairs and Wildcats couldn't stay over us forever. The doors on those after bulkheads to the flooded compartments might go at any minute. And almost a third of *Laffey*'s men were casualties. We had 32 dead and 71 wounded. We were in no condition to meet the Japs again if they came back—and come back we were sure they most certainly would.

Once the decision was made to withdraw *Laffey* from the picket station, it became a fight against time. Tugs *Pakana* (ATF 108), commanded by Lieutenant W. E. White, USN, and *Tawakoni* (AFT 114), with Lieutenant Commander C. L. Foushee, could do a maximum of sixteen knots on their diesel-electric power plants. It would be afternoon before they could reach us. One very long hour went by, then two, then three, each minute dragging like a battleship anchor in deep mud. Our lookouts kept their eyes glued to the skies and the horizon, praying the heavens would stay empty of meatball-marked planes and that the horizon would be broken by the sight of rescue ships. It wasn't especially warm, but I think everyone did a lot of sweating, and not just from the exertion of trying to put *Laffey* in some kind of shape. "When, oh when, would that help arrive," was on every mind.

Except for the planes of our CAP, occasional shouts of our men at work, and the constant churning of the pumps, it was strangely quiet. Too damn quiet. We were a sitting duck and we knew it. The luckiest of us were those who had physical work to do. That at least kept the mind off our situation. But others who didn't and who weren't needed to help out with specific jobs tried to keep busy anyway.

One, Slavomir Vodenhal, an enlisted member of the FIDO team, went aft to the fantail looking for some way to help. On the way he suddenly remembered his seabag with all his belongings, but when he got there he knew he would never see it again. There had been a raging fire in that berthing compartment; it was by then completely flooded. In fact the stern was so low in the water it was almost up to the main deck.

Vodenhal shrugged and was about to turn back toward the forward part of the ship when his eye caught something small and flat floating in the water. Carefully, he inched his way to the edge of the deck and grabbed it. It was a picture of his father and mother that had been in his seabag—the air trapped by the plastic coating had kept it afloat.

Just about that time the mast, forward superstructure, and stacks of a warship appeared on the horizon. She looked like a destroyer—one of ours—and in fact she had been the DD 458. Now she was the high-speed minesweeper *Macomb* (DMS 23) and she was on her way to pick up a pilot who had been shot down. With no tugs yet in sight and with our pumps hardly holding their own against the flooding, I sent *Macomb* a request to have *Laffey* taken in tow. She raced toward us and was soon alongside passing her towing hawser. And then our two rescue tugs hove into view.

Though the tugs were moving at top speed, it took them some time to reach us. Meanwhile, *Macomb* began to tow us. But with one of our rudders jammed hard over, it wasn't an easy job. *Macomb*, like the *Laffey*, wasn't a draft horse. She was a racehorse built for speed, and within an hour we sent her on her way, grateful for her help but just as grateful that the tug *Pakana* could take over the job. The tug had far more towing power, and with the other—the *Tawakoni*—to help her, we could make much faster progress. We could also make safer progress. Both tugs were equipped with large pumps, which they put aboard *Laffey*.

The two tugs took over from *Macomb* about 2:30 in the afternoon; less than an hour later an escort-patrol craft, PCER 851, skippered by Lieutenant Commander Frank S. Bayley, Jr., joined them. Bayley's command was another of those wartime innovations developed by the Navy. She was equipped for rescue missions like a small hospital ship. She came alongside, evacuated our wounded, and then sped off to transfer them to a regular hospital ship.

Just after this it became evident that even with the pumps we had working, the water in our compartments was gaining on us. I went aft and looked the situation over, then contacted the *Tawakoni* and requested more pumping capacity. She secured to our port side near our stern. The tug put her suction hoses into our flooded compartments and used her own pumps. In addition, she sent more electric and motor-driven pumps over to us. Bit by bit, our flooding was controlled, and the water level in our compartments began to go down. At last, *Laffey's* stern rose slowly.

Meanwhile, our jammed rudder was causing towing problems. To counteract these, we backed our starboard engine and went ahead one-third standard (five knots) on our port engine. We were soon making four knots headway.

For the rest of the afternoon and throughout the night, the seas remained calm and the weather clear. Despite our improved circumstances, had they acted up, things could have become chancy. *Laffey* was in no condition to fight a gale and high seas, and all of us knew it. Still, we did not let down our guard. What guns we had left in working order—and there were damned few of them—were kept fully manned during the daylight hours. There was always a chance some suicidal vultures might reappear. But once it grew dark, I released the men from battle stations. The Divine Wind didn't blow at night. Kamikaze pilots weren't trained for it.

For the first time since it had all begun on the morning of April 16, the dark hours of April 16-17 brought us a chance to relax just a little. No, relax is the wrong word. You don't relax on a barely floating junk pile of steel that's being towed through the blackness at four knots in enemy waters. But some of the dread, worry, and tension eased a little. There was time to eat what was available without gulping it down on the run. And there was even some time to talk in something other than the language of reports and orders, and the jargon of naval action, and to start remembering out loud what we all had been through.

I heard how Lieutenant Jim Fravel and his firefighters waded into flames, how Seaman Tom Fern struggled to put out fires until he had to be led away, blinded by smoke and flash burns. There were Pay Youngquist, Charlie Hutchins, and Don Hintzman, rags on burned hands, grabbing hot 40-mm shells to toss them over the side. There was also the story of Hutchins keeping two guns of 40-mm Mount 44 fed with ammunition when the loader of one was wounded. And there was one of Ship's Cook Jerry Pinkoff releasing depth charges grown hot from nearby flames. Had those 300-pound packages of explosives blown, the ship would have been torn apart.

But of all the tales I heard or those my men were telling each other, the most difficult to bear were the ones dealing with injury or death of shipmates. There was Ensign Bob Thomsen taking a hose into the blazing inferno of a berthing compartment just as a Kamikaze hit the after deckhouse, then being trapped and smothered by gasoline fires. There was Falotico shooting to the last until that Jap bomb hit. There was Marvin Robertson, badly wounded in the head and back, carrying wounded Walter Rorie to the wardroom. It went on and on: Jerry Sheets, killed; Cloer, LaPointe, Lehtonen, killed, killed, killed. So many! For their country! For their shipmates! For *Laffey!* A terrible price to pay, yet they would never be forgotten.

A thousand memories had been born during those fearful minutes on radar-picket-station number 1. Bill Kelly couldn't forget the noise, especially the auto-racerlike whining of Japanese aircraft engines. Joe Edmonds remembered the general-quarters alarm that took him to his station in his shorts, pants in hand. Edmonds was in Mount 53's gun crew, one of its few survivors—and only sixteen years old. Young Lake Donald, blasted from a 20-mm gun mount, ended up unhurt, and came to under a torpedo mount. And there were my memories of a hand on my neck, pushing me down to the deck as Jap bullets peppered the *Laffey,* of shouting to make myself heard, of pride and fascination as I saw a five-inch shell from one of our forward mounts meet a Jap plane head on. A thousand memories? No! Each of us had a thousand.

By sunrise *Laffey* was at last safely at anchor off Okinawa. The tug *Tawakoni* fed us our first real meal, breakfast, in almost twenty-four hours. As before, the anchorage was filled with ships, many of them showing combat damage, but this time our reception was a little different. Not one sailor aboard any other ship tried to frighten any of ours with tales of Kamikazes. All they had to do was look at *Laffey* to realize we knew all about Kamikazes. But the fact that men from other ships could look at ours, there off Okinawa, bore witness to something else: It told them we not only knew all about Kamikazes, but that we knew how to beat them.

In the late morning Chaplain Curtis Junker from the *Eldorado* came aboard *Laffey* and held funeral services on our forecastle for those of our men who had been killed or were missing in action. At 11:45 A.M. those of us who were left aboard said a final goodbye to our shipmates who had steamed across their last horizon. We prayed for them, and in our hearts we knew the Almighty had guided them to a safe and peaceful anchorage with Him. It had to be so. They were the very best.

Over the next few days all of us began to regain our sense of proportion and equilibrium again. It's always that way when you've been in a tough battle. It takes a little time to get back on course, back to some kind of regular routine. But our routine wasn't really routine. *Laffey* was supposed to depart Okinawa as soon as she could, and that meant there was a lot of work to be done. There were no drills. It was patch and repair as much as possible so we could make it those thousands of miles across the Pacific. Repair parties from the fleet tugs *Clamp* and *Ute* and the LCI 738 poured aboard to help. But help or not, what we were doing wasn't routine.

During this time I paid a visit to Admiral Turner aboard his command ship, and came away with his hearty congratulations for everyone aboard the *Laffey*. I also paid a visit to my new squadron commander, Captain Beverly Harrison, aboard the *Barton*, in which he flew his flag. Harrison had just recently relieved Bill Freseman; he, Commander Ed Dexter—skipper of the destroyer, and Lieutenant Stuart Cowan—squadron staff communications officer, welcomed me warmly. All of them overwhelmed me with their congratulations for *Laffey*'s exploits.

I'd known Ed Dexter and Stu Cowan for some considerable time, but Captain Harrison was somewhat new to me. However, I quickly discovered that he was a fine man; a good officer with a soft-spoken, unflappable manner; and an excellent superior. By the time I left him I had no doubts that he was willing to recommend the *Laffey* for a Presidential Unit Citation.

This citation was one of the most coveted awards any ship or unit of the Armed Forces could receive; one had been awarded to the original *Laffey* (DD 459). If we received it, every man aboard my ship who had been with her during our struggle up north of Okinawa could wear a special distinctive ribbon. With this in mind, as soon as I returned aboard my ship, I sat down and wrote a letter that Harrison would need to set the process in motion. My men and their ship deserved that citation and I wanted them to have it.

Those days at Okinawa were busy ones for me. In addition to overseeing repairs and writing an official report on the action, I had also to assemble a list of those of my men who deserved individual recognition for meritorious conduct. This was a tough job, because to my way of thinking, all of them did, and trying to single out some seemed an impossible task. But luckily I did not have to do it alone.

I sent for my exec, Lieutenant Challen McCune, and told him to get the officers together and come up with a list of names. In addition, I asked him to see to it that any recommendations for awards made by enlisted men through their division officers be brought to my attention. As a result, for the next several days enlisted man after enlisted man was sent to me so I could personally hear their recommendations.

The job of compiling this list of names and forwarding the recommendations through channels to the Navy Department was a pleasure, but it wasn't an easy task—even with all the help I got. Both then and after, I had a nagging worry that someone had been left off the list who should have been on it. Although this did not happen, there was a tragic oversight. Machinist's Mate John Michel, whose quick thinking and work had helped save the lives of Steve Waite and George Logan, received a Letter of Commendation instead of the medal he deserved. Stalwart John Michel never let on to anyone about this during his lifetime. Not until after his death, caused by cancer in 1971, did we find out about it; and I've never forgiven myself for allowing this slipup to happen. John Michel should have had that medal.

On April 22 at 2:00 P.M. *Laffey* steamed away from Okinawa, bound for Saipan. By no means was she in good shape. Her hull had been patched and her rudder repaired and she was reasonably seaworthy, yet the prospect of an ocean voyage raised no little concern. She had taken a terrible pounding, and there was no way of telling how she might stand up to a storm at sea if we were unlucky enough to encounter one. As always, the sea was the most fundamental and unpredictable challenge.

In spite of her general condition, her lack of radars, and her limited gun power, the minute *Laffey* left Okinawa she was back on duty again. With us was the transport SS *Dashing Wave;* and our sonar gear and depth charges would provide her with antisubmarine protection. Yet frankly, it was a question about who was escorting whom—though not in the mind of Captain Royal W. Abbott, USN, Commander of Transport Division Fifty, who was aboard the *Dashing Wave.* Just before we parted company with him later on, he made this clear by saying, "It was an honor to be escorted by you."

Despite our concern, the trip to Saipan was uneventful. The old devil sea, perhaps out of respect for what *Laffey* had endured, remained quiet and calm. Each day we steamed along with the sun shining down on us from the heavens, our bow splitting the blue-green waters like a hot knife slicing butter, a foam-flecked wake trailing aft from our battered fantail. There were no enemy planes, no submarine contacts. It was peaceful.

At Saipan we stayed just long enough for *Laffey* to get some more emergency repair work done on her fantail and for Matt Darnell and me to pay a visit to our wounded in the hospital there. Like *Laffey*, my men were on the mend, and though still not in the best of shape in some cases, their progress was good. And also like the *Laffey*, I knew that the men would soon be headed for home.

Thereafter, our journey took us on to Pearl Harbor; again, the sea and weather were kind. It was smooth steaming all the way. There was no plunging, pounding, and lifting, no rolling either. The only stress placed on the ship was the thrust of her screws, and this was steady and without interruption.

With so much of the ship still torn up, living conditions were a little spartan and I would hardly term the trip a pleasure cruise. Yet there were no complaints. We had been through so much that any minor discomforts were hardly noticed, and to us the voyage actually was a pleasure.

Our stay at Pearl was a little longer and our welcome was, if possible, even warmer. On arrival, Admiral Nimitz's headquarters sent us hearty congratulations. The Acting Commander, Cruisers and Destroyers, Pacific Fleet, invited the crew to a beer party, and the officers to a party at the Destroyer Officers' Club. I know my men appreciated that message from Admiral Nimitz's headquarters very much, as did all my officers. But in the case of the crew, I strongly suspect that the hamburgers, those hot dogs, and all that beer—as much as anyone could drink, provided free by Rear Admiral W. K. "Sol" Phillips—were appreciated a little bit more.

Of course, I am only guessing. No one told me this. But I knew my men. They liked praise, yet there was something much more satisfying about hamburgers, hot dogs, and beer.

Sol Phillips was an old friend. He had taught me navigation at Annapolis fifteen years before, and it was a great pleasure to see him again. But during our conversation, he threw me a curve. He asked me if I could draw a diagram of the April 16 Kamikaze attacks on the *Laffey*. And he asked me to have it ready by about 8:00 the next morning.

This was a tough one, but thanks to having had time to talk to my officers and men and to having done an official report of the action, the jumbled blur of those minutes had settled into place. Though I was no draftsman or artist, each piece was now in focus. I managed it.

It was well that I did. The next day I was called on to attend a number of meetings and conferences, and was asked to give an account of that action north of Okinawa. For this, the diagram was invaluable. And afterward, Vice Admiral W. W. "Poco" Smith, Commander, Service Force Pacific, introduced me to someone who wanted a copy of it. He was the famous historian Samuel Eliot Morison, who served as a captain in WW II and whose fifteen-volume history of the U. S. Navy's operations in WW II became a classic history of naval warfare. A brief account of *Laffey*'s trial on the picket station and the diagram appeared fifteen years later in Morison's Volume XIV, *Victory in the Pacific*.

Pearl Harbor had excellent repair facilities, but the damage that *Laffey* had suffered was just too extensive for all of it to be handled there. Common sense dictated that the ship be sent on to the West Coast so that she would not tie up facilities at Pearl that could be better used to get less-damaged ships back into action quickly. Some days after we arrived, orders came through for my ship to proceed to the States as soon as further emergency repairs had been completed.

These were absolutely necessary, however, because we could not count on the good weather lasting forever. The explosions and fires had weakened the after part of the ship considerably. Even the relatively minor stresses it had endured on our voyage from Okinawa—the natural vibrations of our propellers and the movements of the rudders—put further strains on her. Shipyard welders at Pearl took no chances. They welded huge I-beams onto *Laffey*'s fantail area just in case we encountered heavy weather. I certainly approved, despite the odd look that they gave her. We had brought her so far and were so close to home, we didn't want to lose her now.

On May 23 we were safely in Port Angeles, in the state of Washington. We had escorted a homeward-bound merchant ship, the *Wisconsin*, from Pearl to San Francisco; then, with our final assignment completed, we'd steamed north to Port Angeles. We off-loaded what little ammunition we had aboard at the St. Clair Inlet ammunition depot. And on Friday, May 25, thirty-nine days after the hell of radar-picket-station 1, *Laffey* was safely alongside Pier 48 in Seattle. We were home, home safe at last, and *Laffey* would eventually sail again.

While we were still at Pearl Harbor, I'd sent Lieutenant Harvey Shaw on ahead to the West Coast by plane with a long list of work that *Laffey* would need to get her in fighting trim again. The day before we moored at Pier 48, Shaw arrived back aboard: What he told us sounded more trying than our struggle north of Okinawa, but trying in a different way. It wouldn't be the Japs this time. It was going to be the public and press. *Laffey* was going to be on display for some days in Seattle and in Tacoma, and all of us were about to become the focus of press attention. High naval officials wanted to convince the public that the war was far from over and that we could not let up on our efforts until it was. Seeing and hearing about *Laffey* could help do that.

It was a worthy objective. There had been some slackening of effort by shipyard and other defense workers ever since VE day on May 8 when the war ended in Europe. Yet though the Japs were reeling from our blows, an invasion of the Japanese home islands might be necessary after Okinawa was secured as a base. It wasn't over—not yet. Still, the idea of being the center of so much concentrated public attention was just a little frightening.

But ... orders were orders, and obey them we did. As it turned out, I think most of *Laffey*'s men enjoyed the experience. Tired as they were and desperately as they wanted leave to be with loved ones, being celebrities—if only for a brief period— turned out to be fun.

The only thing that bothered me about all of this was that there were thirty-two of my men who would never get the chance to share and know the praise heaped on *Laffey*. Back at Okinawa I had written to their families—one of the most difficult tasks any skipper can face. I hated having to do it. I would much rather have brought those men home alive and well aboard the ship they loved so much and gave up their lives to save.

I called Imogen from Seattle on the night of the twenty-fifth. She had heard the story of *Laffey* on the radio news. I was anxious to see her again as soon as I could, but exactly when that would be, I still didn't know. Aside from orders dealing with public display of the ship, publicity interviews, and making arrangements for *Laffey*'s repair, I'd as yet had no hint of what was in store for me. I might be kept in Seattle for some time, involved in a continuing publicity campaign relating to the ship, or I might be given a reassignment.

Though I did not like thinking about the last possibility, I knew that it might happen. Professional naval officers who had had long periods of sea duty were frequently then expected to take command of a desk ashore for a certain period before getting sea duty again. This rotating procedure was quite sensible, because it gave professional officers a variety of experiences which could enhance their worth to the Navy. But to many, being skipper of a desk was not a favorite job. However, it was a possibility I had to face, and there was at least one good thing about it. If I was reassigned to a desk job, I would surely have time to visit Imogen before I took up my new duties.

I could not tell her this on the telephone because such things were covered by security regulations. But I promised her that as soon as I received orders, I would try to get down to Los Angeles to see her. She had moved there from New York some months before in the hope of furthering her career—something she had told me in her last letter.

Imogen congratulated me on *Laffey*'s exploits and said she wanted to see me too; but as I think back on it now, I believe her voice had a note of disappointment or irritation in it. Perhaps the hindsight of years just makes me imagine that this was the case, but at the time, one thing was clear: Something was wrong.

Several days later, I received a letter from Imogen which made me believe all that was nonsense. On May 26 I was contacted and asked to appear on a nationwide network radio program, *We the People.* Being excited about it, I'd sent telegrams to my family, to Bob Montgomery and Pete Newell, and of course to Imogen, alerting them all. All had tuned in on the broadcast, Sunday evening the twenty-seventh, and Imogen wrote that letter immediately after. Again, she congratulated me on our success at Okinawa, and the tone of the letter convinced me that absolutely nothing was wrong between us. Later, when I found out through a letter from Bill Freseman that I was indeed going to be reassigned to BuPers (Bureau of Naval Personnel) in Washington, and called Imogen to say I'd soon have a chance to get to L.A., I was even more convinced that all was well between us.

Wonderful as this prospect of seeing Imogen was, I had mixed emotions when my orders finally came through. I did not want to leave *Laffey* and my men, and turn them over to another skipper. We had been through so much together, and although I knew separation was inevitable eventually, I dreaded its coming. I guess most skippers feel that way about every ship they have commanded, but in the case of *Laffey* and her men, it was something special. Together we'd been tested by the fires of hell and together we had triumphed. It was a bond we would share forever.

In early July the change-of-command ceremony was held on *Laffey*'s forecastle, and I gave my last little speech as the captain of that gallant crew and our ship. It was difficult for me to know what to say. At a time like that words can be so inadequate. But one thing I made sure everyone assembled there understood: *Laffey*'s success was due to the indomitable spirit of her men.

"I will always be proud that I have been shipmates with you," I said. And then, blinking a little because I guess I had something in my eye, I turned over command of the *Laffey* to an old friend, Commander Odale D. "Muddy" Waters.

At the brow after the ceremony, there was a crowd to say goodbye. As I shook each hand, looked into each familiar face, and heard each familiar voice, memories flooded my mind. There was a face, tight-lipped with stress as *Laffey* plunged through a storm north of Bermuda; a voice heard outside my cabin as the ship lay in drydock at Ulithi; an order shouted over the thunder and chatter of our guns as a Kamikaze dove at us. I wanted to stay as long as I could, but I wanted to get out of there too. What would these men think if that lump in my throat got control of me?

And then, suddenly, I was away and walking down the pier, trying to hurry without seeming so do so. But I only got a short distance before I heard a voice calling behind me. I stopped and turned, and in a couple of seconds a running figure caught up with me.

"Captain, sir," the voice said, " I just wanted to say goodbye and thanks." I took his hand, looked into the face. His eyes were full of tears, and I swallowed hard again to keep down that lump in my throat. It was the court-martialed crewman whom I had given another chance, doing his best to let me know how grateful he was for what I had done for him.

I assured him that thanks weren't necessary, that he had done it all himself. He had proven what I believed all along, that he was a good man. Not once since our talk had he been in any trouble, and he'd done his duty as well as any man aboard. I was proud of him, I said.

He thanked me again, and when we parted company there were still tears in his eyes. I turned quickly and walked on down the pier, hurrying a little as I went and trying not to think about it. Suddenly, I felt a little lost, alone. It wasn't the same feeling I had had so long ago about *Aaron Ward*, but it was similar. I knew that never again would I stand on *Laffey*'s bridge as her skipper, and that all those men who played such an important part in my life for so many critical months would no longer be my ship-mates. It was going to take some time for me to get used to the situation.

Still, there was one compensation. My reassignment gave me the opportunity to visit Los Angeles, and that meant I would be able to see Imogen. You can be sure I did not waste any time getting my things together and heading south on my way.

When I had sent the telegram to Bob Montgomery alerting him to my appearance on that radio show, Bob had replied with another containing congratulations and asking me to get in touch with him should I be in Los Angeles. On arriving there, I tried to contact Imogen, but reached Bob first; immediately he asked me to join him and his wife, Elizabeth, for dinner that night. I was on the point of saying I had another engagement but would like to see him later when he added that I was to bring along anyone that I wanted. With that, I accepted.

I was sure Imogen would enjoy meeting Bob and his wife. Both Bob and Imogen were in show business and probably had much in common. Also, I knew Imogen had come to the West Coast to further her career, possibly to get into movies, and Bob had a lot of experience in Hollywood. Once Bob met her—he already knew who she was because he'd seen her picture on my desk aboard ship a number of times—I was sure he would be willing to give her some good advice. And that too would please her.

As a result, I had no qualms about telling Imogen that our first evening together would be spent with some other people. And she, in turn, sounded pleased when I told her who they were. When I hung up, I was sure it was going to be a great evening for both of us.

It didn't start off quite so smoothly. I had trouble finding the place where she lived and by the time I picked her up, I was late. Then we had to rush like the devil to get to Bob's home on time, and we hurried on from there with the Montgomerys to get to the restaurant where we had reservations. In the process, Imogen and I had very little chance to talk.

After dinner we went back to Bob's place. By then, he and I were deep into conversation about the squadron and people in the Navy we both knew. He was especially interested in hearing about good friends like Stuart Cowan, Freseman's staff communications officer with whom he had roomed aboard the squadron flagship. I was happy to report that Stu, the last time I saw him, was in great spirits and had come through unhurt. But I'm not sure how happy Imogen and Elizabeth Montgomery were. They got on fine, but we hardly let them get a word in edgewise.

This didn't change even when actor Jimmy Cagney dropped by. The main topics of conversation continued to be the Navy and the war. Even when Jimmy Cagney talked of movies, they were films dealing with the Navy, films like *The Fighting Lady*, which had just been released. Cagney urged me to see it first chance I got, even though it was about a carrier, not a destroyer.

When Imogen and I said good night to the Montgomerys, I was in great spirits; on the way back to her place, I guess I did most of the talking. Imogen was considerably more restrained. She didn't say much, and she seemed a little preoccupied, as if she had something on her mind. Yet not until we said good night at her door did I sense that something might really be wrong.

I was a little puzzled, and at first I thought it was just the events of the evening. I had been so caught up in the conversation with Bob that I hadn't given her the kind of attention I should have. That, I knew, was unforgivable. But as I drove away and thought about it more and more, I began to realize it was more than that. My worst fears about us had become a reality. Difficult as it was for me to accept, it was all over.

I could hardly believe it, but the more I thought about it, the clearer it all became. Sometime, perhaps months back, Imogen must have decided it just wouldn't work. Fond as we were of each other, she'd apparently reached the conclusion that she was not cut out to be the wife of a professional naval officer. Not only did she have her own career, but even were she to give it up if we married, our basic interests just weren't compatible.

I was upset and depessed, but as time went by, I realized that I was a very fortunate man. During all those months when I had had to face some of the greatest trials and challenges of my life, Imogen had never let me down. There had been no Dear John letters, only those filled with prayers for my safety, and success and encouragement when I needed it most. Even after she must have reached her decision, Imogen had continued to write. Only when I and the *Laffey* were safely home again, and she knew I could manage without those letters, had she indicated to me what she had decided.

I went on to that desk at BuPers in Washington still feeling sad, but with my heart full of gratitude. Imogen, in her own way, like all my men, had helped me save the *Laffey*. Because of that, the USS *Laffey*, DD 724 of the U. S. Navy, met every challenge successfully and did not die on Monday, April 16, 1945. Instead, *Laffey* won, as I'd been determined she would, and came home to eventually receive that Presidential Unit Citation.

That was enough. I could not ask for more.

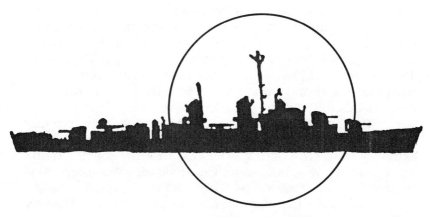

EPILOGUE

That battle up at radar-picket-station 1 north of Okinawa on April 16, 1945, was *Laffey*'s last action in the Second World War. The war ended officially on September 2, and I wish that the ship and all who had been with her on April 16 could have been in Tokyo Bay that day to see the signing of the Instrument of Surrender. But it was impossible. Some thirty-two of our shipmates were dead, killed in that action. Another seventy-one good men were still recovering from wounds, and many of the rest of us were no longer with *Laffey*. And the ship herself wasn't ready. Her repairs were not completed until four days after the signing.

After that the ship spent a relatively peaceful year on duty in Hawaiian waters, but then got involved in a big one. In May 1946 she took part in the atomic bomb tests at Bikini Atoll; but not, thank God, as a target ship like so many of those she had served with in the war. The Navy had her steaming all over the area collecting scientific data on the blasts. Then in 1947 she was decommissioned and became part of the Pacific Reserve Fleet.

During those two years I was in Washington serving in the Enlisted Training Division of the Bureau of Naval Personnel. Though I had no contact with the ship, I was often in touch with some of my officers. Orders for officers emanated from BuPers, and a number of my officers called me with requests for help with new assignments, just as I had called friends there during the war for help myself.

Laffey remained part of the reserve fleet until early in 1951;

and during that period of inactivity, her former skipper was very busy. I spent fifteen tough months working my way through a graduate course in personnel administration at Northwestern University, and then was made executive officer of the cruiser *Manchester* (CL 83). The ship was in Philadelphia, based at the navy yard there, and I was pleased because I had a number of good friends in the area.

Up to then, I had been steaming through life alone, but just by chance I was at a social gathering one day and noticed an extremely attractive young woman across the room. I didn't know who she was, but before the affair was over a very good mutual friend introduced us. This "sighting" proved to be the best one of my life. Her name was Elizabeth Reuss. We got on very well together. And it wasn't very long before we were completely in love and I asked Betty if she would agree to sail in company with me from then on.

Much to my joy, Betty accepted my proposal. We were married six months later, in 1949. Not long after, Betty got her first taste of what it was really like to be the wife of a professional naval officer. We were transferred to Norfolk, Virginia, where I became Commander, Destroyer Division 202, and was involved in a steady round of antisubmarine exercises. After that came two more years in Washington in BuPers.

Laffey was recommissioned January 26, 1951, but I did not become her skipper. She was, however, in good hands. When she went back to war again in 1952, during the Korean hostilities, the man who stood on the starboard wing of the bridge I remembered so well knew her almost as well as I did. Commander Charles Holovak became her skipper; he took her to Korea, where she engaged enemy coastal batteries in Wonsan Harbor and did a lot of those other things she did so well. Who better than Charlie Holovak, my former executive officer, to take the ship Ensign Jerry Sheets had called "our Lady" to sea again? And somehow I had the feeling that Jerry up there was smiling as he watched Charlie do it.

About the time *Laffey* returned from the war, I was promoted to captain and ordered to the Naval War College. And in 1954 when *Laffey*, then operating out of Norfolk, rescued four passengers from the sinking schooner *Able Lady*, off the Virginia Capes, I was skipper of the attack transport *Glynn* (APA 239). I spent fifteen months at sea, some of it following icebreakers through ice fields to deliver Army construction troops to Thule, Greenland. Thereafter, it was back to Washington to the Fleet Readiness Division in the Pentagon.

In 1956 *Laffey* was off again, steaming through waters of crisis. She was part of the Sixth Fleet in the Mediterranean, patrolling the coastline of the Israeli-Egyptian border. She wasn't in battle, but certainly she was as close to it as any ship there. I chuckled when I heard about it. She always seemed to end up someplace where there was trouble in the wind.

After about eighteen months in the Pentagon, I sent in a request for reassignment. In order to qualify for further promotion and have a shot at becoming a rear admiral, I needed command experience with one more qualifying type of warship. I had been in a cruiser and in destroyers. I wanted command of a battleship, and I was greatly elated when I learned I was to become the skipper of the *Iowa*. I took command of this 45,000-ton battleship (BB 61) in December 1956. And before she was finally ordered home to be decommissioned, I too had been out there with the Sixth Fleet in the Mediterranean, in the same waters as the *Laffey*.

In 1959 I was selected for promotion to rear admiral and shortly took over command of Cruiser Division Five in the Pacific. Once again this meant a move to a new home for Betty, but this time at least it was a move to sunny California. Then in 1960, while *Laffey* was still in the Mediterranean area, I became commander of the Mine Force in the Pacific and commander of the Long Beach, California, Naval Base.

I had no contact with *Laffey* in California, but while there I did see Imogen. My wife, Betty, didn't mind a bit because Imogen and her husband were good company. He was a Hollywood movie producer Imogen had married in 1947 when she gave up her career to settle down and have a family; like Betty and me, by then they had two beautiful daughters.

The four of us spent a number of very pleasant evenings together, either at dinner at the Naval Base or at Imogen's home in Encino. There were also some weekend afternoons, too, which our daughter Julie especially enjoyed. Our youngest was very interested in their swimming pool—no doubt because her naval officer father had sailed so many seas.

In recent years we have learned that Imogen has had a new career, this time as a composer, and quite a successful one. Some of her songs have been recorded by singers like Sammy Davis, Jr., and Frank Sinatra. But her only public appearances are talks she gives on music and musical celebrities—such as George Gershwin, whom she knew—at colleges in that area of California.

In 1964 Betty and I and our family were in Omaha, Nebraska, where I served as Commander, Naval Reserve Training, headquartered there. At the same time, *Laffey* had her bow right into it again. There was no shooting; it was all very peaceful. But I doubt that the commander of those Soviet warships training in the Mediterranean really enjoyed being shadowed by the *Laffey*.

I rounded out my active-duty career with two years in Washington, serving as Deputy Inspector General and as Inspector General. But several months before I retired on July 1, 1966, I got a chance to see *Laffey* and a lot of my men again. She was then based at Norfolk, Virginia, and when I found out she would be in port on April 16, the twenty-first anniversary of the Okinawa action, I realized then would be a good time for a reunion.

I got plenty of help. Frank Manson, then a captain, was on duty in Norfolk and volunteered to take care of arrangements there. And Paul Smith, also a captain then, tracked down the whereabouts of a large number of our officers and men.

Over one hundred shipmates and their families poured into a Norfolk motel that Friday to spend the weekend celebrating our anniversary. Betty and our oldest, Hilary, were there with me (Julie was at home); and being still on active duty, I was in uniform. So too were Harvey Shaw, Frank Manson, and Paul Smith, but the rest favored mufti (civilian clothes). No doubt in some cases, there wasn't any choice, because some of my men had lost that trim look that goes with eating Navy chow. But either way, it didn't matter. If anyone did salute anyone, he was saluting an old friend and shipmate. And if some called someone "sir," it was for the same reason. In general, however, greetings tended more toward, "You old SOB! You look great! How the hell are you?"

Very un-naval. But who cared—we were having too much fun!

I guess the only very serious note was struck by a message from Admiral Tom Moorer, Commander in Chief, Atlantic Fleet. (Moorer was later to become Chief of Naval Operations and then Chairman of the Joint Chiefs of Staff.) In part, his message was, "That so many of you have come hundreds and even thousands of miles to see your shipmates and your ship after twenty-one years, testifies to your loyalty and devotion. . . . Those of us on active duty are honored to welcome you as shipmates. We are inspired by your presence."

The next morning we refueled with a good breakfast. Snapshots taken of shipmates those many years ago were passed around from table to table and brought forth the usual joking remarks and nostalgic comments. But there were no photos of the Okinawa action. As far as anyone knew, the only men who might have had cameras handy during those minutes were Jim Fravel and Bob Thomsen. If they had found time to use them, we would never know. Both men had been killed and their cameras destroyed.

We toured the ship that day, welcomed aboard by her skipper, Commander N. L. Kaufman. Then we assembled on the superstructure deck for a memorial ceremony to honor our fallen shipmates. A chaplain said prayers and addressed that crowd of damp-eyed visitors while a helicopter from the Naval Air Station hovered over the water near the stern and dropped a floral cross. Then the ceremony was over; but before leaving, everyone went through the passageway where a bronze plaque dedicated to our fallen shipmates was bolted to the bulkhead. And a lot more eyes grew a lot damper.

We concluded the reunion with a dinner-dance that night. There were a few informal speeches. The music was good and almost everyone found time to dance. There was a lot more reminiscing, a lot more joking, and a good deal of fun. The next morning, everyone said goodbye and headed for home.

This was our first reunion, and the feelings expressed by all who attended were pretty much summed up by my wife. "It was fabulous," she said. But there was something else about it, too. It again made me realize just how much my men loved their ship. When Andy Stash wrote to me later, he put his finger right on it. "She seemed human to most of us, like a long-lost buddy. . . . . How much they loved her and thought about her."

There were more reunions, one in 1970 in Atlantic City, another in 1973 in Alexandria, Virginia. On that one, *Laffey* carried us on a little voyage down the Potomac River, one hundred strong and with families aboard. It was during that gathering that my men first began to express concern about the future of the ship. *Laffey* was then twenty-eight years old; and in terms of a destroyer's life, every year is like three years of human life. Two years hence she would be thirty, the equivalent of a human being ninety years old, and the Navy couldn't keep her too long thereafter.

We agreed then to band together to save the *Laffey*, if we could. We didn't want the breakers to do what the Japanese had never been able to do—finish her. It was our unanimous decision to try and find a city or a state that would accept her and maintain her as a public memorial.

It was the only way our ship could live on—but we knew we were in for a tough struggle. Over the years since WW II there had been so many gallant warships whose men had tried and failed to save them. Could we do it?

Again, the reaction was unanimous. We had done it at radar-picket-station 1 and we'd do it again.

The Navy kept *Laffey* in commission until just after her thirty-first birthday. Yet even by March 29, 1975, when two hundred people assembled at Alexandria for her decommissioning ceremony, the horizon was still full of dark clouds. Though she made a brave sight, with her spotless decks, her flags and pennants fluttering in the fresh breeze off the Potamac, my heart was heavy. She still looked as beautiful and as powerful as the first day I'd seen her, but we had to find her a home. Underneath that brave exterior, she wasn't the same. She'd grown old and tired in the service of her country, and she deserved an honorable place to rest.

Commander John Shewmaker, her last skipper, mirrored my feelings exactly with his words:

"It is with deep personal regret that I haul down the *Laffey*'s commission pennant. With her Presidential Unit Citation, her Meritorious Unit Citation [awarded following the Jordanian Civil War in 1970], four Battle Efficiency *E*'s, four Gunnery *E*'s, four Engineering *E*'s [all for Excellence] she leaves a record for the destroyers of the future to strive to equal."

Then, with colors and pennants lowered and given to Shewmaker, the crew and officers marched off the ship. And Shewmaker, in a kind and very gracious gesture, came over to me and handed me the ship's Presidential Unit Citation pennant. I thanked him, but as I held that blue, gold, and red pennant, I felt very badly. It was over.

Laffey's active career may have come to an end that March 29, but as far as those who loved her were concerned, our fight was just beginning. We were going to save her. We kept at it even though each year brought the sorrowful news that more of our shipmates were gone. Yet we didn't falter. We were not going to abandon *Laffey* as long as there was one of us left to fight for her. And we were going to win.

Win we did, though it took several more years. *Laffey*, the ship that would not die, did not die. She is now in the navy yard in Charleston, South Carolina. Sometime in 1981 she will be moved to nearby Patriots Point, South Carolina's Naval and Maritime Museum in Mount Pleasant, and become a memorial.

White water no longer curls back from our *Laffey's* high, proud bow. There are no men at her throttles or on her bridge, and her guns no longer speak. But she is alive with shades and memories of brave deeds and the brave Americans who did them. They are still with her and will be always. It is my hope that those who visit her, most especially the young, will come to know and perhaps be inspired by them.

If that happens, then what *Laffey* did will not have been in vain.

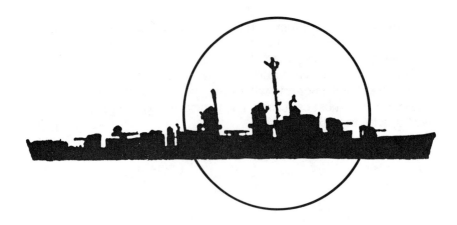

APPENDIX

The survivors of the action—with medals awarded, where applicable; rates within different ratings at the time of the action; plus latest known cities of residence—are listed below. The names of those who have died since World War II are preceded by D.

Adams, William, Machinist's Mate Third Class, St. Charles, MO
Addison, W. T., Lieutenant, USNR, Baltimore, MD
Anderson, Mark G., Seaman First Class, Brooklyn, NY
Andrews, Ralph R., Fireman First Class, Tewksbury, MA
Annino, Calvin W., Seaman First Class, Westfield, MA
Asadorian, Zorob, Water Tender Third Class, Dearborn Heights, MI
Babcock, Myron W., Fireman First Class, Chicago, IL
Bahme, J., Lieutenant junior grade, Houston, TX
Ballenger, Jack A., Fireman First Class, Nashport, OH
Barbeau, William A., Chief Fire Controlman, Bay City, MI
Barber, Harold W., Seaman First Class, Appleton, WI
D   Barlow, Fred E., Seaman First Class, Croydon, PA
Bassett, George E., Radioman Third Class, Torrington, CT
Baumhardt, Arthur, Boatswain's Mate Second Class, Skokie, IL
Beall, George G., Fireman First Class, Arlington, VA
Belk, Ernest E., Seaman First Class, San Diego, CA
Bell, Charles W., Sonarman Second Class, Naples, FL
Bell, James P., Seaman First Class, Northumberland, PA
Bell, John E., Jr., Machinist's Mate Third Class, New Kensington, PA
Bineau, Roland, Seaman Second Class, Biddeford, ME
Boothe, Roy C., Seaman First Class, Vinton, VA
Borcich, Emil C., Seaman First Class, Oak Lawn, IL
Bracci, Vincent F., Seaman First Class, Rochester, NY
Branka, John E., Fireman First Class, Detroit, MI
Brennan, Raymond F., Fireman First Class, Tillamook, OR
Brinkley, Clarence E., Machinist's Mate Third Class, Tampa, Fl

Britton, Robert E., Fireman First Class, Fort Smith, AR
Brock, Isaac, Steward's Mate Third Class, New Orleans, LA
Broussard, Charles A., Seaman First Class, Somerville, MA
Brown, Donald E., Seaman First Class, Grove City, PA
D Brown, James L., Seaman First Class, Converse, SC
D Brusoe, Richard A., Water Tender First Class, Wisconsin Rapids, WI
D Burnett, George R., Fire Controlman Third Class, Somerset, NJ
Bussert, Karl E., Seaman First Class, Lancaster, OH
Cahill, Thomas J., Boiler Tender Third Class, Yonkers, NY
Cain, Joseph F., Radioman Second Class, Adamsville, AL
Calafato, Anthony F., Fireman First Class, Freeport, NY
Calisti, Bruno J., Seaman First Class, Ardmore, OK
Call, Grady E., Fireman First Class, Lexington, NC.
Campbell, Robert L., Water Tender First Class, San Diego, CA
Carlo, Michael A, Jr., Seaman First Class, Rocky Hill, CT
Carney, Robert R., Fireman First Class, Chicago, IL
Carter, Donald, Seaman First Class, Rosholt, WI
Carver, Douglas C., Seaman Second Class, Madison, TN
Cerce, James, Seaman First Class, Portsmouth, RI
Cibulka, John, Jr., Motor Machinist's Mate Third Class, Binghamton, NY
Coffman, Kenneth Dale, Boatswain's Mate First Class—Silver Star Medal,
   Alameda, CA
Cooper, Edwin, Seaman First Class, Hancock, MD
Cronin, John E., Radarman Second Class, Soda Springs, ID
Crump, Douglas C., Fireman First Class, Strasberg, VA
Curtin, David M., Radarman Third Class, Geneva, NY
Danelly, Fitzugh B., Seaman First Class, Pensacola, FL
Darnell, Matthew C., Jr., Lieutenant junior grade, Medical Corps—Bronze
   Star Medal, Lexington, KY
Daugherty, Robert H., Radarman Third Class, Wellsburg, WV
Decker, Norris H., Electrician's Mate Second Class, Battle Creek, MI
Delewski, Lawrence H., Gunner's Mate Second Class—Bronze Star Medal,
   Pottstown, PA
Dickey, Andrew T., Coxswain, Moscow, PA
Dickey, Dennis J., Machinist's Mate Second Class, Neeses, SC
Dixon, Joseph E., Seaman First Class, Rocky Mount, NC
Dockery, Robert W., Seaman First Class, Des Moines, IA
Donald, William L., Seaman First Class, Newberry, SC
Doran, John F., Quartermaster First Class, Greenwich, CT
Dorr, Robert L., Fireman Second Class, Walden, NY
Dorris, Alfred J., Seaman First Class, Elkton, MD
Doyle, Pierce V., Chief Yeoman, Harrisburg, PA
D Dubbs, Carl H., Chief Machinist's Mate, Kulmont, PA
Dunn, John H., Steward's Mate First Class, Louisville, KY
Dunson, Clyde A., Steward's Mate Second Class, New Bern, NC
Earnst, Jack O., Torpedoman's Mate First Class, Haven, KS
Eastham, Lonnie H., Seaman First Class, La Grange, NC
Edmonds, Joe W., Seaman First Class, Eutawville, SC
Englehardt, August G., Radar Technician First Class, Westside, IA
Essig, Daniel M., Ship's Cook Second Class, Flushing, NY
Evans, John B., Seaman First Class, Hasbrouck Heights, NJ
Faginski, Raymond H., Coxswain, South Hadley, MA

Faulkner, William D., Seaman First Class, Charlotte, NC
Fern, Tom B., Seaman First Class—Silver Star Medal, Agawam, MA
Flanders, William A., Seaman First Class, Latham, NY
Foard, Raymond R., Seaman First Class, Charlotte, NC
Fowler, James L., Seaman Second Class, Providence, RI
Freimer, William D., Electrician's Mate Third Class, Brooklyn, NY
Frey, Lyman L., Seaman First Class, Calumet City, IL
Gaddis, Herman S., Chief Signalman, Greenwood, MS
Galvin, Joseph P., Machinist's Mate Second Class, Inglewood, CA
Gauding, Wilbert C., Fireman First Class, Ravenna, OH
Gebhart, Francis M., Gunner's Mate Third Class, Springfield, IL
Gemmell, Fred M., Torpedoman's Mate Second Class, Port Orchard, WA
Giles, Louis F., Seaman First Class, Brooklyn, MD
Glatthorn, John A., Seaman First Class, Darby, PA
Gray, Clarence L., Carpenter's Mate Third Class, Houston, MO
D Griner, Harwell M., Fire Controlman Second Class, Copperhill, TN
Gudelunes, Stanley, Ship Fitter Third Class, Brooklyn, NY
Gulsvig, Clayton A., Fireman First Class, Springfield, OR
Haberkam, John H., Electrician's Mate Third Class, Baltimore, MD
D Haley, Wayne H., Chief Torpedoman's Mate, Brooklyn, NY
Hansen, Raymond A., Torpedoman's Mate Second Class,
  West St. Paul, MN
Hanzel, Frank M., Ship's Cook Third Class, Glendale, NY
Hardway, Carl J., Seaman First Class, Spencer, OH
Harrelson, Doris, Seaman First Class, Newport News, VA
Harris, John W., Seaman First Class, Greensboro, NC
Hearn, George L., Seaman First Class, Merry, NC
Henke, E. A., Lieutenant—Bronze Star Medal, Anacortes, WA
Herold, Ernest C., Machinist's Mate Third Class, New York, NY
Hile, Claude C., Water Tender Second Class, New Orleans, LA
Hilton, Charles E., Seaman First Class, San Diego, CA
Hintzman, Donald J., Machinist's Mate Third Class—Bronze Star Medal,
  Oshkosh, WI
Hoag, Francis G., Seaman First Class, Hatfield, PA
Hogan, Arthur E., Machinist's Mate First Class—Bronze Star Medal,
  Baldwinsville, NY.
Hoopman, Werner F., Fireman First Class, Wheeling, IL
Hudgens, James H., Fireman Second Class, Cordova, AL
Hudgins, James R., Seaman First Class, Roanoke, VA
Hughes, Thomas J., Storekeeper Second Class, Lawrence, MA
Hull, Lloyd N., Lieutenant junior grade, Greenwich, CT
Humphries, S.M., Lieutenant, Athens, GA
D Hungerpiller, Marcellous D., Chief Machinist's Mate—Bronze Star Medal,
  Bethera, SC
Hunt, Lee C., Seaman First Class, Charleston, SC
Hutchins, Charles W., Seaman First Class—Bronze Star Medal,
  Oak Ridge, TN
D Hyson, Richard W., Seaman First Class, Baltimore, MD
D Irving, George, Jr., Seaman First Class, Long Island, NY
Jackson, Ralph D., Electrician's Mate Second Class, Beaumont, TX
Janoski, George, Seaman First Class, Union City, PA

Johnson, Merle R., Seaman Second Class, McAllen, TX
D Johnson, Paul B., Fireman Second Class, Burlington, NJ
Johnson, Raymond T., Seaman Second Class, Allentown, PA
Johnson, Robert C., Seaman Second Class, Framville, VA
Johnson, Robert E., Seaman Second Class, Toledo, OH
Johnson, Tyrus R., Fireman Second Class, Kilgore, TX
Jones, "K". "D"., Jr., Seaman First Class, Asheville, NC
Jump, Morris H., Seaman First Class, Easton, MD
Kachigian, William K., Machinist's Mate Third Class, Taylor, MI
Kaniewski, S. D., Seaman Second Class, Hammond, IN
Kapaldo, Waitman, Ship's Serviceman Third Class, Homewood, IL
Karr, Robert I., Gunner's Mate Third Class, Seattle, WA
Kelly, William M., Signalman Third Class, Belmar, NJ
Kennedy, Earl R., Yeoman Third Class, Mission, KS
Ketron, Stanley H., Gunner's Mate Third Class, Kingsport, TN
Keyes, William J., Chief Boatswain's Mate, Memphis, TN
Klein, Andrew, Radioman Third Class, Glendale, NY
Klein, Gabriel B., Seaman First Class, San Francisco, CA
Klimkewicz, Ambrose J., Seaman Second Class, Garfield Heights, OH
Kmiecik, John J., Seaman Second Class, Chicago, IL
Kodman, Francis, Jr., Chief Pharmacist's Mate, Murry, KY
Kohler, William R., Seaman Second Class, Huntington, WV
Kycia, Edward A., Seaman Second Class, Weathersfield, CT
Langevin, Reginald R., Fireman First Class, Little Falls, NJ
Laskowski, Frank, Water Tender Third Class, Girard, OH
Latwis, Michael, Fireman First Class, Plymouth, PA
D Leary, Howard J., Radioman Second Class, Havre de Grace, MD
Lebrecht, Earl L., Seaman First Class, Palmyra, NY
Lefevre, Walter T., Seaman First Class, Epps, LA
Lesinski, Frank L., Electrician's Mate Third Class, Grand Island, NY
Letourneau, Roland J., Sonarman Third Class, Attleboro, MA
Liller, John F., Jr., Yeoman Third Class, Bronx, NY
Logan, George S., Motor Machinist's Mate First Class—Bronze Star Medal, St. George, UT
Luczkow, Benny, Seaman First Class, Brooklyn, NY
Mackin, William H., Fire Controlman Third Class, South Weymouth, MA
Mallette, Emile J., Seaman First Class, Rockville, MD
Malone, Edwin D., Seaman First Class, Mobile, AL
Malone, Harold J., Ship Fitter Third Class, Cornwall on the, Hudson, NY
Manson, Frank A., Lieutenant—Navy Commendation Medal, Washington, DC
Marini, Olivion S., Radioman Third Class, Woonsocket, RI
Martin, Ralph W., Radioman Third Class, Virginia Beach, VA
D Martin, Ronald G., Seaman First Class, Williamsett, MA
Martinis, Andrew J., Seaman First Class—Bronze Star Medal, Seattle, WA
Masker, William E., Pharmacist's Mate Second Class, Chipley, FL
Matthews, Jim Dan, Ship's Serviceman Second Class—Bronze Star Medal, East Milton, MA
Maxwell, Cornelius A., Torpedoman's Mate First Class, Coatsville, PA
McBryde, Luther B., Seaman First Class, Pine Bluff, AR
McCarthy, Thomas B., Signalman Second Class, Las Vegas, NV

McClafferty, William T., Seaman First Class, Wilmington, DE
McCune, Challen, Jr., Lieutenant, Address unknown
McDonald, James F., Fireman First Class, Somerville, MA
McGinnis, Robert L., Fire Controlman Third Class, Bellefontaine, OH
McIntyre, Clarence B., Chief Commissary Steward, Norfolk, VA
Meier, Welles A., Gunner's Mate Third Class, West Palm Beach, FL
D Michel, John W., Machinist's Mate First Class, Sewell, NJ
Mickle, Ross W., Baker Third Class, Baltimore, MD
D Migues, Joseph C., Coxswain, Jefferson Island, LA
D Miller, James P., Seaman First Class, Moulton, AL
Miller, Leonard B., Electrician's Mate Third Class, Exeter, NH
Miller, Morris, Jr., Fireman First Class, Russellville, AR
Molohan, Michael A., Seaman First Class, Los Nietos, CA
Molpus, E.L., Lieutenant, Savannah, GA
D Morris, William L., Seaman First Class, Fayetteville, GA
Mosher, Albert R., Seaman First Class, Pontiac, MI
Muckerman, Walter B., Jr., Seaman First Class, St. Louis, MO
Murray, Lawrence J., Radarman Third Class, Union, MI
Murray, Patrick J., Seaman First Class, Binghamton, NY
Muskivitch, William E., Seaman First Class, Paramus, NJ
Najork, Jack, Chief Radioman, Lexington, NB
Neifah, Sidney, Radarman Third Class, Bronx, NY
D Newell, Francis P., Coxswain, Philadelphia, PA
Nikirk, John M., Fireman First Class, Bloomington, IN
Nordstrom, Louis D., Sonarman Third Class, Grand Blanc, MI
Nulf, Philip E., Radarman Second Class, Fort Wayne, IN
Nulty, Ward K., Jr., Seaman First Class, Chicago, IL
Odom, Roland, Seaman First Class, Sebring, FL
O'Shaughnessy, William, J., Jr, Seaman First Class, New York, NY
Osman, George G., Radarman Second Class, Thorofare, NJ
Oyer, Herbert M., Jr., Seaman First Class, Lakeland, FL
Pagano, Gilbert A., Radarman Third Class, Massapequa, NY
Palfy, Alexander, Chief Machinist's Mate, Chula Vista, CA
Parino, Frank F., Machinist's Mate Second Class—Bronze Star Medal,
     Haverhill, MA
Parks, Maurice C., Commissaryman First Class, Annapolis, MD
Parolini, G. A. G., Lieutenant junior grade—Silver Star Medal,
     Barrington, RI
Peeler, Elton F., Machinist's Mate First Class—Bronze Star Medal,
     Pasadena, MD
Pelosi, Gaston J., Seaman Second Class, Scranton, PA
Perry, Joseph C., Seaman First Class, Tiverton, RI
D Peterson, Ralph C., Fire Controlman First Class, Carmel, NY
Pezzano, Rocca V., Seaman Second Class, Williamstown, NJ
Phoutrides, Aristides S., Quartermaster Second Class, Portland, OR
Pinkoff, Jerome D., Ship's Cook Third Class, San Lorenzo, CA
Pitta, Kenneth J., Coxswain, San Diego, CA
Pollard, Leonce E., Seaman First Class, Mar-Vista, CA
Porlier, J.V., Lieutenant, Walnut Creek, CA
Powell, Robert W., Seaman First Class, Green Bay, WI
Pressburger, Ramon, Seaman First Class, Southard, NJ

Purrick, Theodore F., Signalman Third Class, New York, NY
Radder, Owen G., Gunner's Mate Third Class, Menominee Falls, WI
D Ray, Robert E., Seaman First Class, Gas City, IN
Redd, James R., Steward's Mate First Class, Washington, DC
Regin, Charles W., Machinist's Mate Third Class, Morton Grove, IL
Remsen, Herbert B., Seaman First Class, Van Nuys, CA
Revels, Leon M., Steward's Mate First Class, Apex, NC
Rick, Herbert J., Yeoman Second Class, Levittown, PA
Ring, Edward L., Jr., Quartermaster Second Class, Ocean City, MD
Robertson, Marvin G., Seaman First Class, Bishopville, SC
Robertson, Shirley D., Seaman First Class, Vinton, VA
D Robinson, Kenneth A., Ship's Servicemen Third Class, Addison, AL
Rooker, Burnard L., Seaman First Class, Jasper, GA
Rorie, Walter, Seaman Second Class, Charlotte, NC
Rosania, Paul, Seaman Second Class, New York, NY
Ross, Frank M., Seaman Second Class, Sumter, SC
Runk, Theodore W., Lieutenant—Navy Cross, San Diego, CA
Rusk, George D., Fireman First Class, Cedar Rapids, IA
Ryder, William D., Chief Quartermaster—Silver Star Medal, Columbus, OH
Saenz, Ernest G., Lieutenant junior grade—Bronze Star Medal, Santa Barbara, CA
Salcido, Felipe., Seaman First Class, Los Angeles, CA
Samp, E. J., Jr., Lieutenant, Cambridge, MA
Samuelian, Frank, Fire Controlman Third Class, Providence, RI
Sattler, Clarence A., Storekeeper Third Class, Meriden, CT
Schenk, Robert L., Seaman Second Class, Elkhart, IN
Schmidt, William S., Machinist's Mate Third Class, Pennsauken, NJ
D Schneider, John F., Torpedoman's Mate Second Class, Roxbury, MA
Scott, Claude E., Electrician's Mate First Class, Riverside, CA
Scott, David M., Machinist's Mate First Class, San Pedro, CA
Secrist, Dale L., Fireman First Class, Fullerton, CA
Setmire, Glenn M., Boatswain's Mate Second Class, Greensburg, PA
Shaw, William H., Lieutenant junior grade—Bronze Star Medal, Gainesville, Fl
Shepard, James I., Machinist's Mate Second Class, Webster, MA
Shepherd, Stanley M., Radioman Second Class, Detroit, MI
Siegrist, Joseph F., Radarman Second Class, Coshocton, OH
Simonis, Cyril C., Sonarman First Class, Bethpage, NY
Skvarka, Cyril M. J., Machinist's Mate Second Class, Barberton, OH
Sloan, Paul V., Seaman First Class, Canton, MA
Smith, Paul B., Lieutenant—Silver Star Medal, Atlanta, GA
Smith, George H., Fireman First Class, Trenton, NJ
Snyder, Jacob L., Jr., Gunner's Mate Third Class, Blain, PA
Spitler, James W., Fire Controlman Second Class, Salem, OR
Spriggs, Oliver J., Fireman First Class, Cincinnati, OH
Stacy, J. L., Gunner, Alma, AR
D Stash, Andrew, Seaman First Class, Ardara, PA
Stein, Derrill W., Torpedoman's Mate Third Class, Klamath Falls, OR
Storm, R. T., Lieutenant junior grade, Glen Ellyn, IL
Strangeff, Joseph R., Seaman First Class, Indianapolis, IN

Strine, Jonathan W., Fireman First Class, Chambersburg, PA
Strozykowsky, S. J., Machinist's Mate Second Class, Glen Burnie, MD
Stuer, Joseph J., Fireman First Class, Johnstown, PA
Sussman, Irving, Radar Technician Second Class, Brooklyn, NY
Swank, James L., Chief Water Tender, West Chester, PA
Taylor, Lester, Seaman First Class, Birmingham, AL
Thompson, Buford L., Machinist's Mate First Class, Pensacola, FL
Thompson, Henry, Carpenter's Mate Second Class, Edison NJ
Thompson, Jay V., Torpedoman's Mate Third Class, Huntington, WV
Thompson, Martin S., Gunner's Mate Third Class, Gilman City, MO
Townsley, James G., Ensign—Silver Star Medal, Middletown, OH
Vece, Samuel, Boatswain's Mate Second Class, North Branford, CT
Vengelist, Anthony, Seaman First Class, Syracuse, NY
Vest, Rex A., Metalsmith Third Class, Renton, WA
Vianest, August E., Water Tender Second Class, Richmond Hill, NY
Vodenhal, Slavomir J., Radarman First Class, Clarkson, NB
Wachsman, Russell H., Seaman Second Class, Parma, OH
Wade, Cecil E., Machinist's Mate Second Class, La Grange, NC
Waite, Stephen J., Machinist's Mate First Class—Bronze Star Medal,
    Woodburn, OR
Walker, Warren G., Chief Gunner's Mate—Bronze Star Medal,
    Manchester, TN
Wallace, Quincie R., Seaman First Class, Statesville, NC
Warner, David L., Fireman First Class, Janesville, WI
D Waters, Earl E., Pharmacist's Mate Third Class, Pueblo, CO
Weiss, Daniel, Seaman First Class, Albany, NY
Weissinger, George N., Seaman Second Class, Rochester, NY
Welch, William H., Baker First Class, Houston, TX
Weygandt, Charles A., Seaman First Class, Belleville, IL
Williams, David H., Storekeeper First Class, Jacksonville, FL
Williams, Edgar E. C., Fire Controlman Third Class, Renton, WA
Williams, Jack E., Machinist's Mate Third Class, Ironton, OH
Williams, Richard, Machinist's Mate Third Class, Darby, PA
Wilson, Henry T., Water Tender Third Class, Philadelphia, PA
Wilson, John G., Seaman First Class, Bronx, NY
Wilson, Lon B., Jr., Seaman Second Class, Gauley Bridge, WV
Wilson, Roscoe S., Steward's Mate First Class, Boston, MA
Wingrove, Samuel F., Water Tender First Class, Virginia Beach, VA
Wix, Fred M., Jr., Seaman Second Class, Candler, NC
Wood, Roy, Chief Water Tender, Nashville, GA
Wright, Merle E., Seaman First Class, New Matamoros, OH
Yazdik, Emanuel J., Radioman Third Class, Honesdale, PA
D Yeagley, Charles J., Sonarman Second Class, Secane, PA
Yuochunas, Thomas C., Water Tender First Class, San Bernardino, CA
Youngquist, Joel C., Lieutenant junior grade—Bronze Star Medal,
    Glendale, CA
Zackerdonski, Daniel, Sonarman Third Class, Pittsfield, MA
D Zebro, Edward V., Gunner's Mate Second Class—Bronze Star Medal,
    Amboy, NJ
Zilempe, Vito J., Water Tender Third Class, Bronx, NY
Zupon, Philip M., Gunner's Mate First Class, Cayuga, ND

THE SECRETARY OF THE NAVY
Washington

The President of the United States takes pleasure in presenting the PRESIDENTIAL UNIT CITATION to the

UNITED STATES SHIP LAFFEY

for service as set forth in the following

CITATION:

"For extraordinary heroism in action as a Picket Ship on Radar Picket Station Number One during an attack by approximately thirty enemy Japanese planes, thirty miles northwest of the northern tip of Okinawa, April 16, 1945. Fighting her guns valiantly against waves of hostile suicide planes plunging toward her from all directions, the U.S.S. LAFFEY sent up relentless barrages of antiaircraft fire during an extremely heavy and concentrated air attack. Repeatedly finding her targets, she shot down eight enemy planes clear of the ship and damaged six more before they crashed on board. Struck by two bombs, crash-dived by suicide planes and frequently strafed, she withstood the devastating blows unflinchingly and, despite severe damage and heavy casualties, continued to fight effectively until the last plane had been driven off. The courage, superb seamanship and indomitable determination of her officers and men enabled the LAFFEY to defeat the enemy against almost insurmountable odds, and her brilliant performance in this action reflects the highest credit upon herself and the United States Naval Service."

For the President,

James Forrestal

Secretary of the Navy

U. S. S. LAFFEY
(DD 724)

IN MEMORY OF THE BRAVE MEN WHO GAVE THEIR LIVES
TO SAVE THEIR SHIP IN THE ACTION BETWEEN U. S. S.
LAFFEY AND TWENTY-TWO JAPANESE AIRCRAFT NEAR
OKINAWA ON 16 APRIL 1945.

JAMES WILLIAM FRAVEL, LT.(JG) USN
JEROME BUTLER SHEETS, LT.(JG) USNR
ROBERT CLARENCE THOMSEN, ENS. USN

HENRY MARSHALL BENSON, EM3c USNR
CHARLES ARTHUR BROUSSARD, COX
   USNR
EDWARD JOHN BROWN, TM3c USNR
FRED DURELL BURGESS, JR., Y3c USNR
CALVIN WESLEY CLOER, BM2c USNR
BERNARD EDWARDS, COX USNR
GEORGE FALOTICO, COX USNR
CHESTER CARLTON FLINT, COX USNR
CONLEY EUGENE FOWLER, F1c USNR
FRANCIS RAY HALLAS, F1c USNR
LA VERNE GEORGE HAZEN, MM3c USNR
WILLIAM ERNEST HEYES, S1c USN
MADOC KENYON IRISH, SF1c USNR
JOHN ALBERT JOHNSON, MM3c USNR
PAUL BUTLER JOHNSON, F1c USNR
LAWRENCE FRANCIS KELLEY, RM3c
   USNR
JOSEPH HILD KLINDWORTH, S1c USNR
JAMES MARCELLE LA POINTE, COX
   USNR
FRANK WILLIAM LEHTONEN, JR., GM1c
   USNR
RONALD GEORGE MARTIN, GM3c USNR
JOSEPH EDWARD MELE, GM2c USNR
WILLIAM LAMAR MORRIS, COX USNR
JACK HARRIS ONDRACEK, TM3c USNR
ROSS EPWORTH PETERSON, EM1c USN
JOSEPH ROGOWSKI, COX USNR
JAMES TRENTON ROTHGEB, F1c USNR
EARL ELDRIDGE WATERS, PHM3c USNR
STANLEY WISMER, GM2c USNR
ROSIER BERNARD WRIGHT, JR., EM3c
   USNR-I